The Voice of Conscience

Univ

Subj

The Voice of Conscience

The Church in the Mind
of Martin Luther King, Jr.

LEWIS V. BALDWIN

UNIVERSITY PRESS

2010

OXFORD
UNIVERSITY PRESS

Oxford University Press, Inc., publishes works that further
Oxford University's objective of excellence
in research, scholarship, and education.

Oxford   New York
Auckland   Cape Town   Dar es Salaam   Hong Kong   Karachi
Kuala Lumpur   Madrid   Melbourne   Mexico City   Nairobi
New Delhi   Shanghai   Taipei   Toronto

With offices in
Argentina   Austria   Brazil   Chile   Czech Republic   France   Greece
Guatemala   Hungary   Italy   Japan   Poland   Portugal   Singapore
South Korea   Switzerland   Thailand   Turkey   Ukraine   Vietnam

Copyright © 2010 by Oxford University Press, Inc.

Published by Oxford University Press, Inc.
198 Madison Avenue, New York, New York 10016

www.oup.com

Oxford is a registered trademark of Oxford University Press.

Library of Congress Cataloging-in-Publication Data
Baldwin, Lewis V., 1949–
The voice of conscience: the church in the mind of Martin Luther King, Jr. / Lewis V. Baldwin.
    p. cm.
Includes bibliographical references and index.
ISBN 978-0-19-538031-6; 978-0-19-538030-9 (pbk.)
1. King, Martin Luther, Jr., 1929–1968. 2. Church. I. Title.
BV600.3.B34   2010
262.0092—dc22   2009027408

9 8 7 6 5 4 3 2 1

Printed in the United States of America
on acid-free paper

For my former professors, Henry H. Mitchell and the late Lucius M. Tobin, who taught me how to view the church and its mission in new ways, and for those teenagers and young adults in the inner cities of this nation who view the church as a sad anachronism.

On lazy summer afternoons and cold mornings, I've seen tall church spires and sprawling brick monuments, dedicated to the glory of God. Often did I wonder, "What kind of people worship here? Who is their God?"

—Martin Luther King, Jr., 3 October 1962

I see the church as the conscience of the community, the conscience of the nation, the conscience of the state, and consequently, the church must be involved in all of the vital issues of the day, whether it's in the area of civil rights, whether it's dealing with the whole question of war and peace.

—Martin Luther King, Jr., 18 April 1966

Foreword

I am unapologetically a fan of Lewis V. Baldwin. Having worked with Martin Luther King, Jr., and lived through the gargantuan struggle to integrate the United States, I feel that I know more about King and his vision for the church than anyone else alive. I have read almost everything about Dr. King in book form, and no one has come close to Lewis Baldwin in deciphering the mystique of the man and his mission.

Baldwin's *There Is a Balm in Gilead*, issued some two decades ago, presented the critical factors that made Dr. King the quintessential prophet of the twentieth century, focusing especially on King's development as an ordained preacher at the Ebenezer Baptist Church in Atlanta, Georgia. Up to that point, most of the "King experts" had either ignored this element of his life or at best made passing mention of it, despite Dietrich Bonhoeffer's and Gunnar Myrdal's insistence that the cutting edge of the religion of Jesus Christ was the black church in America. In *The Voice of Conscience*, Baldwin continues to lay the foundational aspects of King's construct in his mission and person by thoroughly examining his attitude toward and reliance upon the Christian church.

Several biographers of Dr. King have launched investigations into which writings influenced the civil rights leader the most. They have come up with a variety of answers, reflecting the best in Western literature. But when they questioned me about this, my answer startled them. The writings that influenced Dr. King most were the Gospels of Matthew, Mark, Luke, and John, which teach us about the crucified carpenter of Galilee and the sacrificial life that gave birth to the church and inspired much of its mission outreach throughout the centuries. Baldwin knows this well, and his work rightly identifies the church as key to King's strength of spirit against seemingly invincible odds.

The Voice of Conscience makes it patently clear that Dr. King was committed to Jesus' concept of the church and what it should be for the world. At the same time, King was unrelenting in his critique of both the black church and the church universal. Baldwin's book meticulously documents King's perspective on and hope for the Christian church, thereby helping us to better understand how King became a force in establishing justice in an unjust nation.

As Baldwin points out, the church gave Dr. King the spiritual and moral support he needed to withstand the tremendous pressures associated with the movement, including the possibility and eventuality of his own violent death. King often said that the Southern Christian Leadership Conference (SCLC) was "the Home Mission Department of the black church," but he clearly had in mind the importance and potential of the larger church community and culture when he pointed the nation toward a postracial era and a more inclusive, beloved community ideal.

When the writing about King has been distilled generations from now, Baldwin's work, including this volume, will remain the most definitive about the man and his ministry. Baldwin shows us how King, inspired by the church and supported by only a fraction of its leadership, turned the world upside down.

Lewis V. Baldwin is the only authentic "King expert" I recognize.

Wyatt Tee Walker
Former Chief of Staff to Dr. Martin Luther King, Jr.
Southern Christian Leadership Conference
Chester, Virginia

Acknowledgments

This book is largely a product of my own personal struggle with the Christian church and the image it is projecting to this nation and the world at the beginning of this new century and millennium. Increasingly, the church appears more committed to its own institutional structures than it is to the spirit of Jesus Christ. Sadly, Christians too often worship the church and not the Lord of the church; and being in mission is too frequently equated with self-preservation rather than others' preservation. Nowhere is this more evident than in the ways that the church views and relates to what Martin Luther King, Jr., called "the least of these." This book testifies to my conviction that King is as relevant for the church today as he was almost a half century ago, especially if that body is to reclaim, in more authentic ways, its raison d'être.

A great many people were helpful to me in the preparation of this study, thus proving once again that books are always collaborative efforts. I am heavily indebted to a couple of my colleagues, Herbert Marbury and Victor Anderson, for assistance in the conception and writing of parts of this book. Marbury, who teaches Hebrew Bible at the Vanderbilt Divinity School, helped me to better understand King's use of the biblical-prophetic tradition, thereby making it easier for me to explore King's sense of the prophetic church. Anderson, who teaches Ethics and Theology at Vanderbilt, served me so proficiently as a sensitive and constructive critic. He was especially helpful in the completion of the last chapter of this work, which drew substantially on his ideas and insights.

A hearty word of gratitude to the many students who took my courses on King at Vanderbilt University, Fisk University, and American Baptist College over the last decade. My approach to King's ecclesial ideas, values, and vision actually took form gradually as I exchanged ideas with these students, often in informal settings. The many rich, provocative, and probing questions they asked anticipated this volume in interesting and profound ways.

My friend Rufus Burrow, Jr., a Professor of Theological Ethics at Christian Theological Seminary, in Indianapolis, generously shared his thoughts and insights in the early stages of my research, and was always a great source of encouragement. Rufus Burrow also read the completed manuscript and offered insightful and constructive criticisms. He has never hesitated to critique my scholarship on King, but always in a considerate and gentle fashion. I have also benefited from a careful reading of Burrow's outstanding intellectual biography of King, which weaves together crucial threads of the most recent scholarship on the civil rights leader.

Words of appreciation go to Michael Lomax, who helped me to better understand the organization, style, and ethos of the mega-church phenomenon, and why and how it deviates so much from traditions represented by King. Michael first triggered my thinking regarding the many difficulties that mega-churches and their pastors face when it comes to meeting the demands of a truly prophetic ministry. Paula McGee, a young minister and graduate student at Claremont, was also very helpful in this regard. Her papers on mega-church leaders afforded a rich mine of ideas and insights that aided in my effort to critique the mega-church phenomenon based on the ecclesial models of King.

Cynthia Lewis and Elaine Hall, who remain in charge of the library and archives at the Martin Luther King, Jr., Center for Nonviolent Social Change, in Atlanta, were always helpful in locating documents pertinent to this study. I shall never forget the many fruitful and enlightening conversations I had with Cynthia and Elaine at the King Center.

Clayborne Carson and his staff at Stanford University contributed substantially to the completion of *The Voice of Conscience*, primarily by making available six massive volumes of the Papers of Martin Luther King, Jr. These volumes, published by the University of California Press from 1992 to 2007, included numerous sermons, speeches, and writings that yielded rich information on and insights into King's attitude toward and vision for the church. Carson also reviewed my manuscript and offered perceptive criticisms and suggestions for improvement. For this I am eternally grateful.

My dear friend and colleague Walter E. Fluker read and critiqued my material, and generously gave advice regarding possible revisions. Fluker, a King scholar in his own right, really influenced my interpretation in striking ways. His devotion to King's memory and the advancement of his vision for the church is praiseworthy indeed, to say nothing of his deep commitment to scholarly pursuits and integrity generally. Fluker is now involved with the Morehouse College Martin Luther King, Jr., Collection.

A special thanks to the many distinguished persons who endorsed this book with kind and generous comments. Wyatt Tee Walker, who worked closely with King in the Southern Christian Leadership Conference, and who was a pivotal figure in the events surrounding the voter rights campaign in Selma, Alabama, in 1965, graciously agreed to write the foreword. David Buttrick, a Vanderbilt colleague, whose scholarship and teaching in homiletics have won international acclaim, kindly provided an afterword. Buttrick's father, George Buttrick, is known to have greatly influenced the sermonic discourse of King. This work was read and brief reviews were provided by Will Campbell, the highly regarded Southern Baptist preacher, civil rights activist, and author, who was also associated with King in the 1960s; Henry H. Mitchell, the noted preacher, scholar, and dean of black church studies; Leontine T. C. Kelly, the first African American woman elected to the Episcopacy of the United Methodist Church; and Rufus Burrow, Jr. One could not ask for a more illustrious group of supporters.

Daniel P. DuBois, the Assistant Director of Photography Services, Creative Services, and Public Affairs at Vanderbilt, was quite generous with his time and advice when I was struggling with whether or not to include photographs in this book. Vanderbilt is fortunate to have the services of this talented and dedicated young man.

My beautiful wife Jacqueline deserves much praise for assisting me with the typing and organization of this study, often at times when she would have preferred to be preoccupied with other matters. As one who frequently raises deep questions about the direction of the church today and tomorrow, she took a special interest in the topic explored in this work, and offered much encouragement and inspiration.

Many thanks to Theo Calderara, a Senior Editor at Oxford University Press, for expressing a strong interest in this volume and in other pieces of my scholarship on King. Perhaps without knowing it, he, too, has offered much encouragement and inspiration. I was absolutely honored and delighted when Calderara reported that *The Voice of Conscience* had been enthusiastically approved for publication by Oxford. A word of gratitude is also extended to others at Oxford, especially Mariana Templin, Lisbeth Redfield, and Linda Donnelly, who provided assistance at different stages of this project.

Finally, I owe the deepest praise to the God of my ancestors, that magnificent force that kept me motivated, focused, and determined, even when I felt too intellectually and spiritually drained to continue this effort. I have learned yet another lesson about the power of faith to triumph over any deficiency in the human spirit.

Contents

The Voice of Conscience

Introduction

Martin Luther King, Jr.'s importance as a man of faith and as an
exemplary voice and active presence in the life of the church has
been widely acknowledged and approached from different angles by
scholars. Words like *militant, revolutionary, prophet, crusader, reformer,
transformer, nonconformist*, and *activist* have been used to characterize
King's churchmanship and ministry. Among those who stress his
links to African American religion and culture, he is variously
called "the major prophet of the black churches," "the high priest"
or "charismatic leader of the black freedom movement," "the
twentieth century's most celebrated embodiment of the African-
American Christian tradition," and "a pivotal figure" who
"represented a tradition of protest and social action for liberation
that characterized the black church in America from the time of
slavery."[1]

Other scholars highlight King's significance for American
church history, noting how he emerged as "a beacon of evangelically
inspired liberal activism," "introduced a new spirit to America by
invoking the old biblical themes of promise and the dreams of
concord," and "contributed to the transformation of American
religion that began to crest in the sixties."[2] For those interested in
America's public faith, King is viewed as "a religious and political
pragmatist," as a spokesperson for "a bi-racial southern civil
religion," as one who made "tactical use of civil religious rhetoric as a
means of communication with White America," and as "the

virtual personification of a prophetic manifestation of the American civil religion."[3]

The point is that no American clergyman has exceeded the prominence of King. The explanation for his towering significance lies not merely in his prophetic proclamations regarding the most deeply embedded contradictions in the American spirit, but also in the precise and myriad ways in which he challenged the Christian church to act in his own times. By skillfully combining biblical piety and theological liberalism with social analysis and nonviolent activism, King stimulated the thinking and penetrated the lives of millions, exposing their mediocrities and energizing them with a new and more vital sense of what Dietrich Bonhoeffer termed "the cost of discipleship."[4] This is why the civil rights leader's name is routinely included among Christianity's most celebrated saints and sages.

But despite King's place in the pantheon of great Christian thinkers and activists, the literature on his life and work, extensive as it is, does not provide an adequate account of his views on the nature and purpose of the church. Surprisingly, a book-length treatment of this subject has not yet been published.[5] This study is designed to help fill this gap in King scholarship. Its thesis is manifold. First, it contends that church and church-related issues and concerns, inspired by his upbringing and fueled by a certain understanding of scripture and the Christian faith, were always paramount in King's thinking. Thus, the church should be a prominent part of any discussion concerning his growing disillusionment with institutions and structures of power. Otherwise, it is impossible to get anything like a full-orbed understanding of why and how King became the quintessential model of Christian activism in his time.

Second, this work concludes that King's attitude toward the church resulted not only from a life-long intellectual struggle but also from a spiritual pilgrimage and an agonizing voyage of personal self-discovery that began in childhood. To be sure, this is an essential point of departure for studying King's personal formation, as well as his leadership, vision, and call to greatness. The best sources for exploring and developing this angle are King's own writings and those of family and other individuals with personal connections to him.[6]

Third, one finds in King's sermons, speeches, and writings a multiplicity of images and concepts that afford insights into the nature and mission of the church. While King did not develop ecclesiology in the traditional sense and meaning of the word, there is a strong doctrine of the church implicit in his thought and praxis.[7] The word *ecclesiology* almost never surfaced in his public statements concerning the church, but that does not make his reflections on that institution any less profound and erudite. As Henry Bettensen and Chris Maunder have observed, the movement King led "raised profound and radical theological questions regarding the presence of Christ and the true nature of the church."[8] Moreover, one detects in King's ideas and social praxis both a critique of the church and proposals for effecting its spiritual, theological, and ethical renewal. As this study will show, an examination of these matters necessarily requires some attention to related topics, such as revelation, ecumenism, and eschatological concerns.

This book consists of six chapters. Chapter 1 assesses those contextual factors that informed and shaped King's earliest sense of the meaning and purpose of the church. This includes King's birth into "a family of preachers and race leaders" and his upbringing in the Ebenezer Baptist Church in Atlanta, Georgia, the congregation with which generations of his family were affiliated.[9] Equally significant in this regard was the larger black church community of Atlanta, which reinforced the values King imbibed in the King home and from the Ebenezer tradition. It was here that King learned not to separate the church from life.[10] Put another way, it was in this context that King first understood the church as extended familial community, as a vital source of spirituality, as the supreme embodiment of an orally transmitted expressive culture, and as an agency of social service and protest. These images were reinforced in King's consciousness through his exposure to black churches in the North, which occurred during his student days in Pennsylvania and Boston (1948–1954).[11] All of these developments are discussed at some length in this volume, providing support for the claim that familial and church connections proved central to how and why King became a social-change agent. King's early tendency to view the church in dialectical terms, or from the standpoint of its strengths and limitations, is treated seriously as well.

This first chapter is essential in sustaining the view that King never left the church and the church never left him. Indeed, he had a lifelong commitment to the church and to Christian service. Although the precise nature of this involvement and service was not to be defined until his college years (1944–1948), the commitment itself began to take shape, quite unconsciously, when King joined the Ebenezer Baptist Church at age five. That decision, though prompted by "a childhood desire to keep up with my sister,"[12] started him on the path to a radical Christian faith, a process that ultimately placed him in the maelstrom of civil conflict. While the Ebenezer tradition planted the seeds for King's rise as preacher and social activist, his indebtedness, more broadly speaking, was to what Richard Lischer labels "the African Baptist Church," a "world made up of Atlanta's 'Sweet Auburn Avenue,' Ebenezer Baptist Church, Morehouse College, tutors, mentors, role models, and friends—all of whom played a part in bringing him through seminary and graduate school to his first plateau: his pastorate in Montgomery."[13] The African Baptist Church in the South, and most especially Ebenezer, mirrored King's first images of what the church should be.

Chapter 2 examines how King approached the question of the identity, history, and roles of the church in intellectual terms. It will explain how this intellectual quest began at Atlanta's Morehouse College, became more intense during King's years in seminary and graduate school, and reached its highest levels of clarity and sophistication within the context of the civil rights struggle. King grew up in a culture in which the church was variously and commonly identified as "a refuge," "the Lord's house," "the temple of God," "the body of Christ," "the house of prayer," "the chosen of God," "a gathering of the faithful," and "these consecrated walls"; but he never understood that institution as merely a public assembly or an arena for corporate worship. While these images were important, King consistently challenged the church to break out of the stifling and debilitating complacency of its conventional definitions to live out the uncompromising demands of Jesus Christ with every fiber of instinct and conviction. As will be shown, he was primarily interested in the church as a prophetic witness to the gospel, and he was known to characterize that institution as "the conscience of the state," as "the chief moral guardian of the community," and as "the symbol of the beloved community in the world."[14] These and other concepts will come into sharper focus as this study puts King's attitude toward and vision for the church in proper perspective.

King emerges in this second chapter as one who loved, served, defended, and drew on the resources of the church even as he continued to critique it. As will be indicated, when it came to the church, King was not only a loving critic[15] but a critic of rare perception and refinement. He especially targeted those who reduced the church experience to the spiritual realm while ignoring the call to public service, prophetic social witness, and pragmatic activism. Furthermore, King had little use for the usual academic definitions and/or treatments of ecclesiology, which explains why this word rarely appears in his works. His tendency along these lines is the best evidence that his final loyalty was to God, not the church, which he understood to be essentially a human institution guilty of every sin imaginable. King's sermons, speeches, writings, and work in the civil rights field provide a lens through which to not only identify the short-comings of the church in the 1950s and 1960s but also to observe the larger ecclesiastical (i.e., ecumenism, interfaith dialogue, etc.) and theological (i.e., "God is dead," liberation theology, etc.) trends of this period.

Chapter 3 explores King's views concerning the role of the black church in the crusade for freedom, justice, and human dignity in the fifties and sixties. Most of the attention here is devoted to those years during which King served as pastor of the Dexter Avenue Baptist Church in Montgomery,

Alabama (1954–1959) and as co-pastor, with his father and brother, Martin Luther King, Sr., and A. D. King, of the Ebenezer Baptist Church in Atlanta (1960–1968). A range of concerns are addressed. First, King's understanding of the history of the black church in the struggle for freedom and survival in the generations that preceded him is seriously considered. The central claim is that King understood the entire history of the black church in terms of the validity of Henry David Thoreau's assertion that the state is ultimately improved by a creative minority that consistently resists it in the interest of the common good.[16]

Second, King's view of and reliance on the black church as a power base or as a de facto platform to advance the civil and human rights cause are carefully taken into account. This part of the discussion will emphasize the many ways in which King drew on the spiritual and moral disciplines of the black church, or on what Sydney E. Ahlstrom calls "its rich evangelical resources," to "redeem the soul of America," or to create a culture of protest, freedom, equal opportunity, racial inclusiveness, and peace.[17] Thus, the heritage and spirit of the black church as represented more than a century earlier by Richard Allen (1760–1831) and others were reawakened and reclaimed under King's charismatic leadership. Finally, more attention is given to King's ambivalent attitude toward the black church, to his sense of its failures and its redeeming qualities, which became much more informed and pronounced during his years as pastor and civil rights leader.[18]

This third chapter takes issue with two concerns raised in the recent scholarship on King and the civil rights movement. One has to do with the intense focus on King, to the neglect of ordinary people or lesser known figures. It has been said that "King was not necessary to the civil rights movement itself," that "the Movement made Martin, not Martin the Movement," or that one has to see the movement as "picking up King" and not "King as picking up the movement."[19] Scholars should abandon a nondialectical, or "an either/or," approach to reasoning on this question in favor of a dialectical, or "a both/and," approach. The problem is not that too much attention has been devoted to King but, rather, that too little attention has been given to others in the movement, especially local leaders and grassroots organizers.

Also, while King was part of the movement and not the movement itself, it could be argued that he was as important to the movement as the movement was to him. To be sure, the movement made King, but there is also a sense in which King made the movement, for without him the movement would have been something other than what it actually was.[20] Generally speaking, King epitomized the spirit and direction of the movement while having an incalculable effect on the image of the church in his day.[21] Thus, Ronald B. Flowers' and others' descriptions of King "as the person who led the transition from the Negro Church to the black church" is not an overstatement.[22]

The other concern involves what some scholars view as exaggerated claims regarding the significance of the black church as a protest institution, or as a major force in the crusade for equal rights and social justice in the 1950s and 1960s. The argument is that most in the black church refused, for whatever reasons, to actively support the civil rights cause, or that the full power of that institution was never mustered for the benefit of the movement.[23] Such observations are indeed valid for the most part, but this is the nature of social movements. The historic pattern is that such movements always hinge on the resources and contributions of the few and not the many. Hence, the importance of the black church in the civil rights movement should be measured not so much by the number of participants or the amount of material resources contributed, as King himself realized, but by the extent to which that institution became, in the words of Flowers, "the rallying point and source of inspiration for the protesters."[24]

Under the leadership of King and others, the black church was at least as important to the civil rights movement as the church had been to any other major social movement in American history. Moreover, many of those who launched street demonstrations, boycotts, sit-ins, freedom rides, prayer vigils, mass meetings, and other acts of nonviolent protest may not have officially been church members, but they represented the very best elements of the spirit and character of the African American church tradition. King said as much and more when assessing the impact of the church on American life in the fifties and sixties. In fact, Peter W. Williams's description of the civil rights movement as a vital dimension of "the black Christian quest for deliverance" squares very much with King's own assessment.[25]

Chapter 4 discusses King's views on and prophetic challenge to the white church. Fleeting attention is given to his very limited exposure as a youngster to the white church, and to his early struggle with the question of how to reconcile the Christian love ethic with that institution's racist tendencies and practice of segregation. From that point, the discussion turns to King's training in college, seminary, and graduate school, and the impact that had on his developing perspective on institutional expressions of white Christianity. Most of the focus is on how King challenged the white church around the issues of race, poverty and economic injustice, and war and human destruction in the 1950s and 1960s. His sustained, constructive critique of that institution's biblicism, theology, and ethics is highlighted, especially as these related to issues of race relations and the quest for the beloved community.[26] Here, King's work with white liberal Christians and his differences and conflicts with white fundamentalists and evangelicals will surface in profound ways, lending credence to King's belief that the white church was not monolithic when it came to the matter of racial justice and equality.[27]

Several major conclusions are drawn in this fourth chapter. First, King's critique of the white church in America embraced its whole history, extending back to its failure to speak and act prophetically with respect to slavery and segregation in the years before the Civil War. Reflecting on that history as it unfolded up to his time, King, as this chapter also concludes, saw a close correlation between a distorted biblicism and theology and resistance to movements for integration and black liberation and empowerment. Thus, King's "nonviolent Christian critique of and resistance to structural injustice," as Ronald J. Sider describes it, were aimed largely at both the beliefs and the practices of the white church.[28] In King's estimation, the white religious establishment stood as the most glaring and tragic example of a culture awash in hypocrisy, bigotry, and intolerance. The concerns and values implied in this critique are raised most provocatively in King's essay, "Who Is Their God?" (1962) and in his "The Letter from the Birmingham Jail" (1963).[29]

Equally significant is the conclusion that King essentially failed in his efforts to move the white church toward renewal and a more vital and prophetic role in the crusade to redeem and transform America. While he encountered isolated, prophetic voices in the moderate and liberal wings of the white church that gave him some basis for hope, it was, generally speaking, white Christians' devotion to the status quo that compelled him to assign a unique vanguard role, and indeed a messianic role, to the black church in the unfolding history of humankind's redemption and transformation.[30] Even so, this study will not ignore King's perspective on those cooperative, inter-church and interdenominational efforts that united black and white Christians in the civil rights and peace movements, especially as revealed in the activities of groups such as the National Council of Churches, Clergy and Laity Concerned, and the National Conference on Religion and Race.

Chapter 5 traces the development of King's thinking as it related to the Christian church and its mission in a global context. While his view that the black church has a message for the world will not be ignored, of particular significance is his understanding of the roles that the church as a whole should assume in the lives of people outside the United States—in Africa, Asia, Europe, and other parts of the world. The contention here is that King challenged the Christians of the world to not only eliminate racism, poverty, and war on an international scale but also to engage with each other and those of other religions to shape a positive pluralism. This was most evident not only in King's challenge to the World Council of Churches but also in his employment of the metaphors of "the world house" and "the worldwide neighborhood."[31]

Moreover, King's references to Mohandas K. Gandhi, a Hindu, as "the greatest Christian of the modern world" should not be taken lightly, for it shows that King was not confined by narrow and traditional perceptions of what it means to be the church, or to act in the servant style of Jesus Christ.[32] It also reveals King's potential fruitfulness for interfaith or ecumenical dialogue.[33] Indeed, King, to a greater extent than many fundamentalists and evangelicals in his time, understood the mission of the church in universal and inclusive terms; and he was far more concerned about the advancement of practical or applied Christianity than about the spread of doctrinal or missionary Christianity.

Chapter 6 will identify the most relevant features of King's thinking for the construction of what might be called a liberating and empowering church for the twenty-first century. It holds that an assessment of King's legacy as it pertains to the nature and mission of the church is possible, and that, through a close examination of his ideas and concerns, a doctrine of the church emerges that is meaningful for today.[34] In other words, when it comes to the question of the church's role in the contemporary society and world, King is a model for reflection. Christians can get special insights and lessons from the type of energetic, creative, and prophetic ministry model he so brilliantly articulated and exemplified because the religious establishment of our time is not vastly different, at least in some respects, from that of his own. This chapter, then, suggests the need for a reappropriation of King's ideas for the contemporary and future church.

This sixth chapter is representative of a conscious effort to take King beyond his own context while situating him in other, more recent contexts in which he is still meaningful. The view is that his constructive reflections on and critique of the church transcend the immediate historical setting in which he spoke, wrote, and struggled. Even so, any serious endorsement of King for our time must also reckon with King in his own time. The central point is that in these times, when many are questioning the relevance and reformability of the church in light of human needs, King remains a powerful prophetic voice and a paragon of Godly devotion.[35] This is true in part because King's activism was ultimately determined by the example of Jesus Christ and/or the needs of society, and not by the norms of the church and the academy. Be that as it may, King demonstrated what can happen as a result of the multifaceted interaction of the church and society, culture, and politics.

This book testifies to the enduring power of King's thought and activism. A part of its aim is to make available to a new generation of church-persons the thought of one of the most penetrating and insightful minds of the twentieth century. It is also designed to contribute to the enrichment and extension of current discussion and debate about the intellectual legacy of King, and about the relationship of the church and religion to public life and society.[36]

This book is not the final word on King's definition and descriptions of what the church should be in this nation and the world. It is hoped that it will help many to better understand King as a serious person of ideas while exposing key issues that call for further investigation. At the same time, it is hoped that this work will contribute to the expanding body of literature on both King and the church. If this occurs, the effort will be well worthwhile.

1

The Roots Factor

The Church as a Second Home

When discussing the Negro church as it is and as it might come to be, it must never be forgotten that the Negro church fundamentally is an expression of the Negro community itself.

> —Gunnar Myrdal, "The Negro Church: Its
> Weaknesses, Trends, and Outlook"

The church has always been a second home for me. As far back as I can remember I was in church every Sunday.

> —Martin Luther King, Jr.

The Black Church has been womb and mother to a vast spectrum of black leadership in every generation since its inception.

> —C. Eric Lincoln, *Race, Religion, and the
> Continuing American Dilemma*

Traditionally the black church has been an extended family and the family has been a "domestic church."

> —J. Deotis Roberts, *Roots of a Black
> Future: Family and Church*

The life of Martin Luther King, Jr., may be viewed as a continuing commitment to the advancement of the ministry and mission of the Christian church. The son, nephew, grandson, and great-grandson of Baptist preachers and pious, God-fearing, and church-going women,

King was literally born in the church, and the church figured prominently in his earliest conception of place in a southern context.[1] Moreover, the church shaped his identity, rooted him in strong moral and spiritual values, and instilled in him a sense of direction and purpose.

This opening chapter traces the origins of King's understanding of the church back to his childhood. Special attention is devoted to his upbringing in Ebenezer Baptist Church and the surrounding culture in Atlanta, Georgia, and the ways in which that informed his developing perspective on the church as a whole. King's experiences as a young minister at Calvary Baptist Church in Chester, Pennsylvania, and at Twelfth Baptist Church in Boston, Massachusetts, are also discussed, especially in terms of how they reinforced images of the church that he had brought from his background at Ebenezer.[2] The central point is that black congregations afforded the models for King's earliest sense of the identity and function of the church. However, as this chapter concludes, this did not occur in isolation from King's extensive exposure to liberal-modernistic thinking at Morehouse College, Crozer Theological Seminary, and Boston University—training that led him to raise critical questions about even some of the most fundamental church teachings and practices.

The Ebenezer Tradition: The Making of a Church Culture

Martin Luther King, Jr.'s earliest awareness and understanding of the church owed much to what might be called the "Ebenezer tradition."[3] Atlanta's Ebenezer Baptist Church, the home church of King and generations of his forebears, was founded in 1886 by blacks who were not far removed from slavery and who were convinced that autonomous religious and/or ecclesiastical institutions had to be created to serve the peculiar and manifold needs and aspirations of African Americans. King's maternal grandfather, Adam Daniel Williams, became the second pastor of Ebenezer in 1894, succeeding John A. Parker, and King's father, Martin Luther King, Sr., assumed the pastorate of that congregation in 1931, following the death of Williams.[4] During the many years that Williams (1894–1931) and King, Sr., (1931–1975) served Ebenezer, they became widely known for their civil rights activities, social service ministries, and persistent efforts to make the church responsive to the social, political, and economic realities of their times.[5]

As artists, orators, and members of various social clubs and church auxiliaries, King, Jr.'s maternal grandmother, Jennie C. Parks Williams, and his mother, Alberta Williams King, also contributed substantially to making Ebenezer a force for change, thus reinforcing the idea of church as an active presence in the total life of the community.[6] Raised in a culture in which the church was a prime locus for storytelling, King, Jr., became quite familiar with this history, and his sense of the inextricable links between Ebenezer Baptist Church, the King family, and the quest for black freedom and self-determination helps explain why he, even as a boy, was uncomfortable with narrow and self-centered images and definitions of the church.[7]

King, Jr., embraced Ebenezer's history as part of the air he breathed and the ground he walked on as a child, and consequently, the past for him became a part of the present. Pursuing an official membership at Ebenezer while still very young, he was unaware in any theoretical sense of the meaning of the church:

> I joined the church at the age of five. I well remember how this event occurred. Our church was in the midst of the spring revival, and a guest evangelist had come down from Virginia. On Sunday morning the evangelist came into our Sunday School to talk to us about salvation, and after a short talk on this point he extended an invitation to any of us who wanted to join the church. My sister was the first one to join the church that morning, and after seeing her join I decided that I would not let her get ahead of me, so I was the next. I had never given this matter a thought, and even at the time of my baptism I was unaware of what was taking place. From this it seems quite clear that I joined the church not out of any dynamic conviction, but out of a childhood desire to keep up with my sister.[8]

Ebenezer Baptist Church became a learning community for young King, sharing that role with his home, both of which existed on Atlanta's Auburn Avenue, less than two blocks apart. His earliest letters to his parents, some of which were written when he was only eleven, reflect the educational value of his Ebenezer experience, for they "convey an intimate knowledge of Baptist church life, including such details as congregational governance, ward meetings, church finances, and social events."[9] The youngster got a superb artistic education as well because, in church and at home, there were his maternal grandmother's and Aunt Ida Worthem's "interesting stories," his father's dynamic hellfire and brimstone proclamations of the gospel and the biblical revelation, and his mother's singing, almost always accompanied by brilliant displays of her skills on the piano or organ. Also, King, Jr.'s earliest moral and religious education occurred in both contexts, in which sacred space was provided for the exploration of controversial topics and ideas regarding the human condition and human responsibility. Here he gained an experiential knowledge of the power of love. The lessons he learned at the dinner table were reinforced by his Sunday school teachers and other adult figures at Ebenezer, all of whom had the freedom to discipline the boy if the need arose.[10]

Though he was introduced as a child to a church culture that was decisively fundamentalist or evangelical in terms of its faith, doctrine, and practice, there was much tangible in King, Jr.'s boyhood to indicate that he would become not merely a strong supporter but also an uncompromising critic of the church. The fact that he was reciting biblical passages and singing, "with rollicking gospel beat," "I want to be like Jesus" before he reached age six is telling enough, but the youngster's uneasiness with Baptist theological orthodoxy had surfaced by the time he reached his teens, to say nothing of his inability to reconcile certain church teachings with his own sense of reasoning:

> The lessons I was taught in Sunday school were quite in the funda-
> mentalist line. None of my teachers ever doubted the infallibility of
> the Scriptures. Most of them were unlettered and had never heard of
> biblical criticism. Naturally, I accepted the teachings as they were
> being given to me. I never felt any need to doubt them—at least at
> that time I didn't. I guest I accepted biblical studies uncritically until
> I was about twelve years old. But this uncritical attitude could not last
> long, for it was contrary to the very nature of my being. I had always
> been the questioning and precocious type. At the age of thirteen, I
> shocked my Sunday school class by denying the bodily resurrection
> of Jesus.[11]

This early tendency to question certain traditional or orthodox church teachings while maintaining an active membership at Ebenezer Baptist Church was indicative of the kind of ambivalence that would characterize King, Jr.'s attitude toward and approach to the church in general. This spirit of ambivalence was heightened significantly by the youngster's inability to come to terms with what he perceived to be a powerful residue of anti-intellectualism and unbridled spiritual emotionalism in the church, and especially in southern black Baptist Protestantism:

> I had seen that most Negro ministers were unlettered, not trained in
> seminaries, and that gave me pause. . . . I had been brought up in the
> church and knew about religion, but I wondered whether it could
> serve as a vehicle to modern thinking. I wondered whether religion,
> with its emotionalism in Negro Churches, could be intellectually
> respectable as well as emotionally satisfying. I revolted against the
> emotionalism of Negro religion, the shouting and the stamping. I
> didn't understand it and it embarrassed me.[12]

Ashamed of the seeming excesses of black Christians while singing and shouting, King, Jr., failed to perceive the legitimacy of these means of artistic expression on black or any other terms. Indeed, he demonstrated an inability to embrace some of the most vital forms of African American culture, for Ebenezer Baptist Church itself, like other black congregations in and around Atlanta, afforded virtually all the ingredients that W. E. B. DuBois associated with the slave church—namely, the preacher, the frenzy, and the music. Thus, it is not surprising that King, Jr., saw variants of the shout as his mother, Alberta King, played the piano and sang at Ebenezer, or during the sermons of his father, King, Sr., who was known for his "prancing" and "walking the benches" with his parishioners.[13] Though often confusing and embarrassing, such experiences taught King, Jr., something quite profound not only about the rich emotive qualities of the black church, which he would ultimately affirm on some levels, but also about its personalist and therapeutic tendencies, or its significance in affirming personhood by offering to the folk a means of catharsis, of release and healing, for deep-seated, pent-up frustrations and emotions.[14] In short, Ebenezer afforded examples of how the church might best function as a therapeutic community.

Ebenezer reflected the sort of expressive character that had long been associated with church life across racial boundaries in southern history and culture.[15] But, significantly, King, Jr., never reduced that congregation's expressive role nor its worship experience to merely soul-stirring sermons and spiritual or gospel songs swelling and overflowing into joyous shouts. Informality of style and joyous expressions of faith constituted for him a very small part of the liturgical life of the black Baptist church, or of what the church was about generally. The church and the worship experience in its wholeness were about coming to terms with the contradictions of human existence, feeling a sense of power and fulfillment that were so often denied in the empirical realm, and finding answers to many of the proximate and ultimate concerns of life. This is why King, Jr., never lost interest in the church as a child, despite what he deemed to be its most unattractive features. King, Sr., reported that the boy "loved the church in a way I could recall in myself, the feeling for ceremonies and ritual, the passionate love of Baptist music." This led King, Sr., affectionately called Daddy King, to "believe through" King, Jr.'s "earliest years that" the youngster "would evolve more naturally than" his younger brother A. D. "to a place in the pastorate of Ebenezer" Baptist Church.[16]

Ever mindful of his people's deep yearning for the infinite presence of the spirit of God, and for a context in which to experience personal solace, King, Jr., understood the need for the church to serve as the organizing center and font of spirituality. His experiences at Ebenezer convinced him that the church was not merely an organizing institution and a stable foundation for black communities but also the most attractive mechanism for extending the influence of religion and spiritual values to the ranks of the folk. This perspective also grew naturally out of King, Jr.'s association with ordinary church folk, and out of a kind of revivalist ethos and tradition that nurtured him and generations of his forebears. Church life, then, was about lifting up an abused and despised people into a transcendent moment, thus affirming both their spirits and their spirituality. King, Jr., actually grew up with the sights and sounds of people surrendering themselves in praise and petition before God, and Ebenezer Baptist Church mirrored for him this image of the church as the custodian of a deep and vital spirituality.[17]

The same could be said of King, Jr.'s early sense of the church as a refuge for his people.[18] Mainly through stories passed down from the pulpit and the dinner table, he learned that the church had always been an institution of recognizable influence and proved staying power for people who often had no other source of protection. He heard from King, Sr., and Mama Alberta accounts of how the church, along with black colleges, "had provided a safe sanctuary" for blacks determined to escape the wrath of vicious white mobs during the Atlanta riots of 1906. A. D. Williams, King, Jr.'s grandfather, had "experienced the terrible racial violence," when "several Negroes were killed and many more were attacked and injured by the police," and this prompted him to unite with other black clergymen in forming the Atlanta Civic League, "an advisory board that met with city officials to curb any racial conflict in the city."[19] The 1906 Atlanta riots tested Ebenezer's social and political commitments in serious and perhaps even unprecedented and unimaginable ways, and Williams, from that point, was apparently compelled to think more intensely about how the relevance and effectiveness of the church as a prophetic voice and presence could be significantly enhanced. But the image of the church as a refuge was such that even those black preachers who, unlike Williams, avoided activity in the streets or the public domain provided vital pastoral ministries that helped their people to deal with adversity, tragedy, and uncertainty. Hence, the ministry of the church was social even when it did not explicitly find expression in social action. The complexity of the church at this level was probably never detected to any great extent by King during his childhood.

There were other accounts known in King family circles of how the church shielded their ancestors from the violence and contempt of the white South—accounts that helped give shape and meaning to not only King, Jr.'s understanding of the Ebenezer tradition but also to his sense of himself, the church as a whole, his culture, and the world around him. King, Jr., was informed that the church had "offered relief from this life of hardship" for Delia King, his paternal grandmother, and her children, as they were abused and exploited under a sharecropping system in Stockbridge, Georgia. Referring to those times, King, Jr.'s father noted that "Church was a way to ease the harsh tone of farm life, a way to keep from descending into bitterness."[20] Living in the long shadow of slavery and in a period marked by Jim Crowism and violent lynchings—in a world in which reality was so often vague, inconsistent, and capricious—the church helped King, Sr., and his mother and siblings to navigate through the shadows of a dark and chaotic existence. King, Sr., and King, Jr., would later bring this sense of the church to their pastoral experiences at Ebenezer Baptist Church.

Thus, King, Jr., was made to see that the church was the raison d'être for his people, or that source that helped them to handle tragedy and that provided an anchor for meaning in daily life. People looked for hope and new life in the church, and there they found the strength to survive from one week to the next. What happened in the worship experience nurtured their search for answers, hope, and some sense of assurance that tomorrow would be better, for the church always communicated the promise that justice can be achieved and the persecuted redeemed. This was never lost in a culture in which the Exodus story in the Bible, which features God's setting the captive free and imposing judgment and retribution on the oppressive system of the Pharaoh, had such strong resonance. The image of the black Baptist church as a refuge remained deeply etched in King, Jr.'s consciousness, and it actually reinforced his awareness of the larger, historic role of the church as a bulwark against the discrimination and dehumanization inherent in white society's values and institutions.[21]

Equally important for King, Jr., were the ways in which the church kept people together in the face of bigotry and intolerance and gave them a healthy sense of themselves. He discovered in Ebenezer Baptist Church an important symbol of community, for it was there in Sunday school that he not only developed "the capacity for getting along with people" but also witnessed firsthand how the church functioned as a unifying force. Ebenezer was not just a community of faith but, by definition, also a shared community experience—a congregation that planted itself firmly within the life of the broader community it served. Bound together by a common experience and devotion, by the need for communal interaction and support, and by a consensus of beliefs, attitudes, and expectations, the members of Ebenezer enjoyed the benefits of a church fellowship that extended into the King home a block or so away. As King, Jr., explained in his "Autobiography of Religious Development" (1950), in which he mined the terrain of his own religious upbringing, the importance of this kind of ecclesial context for shaping his earliest conception of community could not be overstated.[22]

For King, Jr., the name of Ebenezer Baptist Church conjured up images of not just local autonomy and freedom but also of church conferences, family reunions, and communal feasts—experiences animated by a lot touching, hugging, storytelling, laughter, holy kissing, and the sharing of handshakes and other warm greetings. Ebenezer was for him a critical part of an extended familial community, for members of that congregation were present at virtually every major turning point in his life, from birth to death. This is why the youngster regarded the church as "a second home."[23] The testimony of his father, King, Sr., concurs, for he reported, recalling the times extending back to his father-in-law A. D. Williams's pastorate at Ebenezer, that in the church, "Negro people had a closeness and sense of family that made for very strong bonds of emotional security."[24] Small wonder that the church and family were so inextricably intertwined in King, Jr.'s consciousness, and that together they formed the communal ethical standards that shaped his upbringing, and that of his black playmates as well.[25] Generally speaking, the Ebenezer experience taught King, Jr., a lot about the significance of the extended family structure—about its history, its values and traditions, and the manner in which it functioned in African American life and culture.

As King, Jr., would discover, Ebenezer's place in the community confirmed so much of what scholars like W. E. B. DuBois, Carter G. Woodson, and Benjamin E. Mays were saying in the early twentieth century about the social role and significance of the black church in history.[26] Not only was "Social life built completely within the framework of the church," as Daddy King observed, but many felt that the church had to become a prophetic voice in addressing and eliminating social evil.[27] King, Jr., came to see this very early in life, despite being exposed to congregations that attached more significance to evangelism, revivalism, proselytizing, and a puritanical moral code than to efforts to mobilize people against poverty and oppression. Ebenezer Baptist Church was the context in which he first developed the idea of the congregation as a site for both religious and social actions.

Ebenezer's tradition of service to the community and race, which would become a major source of pride and inspiration for King, Jr., extended at least as far back to A. D. Williams, who measured up to heroic standards of virtue while combining a biblical-theological conservatism and fire-and-brimstone preaching with a reform, activist ethic. Functioning in an era when Social Gospelers like Walter Rauschenbusch, Washington Gladden, and Reverdy C. Ransom were highlighting Christianity's responsibility for social problems, Williams, commonly referred to as "one of Atlanta's most prominent and respected ministers," absolutely refused to allow Ebenezer to become a tool of the status quo or the white power structure. He determined instead that the congregation establish a model of the church as crusader against bigotry, exploitation, and injustice. Williams embodied Ebenezer's prophetic spirit and social agenda in ways that would later benefit King, Sr., and King, Jr., as they sought to use that church as a platform from which to launch their own social activities.[28]

Under Williams's leadership, Ebenezer developed the financial resources and the structures of congregational life that enabled it to support ministries geared to political and social change. In 1906, Williams united with some five hundred blacks in Georgia in forming the Georgia Equal Rights League, an organization that protested the white primary system and addressed issues ranging from lynching to the exclusion of African Americans from juries and the military. In 1917, Williams participated in the organization of the Atlanta branch of the National Association for the Advancement of Colored People (NAACP), and was active as a member and president of that organization, often holding meetings at Ebenezer and in his home.[29] In that capacity, he supported the struggle for racial justice through legal channels while leading voter registration rallies, thus prefiguring both King, Sr., and King, Jr., who, much like Williams, also believed that litigation had to be combined with political strategies, moral suasion, and social protest in the struggle to win freedom and justice. In the 1920s, Williams led Atlanta's black community in a boycott of local stores and businesses that supported *The Georgian*, a newspaper known for its casual use of racial epithets in its references to African Americans. He later spearheaded a drive to stop a municipal bond issue because it contained no provisions for black high school education.[30] Clearly, Williams used the church as a power base and rallying point for such activities, an approach that would also be used by King, Sr., and King, Jr.

Apart from his challenge to white power, Williams was stubborn in his conviction that his church should never abandon charity or social service ministries aimed at improving the general quality of life for people. Thus, Ebenezer Baptist Church would become, in effect, a social welfare agency during the 1920s and 1930s, sharing that distinction with other black congregations in the urban South and North, especially those that struggled to meet the challenges resulting from the Great Depression and the mass exodus of blacks from the rural South.[31] King, Sr., related the following about the ingenuity his father-in-law displayed in devoting the resources of Ebenezer to meeting a multitude of needs in the community, an account he must have shared many times with King, Jr.:

> They were a generous congregation, and what money Reverend
> Williams could take in he poured back into the community to make
> food available to the hungry and clothes to those without them. We
> kept children while mothers worked. The church bought and

supplied medicines. Ebenezer tried to be an anchor as the storm rose. And we did well—nothing fancy, no frills. But the church helped as many in need as the church could reach. And the church grew stronger.[32]

The speech Williams gave at the NAACP national convention in Cleveland in June 1919, which focused on black voter registration and the wise use of the ballot, afforded more proof that he, unlike so many other black clergymen in his time, rejected the notion that the church should simply spread the gospel and save souls, and not get tangled up in transitory social and political problems.[33] For Williams, the biblical-theological concept of the kingdom of God was not simply about personal salvation, otherworldliness, and compensatory hope; it was also about the church's challenging and transforming social, political, and economic structures. Convinced that a civil rights–social justice tradition is not necessarily incompatible with a conservative theology, he sounded a social gospel note as he instructed his son-in-law and assistant minister, King, Sr., concerning the proper role of the church and its ministry:

It was through him that I came to understand the larger implications involved in any churchman's responsibility to the community he served. Church wasn't simply Sunday morning and a few evenings during the week. It was more than a full-time job. In the act of faith, every minister became an advocate for justice. In the South, this meant an active involvement in changing the social order all around us. . . . Reverend Williams made it clear to me from the time I moved into his house that he felt no sympathy for those who saw no mission in their lives, who could not understand, for instance, that progress never came without challenge, without danger, and, at times, great trial. These obstacles, however, could not stop the true man of God. A minister, in his calling, chose to lead the people of his church not only in the spiritual sense, but also in the practical world in which they found themselves struggling.[34]

Williams was part of an age in which black ministers viewed themselves as the chief moral guardians of society, and he understood the importance of centering the worship and witness of the church on the general quest for a better society. In presenting such a vision of the social mission of the church, he was not only setting an example for King, Sr., and King, Jr., but also standing in the best tradition of his forebears, for black churches originated out of the conviction that worship and the private devotional life cannot be legitimately separated from public duty and corporate responsibility. Therefore, the Christian command for racial justice remained imperative, as the early black church fathers and mothers, much like Williams in later times, sought to implement their faith in very practical ways.[35] Ebenezer Baptist Church offered a window through which to view the symbolic, ideological, and political roles that black churches had assumed since their beginnings, for they were never merely imitations of white models.

Williams's belief that the church is called to serve simultaneously as a religious body and as a social center was one of the key ideas he passed on to his son-in-law, King, Sr., who in turn introduced it to his son, King, Jr. When it came to the whole question of the role of the church in public life, Williams—whose influence extended beyond Ebenezer into the Georgia Baptist State Convention and the National Baptist Convention, USA—was perhaps King, Sr.'s greatest single influence.[36] When Williams died in 1931, King, Sr., succeeded him as Ebenezer's pastor and as a vocal presence in the Georgia State and National Baptist Conventions, and the mission priorities he pursued for the next forty-four years recalled those of his father–in-law. Both were subscribers to what has been variously called "social gospel Christianity," "a homespun social gospelism," and "a distinctive African American version of the social gospel," thus anticipating King, Jr. in striking ways.[37] As was the case with Williams, the biblical call to social justice was at the core of King, Sr.'s proclamations and the driving force behind his social activism. King, Sr., was unalterably convinced that there were strong scriptural warrants for enacting progressive social policies that encourage peaceful human relations, equality of opportunity, and a better sharing of the earth's goods, and that the church's mandate is to make that known in word and deed.

In keeping with this conviction, King, Sr., consistently challenged the white supremacist values and institutions that attempted to silence his voice and to limit black political and economic opportunities, and, in so doing, he always drew on the rich moral, spiritual, and material resources of Ebenezer Baptist Church. Determined to have full access to the ballot, King, Sr., defied Atlanta's city hall "by riding the whites-only elevator to the registrar's office," and in 1935, he actually "led a public protest against the segregation of elevators at the Fulton County Courthouse." Like A. D. Williams, he served the Atlanta NAACP as a faithful member and as president, and greatly assisted that organization's voter registration drive and its protest of a bond issue that disallowed sufficient funds for black schools. In the late 1930s, King, Sr., worked with the Atlanta Civic and Political League in launching voter-registration drives, and as head of the Atlanta Baptist Ministers Union, and despite resistance from whites and blacks, he led a march in support of that cause. As chair of the Committee on the Equalization of Teachers' Salaries, he protested policies "that paid higher salaries to white teachers than to blacks with equivalent qualifications and experience."[38] Moreover, King, Sr., was known for his bold and uncompromising responses to white policemen who dared to call him "a boy" and to shoe salespersons who insisted that he sit in the colored section before being served. Even as a child, King, Jr., knew of his father's assault on personal and institutional racism on many fronts, and he would suggest, once he reached adulthood, that King, Sr., always viewed his roles as church pastor and social activist not as separate spheres or polar opposites but as extensions of each other:

> From before I was born, my father had refused to ride the city buses, after witnessing a brutal attack on a load of Negro passengers. He had led the fight in Atlanta to equalize teachers' salaries, and had been instrumental in the elimination of Jim Crow elevators in the courthouse. As pastor of Ebenezer Baptist Church, where he still presides over a congregation of four thousand, he had wielded great influence in the Negro community, and had perhaps won the grudging respect of the whites. At any rate, they had never attacked him physically, a fact that filled my brother and sister and me with wonder as we grew up in this tension-packed atmosphere.[39]

King, Sr., insisted that one who commits to the church necessarily becomes an agent of social change. Quoting from Luke 4:18–19, he asserted: "We are to do something about the broken-hearted, poor, unemployed, the captive, the blind, and the bruised. How can people be happy without jobs, food, shelter and clothes?"[40] Although quite mindful of how the mere struggle for survival absorbed what little reform energies many black congregations had, Daddy King—living in an era marked by what has been labeled "the deradicalization of the black church"[41]—nevertheless had little patience for a socially inactive or dysfunctional church, and virtually none for the church that was concerned only with its own institutional maintenance. He lamented the fact that so many churches flatly rejected prophetic, social gospel Christianity while retreating into enclaves of a narrow moralistic, fundamentalist Christianity, a problem that stifled the creative potential of the church as a whole in the 1930s and 1940s. While agreeing with the prevailing concern to preserve the fundamentals of the faith (i.e., virgin birth, the resurrection and deity of Christ, his substitutionary atonement, the second coming, and the authority and inerrancy of the Bible), King, Sr., insisted that this alone did not constitute the essence of the church. In a speech at the Atlanta Missionary Baptist Association meeting in 1940, he declared:

> The church is to touch every phase of the community life. Quite often we say that the church has no place in politics, forgetting the words

of the Lord: "The spirit of the Lord is upon me, because he hath anointed me to preach the Gospel to the poor; he hath sent me to heal the broken-hearted, to preach deliverance to the captives, and the recovering of sight to the blind, to set at liberty them that are bruised, and to preach the acceptable year of the Lord."[42]

King, Sr., was actually echoing Carter G. Woodson's claim, set forth in a 1939 essay, regarding the black church as "all-comprehending institution."[43] The idea here is that the influence of the church extended beyond the strictly spiritual and ecclesiastical into virtually all spheres of African American life—from the personal dimensions of everyday existence to public affairs and issues of public policy. The church set the community's moral and ethical standards, and was the center of everything from philanthropy to political organizing to business endeavors and land ownership. It taught the values of education, entrepreneurship, and civic responsibility, and it inspired the contributions made by African Americans from across the spectrum in the arts, from theater to music, painting to poetry, and everything in between. It encouraged the folk to excel in almost every sphere of endeavor and was *the* force in the lives of many who acquired notoriety and respectability in academics, the arts, business, entertainment, and other fields. Obviously, this unique and pivotal role of the church meant that religion penetrated every seam of the black cultural fabric and touched every corner of black society, from the church sanctuary and the concert hall to the ball park, and from the school playground to the pool room and the night club. Ebenezer Baptist Church was a living, institutional symbol of this, thus making it impossible for King, Jr., even as a child with no clear definition of the Christian faith, to think of the church as being separate from life itself.[44]

King, Jr.'s social sensitivity was sharpened as he grew up with the knowledge of his grandfather's and father's activities in the church and community. Largely because of the work of A. D. Williams and King, Sr., Ebenezer became literally a benchmark for congregational and ecclesiastical activism, and a congregation quite conscious of its traditions and its role in the struggle. It was here that the Christian life was understood in terms of unconditional love and service to others, and King, Jr., absorbed this lesson almost unconsciously. Ebenezer also afforded a vital context in which he not only experienced lively worship but also learned much about racism and poverty, and about religion as a resource for mobilizing people in the interest of social change.[45]

The Ebenezer tradition helps explain why race and class figured into King, Jr.'s earliest sense of Christian ethics, and why his challenge to the fundamental structure and ethos of southern society began when he was still essentially a child. At age six, he was taught, despite bouts with white supremacy, that "I should not hate the white man, but that it was my duty as a Christian to love him." When he was only fifteen, in a speech called "The Negro and the Constitution," he addressed the problem of race as America's chief dilemma, pointing to the paradox of a nation born in freedom and claiming Judeo-Christian values while holding black human beings in bondage.[46] At age seventeen, King, Jr., wrote a letter to the *Atlanta Constitution*, insisting that his people be given the ballot, "equality before the law," and "equal opportunities in education, health, recreation, and similar public services." In a paper on "The Economic Basis of Cultural Conflict," he spoke to the links between racial and economic injustice.[47] In these and other actions taken by King, Jr., very early in life, one detects the influence of the Ebenezer Baptist Church's powerful legacy of social concern and activism.

The impact of the Ebenezer tradition on the shaping of King, Jr.'s concept of the church came not only through the leadership and activities of A. D. Williams and King, Sr., but also through the rich insights and contributions of Jennie C. Parks Williams and Alberta Williams King, his grandmother and mother.[48] Big Mama Jennie, as she was often called by King, Jr., and his siblings, Alfred Daniel and Christine, was "prominent in city, state and national religious affairs for more than forty years," and was also known and admired in many circles for the support she gave her husband in the crusade for racial justice and equality of opportunity. Aside from serving as president of the Missionary Society at Ebenezer and the Fifth District of the State Baptist Convention, and as a member of the Ministers' Wives Coterie and the Executive Board of the State and National Baptist Conventions, she was an orator, a widely celebrated speaker at church and civic events, and a gifted storyteller, and was also "involved in most aspects of church governance" at Ebenezer.[49] Her death in 1941 created an emptiness in young Martin's life and deprived him of one of his earliest and most significant intellectual, spiritual, and moral sources. Referring to Big Mama Jennie as "a saintly grandmother," King, Jr., discovered in her not only a powerful example of the Christian life but also a deep source of wisdom and a pillar of strength as he struggled to understand the church and his place in both that institution and the society as a whole.[50]

Affectionately referred to as Mother Dear by her children and Bunch by King, Sr., Alberta King was no less important as a strong and enduring influence on King, Jr. Widely hailed as "a dedicated church worker," as one "who figured prominently in social circles," as "a tribute to the foundation on which Ebenezer stands," and as "a loving source of strength to her family, her congregation, and her community," Alberta taught King, Jr., and her other children that "hatred and violence must be replaced by love."[51] Alberta's and King, Sr.'s teachings on the importance of embracing the love ethic in human relations, shared at both Ebenezer and in the King home, freed King, Jr., of what could have been a lingering bitterness toward whites and led him to look out on the world with a lot of optimism and hope. When six-year-old King, Jr., experienced the breakup of a friendship with a white playmate owing to the racism of the boy's parents, it was Alberta who sat the child on her knee and explained racial discrimination "as a social condition rather than a natural order."[52] She then insisted that he should never feel more or "less than anyone else," and implied that he should always be guided by the Golden Rule in his dealings with others.[53] Apparently, Alberta reinforced in King, Jr., that self-confidence, sense of somebodyness, and altruistic spirit that were typically instilled by Ebenezer Baptist Church and in black church culture generally.[54]

Aside from giving King, Jr., one of his first lessons on race, Alberta, an organist and choir director at Ebenezer, and also a leading musician for the Women's Auxiliary of the National Baptist Convention, greatly inspired him through her musical talents, thus contributing to his appreciation of black art and his early sense of the cultural significance of the church. Alberta's contribution in this regard was immeasurable, especially since singing and reciting Bible passages, which King, Jr., did with her encouragement in church and over meals at home, proved to be powerful incentives in absorbing the features of black culture.[55] Moreover, by observing Alberta's and Big Mama Jennie's many involvements and activities, King, Jr., grew conscious of the importance of church work in creating public roles for African American women, especially in black Baptist church circles in the South.

King, Jr., was profoundly affected by his family's long history of devotion to the church, and his earliest thoughts about how he might best meet the challenge of racial injustice were based largely on the example provided by his grandparents and parents.[56] Although King, Jr., was only a year old when A. D. Williams died, and twelve when he lost Big Mama Jennie, he found in King, Sr., and Alberta King echoes of their refusal to bow to white people and their oppressive routine. Hence, their spirit of resistance, supported by the teachings and resources of the church, became King, Jr.'s own:

> With this heritage, it is not surprising that I had also learned to abhor segregation, considering it both rationally inexplicable and morally unjustifiable. As a teenager I had never been able to accept the fact of having to go to the back of a bus or sit in the segregated section of train. The first time that I had been seated behind a curtain in a dining car, I felt as if the curtain had been dropped on my selfhood. Having the usual growing boy's pleasure in movies, I had yet gone to

a downtown theater in Atlanta only once. The experience of having to enter a rear door and sit in a filthy peanut gallery was so obnoxious that I could not enjoy the picture. I could never adjust to the separate waiting rooms, separate eating places, separate rest rooms, partly because the separate was always unequal, and partly because the very idea of separation did something to my sense of dignity and self-respect.[57]

Rooted in the values of both church and family, the Ebenezer tradition impacted King, Jr.'s life in other ways, as well. It was a driving force behind his decision to pursue training at the college, seminary, and graduate-school levels, and it nurtured and directed his proclivity toward church and race leadership. King, Jr., became a freshman at the all-black, all-male Morehouse College in Atlanta in 1944, the institution at which his maternal grandfather, father, and brother A. D. also matriculated. After graduating from Morehouse with a degree in sociology in 1948, King, Jr., studied theology at Crozer Theological Seminary in Chester, Pennsylvania, and later completed Ph.D. work at Boston University in that same field. While he delighted in the treasures of learning, the Ebenezer influence was such that he tailored "his academic training" at all levels to fit his needs as a pastor of a black Baptist congregation.[58]

The Ebenezer tradition also helps explain why King, Jr., chose to answer the call to ministry in 1947, when he was only eighteen, instead of pursuing his initial plan to become either a lawyer or a physician. A senior at Morehouse at the time, King, Jr., related the experience in these terms:

It was in my senior year of college that I entered the ministry. I had felt the urge to enter the ministry from my latter high school days, but accumulated doubts had somewhat blocked the urge. Now it appeared again with an inescapable drive. My call to the ministry was not a miraculous or supernatural something; on the contrary it was an inner urge calling me to serve humanity. I guess the influence of my father also had a great deal to do with my going into the ministry. This is not to say that he ever spoke to me in terms of being a minister, but that my admiration for him was the great moving factor. He set forth a noble example that I didn't mind following.[59]

Having a mounting interest in eliminating bigotry and intolerance and in creating human community, it is not surprising that King, Jr., followed in the footsteps of A. D. Williams and King, Sr., for he knew very early on that any viable movement on the part of blacks for freedom and justice had to be based in the church.[60] He also understood that the black pulpit, a setting in which the stories and characters in the Bible came alive, and an arena in which the inter-sections between speech and performance, between word and ritual, were always remarkably evident, provided the conduit, and indeed the best means, through which liberating social, economic, and political ideas entered into and circulated within the community. This could not have been more important for a young man imbued with the determination to change the conditions under which his people lived. The fact that King, Jr., chose ministry speaks not only to the enduring influence of Ebenezer but also to his belief that the church would afford a degree of access to the people that was quite untypical of other settings. His thoughts along these lines proved far more compelling than any reserva-tions he had about the potential of the church and its ministry as an avenue to modern thinking and/or intellectual freedom.[61]

King, Jr., grew up with preaching and preaching legends all around him, but his earliest lessons in preaching as both the spoken word and the per-formed art came under the tutelage of his father at the Ebenezer Baptist Church. It has been said that he "absorbed the slaves' worldview at Ebenezer Church," and that "the religion of Ebenezer Church" was "the earliest and most signifi-cant influence on his language."[62] This was evident from the time he preached his trial sermon at Ebenezer, an event that drew a crowd so large that it had to be moved from the church's small auditorium to its main sanctuary.[63] Soon thereafter, in February 1948, King, Jr., was ordained at Ebenezer; and from that point, he, being quite tradition-minded, set out to master the pulpit as he had come to know it.[64] Serving as an assistant minister to King, Sr., in those days, his deep desire to achieve excellence on this level would not be easy, for he had to deal with Daddy King's "old school" convictions and authoritarian approach to pastoring, both of which contributed to the idea that very young men who entered the ministry had to be constantly monitored, tested, and brought along slowly and carefully. A key issue here was church discipline, which A. D. Williams had also upheld in supreme fashion as he nurtured a young King, Sr., for ministry.[65]

Although King, Jr., preached occasionally at Ebenezer and other black churches in the Atlanta area, many of his earliest sermons have not survived. Even so, certain claims can be safely made regarding his approach to preach-ing. One is that his "style of preaching grew out of the tradition of the southern Baptist ministers, with cadences and timing which he had heard from his father and other ministers as long as he could remember."[66] This, perhaps as much as anything else, contributed to King, Jr.'s exceptional persona and his ability to communicate in the clearest and most eloquent terms. But King, Jr.'s unique and superb grasp of the art and practice of oratory would in time distin-guish him from his father and many other preachers in that generation, and this would prove most beneficial in the largely oral, storytelling culture in which he lived and functioned as a civil rights leader. The Ebenezer Baptist tradition helped prepare the ground for King, Jr.'s mastery of the sermonic art, with all of its power, poetic cadences, and rich metaphors and imagery.[67]

That tradition also brought to his preaching a social dimension that was often missing even in the sermons of well-established black preachers in the South in those times. Given King, Jr.'s links to both the Ebenezer Baptist Church and the black experience, it would have been only natural for him to speak in his sermons to the very same issues of racial injustice that he had already addressed in his writings and speeches in his early teens.[68] After all, Ebenezer afforded the kind of context that made prophetic preaching possible. In this regard, and indeed in other respects, Ebenezer epitomized the vitality of the church in the African American experience, for no institution was more significant in terms of the transmission of culture and cultural values from one generation to the other.

Ebenezer Baptist Church lived in King, Jr.'s memory, even as he sought to adapt to new and different surroundings. But Ebenezer was not merely a place of sacred memories and dreams for the youngster; it was also the setting in which a powerful core of values and traditions were nurtured. It was so much a part of the daily rhythm of King, Jr.'s early life in the South, and it was also at the center of that vast complex of forces that made him secure in a dangerously insecure world. Also, Ebenezer figured prominently in his decision to embrace the challenge of race leadership, and it would become a supporting framework for his life of activism and service to humanity.[69]

But that community of faith that informed and helped mold King, Jr.'s thinking concerning the image and function of the church was not confined to Ebenezer Baptist Church. The young man benefited from a larger church community that included not only other black congregations of different denominational affiliations along Auburn Avenue and in other parts of Atlanta and the South, but also Morehouse College, where he first learned to think of the church in theoretical terms, and black Baptist congregations in the North, at which he preached and fulfilled apprenticeships.[70] It is to this larger church community that the discussion now turns.

Beyond Ebenezer: The Larger Church Community

Martin Luther King, Jr., discovered in Atlanta, and the South as a whole, a vast and varied cultural and religious landscape that he regarded as sacred space. Atlanta was a center of thriving black church life in the 1930s and 1940s. Along the northeast side of "Sweet" Auburn Avenue, with its visible but complex webs of familial and neighborly relations, the Big Bethel African Methodist Episcopal Church (AME) and the Wheat Street Baptist Church existed in close proximity to the Ebenezer Baptist Church and the King's home.[71] These large congregations were home to a proud and burgeoning black elite that included not only preachers and accomplished musicians but also physicians, college professors, bankers, morticians, and specialists in other fields, all of whom were success symbols and role models for King, Jr.[72] This helped account for King's enormous drive and ambition to succeed in life.

But small-membership congregations tended to be the norm, and both neighborhood churches and churches consisting largely of kinfolk were quite common on Auburn Avenue, throughout Atlanta, and across the South. Unlettered preachers frequently roamed from church to church, either seeking pastoral appointments or on the prowl for sermonic content and illustrations. The churches, pervaded by the kinlike atmosphere, became the repositories of black identity, the prime institutional embodiments of folk values, and the treasures of religious folk life.[73] Thus, King, Jr.'s early sense of the church stretched beyond Ebenezer Baptist Church and his own extended family to include the larger black community of Atlanta and the South, for it was in this broader setting that the full range of culture found its most powerful expression.

King, Jr.'s earliest awareness of the church was deeply rooted not only in personal experience but also in a consciousness of place and time. He vividly recalled the impact of the church on the social, moral, and spiritual life of his neighborhood:

> This was a wholesome community, notwithstanding the fact that
> none of us were ever considered members of the "upper upper class."
> Crime was at a minimum in our community, and most of our
> neighbors were deeply religious. I can well remember that all of my
> childhood playmates were regular Sunday School goers, not that I
> chose them on that basis, but because it was very difficult to find
> playmates in my community who did not attend Sunday School.[74]

Big Bethel A.M.E. Church and the Wheat Street Baptist Church loomed large in that circle of congregations that so decisively impacted and reflected the culture of black Atlanta during King, Jr.'s childhood. Like Ebenezer, both of these churches had long stood at the vanguard of social justice advocacy.[75] In September 1906, as blacks faced some of the worst terrorism and mob violence from whites in Atlanta's history, Big Bethel hosted the seventh annual convention of the National Negro Business League, a meeting at which Booker T. Washington, the group's only president up to that point, was reelected.

Meetings of the local NAACP occurred at both Big Bethel and Wheat Street Baptist Church in later years, as was the case also with Ebenezer. One of the most important meetings of the NAACP was held at Wheat Street in January 1932, where the delegates seriously addressed the "local conditions affecting the fundamental rights of the colored citizens of Atlanta."[76] Growing up in the shadow of Big Bethel and Wheat Street, and having a keen knowledge of the Ebenezer tradition, King, Jr., would never have problems "with the principle that the church had to speak for the political and social aspirations of the community."[77]

Located only a block from Ebenezer, the Wheat Street Baptist Church was especially important as a symbol and an active presence for King, Jr. The church's influence on young King came primarily through its pastor, William Holmes Borders. Borders had presided at King, Jr.'s maternal grandmother's funeral at Ebenezer in 1941,[78] and his wife, Julia P. Borders, whom King, Jr., respected for "her devotion to Christ and his church," was the boy's eighth-grade English teacher.[79] Viewing Borders as "a colorful pulpiteer" and a leader of his people, King, Jr., admired and respected the ways in which this pastor put the church to the service of the race, and the youngster "used to go to the church next door and slip back home before his father missed him." Apparently, Borders' persona, charisma, and style of ministry became a critical part of King, Jr.'s personal development, ministerial identity, and understanding of the church.[80] Under Borders' leadership, Wheat Street stood as living proof of the power of lessons King, Jr., was always taught at Ebenezer—namely, that the church assumes meaning in the service of a cause. Borders was essentially as much a personification of this principle as King, Sr., and A. D. Williams.[81] Hence, Wheat Street became a vital part of that larger church culture that sensitized King, Jr., to the dimensions of the racial justice issue, and that would in time make him so receptive to church-based social gospel advocacy and progressivism.

There was a familial quality to that broader church culture that affirmed King, Jr.'s personhood, humanity, and early thirst for community, and that helped him to make some sense of the paradox of a society supposedly rooted in Judeo-Christian values while sanctioning structures of white supremacy and black subordination. Therefore, when King, Jr., identified the church as his "second home," he had in mind this wider church culture, and not simply Atlanta's Ebenezer Baptist Church. While churches like Big Bethel and Wheat Street differed in terms of denominational identity, polity, doctrine, and standards of discipline, they never lost that sense of being a part of an extended familial community, and they were nonetheless able to establish, at least on some levels, a broad, interdenominational tradition of shared involvement in the crusade for a just and inclusive society. The heavy involvements of Big Bethel, Wheat Street, and Ebenezer with the NAACP and in the larger struggle against racial discrimination became shining examples of how such cooperative ventures occurred.[82]

Herein lies much of the explanation for King, Jr.'s lifelong refusal to become obsessed with church labels and his own denominational identity. It was apparent to him, even as a child, that the very nature of the black condition demanded inter-church and interdenominational cooperation.[83] Indeed, King, Jr.'s early egalitarian views and spirit of ecumenism were tempered by that larger church culture to which he was exposed, and he, as a consequence, developed an openness to the concept of cooperative Christianity long before he engaged in a serious study of Walter Rauschenbusch and the Social Gospel movement.

For King, Jr., the church life of Auburn Avenue essentially mirrored the religious dynamics of the black South as a whole. People were drawn together in a cultural affinity of shared experiences, of shared values and traditions, mainly because of a common condition rooted in oppression. Spiritual values, which extended beyond any particular concept or image of the church, paraded as the key force in providing social cohesion and stability under difficult circumstances, and also in fostering a strong group consciousness among the folk. Cut off from most areas of social and political life in the South, the church was the place in which African Americans sought shelter in their common grief and frustrations, and there they found limitless opportunities not only for self-help and self-expression but also for recognition and leadership. The values of individualism and materialism were often discouraged, and the church lifted up a vision of true humanity characterized by the beloved community.[84] It could not have been otherwise in a culture in which people expected a church experience that offered genuine Christian sharing, nurturing, and discipleship, in addition to celebratory worship. Knowing the social dynamics in the South, and especially the racial terrain on which blacks and whites related to one another, King, Jr., found this function of the church as extended family and as a pivotal symbol of community to be most appealing and indeed indispensable. This was only natural for one who spoke to the need for African American unity long before graduating from college.[85]

Although King, Jr., occasionally accompanied his parents on trips to local and regional church activities as a child, his most extensive contact with the larger black church community and culture of the South occurred in the late 1940s, while he was matriculating at Atlanta's Morehouse College. As a member of both the College Glee Club and the Atlanta University-Morehouse-Spelman Chorus, and as an aspiring young preacher, King, Jr., sang and spoke widely, at church and community events, especially during the six months after his ordination, when he served as an assistant minister with his father at Ebenezer.[86] Being Daddy King's son alone carried considerable weight in church circles, and this often translated into invitations to sing or speak. King, Jr., was thoroughly introduced to urban and rural congregational life in various parts of the South, and this exposure undoubtedly sharpened his vision of how the church might best relate to the personal and collective lives of blacks in diverse settings.

King, Jr.'s exposure to and involvements with music and preaching were a critical component of his introduction to the artistic qualities so powerfully displayed in the life of southern black churches. His early fascination with gospel music, the spirituals, and the great hymns of the church was nurtured in a black church community in which sacred music and sound musical education were virtually a part of daily life. King, Jr.'s exposure to instrumental and vocal music at Ebenezer and in the King home, alluded to earlier, was extensive enough, especially since the youngster was also required to take music lessons, but there were other church influences that he could never fully escape. In the 1930s and 1940s, the Big Bethel AME Church, slightly more than a stone's throw from Ebenezer, became widely known for black sacred music of the highest quality, and especially *Heaven Bound*, which was written and performed by the congregation. "Utilizing many of the old spirituals in the form of the miracle play," this piece attracted large crowds in numerous performances, some of which were undoubtedly attended by the Kings. Moreover, Kemper Harreld, the Director of Music at Morehouse College in the early 1940s, did outstanding work with orchestras and glee clubs in various churches and schools, thus adding to the rich musical traditions of black Atlanta and the South.[87] So when it came to the whole question of the potential of the church for artistic creativity, or as a symbol of expressive culture, Ebenezer, Morehouse, and southern black churches generally came together in King, Jr.'s consciousness. Early on he realized that the black church was unique in the exceptional quality and variety of talent it provided and that its values of freedom and self-determination, advanced most prominently through religion and art, sufficiently distinguished that institution from the white church in the South.

Perhaps more important for King, Jr., was the hegemony that the church and spiritual values held in southern black life. In a culture in which he absorbed much of the atmosphere of southern revivalism, the church brought to mind not only a rare enthusiasm for the truths of scripture, the spoken word, and fire-and-brimstone preachers who danced in the aisles under the power of the Holy Spirit but also a simple, direct, and homey preaching of the gospel, with the accompanying punctuations of "Amen" and "hallelujah" from congregations.

Equally important were the ceremonial and ritual aspects of music and the frenzy, which heightened the possibilities for spiritual ecstasy, and Christian teachings that informed day-to-day life among the folk. Although King, Jr., failed to understand in those early years the extent to which spirit possession, shouting, sacred dance,[88] and the orally transmitted expressive culture of the South[89] as a whole, were linked to African cultural forms, as W. E. B. DuBois and others had long noted, he always turned to the church as the arena in which to reaffirm his identity and to refocus and revitalize his spiritual life. Indeed, King, Jr., found an enormous measure of strength and security in knowing that the southern black church stood as a caretaker of the sacred truths of scripture, a preserver of cultural values and traditions, and a reservoir for spiritual renewal.

But even as King, Jr., drew power and inspiration from the southern black church, there remained much about that institution that he personally found unacceptable and at times frustrating. As previously indicated, his dislike for what he regarded as the rigid biblical fundamentalism and extreme emotionalism he witnessed could not have been more evident,[90] but there were other concerns as well. He must have struggled with the thought that so many black congregations, led by unlettered and narrow-minded preachers, and deterred by a fear of political and economic reprisals, refused to embrace a reform-activist ethic and tended to stress salvation in the afterlife while neglecting the moral and physical struggle for liberation in this life. King, Jr.'s knowledge of the Ebenezer tradition alone would have demanded this much of him, and perhaps considerably more. The contradictory tendencies he saw in the life of the church contributed immeasurably to his growing awareness of his own personal dilemma as a black southerner, and of the dialectical character of the world around him.[91] As one who experienced community with southern blacks and noncommunity with southern whites, and who saw segregation even in the church,[92] King, Jr., would not have been overwhelmed or deterred by churches that highlighted issues of conversion, individual salvation, and matters of personal ethics to the exclusion of both a sense of corporate responsibility and the need to work for social, political, and economic change.

King, Jr.'s problems with the church were not limited to its biblical fundamentalism, unbridled emotionalism, and tendency to disconnect the spiritual and the ecclesiastical from the social and political. He also confronted the hyper-moralism of the southern black church, an issue that would have been problematic for any youngsters who, like himself, were prone to raise critical questions about traditional church teachings.[93] Daddy King remembered that "Church folks then didn't drink or smoke or dance with each other,"[94] and congregations routinely attacked alcohol consumption, gambling, secular dancing, theater going, card playing, and Sunday sports as though they were the greatest sins in society.

King, Jr.'s lively personality and youthful love for partying and the nightlife inevitably conflicted with this puritanical moral code as it was sanctioned at Ebenezer Baptist Church and in church culture generally. Walter McCall, another young minister who was King, Jr.'s friend and classmate in college and seminary, recalled that many times Daddy King "opposed our dancing and things like that," but "we would slip off anyway and go. Many times he and I as well as his sister and some more girls would congregate at his house while his Daddy was at church and we'd put on a party."[95] "On one occasion at the local YMCA, an enraged Daddy King," according to one report, "dragged an embarrassed Martin from the dance floor."[96] In a culture in which the quality of one's personal life was commonly judged by churchly standards, secular dancing was at the very least inappropriate for laypersons and virtually unthinkable for a young minister. But King, Jr.'s love for what has been called "the light side of life" never really faded,[97] even as he appreciated the image of the church as the supreme guardian of moral values and also its well-established practice of framing moral arguments about personal life in biblical terms.

King, Jr.'s early dialectical attitude toward the black church found expression in a period during which many easy caricatures of that institution were projected in folklore, film, and literature. Anti-intellectualism and excessive emotionalism were stereotypes that persisted in popular portrayals of the black church, and even African American scholars freely criticized that institution and its leadership as being too exploitative, self-serving, and out of touch with the realities of black existence.[98] It would have been most difficult, if not impossible, for King, Jr., to escape the impact of these images, consciously or unconsciously, but he never left the black church. Moreover, he continued to believe in the power and potential of the church as a liberating force for his people.

Much of this attitude resulted from the strong influence of preacher-intellectuals who mentored King, Jr., as he pursued his studies at Morehouse College from 1944 to 1948. Chief among these seminal influences were Benjamin E. Mays, Morehouse's president, and George D. Kelsey, its professor of ethics, both of whom were actively involved in civic, local church, and denominational affairs, and were also known for their moral courage and commitments to social change. King, Jr., took a course in Bible from Kelsey and was almost always present for Mays's Tuesday morning chapel addresses; and the youngster admitted admiring "them both very much" because of "their ability to interpret the Christian gospel."[99] Kelsey was known for his sharp critique of the church, and especially Protestant liberalism, in his articles, and Mays wrote books and essays that highlighted the dilemma facing the Negro church in a racist society.[100] Even if King, Jr., neglected to read these works, he would have heard their content in Kelsey's lectures and Mays's chapel talks. Moreover,

Kelsey's efforts to build strong black church leadership and Mays's work to improve race relations through both the church and the interracial Southern Regional Council were quite well known, and this, too, would have caught King, Jr.'s attention.[101] In any case, King, Jr., found in Mays and Kelsey towering figures who never absolved themselves of the moral responsibility to not only pass judgment on the social world in which they lived and operated but also to transform that world through prophetic witness and church-centered activism.

Additionally, Mays and Kelsey represented a more enlightened perspective and tradition in the southern black church, thus contributing to young King's sense of the ambivalent side of that institution. Typical church-going pillars of the community, but with deep ties to both the academy and the church, Mays and Kelsey also reflected the unique power and resources lying fallow in the

FIGURE 1.1. Benjamin E. Mays (1894–1984), Baptist minister, Morehouse College President, and "spiritual mentor" and "intellectual father" to King.

FIGURE I.2. George D. Kelsey (1910–1996), Baptist minister and educator
who mentored King at Morehouse College.

historical and ethical strands of southern black Baptist Protestantism. They
were intellectual and cultural influences who challenged young King on the
issue of race, and around the whole question of the moral responsibility of the
church in a racist society, a contribution of enormous proportions since being
black in the South had much to do with a distinctive psyche, mindset, and
ethos. Mays and Kelsey helped King, Jr., to better understand the southern
black church in all its richness and complexity. Moreover, they were, for King,
Jr., living reminders that the black church was not totally devoid of a Social
Gospel tradition,[102] and they, along with King, Sr., and the Ebenezer tradition,
would loom large in King, Jr.'s decision to serve his people under the auspices
of the church.

King, Jr., said on many occasions that his decision to become a minister
owed much to the influence and example of Mays and Kelsey. Noting that they
"made me stop and think," King, Jr. went on to remark: "Both were ministers,

both were deeply religious, and yet both were learned men, aware of all the trends of modern thinking. I could see in their lives the ideal of what I wanted a minister to be."[103] By word and deed, Mays and Kelsey further convinced King, Jr., that the Christian ministry stood as the noblest of all callings, or the type of calling that made a claim on one's very soul. Thus, when King, Jr., spoke of his "call to preach" as not "some miraculous vision" or "blinding light experience on the road of life," but as "an inner urge" and "a desire to serve God and humanity,"[104] there were echoes here of the lessons he had learned from Mays, Kelsy, and, of course, Daddy King, all of whom were steeped in southern black Baptist Protestantism.

At the same time, King, Jr., was driven by something deep in the recesses of his own being, for he, by his own admission, "had felt the urge to enter the ministry from my high school days."[105] The urgent sense of mission he felt through the church and to the world in which he lived afforded a revealing glimpse of at least some of the qualities that would lead to his greatness,[106] though the events that would make him into a national and international figure could not have been foreseen. Be that as it may, Mays and Kelsey helped King, Jr., to overcome many of his doubts and reservations about the church and ministry, and they also contributed to his earliest sense of how to move congregations from vital faith to positive and concrete social action.

Needless to say, the Morehouse experience was of primary significance in King, Jr.'s effort to understand the church in intellectual terms. At Morehouse, he was exposed to different ideas about what it means to follow Jesus in faith, and he began to struggle with the political implications of his ecclesiological and theological convictions. There were lessons on the merits of cooperative Christianity, and King, Jr., read Henry David Thoreau, the nineteenth-century American essayist and social critic who had challenged the church and society around the concept of noncooperation with unjust governments and laws.[107] It is also conceivable that King, Jr., may have heard of Mohandas K. Gandhi's life and work for the first time. After all, Gandhi's ideas and activities had been widely publicized in one of Atlanta's major black newspapers as early as 1931,[108] and they were commonly discussed among African American intellectuals and preachers at Morehouse. Moreover, Benjamin Mays, who visited Gandhi in India in 1936, must have referred to his experience in his Tuesday morning chapel speeches in the late 1940s.[109] In any case, Morehouse, under Mays's leadership, provided the type of academic atmosphere that reminded King, Jr., that the church did not have to compromise its spiritualizing proclivity in order to be a forum for new and creative ideas and a transforming force in the socio-political arena. Therefore, it is not surprising that King, Jr., would later use some of the idioms of Mays, Kelsey, and other preacher-intellectuals at Morehouse in his writings and speeches about religion and the church.[110]

Apparently, Morehouse College was a critical part of King, Jr.'s family and church traditions.[111] A. D. Williams and Martin Luther King, Sr., studied at that institution, prompting King, Jr., to indicate on one occasion that "Morehouse has had three generations of Kings."[112] Mays, Kelsey, Samuel Williams, Lucius M. Tobin, and other preacher-intellectuals at Morehouse, all of whom were Baptists, frequented the King home, appeared and spoke at Ebenezer Baptist Church from time to time, and were considered a part of the King's extended family. Consequently, the values and traditions of Morehouse, Ebenezer, the King family, and the larger black community of Atlanta and the South came together in King, Jr.'s consciousness as he thought more seriously about the church from an ethical, philosophical, and theological standpoint.[113]

But there was yet another part to this equation that merits careful consideration—namely, the ways in which King, Jr.'s exposure to and affiliation with black churches in the North from 1948 to 1954 impacted his expanding attitude toward the church in general. Attention to this subject has too often been overshadowed by the growing tendency to southernize or regionalize those major formative influences in King, Jr.'s life.[114] From the fall of 1948 to the spring of 1951, as King, Jr., studied at Crozer Theological Seminary in Chester, Pennsylvania, he also worshiped at the Calvary Baptist Church in that city, sometimes assisting its pastor, J. Pius Barbour, who had long been a dear friend of the King family. Born in Texas, Barbour had been raised in southern culture and trained at Morehouse and Crozer as well, and he had also taught at Tuskegee Institute and pastored churches in Texas, Alabama, and Indiana.[115] Significantly, Barbour's life had intersected at many points with that of King, Sr., and King, Jr., strongly admired his personality and intellect. "He is full of fun, and he has one of the best minds of anybody I have ever met," said King, Jr., of Barbour in a letter to his mother during his first year at Crozer.[116] Deeply grounded in the culture and politics of the African American community in Chester, and known for a rare ingenuity and a virtuosity of talent, Barbour spoke widely in the United States and abroad on "The American Race Question" in the late 1940s, thus becoming yet another tremendous moral, spiritual, and intellectual source for King, Jr., as he thought about the proper mission of the church and its leadership in human affairs.[117]

Calvary Baptist Church became King, Jr.'s home away from home. The church had been founded in Chester in 1875 by African Americans who, like King, Jr.'s own forebears in Georgia, were inspired by the slave experience; and many of its members across generations came to Chester from points in the South during the Great Migration, bringing with them a southern sense of place.[118] Hence, there was much about Calvary that recalled King, Jr.'s own experiences at Atlanta's Ebenezer Baptist Church: the rich enthusiasm for the

FIGURE 1.3. Josephus Pius Barbour (1894–1974), pastor of Calvary Baptist
Church, with whom King worked as an assistant minister during his
Crozer years.

Bible and the spoken word, songs and testimony that echoed with a strange
amalgam of heartache and hope, worship filled with ecstasy and passion, the
healing power of laughter and friendship, the centrality of family and community, and more generally speaking, the complex interplay of spiritual and cultural values. King, Jr., became one of "the sons of Calvary," and it is said that his
ties with Barbour "was like a father-son relationship."[119] The youngster
frequently dined at Calvary and at the home of Barbour and his wife, Olee
Littlejohn, and there were many "philosophical and theological discussions" or
"'bull sessions' about religious topics."[120]

King was adopted by others at Calvary as well, as "he would go from house
to house looking for food and fun." Sara Richardson, who was very active at
Calvary, recalled that she would always leave her key "under a brick so" King,

Jr., "could get into my house when I was away." She continued: "He would come in and cook. Having a love for sports, he would come to my house on Wednesday nights to watch boxing matches and to eat with his friends."[121] Emma Anderson, another spiritual force in the life of Calvary at that time, remembered that King, Jr., "was very fond of the Talley family, and he called Esther Talley, one of Calvary's elders, 'Mother'."[122] Calvary and the larger black community of Chester gave King, Jr., a feeling of "at homeness,"[123] and the idea of church as family was reaffirmed in his thinking. This explains why King, Jr., who was only nineteen when he went to Crozer, escaped the spiritual pain that would have otherwise characterized his transition from Morehouse and the larger black culture in Atlanta to life on an essentially white seminary campus.[124]

The artistic side of church life in Chester fulfilled a certain need that King, Jr., had brought from Ebenezer and Morehouse. The sermonic style of Barbour, which often combined folktales and songs with stories from the Bible, was undoubtedly stimulating, enriching, and edifying. Moreover, King, Jr., delighted in the singing of Olee Littlejohn Barbour, who was known for powerful renditions of the spirituals and gospel songs, and who had musical talents equal to those of Alberta King, his own mother.[125] For King, Jr., Calvary, like Ebenezer, brought to life the extraordinary artistic and cultural heritage of the folk. Such an environment afforded opportunities for the young man to develop and refine his own skills as a preacher and singer, even as he enjoyed other aspects of the cultural life in Chester.[126] Calvary was actually King, Jr.'s connection to the broader reaches of black culture in Chester, which included music and dance in sacred and secular forms. His awareness of the often veiled links between the church and secular cultural forms in the black community, which had been quite evident in Atlanta, was reinforced, and so was his sense of the church as the fountainhead of culture.

King, Jr.'s exposure to black church culture in the North continued as he pursued doctoral studies at Boston University from the fall of 1951 to mid-1954. During much of this time, he affiliated and worked with Twelfth Baptist Church in the Roxbury section, a congregation that assumed much of the same role in his life as that undertaken by Ebenezer in Atlanta and Calvary in Chester. Twelfth Baptist had originated as part of the separate and independent African Church movement in Boston in 1840, and was celebrated for its active involvement in the abolitionist crusade.[127] Many of its members in the early 1950s, much like King, Jr., had come from the South, were steeped in the values and traditions of southern black culture, and managed to recreate in their new environment a southern sense of place.[128] Twelfth Baptist was steeped in the revivalist ethos that King, Jr., had come to know so well, and there he was exposed to vigorous proclamations of the divine inspiration and authority of scripture; songs full of joy, power, and heartbreaking pathos; lively and celebratory worship; delicious food and a festive spirit; a familial quality that met his need for connectedness and belonging; and vital displays of spirituality, art, folklore, and material life. Images of the church and the South in King, Jr.'s thinking were replicated at Twelfth Baptist and in Roxbury's black community. Affectionately referred to as an "adopted son" of Twelfth Baptist,[129] King, Jr.'s life in Boston mirrored the significance of the church as a source of adaptation to new and different circumstances.

Twelfth Baptist Church's influence on King, Jr., was filtered primarily through its pastor, William H. Hester, who was "an old friend of King, Sr."[130] A native of North Carolina, Hester was a man of moral passion and high ideals, a living embodiment of the Christian faith and commitment, and one who

FIGURE 1.4. William Hunter Hester, pastor of Twelfth Baptist Church (1924–1964), with whom King worked as an assistant minister during his Boston years.

remained uncompromising and undaunting in his pursuit of the public good. Hester "was particularly supportive of King," and allowed the young man to occasionally preach and minister to youth.[131] Hester also kept King, Sr., updated on his son's progress as a preacher.[132] King, Jr., was constantly reminded of the centrality of preaching in the life of the church, and of the need to further develop and refine his sermonic content and style.[133] In this respect, Hester was as important for King, Jr., as King, Sr., William Holmes Borders, and J. Pius Barbour had been up to that point.

King, Jr.'s growing reputation as a preacher led to speaking engagements at a number of churches in the Boston area.[134] Single and quite mature in mind and spirit, and functioning in a culture in which the unattached commonly met their mates in church, his preaching ability often caught the attention and interest of attractive young females. But King, Jr., did not meet Coretta Scott, the woman who would become his wife, in church. In fact, Coretta, an Alabama native and member of the African Methodist Episcopal Zion Church (AMEZ), and one who held stereotypical views of ministers and the Baptist Church, was initially turned off when told by Mary Powell, a King family friend who introduced her to King, Jr., that the young man was a minister from a Baptist Church in Georgia.[135] In 1953, however, King, Jr., and Coretta were married, and the two, owing largely to King, Jr.'s influence, ultimately found common ground in the belief that the church functions and serves best when it is not obsessed with denominational labels and barriers.[136]

King, Jr., and Coretta shared a southern sense of place that took seriously the intertwining and stabilizing influences of church and family.[137] Moreover, Coretta, who was a student at the New England Conservatory of Music in Boston when King, Jr., met her, had a strong love for and devotion to the liturgical and artistic sides of church life. For King, Jr., this was enormously impressive. He consistently encouraged Coretta in her studies and voice lessons, for she, much like Alberta King and Olee Littlejohn Barbour, was for him not only an artist of considerable talent but also a living example of both the power of black art and the vitality of the church in the African American experience.[138]

Clearly, the black community in Boston was part of that world that shaped King, Jr.'s concept of the church. The youngster found in Boston, as he had in Atlanta and Chester, the preachers, intellectuals, and artists who embodied what he considered the true spirit of the church and with whom he could discuss the meaning and mission of that institution in highly critical and sophisticated terms.[139] Also, King, Jr., found reinforcement for his desire to return to the black church in the South. "He wanted this," Coretta remembered, "because it would bring him into close contact with the people to whom he wanted to devote his life."[140] It was this deep concern for the masses, or those who struggled in life's valley, that compelled King, Jr., to claim the southern black church as the place "where I plan to live and work." This choice alone shows that he was not some child of privilege who had absorbed uncritically the middle-class ethos and values.[141]

The Church and the Academy: Negotiating Boundaries

Martin Luther King, Jr.'s attitude toward the church found greater shape and clarity as he moved "from teenage religious skepticism toward a theological eclecticism that was consistent with his Baptist religious roots."[142] Having denied the bodily resurrection of Jesus at age thirteen, by the time he went to Morehouse, King, Jr., had become known in church and family circles for his unusual idealism, his intellectual energy and independence, and his tendency to challenge or question traditional Christian teachings. Clearly, King, Jr., was quite liberal before he left Ebenezer. Be that as it may, his youthful religious skepticism and inquisitive spirit were further awakened at Morehouse, as he was introduced to philosophical and theological liberalism and as new ideas fell on fertile ground. Referring to the impact of this on his perspective on the church and the Bible, King, Jr., himself asserted:

> At the age of fifteen I entered college and more and more could I see
> a gap between what I learned in Sunday School and what I was
> learning in college. . . . My college training, especially the first two
> years, brought many doubts into my mind. . . . It was then that the
> shackles of fundamentalism were removed from my body. . . . The
> conflict continued until I studied a course in Bible in which I came to
> see that behind the legends and myths of the Book were many
> profound truths which one could not escape.[143]

Morehouse proved to be a soul-searching as well as an intellectually sobering experience for King, Jr., for that was the first academic context in which he seriously and critically engaged concepts of the church in intellectual terms, and especially in philosophical, ethical, and theological terms. As he himself put it, "Doubts began to spring forth unrelentingly," compelling him to raise new and more critical questions about the meaning and relevance of the church, particularly from the standpoint of its teachings and doctrinal claims. While he studied and eagerly embraced Henry David Thoreau's thoughts on civil disobedience or noncooperation with evil as a perennial challenge to the church, and "absorbed Jesus' teachings with his whole being,"[144] his rebellion "against the more conservative notions of his evangelical boyhood church" surfaced in a most interesting way in February 1948, during his last semester at Morehouse. As King, Jr., sat before an ordination committee that included King, Sr., Lucius M. Tobin, Paul H. Henderson, Benjamin E. Mays, Samuel W. Williams, J. H. Edwards, and several other ministers,

> the committee asked him about the Virgin Birth. He denied that Jesus was born of a virgin. Edwards, King, Sr., and other members of the committee disagreed with the younger King's refusal to accept the entire Bible as literally true. But, despite this difference, they had no trouble ordaining him as a minister.[145]

Keith D. Miller's suggestion that Daddy King and the other ministers decided to ordain King, Jr., "because, unlike fundamentalists, they did not regard Biblical literalism as a litmus test of true Christianity" is not at all persuasive. Biblical fundamentalism, particularly in terms of doctrinal conformity, was routinely a litmus test for the ordination of ministers at Ebenezer and at other black churches in Atlanta and throughout the South at that time. But young King was the son of Martin Luther King, Sr., one of the most prominent preachers in the South, and this consideration seems to have assumed priority over all other concerns, including the fact that King, Jr., denied the virgin birth. That pivotal moment, during which the son was ordained despite doctrinal disagreements with his father, was quite revealing in terms of the politics of the southern black church. It is also conceivable that King, Jr.'s ordination committee was heavily influenced by the presence and input of preacher-intellectuals like Mays and Tobin, who had studied biblical criticism and who were receptive to aspects of Protestant liberalism.[146]

At any rate, King, Jr.'s struggle to reconcile what he was studying in academic circles with the ideas he had gotten from his parents and Ebenezer Church continued at Crozer Theological Seminary and Boston University. In fact, Morehouse was far more instrumental than King, Jr.'s parents and Ebenezer in preparing him for training at Crozer and Boston. "This is why, when I came to Crozer, I could accept the liberal interpretation with relative ease," King, Jr., recalled.[147] Much of what he learned and embraced from biblical critics and liberal theologians at Crozer were unheard of in black church culture in the South generally, and he noted, during his second year at that institution, that "Today I differ a great deal with my father theologically."[148] The problem stemmed primarily from King, Jr.'s rejection of scriptural inerrancy and literalism.

In any case, the disagreements between the father and the son could not have been more evident during King, Jr.'s Ph.D. studies at Boston, where his exposure to biblical criticism and Protestant liberalism not only continued but also increased, even as he found a sobering influence in the Christian realism of Reinhold Niebuhr. Although King, Sr., admired his son's "mind's receptivity and the genuine passion he had for learning," and thought that many of "his arguments, theological or not, were precisely constructed and convincing," the elder King did not hesitate to voice displeasure when King, Jr., fell under the influence of Karl Marx, a development that would have enduring implications as far as the youngster's critique of the church was concerned. Concerning King, Jr.'s movement along these lines, King, Sr., recounted:

> Politically, he often seemed to be drifting away from the basics of capitalism and Western democracy that I felt very strongly about. There were some sharp exchanges; I may even have raised my voice a few times. But mainly it was a rich period in my life, when a wealth of knowledge from around the globe could be imparted by a son to his father.[149]

While embracing the vocabulary and some of the values of theological liberalism,[150] King, Jr.'s attachment to many of the enduring lessons of faith he received from his parents and Ebenezer Church remained undimmed. "At present I still feel the effects of the noble moral and ethical ideals that I grew up under," he commented in a paper written at Crozer in 1950. "They have been real and precious to me, and even in moments of theological doubt I could never turn away from them."[151] The young man "did not lose his faith" and his attraction to the power "of traditional evangelical Christianity,"[152] despite his reservations about its emotionalism, its biblical fundamentalism, its hyper-moralism, and its failure to embrace what he considered important trends in modern thought.

Although Friedrich Nietzsche's critique of the Christian love ethic, to which King, Jr., was exposed at Crozer, resonated in some ways with him as a disempowered black man from the South, he remained open to the belief that that ethic afforded endless possibilities for positive and constructive change. Moreover, King, Jr., never lost respect for the authority and charisma of the church, and for the view, advanced so consistently by A. D. Williams, King, Sr., and others before him, that the church should address the needs of the abused and outcast while never cooperating with evil systems and laws. Significantly, King, Jr.'s family and church remained primary influences on his theological perspective, particularly as it related to the personal God who acts in history to bring the disjointed elements of reality into a harmonious whole.[153]

King, Jr., never failed to keep the liberal theology he studied "in touch with the Baptist nurture of his youth."[154] He actually tested "the Western theological traditions he encountered against his African American background."[155] At Crozer, he found in his studies of Walter Rauschenbusch, George W. Davis, and other liberal theologians and ethicists the type of language and concepts he needed to explain the Social Gospelism he inherited from the religious-ethical tradition of the black church at the highest levels of society, and especially in academic and liberal church circles. It was also at Crozer that King, Jr., engaged in "a serious intellectual quest for a method to eliminate social evil"[156]—a quest inspired chiefly by the church and by his experiences with the black communities of Atlanta and Chester, and to some degree by the sermon he heard on Gandhi in Philadelphia in 1950, which was given by Mordecai W. Johnson, the African American theologian and president of Howard University.[157] The Crozer environment was intellectually stimulating, a setting in which the theoretical and practical aspects of ministry were heavily emphasized, and King, Jr., regarded it as yet another context in which to explore questions concerning the social roles of the church.

The same applied in the case of Boston University's School of Theology, a setting in which many of the core ideas and values of King, Jr.'s church and cultural heritage found affinity with different strands of liberal Protestant thought. The personal idealism he studied stressed the personal God of love and reason and the sacredness of all human personality—principles proclaimed in the preaching of A. D. Williams and King, Sr.; affirmed at Morehouse; and practiced in traditional black church life. Understandably, personalism became not only King, Jr.'s "basic philosophical position" but also part of a refining process for ideas and values he would consistently advance in the black church and in the larger sphere of his activities.[158]

King, Jr.'s search for philosophical and theological answers to the problem of race, which had begun on a serious note at Morehouse, continued at Crozer and Boston.[159] His encounter with Reinhold Niebuhr's Christian realism, and especially his thoughts on the glaring reality of evil at every level of human existence,[160] proved quite relevant and useful in this regard. In fact, King, Jr., himself acknowledged that his high regard for Niebuhrian neo-orthodoxy "may root back to certain experiences that I had in the south with a vicious race problem."[161] From an ethical and theological standpoint, neo-orthodoxy helped King, Jr., to put the race problem in proper perspective and also to maintain a firm ideological grounding between the extremes of fundamentalism in the black church and the excesses of liberalism in the academy.[162]

The ways in which King, Jr.'s studies impacted his style and image as a preacher are no less important. The young man was exposed to preacher-intellectuals at Morehouse, Crozer, and Boston, and was thus convinced that preaching could be theologically sound and "intellectually respectable," as well as dynamic and entertaining. "When he accepted this fact," said Coretta of her young husband, "it opened the way for him to go into the church." It also provided the angle necessary for King, Jr., to appeal to the head and the heart in his sermons. "The balance between mind and soul, intellect and emotion," continued Coretta, "was what he would strive to achieve."[163] Strangely, King, Jr.'s early success in this capacity was significantly enhanced by his tendency to appropriate the words, phases, images, and illustrations of other preachers and intellectuals, often without proper attribution. Having grown up "in a culture in which homiletic borrowing was commonplace,"[164] and was not considered necessarily unethical or intellectually dishonest, King, Jr., was able to master the art of preaching with relative ease, especially in church settings. Even so, his attitude toward borrowing underscored the tension that existed between black-church standards and the demands of the academy, in which there were clearly defined and established canons of scholarship. Apparently, King, Jr.'s borrowing essentially demonstrated that when it came to the question of ethical standards in preaching and writing, he was more indebted to black church culture than to the culture of the academy.[165]

There was a direction to King, Jr.'s studies at Morehouse, Crozer, and Boston that grew out of his encounter with place, the church, and the full range of southern life and culture. Refusing to think in terms of a strictly academic career, his desire was to "go back home" and to share "his broader contacts and educational experience" in the North as part of an overall effort to solve the race problem through the ministry and mission of the church. For King, Jr., it was never really a matter of choosing the church over the academy or vice versa, but of bringing the resources of both to bear on the human condition in his time. Obviously, he felt that the fruits of his training could be instrumental in redefining and reshaping the values and institutions that, after all, made him who and what he was—namely, a southern black Baptist preacher.[166]

Although the more critical approach in the academy made King, Jr.'s faith stronger and more secure, Crozer and Boston could not have prepared him for a pastoral role in the black church. This is why he remained steeped in the black church while also fulfilling his academic requirements. He filled in for his father at Ebenezer during the summers, served apprenticeships at Calvary and Twelfth Baptist while in Chester and Boston, and preached at other churches in the North and South during those years.[167] This constant involvement and exposure helped him to properly negotiate the boundaries between the church and the academy, and also kept him from being drawn into patterns and categories of thought foreign to his own. Moreover, King, Jr., fully understood that much of what he learned, discussed, and debated in the academic world would not register well in the church, where the folk were more interested in affirming and celebrating faith than in asking open-ended questions, thinking critically, and engaging in the free play of ideas.

Morehouse, Crozer, and Boston were necessary steps in King, Jr.'s spiritual and intellectual odyssey. Largely because of these citadels of academia, he was able to bring to the pulpit and to his sense of the church an intellectual interest and passion. Furthermore, he was, owing to the combined influences of the church and the academy, quite successful in forging a synthesis that involved an eager acceptance of the richest insights of biblical criticism and liberal theology, as well as a deep appreciation for the "profound truths" of scripture and the evangelical style.[168]

It was in his capacities as preacher and intellectual that King, Jr., set out to define the nature and purpose of the church. The thought processes for him began at Morehouse College and extended through his years as a seminarian, graduate student, pastor, civil rights leader, and world figure. During these stages in his life, various concepts and images of the church coursed through his sermons, speeches, and writings. Those concepts and images are the subject of the next chapter.

2

The True *Ekklesia*

Toward a Definition of the Church

The Church is not only the community of the New Being; it is also a sociological group immersed in the conflicts of existence.

—Paul Tillich, *Systematic Theology:*
Three Volumes in One

The projection of a social gospel, in my opinion, is the true witness of a Christian life. This is the meaning of the true *ekklesia*—the inner spiritual church.

—Martin Luther King, Jr.

If the very existence of the Church is meant to be leaven in the dough, salt in the meal, and light for all those who dwell in the human household, then the ecclesial community must accept the obligations that derive from its essential function.

—Juan Luis Segundo, *The Community*
Called Church

The Church exists not for itself, but to serve the revolution.

—Rosemary Ruether, *Liberation Theology:*
Human Hope Confronts Christian History
and American Power

Martin Luther King, Jr., always questioned narrow and conventional understandings of the church. Having an uncanny gift for conveying in word and deed what it means to live the Christian faith, he consistently critiqued the powerful and entrenched models of the church as bureaucracy and institution while fully embracing the idea of church as movement.[1] Moreover, King believed that the mission of the church is never in and to itself as a body but, rather, in and to the world in which it claims legitimacy and relevance.[2] Thus, much of his life was devoted to exploring ways in which the church might maximize its potential and effectiveness as a positive force in society.

For King, the church was defined largely by the values that adorned its life. More specifically, this meant that any ecclesiastical body or structure that presumed to represent and speak for God had to struggle daily to understand not only human sinfulness and divine grace, but also the social, political, and economic realities that gather at their intersection. Authentic discipleship, in King's estimation, demanded consistency and a direct correlation between what the church claimed to be and how it functioned.[3] His thoughts on these matters could not have been more challenging, especially in an era when the tasks confronting the church seemed almost insuperable and when too many clerics were insisting that that institution functions best in a social and political void. But nothing less could have been expected from one who was, unarguably, the most visionary church leader of his generation and who was so uniquely positioned at the crossroads of religion, politics, and social activism.[4]

This chapter explores King's approach to the question of the identity and mission of the Christian church in intellectual terms. The discussion develops along several lines. First, considerable attention is given to King's training at Morehouse College,[5] Crozer Theological Seminary, and Boston University—academic institutions that afforded the kind of contexts he needed to struggle with concepts of the church, its values and traditions, and its structures of authority, before using that institution as a power base for his activities in the areas of civil rights, social justice, and peace.[6] King's studies in college, seminary, and graduate school are viewed here as a proper point of departure for any serious discussion of how he understood the church in both theoretical and practical terms. Second, King's perspective on the various images and/or models of the church is seriously treated. Finally, his sense of how the church might best move from faith to praxis in its ministry and mission is examined. At these junctures, there is a significant focus on King's years as a public figure and activist, a period during which he brought the greatest clarity and sophistication to his understanding of the meaning and purpose of the church. Also, at various points in this chapter, King's constructive critique of the Christian church is discussed, with special attention to how he challenged what he considered to be the church's stifling complacency in an age of both peril and promise.

The Meaning of the Church: An Intellectual Odyssey

Martin Luther King, Jr., studied in various intellectual environments that were charged with great interest, not only in the history and traditions of the church but also in how it organized its life and practiced its mission. From Morehouse (1944–1948) to Crozer (1948–1951) and Boston (1951–1954), King had classmates and professors who shared his deep roots in and love for the church, and who were always willing to discuss that institution in intellectual terms, and especially in relationship to the practical problems of everyday life. Thus, it is not surprising that King devoted considerable time to thinking and writing about the church and its place in history and in the society and culture.

At Morehouse, the church was as vital a part of King's education as his courses in sociology, philosophy, and other subjects. Some of his work in that setting reflected an interest in various church teachings and practices. In a paper on sacred and secular rituals, written during his last year at Morehouse, King discussed the ritualistic aspects of church life, giving special attention to holy days and to the sacraments as understood and administered from the time of the Apostle Paul up to the present.[7] In the Bible courses he had with George D. Kelsey, his participation on some levels revealed an intense interest in the teachings and mission of Jesus and the early church.[8]

Also at Morehouse, King's vision for the church was informed by his exposure to social realism in the lectures of his philosophy professor Samuel Williams and his sociology professor Walter Chivers, and by the personalistic ideas to which he was introduced in the chapel sermons of Benjamin E. Mays. Thus, it was there that King first became familiar with much of the intellectual language and the conceptual categories he needed to articulate, in very sophisticated ways, the type of "homespun Social Gospelism" and "homespun personalism" he had inherited from family and the Ebenezer tradition.[9]

Beyond this, young King continued to display a keen interest in the practical dimensions of church activity, and especially in how the church might transform society in the interest of the common good. His decision to enter the ministry, to seek the best possible training, and to affiliate with the Morehouse Chapter of the National Association for the Advancement of Colored People (NAACP) more than testified to his conviction that the combined resources of the church, the academy, and civil rights organizations had much to offer in this regard.[10]

Clearly, the theoretical and the practical came together in King's consciousness as he struggled with how the church might best be defined in historical, traditional, and ethical terms.[11] This was only natural considering his exposure to preacher-intellectuals like Kelsey and Benjamin E. Mays, who, aside from being men of ideas, offered living lessons in the true meaning of the church. Be that as it may, the Morehouse experience proved foundational for King as he explored a range of questions regarding the spiritual, ritualistic, and intellectual traditions and resources of the church, and as he considered the church's potential as an agent of social change.

Morehouse prepared the ground for King's more serious intellectual engagement with questions at Crozer and Boston about the church.[12] At Crozer and Boston, King's emerging sense of the church was heavily influenced by his studies in liberal Christian theology and ethics, and especially the Social Gospel movement and personal idealism. He accepted Social Gospel liberalism at Crozer with, as he put it, "relative ease," and was calling himself "a profound advocator of the social gospel" almost from the point of his matriculation there.[13] But King never accepted uncritically Social Gospel liberalism's superficial optimism concerning human nature and the human capacity to bring the kingdom of God to earth, a tendency that owed much to the influence of the Christian realism of King, Sr., Morehouse's President Benjamin E. Mays, Morehouse professors George Kelsey, Walter Chivers, and Samuel Williams, and later to King's study of Reinhold Niebuhr.[14] Needless to say, all of this would have profound implications from the standpoint of King's views on and expectations for the church.

The Social Gospel movement was not new to the traditions of the black church, for King had seen it at work in the ministry of King, Sr., and in the activities of George Kelsey and Benjamin Mays. But King's reading of Walter Rauschenbusch's *Christianity and the Social Crisis* (1907) at Crozer presented certain intellectual challenges around the whole question of the meaning and relevance of the church universal throughout the ages, and especially in modern times. Rauschenbusch's work, which advocated Christianizing society by applying the biblical principles of love and justice to the transformation of the state, economy, family, church, and other institutions, gave King much of the theological basis for his understanding of the social roles of the church.[15] But the youngster read Rauschenbusch dialectically, accepting many of his ideas while noting, on the other hand, that Rauschenbusch had come "perilously close to identifying the Kingdom of God with a particular social and economic system," a "tendency which should never befall the Church."[16] In any event, King, from his Crozer years, used Raushenbusch and the Social Gospel movement to frame virtually all of his ecclesiological concerns.

The same might be said of the personalism that King studied at Crozer and, to a much greater degree, at Boston University. Exposed to Personalists like Edgar S. Brightman and L. Harold DeWolf, King found concepts in personal idealism that resonated with core values in both the Social Gospel

FIGURE 2.1. Walter Rauschenbusch (1861–1918), exponent of the Social Gospel, and an intellectual source for King's views on the social role of the Christian Church.

movement and the black church, chief among which were the personal God of love and reason, the dignity and worth of all human personality, and the need for persons to live in community.[17] DeWolf's provocative work, *A Theology of the Living Church* (1953), which vehemently denounced hypocrisy in church culture, became an important source for King as he, during his last year at Boston, considered how the church might benefit from a more genuine embrace of the insights of both personal idealism and Social Gospelism.[18]

King wrote extensively on many aspects of church life while at Crozer and Boston. In a paper written during his second year at Crozer, he attempted to define the church in historical terms, or "in a very catholic and comprehensive manner," noting particularly its role as "the sum of those organizations" formed "to serve as organs of Christ, for the expression and promotion of his religion." Mindful of the interplay between the human and divine in the church's life,

King went on to establish that that body "is not assured of unfailing correctness in thinking" nor "absolute truth," that it "is in history" and must therefore "deal with the relative." But "the Holy Spirit is steadily leading" God's people, he concluded, moving them toward "the perfect truth in the highest and most practical realm."[19]

Much of what King wrote amounted to a rehearsal of pivotal figures, events, and dates that marked the evolution of the church from the apostolic age to his own time. A number of his seminary and graduate-school papers highlighted the various images and traditions of the church that had extended from Christ and the Apostles to Martin Luther, John Calvin, Friedrich Schleiermacher, Walter Rauschenbusch, and a host of Christian thinkers in his own time.[20] As a young academic and preacher with aspirations toward the pastorate, King grasped the importance of knowing how the Christian church had originated and developed through the ages, not only with regard to its chief spokespersons, its most celebrated sages, and its most persistent critics, but also from the standpoint of its history, dogma, doctrine, sacraments, morality, and practices.[21] Significantly, King's knowledge in this area was virtually assured in contexts in which his peers and professors saw no necessary tension between faith and learning, and in which all were expected to strike a careful and proper balance between practical spirituality and the academic life.

King repeatedly alluded to the normative authority of the early church in his academic writings. In a handwritten outline for a course on "The Preaching Ministry of the Church" at Crozer, he alluded to the importance of the Apostolic Fathers and the Christian Apologists in shaping the life and thought of the young church.[22] In papers at Crozer and Boston, King made numerous references to the early church's struggle with concerns ranging from Judaizing influences, revelation, and eschatology to Christological and trinitarian debates, and the names and contributions of the Apostle Paul, Tertullian, Irenaeus, Origen, Arius, Augustine, Pelagius, and other Christian pioneers and thinkers were often mentioned. Perhaps more significant for King were the early Christian martyrs, who refused to bow to the emperor or to go to war, and who suffered and died for their faith. Small wonder, then, that the strict discipline of devotion and restraint among the early Christians would later become one of the prime motivations for King's acts of nonviolent civil disobedience.[23]

The medieval church occupied an important but less favorable place in King's thinking as a student. In a paper at Boston, he referred at some length to St. Augustine, in whom the main currents of both early and medieval church thought converged, and from whom flowed much of the streams of medieval scholasticism, Protestant Reformation theology, and neo-orthodoxy.[24] King also wrote about Peter Lombard, Bernard of Clairvaux, St. Anselm, St. Thomas

Aquinas, John Duns Scotus, and other ecclesiastics who systematically applied reason to revelation in the age of medieval scholasticism.[25] Although King would ultimately draw on St. Augustine and St. Thomas Aquinas in defending his protest against unjust laws,[26] while at Crozer and Boston, he found little in the church of the Middle Ages to support his mounting intellectual quest for a method to eradicate social evil.[27]

The Protestant Reformation of the sixteenth century was probably more significant for King in this regard. King described the Reformation as "a significant trend" in the history of the church, and he credited Martin Luther and the other reformers, whom he labeled "doctrinal preachers," with destroying "the Church as the central religious authority" and putting "the Bible in its place." "Although they [considered] the Church important and even necessary," said King of the reformers in papers at Crozer, "they never [gave] it the authoritarian position that it held in Roman Catholicism." "It was Christ that was supreme for them," King added, "not the Church of the Pope."[28] Concerning Luther's doctrine of the church, King, in a written assignment at Boston, stated:

> He speaks of the Church in a twofold manner. On the one hand . . . , there is the visible church which is an outward reality with action and clergymen. On the other hand there is the invisible Church which is composed of all in spiritual fellowship with Christ. . . . It is quite possible, argues Luther, to be in the visible Church without being in the invisible Church. However, this assertion never caused Luther to think of the visible Church as being separated from the invisible Church; the two are together like body and soul. The invisible Church exists within the visible Church. Needless to say that Luther sees no earthly head of the Church. Christ alone is the head of the Church.[29]

To further explain this idea of church as "invisible" and "visible," images that extended at least as far back as St. Augustine,[30] King further underscored Luther's distinction between "the spiritual, inner Christendom" and "the bodily, external Christendom." Quoting Luther, King asserted that "The first [is] the natural, essential, real and true one," and "The other," spoken of by the Apostles, is "man-made and external."[31] For King, John Calvin's doctrine of the church echoed this twofold vision of that institution, as the French-born Genevan reformer melded his own thoughts with those of Luther and other Christian thinkers of the fourteenth, fifteenth, and sixteenth centuries:

> Calvin's doctrine of the Church is quite similar to Luther's. According to Calvin the Church is the means by which we are nourished in the

Christian life. . . . Following the line already marked out by Wyclif,
Hus, and Zwingli, Calvin defines the Church as "all the elect of God,
including in the number even those who have departed this life."
Like Luther, he sees the Church as both visible and invisible, and its
marks are the word and the sacrament. Where the word is truly
taught and the sacrament rightly administered there is the Church,
and outside of it there is no salvation. Calvin is very insistent upon
this point.[32]

Calvin's view of God as "father" and the church as "mother" registered well
in young King's consciousness, especially since he had grown up with these
concepts at Atlanta's Ebenezer Baptist Church. Steeped in traditions that
employed maternal imagery to describe the church, King the academic could
easily accept Calvin's use of "the title mother" in his ecclesiological language,
especially since the reformer highlighted the notion that true believers are born
of the church, "nourished at her breast, and continually preserved under her
care and government till we are divested of this mortal flesh, and become like
Angels."[33]

For King the graduate student, the Reformation thinkers recaptured much
of the spirit of the early Christians in their protest against the abuses of medieval Catholicism; in their willingness to challenge misguided power and evil
structures even at the risk of their lives. In King's references to the protest
activities of the Reformers in his papers, one finds a clue to why he would later
echo Luther's famous words—"Here I stand; I cannot do otherwise, so help me
God"[34]—in his celebrated "Letter from the Birmingham City Jail" (1963), a document that adamantly affirmed the Christian's call to always act on conscience
and with the goal of uplifting humanity. Also, King saw that the Reformers, by
restoring a sense of the centrality of scripture[35] and the laity in the church, not
only challenged the legitimacy of the Catholic doctrine of the church but also
reclaimed the image of the church as the whole people of God. King perceptively acknowledged Calvin's significance in this respect:

The visible church is properly governed only by officers of divine
appointment made human in the New Testament. There are pastors,
teachers, elders, and deacons,—partly clerical and partly lay office
bearers, for in Calvin's system the recognition of the rights of the
laymen, characteristic of the whole Reformation movement, comes to
its completest development. This recognition received further
illustration in that the officers of the Calvinistic Churches, unlike
those of the Roman, Lutheran, and Anglican communions, enter
their charges only by the consent of the people whom they serve.

Their call is twofold,—the secret inclination which has God as its
author, and the election "on the consent and approbation of the
people."[36]

King noted that the Reformers shared much with the Catholics when it
came to church traditions, especially as they unfolded in the Christological and
trinitarian decisions of the early church councils. But apparently, King found
the Reformers' definitions of the church far more legitimate and appealing
than that of the Catholics. Ever mindful of the hierarchical church model
embraced and imposed by the Catholic tradition, King, in response to an examination question at Boston, observed:

> The Roman Catholic view of the Church hinges around the
> infallibility of the organized Church. It is held that this Church was
> organized by Christ, who in turn gave Peter the keys to the kingdom,
> making him the first Pope. Now all of this strikes me as erroneous
> and unhistorical. So long as the Church is an organized historical
> institution, it can never be infallible. Moreover, it must be affirmed
> that it is as erroneous to think of Christ as deliberately organizing the
> Church. It might be true to say that he believed in organization, the
> mere fact that he organized his disciples, but to say the Christ
> consciously organized the Church and made Peter the first Pope is to
> push the record to false proportions. . . . So we affirm that the
> organized Church is fallible. This, however, does not mean that the
> organized Church isn't necessary. It is absolutely necessary. Its
> primary purpose in history is to keep the fellowship of love alive in
> history, to exhort and teach doctrine, and to raise its voice against
> social evils wherever they may exist.[37]

King's papers at Boston revealed a deep interest in the locus of church authority as it extended through the Protestant Reformation up to George Fox,
Friedrich Schleiermacher, Walter Rauschenbusch, Karl Barth, Reinhold Niebuhr, Paul Tillich, and other more contemporary Christian thinkers. King's
own concept of the church as a student, while rooted in African American cultural influences, assumed intellectual structure in the context of his reading of
these sources. Clearly, that concept also owed much to the Social Gospelism of
Rauschenbusch, the personal idealism of Brightman and DeWolf, and the
Christian realism of Niebuhr, which addressed both the redeeming features
and the human limitations of the church; but it was ultimately the product of
King's intellectual engagement with the entire Christian tradition, including
the heritage of the Protestant Reformation:

> For me the Church is both visible and invisible or, to put it otherwise, both organized and spiritual. The organized Church is that fallible historic Church filled with many of the evils of history. The spiritual Church is the great fellowship of sharing under the guidance of the Holy Spirit. It is the koinonia. It is in a sense the Kingdom of God on earth. . . . The true Church is the spiritual Church. If there are any claims to infallibility, it is here. It is in the spiritual Church that we witness the Kingdom of God on earth. It is the true body of Christ. The organized Church is divided. But the spiritual Church is united.[38]

Constantly challenged to think of the church's present and future in relation to its past, there emerged in young King's consciousness a sense of the church as tradition. In a statement, "What Shall We Think About the Church?," written as part of a longer essay at Crozer, King identified the "church as a religious institution for the perpetuation of a religious tradition." In more specific terms, while acknowledging the church's failures as a bearer of tradition, he further elaborated the point:

> The church is the institution which has gathered together the various insights of spiritual giants through the ages and welded them into a body of belief and conviction which has passed from one generation to another with cumulative conviction. Without the institution working through the centuries, these insights would have perished long ago. . . . This does not mean that the church perfectly perpetuates the ideal for which it stands. It is an obvious fact that the church, while flowing through the stream of history, has picked up the ends (evils) of little tributaries, and the evils of these tributaries have been so powerful that they have been able to overwhelm the main stream. But amid all of its weaknesses, we must admit that the church enlarges our sympathy and reinforces our power by uniting us with those who have followed Jesus before us, or who will follow him after us.[39]

Clearly, King came to see that church history is as much real history as it is sacred history. Therefore, even before pursuing seminary and graduate school training, he never subscribed to romanticized and sanitized notions of what the church is or should be. This was even more typical of King the seminarian and graduate student, who understood well the Barthian conception of the limitations imposed by human sinfulness, and who wrote papers about Reinhold Niebuhr's great sensitivity to the subterfuges of human frailty.[40] But eminently more important for King was the need for the church to always acknowledge its ambivalent side, or its divine and human dimensions, while remaining open to renewal in every age.

King's academic papers contain descriptions of the church that he would build on and advance with greater analytical depth and clarity as a pastor and civil rights leader. The young man was apt to portray the church as the body of Christ, a spiritual gathering, or the community of faith in his writings and sermons. Other concepts surfaced as well. In one essay outline at Crozer, King described the church as "a religious communion," "the light-bearer of mankind," called to confront humans "with the fact of the living God." "The church is the disciples listening to the sermon on the mount, or following Jesus along the roadways of Palestine," he declared. "It is Peter and his comrades eyeing the leaders of Judaism and saying, 'We must obey God rather than man'."[41]

In that same outline, King reflected on "the church as a nucleus of fellowship." Perhaps with vivid memories of his own upbringing at Ebenezer, he noted that "It is the place of the church to make people feel at home, not in a superficial sense but in the deep and abiding sense of finding peace in the fellowship which we have one with another." "The church must stress fellowship as being more important than creeds, and experience as being more important than doctrinal uniformity,"[42] King added. This idea of the church as "home" and "fellowship" revealed much about King's early intellectual struggle with the meaning, character, and significance of human community. As a seminarian and graduate student, he obviously gave serious consideration to the church as a critical force in overcoming the many artificial barriers that separated people. This was more than substantiated in King's occasional use of the word *koinonia*, which, from the New Testament Greek, means fellowship or reconciliation in the context of the *ekklesia*.[43] In a short piece on "What a Christian Should Believe About Himself," written for a theology course at Crozer, King raised the idea of church as family, an image that also reflected his early communitarian vision:

> Each Christian should believe that he is a member of a larger family
> of which God is Father. Jesus expresses the view throughout the
> Gospels that we are members of one family, meant to live as brothers
> and to express our brotherhood in helpfulness. A failure to realize
> this truth is a failure to realize one of the main tenets of the Christian
> religion. The Fatherhood of God and the Brotherhood of man is the
> starting point of the Christian ethic.[44]

Convinced that "The thesis of the Christian ethic is the endless possibilities for the fulfillment of brotherhood in history,"[45] King raised the need for the church to seriously combat oppression and social injustice in his papers and in his conversations with his fellow students and professors at Crozer and Boston. In such instances, the challenge that various forms of bigotry and intolerance presented for the church loomed large in King's consciousness, as had been the case during and even before his Morehouse years.[46] In a paper that addressed the question, "Is the Church the Hope of the World?," prepared at Crozer, King lamented the thought that the church was "one of the chief exponents of racial bigotry" and other forms of prejudice and injustice.[47] Instead of hating "members of another race, or another nationality, or another religion," the young seminarian maintained in a document for a preaching course, the church should follow the example of the Good Samaritan, who acted in love while looking beyond the many chasms that separated Samaritan and Jew.[48] Although King's view of the church as Good Samaritan, which would be advanced with greater clarity and sophistication in later years, owed much to the kind of liberal Christian theology and ethics the young man was studying at Crozer,[49] it also revealed his enduring indebtedness to the black church, and especially the Ebenezer tradition.

King also thought in terms of the church's responsibility to address the problems of poverty and the needs of the poor. As he understood it, the role of the church historically had to be viewed largely in these terms. For him, the very thought of the church existing as one of the richest institutions, and thriving in the midst of grinding poverty, proved quite unsettling. "While somewhat extravagant, there is a healthy warning in the statement, Christianity was born among the poor and died among the rich,"[50] he wrote in a paper at Boston University. King went on to associate "the greatest service of the poor" with a movement toward "the greatest attainment of truth,"[51] and he insisted that the Prophet Amos, who decried the mistreatment of the poor by the rich, properly proclaimed that "justice between man and man [is] one of the divine foundations of society" and "the root of all true religion." King added: "This high ethical notion conceived by Amos must always remain a challenge to the Christian church."[52]

As a graduate student, King indicted the church for its long history of sanctioning monopoly capitalism[53] and of betraying the concerns of the needy, and he asserted that congregations should reclaim a sense of "the value of persons" and "stop trying to outstrip each other" in the number of their converts, the size of their sanctuaries, and the abundance of their material resources.[54] King was absolutely convinced that the church embodied the resources needed not only to meet human needs on many levels but also to motivate people to new heights of self-esteem, achievement, and self-uplift. He wrote: "The church holds before us this fact—confirmed in the lives of Paul, Augustine, John Wesley, Tolstoy, and Schweitzer in Africa—that you can be more than a conqueror, and that life can be what you choose to make it."[55]

Not surprisingly, King confronted forthrightly the whole question of the educational value of the church throughout his student days. It was his conviction that the church should be a forum for the exchange of ideas and the advancement of learning. In emphasizing the church's educational function, he did not have in mind merely an arena in which creeds and dogma are shared and learned. Also, he did not mean a context in which absolute truth is conveyed, though he did speak to the importance of the church as an interpreter of God's revelation in the Bible, which he called "a sacred book of the Christian church."[56] In a paper on the ministry of the church at Crozer, King held that the church's leadership is mandated to present theology "in light of the people's experiences," not to "leave the people lost in the fog of theological abstractions." "It is my conviction," King continued, that the leadership of the church "must somehow take profound theological and philosophical views and place them in a concrete framework." Also in connection with this educational role, King maintained that "One of the basic functions of the Christian Church is to keep alive a certain degree of moral sensitivity," or to "urge men to be good, to be sincere, to be conscientious."[57]

Social Gospel liberalism and personal idealism provided the kind of intellectual structure and conceptual framework King needed to challenge the widely held view that the church should ignore the social life while promoting soul-winning preaching, inspiring conversions, and preparing individuals for personal salvation. While this view was quite common even in black-church circles, King never really took it seriously, let alone subscribed to it. Knowing that any attempt to separate the personal from the social inevitably led to a distortion of what the church and its ministry should involve, King, in a statement at Crozer, offered reflections that would be shared repeatedly when he became a civil rights leader:

> Above all I see the preaching ministry as a dual process. On the one hand I must attempt to change the souls of individuals so that their societies may be changed. On the other I must attempt to change societies so that the individual soul will have a change. Therefore, I must be concerned about unemployment, slums, and economic insecurity. I am a profound advocate of the social gospel.[58]

With the whole history of the church in mind, King reasoned, in a paper outline at Boston, that that institution had always been the strongest and most vital in character when it embraced unequivocally the demands of a Social Gospel:

Whenever Christianity has remained true to its prophetic mission, it has taken a deep interest in social justice. Whenever it has fallen short at this point, it has brought about disastrous consequences. We must never forget that the success of communism in the world today is due to the failure of Christians to live to the highest ethical tenets inherent in its system.[59]

In a paper on "Reinhold Niebuhr's Ethical Dualism" at Boston, King elaborated further on what it meant to engage both the personal and the social in the life of the Christian church. Drawing on Niebuhr, he commented:

The Christian, being in though not of this world, is never fully free from the complexities of acting as a vicar of Christ in his intentional life and a social and political agent in his actual life. The more aggressively one relates the gospel to life, the more sensitively he realizes that the social unit can accommodate only justice, not agape. Agape is always a possibility/impossibility. It remains perennially relevant in society as the regulative principle of morals, but it is realized in society only through infinite degrees of justice.[60]

Equally significant for King was the ever-present need for the church to properly distinguish between its ethical responsibility and the ceremonial and ritualistic aspects of its life. Exposed to the works of Walter Rauschenbusch from the time he entered Crozer, King was not likely to define the church at its best in liturgical terms. Although he always valued and participated in the worship life of the church, he, like any other student of evangelical liberalism in his time, was apt to assign a much higher priority to the church's ability to meet the ethical demands it confronted. In other words, young King understood the church primarily in socio-ethical terms, especially as he continued to reflect upon that unbroken tradition stemming from the ancient Hebrew prophets up to the time of Jesus and the Apostolic church. In a statement at Boston in 1953, King used Amos 5:21–24 to proclaim that "God demands justice rather than sacrifice; righteousness rather than ritual." While admitting that Amos was not against all ritual and sacrifice, which he associated with worship, King maintained that the prophet's primary concern "is the ever-present tendency to make ritual and sacrifice a substitute for ethical living." He continued: "The most elaborate worship is but an insult to God when offered by those who have no mind to conform to His ethical demands. . . . Unless a man's heart is right, Amos seems to be saying, the external forms of worship mean nothing."[61] Here the influence of both King's black church heritage and the Social Gospel of Walter Rauschenbusch is abundantly evident.

King's perspective on this level drew much from the insights of the African American thinker Howard Thurman, the Dean of Marsh Chapel at Boston during King's last year in residence there, and one who had long preached, lectured, and written concerning the ethical responsibility of the church in the contemporary age. When it came to this particular concern, Thurman's *Jesus and the Disinherited* (1949) was perhaps as important for King as any other intellectual source he studied at Boston. Once King became a civil rights leader, he was known to take a copy of the book with him as he moved from airport to airport. Apparently, preacher-intellectuals like Thurman, and to a considerable degree J. Pius Barbour and William Hester, were a constant and enduring influence on King's thinking regarding the church during his Boston years. They helped assure that the black church would remain a significant frame of reference for King's understanding of what the church as a whole should be, even as he studied the ecclesiological perspectives reflected in various streams of Western ethics, theology, and philosophy.

The intellectual atmosphere at Crozer and Boston proved ideal for critical and inquiring young minds, and this is why King seldom hesitated to speak and write about what he perceived to be the church's greatest failures in history.[62] While his critiques occasionally targeted the black church and the white church, he usually spoke and wrote with the church universal in mind. In sermon outlines and essays at Crozer, King chided the church for its obsession with doctrine, dogma, authority, and other matters he felt had "no essential place" in human salvation. In a paper on "The Purpose of Religion," he questioned the Catholic view that "the church, its creeds, its popes and bishops have recited the essence of religion and that is all there is to it."[63] Convinced that the meaning of the church had to be interpreted for each age,[64] King was, as indicated previously, prone to associate that institution at its best with practical or applied Christianity, and not with the values of tradition, authority, and hierarchy.

For King, the church's preoccupation with the nonessentials of traditionalism and authoritarianism had long made it unappealing in the eyes of many who would have otherwise embraced it. In an essay at Crozer, he spoke to the church's failure to prepare individuals for a genuine response to the call of Christ. Referring to the ecclesial vision of the neo-Reformed theologian Karl Barth, King spoke forthrightly to the glaring limitations of the church:

> He uses the church as an example. Today she calls men to
> thanksgiving, repentance, and prayers. But when the church says
> something, it is always an open question. Repentance must go
> beyond the church, for in many instances the church is the greatest

hindrance to repentance. The church, in many instances, has
betrayed God to the needs and humours of men. If we want to hear
the call of Jesus we must hear it despite the church.[65]

King was equally blunt in his assessment of how the church had so often
served as a barrier rather than a bridge to human community. Viewing the
church in its broadest historical context, he explained how that institution had
too frequently been more of an oppressor than a liberator, and a persecutor
instead of a promoter of peaceful coexistence. Describing Christianity in its
very essence as "a value philosophy" in which "All human personality is
supremely worthful," King declared:

I am cognizant of the fact that the record of the Christian Church has
been smeared in the past by infamous persecutions and the irremov-
able strain of the inquisition, but even so, Christianity at its best has
never let go the ideal that man is an end because he is a child of God,
and that the end of all life is the glory of God. The Christian ethic
would affirm that destructive means can never justify constructive
ends, because in the final analysis the end is pre-existent in the
means.[66]

In "Facing Life's Inscapables," a written assignment for a preaching
course at Crozer, King advanced this point in greater depth, lashing out at the
church's age-old tendency to condemn and to participate in exclusionary practices. "When we would criticize others for their shortcomings and insist that
they be turned out of the church," he observed, "we hear Jesus saying, 'he who
is without sin cast the first stone.'"[67] Referring once again to the parable of the
Good Samaritan to illustrate his point, King suggested that the church is true
to its calling to the extent that it becomes a whosoever-will-let-him-come
church.[68]

The problems of religious bigotry and self-righteousness were not ignored
in young King's critique of the church. In its quest for souls, he maintained,
the church had so often emphasized denominational identity and unscrupu-
lous competition to the neglect of much-needed mission priorities:

Now we are bogged down in competitive denominationalism which
is destroying the warm blood of the Protestant Church. "Which of
them should be accounted greatest?" Let the churches stop trying to
outstrip each other in the number of their adherents, the size of their
sanctuaries, the abundance of their wealth. If we must compete, let
us compete to see which can move toward the greatest attainment of
truth, the greatest service of the poor, and the greatest salvation of the

souls and bodies of men. If the church entered this kind of competition, we can imagine what a better world this would be.[69]

King's sharpest critique was aimed at the church's tendency to parade as a supporter and archdefender of the status quo. He pointed out, in a paper on the Prophet Jeremiah at Crozer, that "the worst disservice that we as individuals or churches can do is to become sponsors and supporters of the status quo."[70] In other writings at Crozer, King further stated the case, claiming that the church "has too often been an institution serving to crystallize the patterns of the status quo." In his estimation, such a tendency undermined the church's potential as "the hope of the world."[71] Even in that early period, there was the suggestion in his writings that the church as a prophetic witness to truth must always be in healthy tension with the demands of the state, a position he, drawing heavily on both Judeo-Christian traditions and the symbols of American participatory democracy, would later articulate in greater detail.[72]

Like many of his classmates and professors at Crozer and Boston, King was quite concerned about the whole question of the communist challenge to the church. In sermons and essays at Crozer, after reading Karl Marx's *The Communist Manifesto* (1847) and *Das Kapital* (1867), he labeled communism "the only serious rival to Christianity" and "a necessary corrective for a Christianity that has been all too passive."[73] The church's only logical response to this challenge, King contended, was to take seriously and promote equal rights and social justice. While arguing that "Christianity and Communism are incompatible," he felt that the church had much to learn from Marx's passion for the uplift of the poor and exploited. "The *Communist Manifesto* might express a concern for the poor and oppressed," King wrote, "but it expresses no greater concern than the Manifesto of Jesus," whose challenge to the church is "to preach the gospel to the poor," "to heal the broken-hearted," "to preach deliverance to the captives," "to give sight to the blind," "to set at liberty them that are bruised," and "to proclaim the acceptable year of the Lord."[74] Interestingly enough, the young man's sermon, "The Challenge of Communism to Christianity," preached occasionally during his Boston years, was quite well received by some at Atlanta's Ebenezer Baptist Church.[75] That sermon would become foundational for messages King would deliver on communism's challenge to the church during his leadership in the civil rights movement,[76] a period during which he was compelled to refute the charge that his activities were not genuinely church-based but communist-supported and inspired.

As previously noted, King pursued academic training with a sense of how it might be applicable to his needs as a pastor in the black church in the South. He was convinced that his future rested with that institution,[77] despite the fact that he was offered pastoral appointments at black churches and faculty and administrative positions at predominantly white academic institutions in the North.[78] This conviction owed much to his experiences with racism in the South and the North, and it also developed out of his sense that southern black congregations stood in greater need of trained leadership than churches and academic institutions in other regions of the country.

King also approached his studies in the academy with a concern for how this might prove useful in his people's struggle against racism and injustice. Clearly, his exposure to the ideas of great ethicists, philosophers, and theologians increased his uneasiness about many of the South's values, practices, and institutions, thus reinforcing his determination and quest to eliminate social evil under the auspices of the church. As King himself would put it, a portion of his training in the North would be put to the service of eliminating the problem of race, a problem which he, from his years in high school, had viewed as the central paradox of both southern and American life and culture.[79]

Although King completed the requirements for the Doctor of Philosophy degree in philosophical theology at Boston University in 1955, he never lost his appreciation for a dynamic intellectual environment and the possibilities this held for church growth and renewal. Moreover, King kept abreast of certain developing trends in biblical-theological scholarship, and he always sought to apply the fruits of scholarship and learning to his ministry in the church[80] and to the practical realities of everyday human existence. Thus, after he finished his studies in the academy and assumed a pastoral role in the church and a place in the black-freedom struggle in the mid-1950s, he increasingly became a more mature, perceptive, and constructive critic of institutions, and his reflections on the church became all the more interesting and provocative.

In the Service of the Lord: Images of the Church

Martin Luther King, Jr.'s views on and attitude toward the church were further clarified and refined in the context of his roles as pastor and social change agent. He became the pastor of Dexter Avenue Baptist Church in Montgomery, Alabama, in April, 1954, and was catapulted to a leadership role in the Montgomery bus boycott in December 1955.[81] From that point on, King was compelled to think even deeper about how the church's mission should relate to the broader issues and concerns of society. In his own thinking, his pastoral role in the church was never antithetical to his involvements in the sociopolitical arena, for both were extensions of his training and ministry. Needless to say, this perspective had significant implications as far as King's conception of the church was concerned. The discussion that follows will make this clear, while highlighting the various images that King, in his capacities as pastor and social activist, associated with the church.

King arrived at Dexter in Montgomery with a sense of the church as community-connected rather than race-based or class-oriented. Thus, from the beginning of his pastorate, he recommended that the congregation create a cultural committee and membership, courtesy, and birthday clubs, "in order that every member of the church shall be identified with a smaller and more intimate fellowship of the church."[82] King also formed "a Social Service Committee" to "channel and invigorate services to the sick and needy," and that step, in addition to his strong efforts to secure a life membership in the NAACP for Dexter, further reflected his view that the mission of the church must never be separated from the larger community in which it exists—that the church must always engage the cultural, social, intellectual, economic, and political concerns and needs of the masses.[83] The same might be concluded from King's decision to work with the local NAACP, the interracial Alabama Council on Human Relations, and other city and state-wide social and political action groups.[84]

Taking seriously "the whosoever will, let him come doctrine,"[85] King lifted a vision of the church that transcends bureaucracy, gratuitous regulations, and artificial human barriers in the interest of enhancing genuine fellowship and unity:

> I've been to churches, you know, and they say, "We have so many
> doctors, and so many schoolteachers, and so many lawyers, and so
> many businessmen in our church." And that's fine, because doctors
> need to go to church, and lawyers, and businessmen, teachers—they
> ought to be in church. But they say that—even the preacher
> sometimes will go all through that—they say that as if the other
> people don't count. . . . And the church is one place where a doctor
> ought to forget that he's a doctor. The church is the one place where a
> Ph.D. ought to forget that he's a Ph.D. The church is the one place
> that the schoolteacher ought to forget the degree she has behind her
> name. The church is the one place where the lawyer ought to forget
> that he's a lawyer. And any church that violates the "whosoever will,
> let him come" doctrine is a dead, cold church, and nothing but a little
> social club with a thin veneer of religiosity. . . . When the church is
> true to its nature, it says, "Whosoever will, let him come. . . ." It's the
> one place where everybody should be the same, standing before a
> common master and savior.[86]

This is how King understood the New Testament's call to *koinonia*. He insisted that the church is the whole people of God (*laos*), and not some hierarchical arrangement centered exclusively in the clergy. Moreover, as had been the case as far back as his Morehouse years, he took seriously the Reformation concept of the priesthood of all believers, or the conviction that ministry is the business of not merely the clergy, but of the laity as well. Even so, when it came to the question of where authority lies in the church, King harked back to the view, held as far back as the Protestant Reformers, and rooted deeply in the traditions of southern black Baptist Protestantism, that God chooses from that universal priesthood persons who are divinely called and commissioned by the institutional church to lead and to do ministry in a special way. Thus, the pastor, according to King, is vested with authority on two levels:

> First of all, his authority originates with God. Inherent in the call
> itself is the presupposition that God directed that such a call be made.
> This fact makes it crystal clear that the pastor's authority is not
> merely humanly conferred, but divinely sanctioned. . . . Secondly, the
> pastor's authority stems from the people themselves. Implied in the
> call is the unconditional willingness of the people to accept the
> pastor's leadership. This means that the leadership never ascends
> from the pew to the pulpit, but it invariably descends from the pulpit
> to the pew.[87]

Mindful of the traditions and values that influenced his father and the previous generations of black preachers, and with the precision of an accomplished engineer, King further explained his point:

> This does not mean that the pastor is one before whom we blindly and
> ignorantly genuflect, as if he were possessed of some infallible or super-
> human attributes. Nor does it mean that the pastor should needlessly
> interfere with the deacons, trustees or workers of the various auxiliaries,
> assuming unnecessary dictatorial authority. But it does mean that
> the pastor is to be respected and accepted as the central figure around
> which the policies and programs of the church revolve. He must
> never be considered a mere puppet for the whimsical and capricious
> mistreatment of those who wish to show their independence, and "use
> their liberty for a cloak of maliciousness." It is therefore indispensable
> to the progress of the church that the official board and membership
> cooperate fully with the leadership of the pastor.[88]

Here King upheld the notion of the church as a democratic institution, even as he affirmed the authoritative and leadership role of the pastor. Clearly, he opposed the idea of unrestricted authority and leadership on the part of the pastor, knowing that this could undermine order and discipline in the life of the church. In his own mind, the church functioned best when the ministries of the clergy and laity complemented and strengthened each other. The image of wholeness is of paramount importance here. Be that as it may, King evidently felt that he was being quite biblical in his approach to issues of church authority and leadership, even as he drank from the wellsprings of both the Protestant Reformation and black church traditions.

King called for profound changes in the ways in which Christians and the society as a whole thought about the church in the 1950s and 1960s. He refused to associate the essence of the church with buildings or other material things,[89] though his personal idealism did lead him to believe that church property, as all other property, has instrumental value and is therefore worthy of great care and consideration. Also, the church for King was more than a gathering, an authority structure, programs, and services rendered to a specific constituency in a particular geographical area. Equally problematic for him were the traditional models of the church as institution and organization, despite his occasional references to the church in these terms. In King's estimation, institutional and organizational self-centeredness, revealed most prominently in the preoccupation with growth and numbers, loomed as a serious threat to the very life and relevance of the church. What mattered most to him was not the institutional and organizational life of the church but, rather, the concept of the church as mission and movement, a perspective that also owed much to his black church background and his exposure to Walter Rauchenbusch and the Social Gospel.

A plethora of other images of the church surfaced in King's sermons, speeches, writings, and interviews with representatives of the media. Biblical-historical images of the church as covenant, rooted in the traditions of ancient Israel and the divine promise to deliver God's people, and in the new covenant God made with God's people through Jesus Christ, were occasionally highlighted by him. For King, the Apostolic church epitomized the covenantal relationship between God and humanity, one grounded in Christ's redemptive activity on the cross, in the obedience of the faithful, in the Holy Spirit as guide and comforter, and in the conviction that God's kingdom would come to earth. Thus, King had no problem with definitions of the church as the New Israel, the chosen ones, the people of God, the company of the faithful, the bride of Christ, and the body of Christ.[90] These images best captured for him that sense of the church as the covenantal ideal. Such images, King believed, were also applicable to the church in all ages. But interestingly enough, he frequently used the early church as a model when explaining the kind of covenantal relationship that should exist between God and the contemporary church. Moreover, he delighted in thinking of the church in his own time as a living covenant, or as a compact or co-worker relationship between God and individuals who are committed to the actualization of God's plan for God's creation.[91]

Of all the diverse faces of the church, King was probably most familiar with its life as liturgical event and activity. After all, he grew up in a culture in which worship, centered largely on preaching and music, was widely understood to be the central task of the church. Defining worship as "a silent communication with God," or that which "helps us transcend the hurly-burly of everyday life and dwell in a transcendent realm," King held that "This tendency to worship is one of the elemental functions of human life."[92] Having deep roots in the church, so much of what he said and wrote offers an informed and insightful glimpse into its liturgical life. The "esthetic response to Christ," he declared, "is bound up in the beauty of the worship, the moving anthems and ceremony which the church has created about His life."[93]

Though convinced that the liturgical experience must involve celebration, that it must be dynamic and moving, King strongly rejected the tendency to equate vibrant worship with entertainment. Noting that "many of our churches would leave us with the impression that worship is entertainment," he insisted that the liturgical church at its best is never "an entertaining center," but a "fellowship" in which the hearts and minds of persons are nurtured through an exercise of their artistic, ritualistic, and intellectual gifts and talents. He denounced ministers "who are mere showmen giving the people what they want rather than what they need," and who ascend "the pulpit depending on the volume" of their voices "rather than the content" of their messages. Equally disturbing for King were "prayers uttered for the entertainment of the listeners rather than for the sincere communication with God," and songs that "appeal to the feet and hands rather than to the heart and mind":

> This tendency to reduce our worship periods to mere entertaining
> periods has sapped the very vitality of spiritual fervor from the root of
> the Church. The living water of the Holy Spirit fails to flow through
> the stream of our churches. Of course the irony of the whole matter
> is that the very people who make worship an entertaining center are
> the people who are convinced that their actions reveal the Holy Spirit.
> They have confused overt emotionalism with the true Holy Spirit.
> This misinterpretation of the Holy Spirit has caused many to fail to
> see the value of a sensible sermon. Moreover, it has caused many to
> lose appreciation for real music. We have strayed away from those
> songs that were written out of the souls of men, and jumped to those
> songs which are written merely for commercial purposes. At this

point there is a great deal that we can learn from Catholicism. No one can doubt the fact that the Catholics have mastered the art of worship. On many occasions I have been in Catholic churches and it felt as if the very atmosphere blew the wind of the Holy Spirit. There was something in the very atmosphere that motivated one to worship.[94]

Although King understood the worship experience as part of the interior and private life of the church,[95] as indicated earlier, he did not associate this merely with ritualism, ceremonialism, or a solemn assembly or sacred arena in which confession, witness, prayer, meditation, Bible study, and family devotion occur. As King occasionally pointed out, Jesus condemned the Pharisees because they confused "ceremonial piety" with authentic worship and "genuine religious living."[96]

In King's thinking, worship constituted "a public affair" in which the faithful gather not simply to celebrate sacred liturgy or to partake of the sacraments but also to bear witness to the gospel and to be called into being and activity through faith in the living, risen Christ who saves, liberates, and empowers. In other words, worship is a call to service, but it is, as King wrote, "not to be confused with service." "When one worships God he is not necessarily serving God," said King. "Worship only prepares one for service." He further remarked: "We must not think that after we worship we have totally fulfilled our Christian duty. If worship does not cause us to serve our fellow man in everyday life and see the worth of human personality, then the whole process is as 'sounding brass and a tinkling cymbal.'"[97] Stressing this distinction between worship as "private" and "public," King went on to explain:

> Although private worship is significant and uplifting it must not be a stopping point. A worship period on the radio cannot be a substitute for a worship period in a church. Worship at its best is a social experience where people of all levels of life come together and communicate with a common father. Here the employer and the employee, the rich and the poor, the white collar worker and the common laborer all come together in a vast unity. Here we come to see that although we have different callings in life, we are all the children of a common father, who is father of both rich and poor. This fellowship and sense of oneness that we get in public worship cannot be surpassed.[98]

For King, the liturgical function evoked images of the church as the temple, a believing community, the household of faith, a nurturing presence, a witnessing and ritual community, the fellowship of the Holy Spirit, and a center of proclamation (*kerygma*) and celebration. Although mindful and appreciative of the great resources of power in the worship life of the church,[99] and of the diverse gifts it received from God through the Holy Spirit and its continuing, vital presence, King was not prone to spiritualize the meaning of the church. As he saw it, the church, while nurturing the spiritual lives of the faithful, is more than a mere means to a spiritual end.[100] This is essentially what he sought to convey in word and deed.

King was no less intentional when it came to the concept of the church as teaching agent, or as a significant force in the cultivation of the mind.[101] Ever mindful of the intellectual, psychological, and material effects of so much of the miseducation promoted in the church, he spoke of teaching and counseling as a vital part of the church's raison d'être.[102] While agreeing that the church is not, first and foremost, an intellectual center, King nevertheless asserted that its identity is largely established by *what* and *how* it teaches. As he saw it, engagements with scripture, creeds, liturgical statements, the mechanisms of doctrine, and the biblical imperative to proclaim the gospel (*kerygma*), were only a part of what should be expected of the church as an educative force in society. The church is also an incarnate community which receives the Word of God in Jesus Christ, and which instructs and demonstrates in practical ways its values of love, mercy, nonviolence, justice, forgiveness, and reconciliation.[103] In this respect, King felt, the church best lives up to its claim of being a witnessing community.

King believed that the church's role as teacher invariably meant that it had to be in the business of serious theological reflection. In other words, the church, as he occasionally suggested, had to become infused with a dynamism of relevant theological discussion, but he knew that this would require more trained leadership, a concern he periodically raised and eagerly supported.[104] He brooded over the fact that the church of his time was essentially out of touch with the "death of God" thought and other emerging trends in theology—developments he viewed as a healthy challenge to the church's complacent theism.[105]

In contrast to Christian fundamentalists, King maintained that it was indeed possible to be a devoted churchperson and a strong and polished intellectual at the same time. This point necessarily had to be shared and reshared, he thought, especially in ecclesial contexts in which interpretations of the Bible were too often personal, subjective, and not informed by critical commentary, and in which a blind acceptance of dogma impeded understanding and progress.[106] Thus, bringing a higher level of intellectual vitality to church life could not have been more pressing for King. Moreover, the church had to assist people in keeping open, critical, and analytical minds. But King knew that this was easier said than done in a culture in which the most serious quests for erudition and maturity in the realm of biblical and theological studies were commonly left to church-based or related academic institutions. While appreciating divinity schools and seminaries as centers of creative and critical discourse,[107] King felt that the church's significance as a force in the enlightenment of the mind was too frequently compromised because too many of its best minds were confined to the isolated corridors of these types of academic institutions. Such an analysis could not have been more perceptive, coming, as it did, from one who held a Ph.D. in philosophical theology and who was one of the most fertile ecclesiological minds of the twentieth century.

The idea that the church has everything to teach and nothing to learn from society and culture was categorically rejected by King. He held that even as the church fulfills its teaching responsibility, it must remain open itself to understanding, development, and renewal.[108] In King's thinking, this is part of what the church had to do in order to remain faithful to the cause of the gospel. Clearly, he was envisioning and calling for a model of the church that looks beyond the church, or a church that is as receptive to learning from the world as it is of offering its own wisdom, values, and resources to that world. Perhaps this explains, at least in some measure, King's extraordinary ability to inspire public debate around the whole question of the meaning of the church and its relationship to the world.[109]

The image of the church as a vehicle of missionary outreach loomed large in King's consciousness whenever he spoke of that body's task of witness and service to humankind as a whole. Like other pastors in the 1950s and 1960s, he took seriously the enormous challenge implied in the Great Commission (i.e., Matthew 28:19–20), and understood disciple making to be at the core of the church's identity. King typically extended the call to discipleship in churches after preaching,[110] but he believed it was far more important to attract believers by example. He also stressed the salvific and transforming significance of the gospel, advanced the need for a conversion or new birth experience, and baptized new converts. But even as he included missionary and evangelistic activity among the church's most defining vocations,[111] he lamented that Christian missions abroad too often amounted to merely cultural imperialism. Thus, he refused to share the deep sense of missionary urgency and compassion that pervaded so much of evangelical church life in the United States. In King's estimation, the church as messenger of the good news, as missionary presence, or as an avenue for the spread of the Christian faith legitimately involved not the imposition of America's values and traditions on other peoples and parts of the world but, rather, sincere efforts to be Christ to the world,[112] an issue that will be treated at greater length in Chapter 5 of this work.

King submitted that the church should be at its most vigorous when serving in its capacity as moral crusader and authority. The church becomes what King would call "a moral power," not by functioning as a self-interested institution but by leading people to live genuinely ethical lives and by confronting forthrightly and courageously the moral issues of its age. "Whenever a crisis emerges in history," King declared, "the Church has a role to play." He continued: "The Church can never evade any moral issue, because this is its primary concern."[113] King probably said more than any church leader of his time about the ethical task and significance of the church, and about the roles it might possibly play in morally changing individuals as well as social groups.

King often called the church "the chief moral guardian of the community,"[114] suggesting that it is by both definition and nature an ethical community. As such, it should, King argued, not only parade as an arena of moral discourse, or as the setting in which serious reflection upon the moral claims inherent in the gospel occurs, but must also assume leadership in setting, embracing, and advancing the highest standards of both personal and social morality.[115] This could not have been more important for King, for he consistently urged the church to be the vanguard in a new awakening of America's moral consciousness, especially around the issues of racial discrimination, economic exploitation, and violence and human destruction. "Because of this crisis those of us who are Christians are challenged more than ever before to make the Christian ethic a reality," asserted King in 1963.[116]

As King determined, the church actually betrayed its own moral and spiritual foundations whenever it ignored, tolerated, or compromised and cooperated with evil in any form. He sadly acknowledged that this, unfortunately, had too often been the case. "So the church," he declared, "must acknowledge its guilt, its weak and vacillating witness, its all too frequent failure to obey the call to servanthood":

> We must all admit that in the midst of many of the great issues of
> life there have been those moments when we in the Church have
> been all too silent and apathetic. There have been those moments
> when we have stood idly by mouthing pious irrelevancies and
> sanctimonious trivialities. There have been times when we remained
> silent behind the safe security of stained glass windows. But now
> more than ever before there is a need for all people of goodwill and
> all Christians to stand up.[117]

King warned, with the church uppermost in his mind, that if America continued to follow a path of silence, apathy, and neutrality in the face of social evil and injustice, it would face "an inferno such as even the mind of Dante could not imagine."[118] The very salvation of the church as the body of Christ, then, inhered, as King so often stated, in its effectiveness as a critic and transformer of culture. Here his thoughts recalled H. Richard Niebuhr's references to the church in his *Christ and Culture* (1951). Convinced that the ecclesial community should always be in creative tension with culture, and especially with "the powers that be," King, with the insight of an astute therapist, stressed the significance of what Harry Emerson Fosdick called the transformed nonconformist church, or the church as disturber of the status quo:

> It has always been the responsibility of the church to broaden horizons, challenge the status quo, and break the mores when necessary. In the words of the Old Testament, the church is "set over nations and over kingdoms, to root out and to pull down, to destroy and to overthrow, to build anew and to plant." We are called to be thermostats that transform and regulate the temperature of society, not thermometers that merely record or register the temperature of majority opinion.[119]

Noting that "Christians have a mandate to be nonconformists," King held that "The church must be reminded that it is not the master or the servant of the state, but rather the conscience of the state." "It must be the guide and critic of the state," he added, "and never its tool."[120] As "the conscience of the community, the conscience of the nation, the conscience of the state," the church's nonconformity and uncompromising posture, King believed, was indispensable in what he termed "this very tense period of transition," in "order to make it possible for us to move from the old order into the new order."[121] In other words, radical discipleship was for him a precondition for the kind of authentic churchmanship that redeems and transforms.[122]

Perhaps King's harshest critique was aimed at the church's tendency to serve as "an archdefender of the status quo." "Far from being disturbed by the presence of the church," King lamented, "the power structure of the average community is consoled by the church's silent—and often even vocal—sanction of things as they are."[123] While admitting that he knew Christians who risked life and limb in resisting the existing social and political order, King was most troubled by that side of the church that appeared too willing to render to the state and the status quo a reverence due to God alone:

> But I understand that there are many Christians in America who give their ultimate allegiance to man-made systems and customs. They are afraid to be different. Their great concern is to be accepted socially. They live by some such principle as this: "Everybody is doing

it, so it must be all right." For so many of you morality is simply group consensus. In your modern sociological lingo, the mores are accepted as the right ways. You have unconsciously come to believe that right is discovered by taking a sort of Gallup poll of the majority opinion. How many are giving their ultimate allegiance to this way?[124]

"The Christian owes his ultimate allegiance to God," King remarked, "and if any earthly institution conflicts with God's will it is your Christian duty to take a stand against it." In this regard, King contended, the early Christians had afforded the best model for the contemporary church, for they had been "willing to face hungry lions and the excruciating pain of chopping blocks rather than submit to certain unjust laws of the Roman Empire."[125] Hence, the very idea of a status quo church had to be rejected because it was not in the best tradition of the church, a claim King made consistently as he reconciled his own church-manship with his willingness to resist unjust governments and laws. The civil rights leader insisted that:

> The church must remind its worshipers that man finds greater security in devoting his life to the eternal demands of the Almighty God than in giving his ultimate allegiance to the transitory demands of man. The church must continually say to Christians, "Ye are a colony of heaven." True, man has a dual citizenry. He lives both in time and in eternity; both in heaven and on earth. But he owes his ultimate allegiance to God. It is this love for God and devotion to His will that casteth out fear.[126]

King also criticized the tendency of the church to draw "a strange, un-Biblical distinction" between the religious and the political, the secular and the sacred, and the body and soul, and he chided that institution for encouraging a strictly otherworldly outlook and compensatory hope, thus relegating public service and human welfare to secondary status or no place at all.[127] King identified this as part of a "lopsided theology" that causes the church to ignore "the here and now," while promoting the false notion that "man must lie still purely submissive" and wait on "God in His good time" to "redeem the world." Such a church, in King's opinion, epitomized an unhealthy escapism, and it encouraged the kind of apolitical spirit that is perhaps even more frustrating than outright, uncritical loyalty to the state:

> Of course, there are always those who will argue that the Church should not get mixed up in such earthly, temporal matters as social and economic improvement. There are still all too many churches

following a theology which stresses the total and hopeless depravity of all mundane existence and which admonish men to seek salvation in escape from social life and in preparation for an hereafter wherein all wrongs will be automatically righted. But however sincere, this view of religion is all too confined.[128]

Knowing that the church of his day was increasingly becoming "an irrelevant social club with no moral or spiritual authority," King frequently recommended that it "recapture its prophetic zeal."[129] He cherished the image of the church as a prophetic voice and witness, in part because he felt that it was highly established in scripture, and especially in the lives and activities of the ancient Hebrew prophets, Jesus, and the Apostolic church. Simply put, King actually thought of the church as a prophetic witness to the prophetic tradition of the Hebrew prophets, Jesus, and the early church.[130] That image of the church was deeply rooted in his own church heritage and supported by personal idealism, Social Gospelism, and other trends in theology and ethics to which he had been heavily exposed. Steeped in this range of traditions, King understood the role of the prophet as a mouthpiece for God, or as one who, as he put it, "tells the truth."[131] "The prophets remind me that somebody must bring God to man, and say thus sayeth the Lord," said King, and he went on to state, referring to himself, that "in the prophetic role I must constantly speak to the moral issues of our day far beyond civil rights."[132]

Apparently, King felt that every minister of the gospel becomes a prophet by virtue of his calling; that "no one fills this need so perfectly as clergymen."[133] Small wonder that he was so critical of clergymen who, as he himself indicated, "remained silent behind the safe security of stained glass windows."[134] Such an indictment would have been expected from one who, through word and deed, "taught us that ministry without prophetic activity is less than ministry."[135] But what did this mean for the church as a whole?

King saw the prophetic function as unifying, primarily in the sense that it brings together clergy and laity, or the entire church community. In other words, the prophetic is a role that the whole church assumes. Thus, when King told the ministerial staff of SCLC in 1967 that "I want you to help me as God's prophets,"[136] his challenge had meaning for the church as a totality, or as an inclusive body. In King's way of thinking, the church as the people of God, unified under and with God, becomes a prophetic community led by a prophetic preacher. This view of the church, however perceptive, proved too demanding for most Americans in the 1950s and 1960s, and it was obviously at the root of much of King's conflict with the state and the more conservative wings of the church.[137]

Repelled by the excessive emphasis on individual salvation, King tended to see the church primarily as a social center and mission. In this capacity, said he in 1964, the church becomes "a vital force" not by merely criticizing unjust social structures and dramatizing and exposing social evil but also by challenging "its worshipers to remain awake through this great social revolution."[138] But even this was only a part of the challenge as King saw it. "The church," he claimed, had to also "take the lead in social reform,"[139] or in the business of creating and nurturing communities for social service and change. In more specific terms, King, who fully embraced the dynamic, functional model of church activism, explained:

> The churches must become increasingly active in social action outside their doors. They must take an active stand against the injustices and indignities that the Negro and other non-white minorities confront in housing, education, police protection, and in city and state courts. They must support strong civil rights legislation. They must exert their influence in the area of economic justice.[140]

When it came to the social role of the church, King's standards were in the stratosphere. As he viewed the situation, the civil rights movement was the moment of decision as to where the church stood on a range of social justice issues.[141] Unity in social witness and practice on the part of the church, he noted, did not require a uniformity of doctrine, liturgy, and polity. But King also knew that the church's potential for radical social transformation hinged largely on its ability to recover a proper balance between evangelism and social action. This need could not have been greater, for the church as a body, as he stated in so many ways, had too long lacked a faith-based social ethic, a biblically grounded ethic of social justice, or an *agape* ethic that embraced life's social dimension. In other words, the church had failed in relating biblical, ethical, and theological insights to the need for social change.[142] According to King, this is largely what accounted for the ineptness of the church as a social institution.

The image of the kingdom of God was key to King's understanding of the church and its social dimension and mission. Put another way, his idea of church was centered in a theological vision of the kingdom of God on earth. The church excels as an agent of change, King believed, by affirming the kingdom of God on earth and by becoming a symbol of that kingdom. In response to the church's tendency to turn Jesus' preaching about the coming of the kingdom into an individualistic gospel of salvation, King eagerly and consistently proclaimed that the kingdom is not merely about the afterlife but about the power that can change lives and relationships, laws, structures, and institutions in the here and now. Here, King's indebtedness to the Social Gospelism of Walter Rauschenbusch and to his own church traditions became, once again, quite evident.[143]

Although the church for King was called to be the locus of God's liberating and humanizing activity on earth, his view of the kingdom of God compelled him to think in terms of a co-worker relationship between God and the church in the interest of improving the human condition. As he put it at times, the point is that God is immanent in the world and in human experience, working through and with devoted persons and a committed church for the actualization of the divine purpose in history.[144] This idea formed the basic conceptual framework of King's paradigm for ecclesial action.

To be sure, this kind of theological outlook proved immensely significant in terms of King's concept of the church as a symbol of the beloved community.[145] For King, the theological vision of the kingdom of God on earth and the ethical goal of the beloved community were synonymous, for both "expressed an optimism about the future of society and historical progress."[146] Not apt to identify the church with any company of the elect, though he did speak occasionally of Christians being called or chosen, King thought of the church in communitarian and/or inclusive terms, variously viewing it as a symbolic expression of the beloved community, as a cooperative fellowship, as an alliance of conscience, as "a great fellowship of love," or as an agent or catalyst for reconciliation.[147] King was actually speaking of an expansion of the New Testament concept of *koinonia* in light of the contemporary human condition.

In broad theological language, the beloved community ideal for King implied that the church should be the primary means by which humans are reconciled to each other and restored to fellowship with God. Sociopolitically speaking, it suggested that the church, by affording richer possibilities in its own internal life for love, reconciliation, and unity in diversity, could contribute to the civil rights movement's ultimate goal of integration—of mutual acceptance, interpersonal and intergroup living, and shared power.[148] In short, King reasoned that the ecclesial community had much to gain and share by creating community, and he used the beloved community, or the completely integrated society, as a motif for urging a social awakening upon the churches.

King lived and functioned in a culture in which there were competing discourses concerning how the church might best achieve the beloved community. As a theological liberal, he pointed the church toward a vision of sustainable community, urging it to become a major factor in overcoming racism, classism, and other artificial human barriers.[149] Consequently, the church as the beloved community probably represented the most enduring aspect of

King's ecclesiological rationale, but there were questions: Is the beloved community empirically possible, or can it be grounded in empirical reality? Is it
essentially inconsistent for the church to affirm and pursue the highest communitarian ideal while, at the same time, celebrating its historical, liturgical,
and ecclesiastical diversity?

King answered these questions in the affirmative, and he viewed the
church-centered civil rights movement, which reflected both heterogeneity and
obvious unity among its participants, "as a microcosm of the Beloved
Community."[150] So the beloved community for King was not just some "abstract
ideal"; it could indeed be actualized in history.[151] He knew that barriers existed
at every level of human achievement to the beloved community, but he felt that
the possibilities of overcoming them are limitless. Undoubtedly, he was
convinced that the Christian faith, in its true genius, offered the church a promising way of eliminating all barriers to the realization of the beloved community. Perhaps more important, King affirmed that "there is a personal power in
this universe that works to bring the disconnected aspects of reality into a harmonious whole,"[152] a conviction that could have profound implications for the
church as it sought to live in meaningful community.

"The cross," King explained, "is the revelation of the extent to which God
was willing to go to restore broken community."[153] It was in this connection that
he spoke of the sacrificial church, or the church as suffering servant.[154] This
stands as perhaps King's most striking image of the church. Tenacious and
nuanced enough to grasp what is at stake for those who resolve to live in the
servant-style of Jesus Christ, King employed a Christological hermeneutic that
highlighted the need for the church to shoulder the cross, or to offer itself as a
living sacrifice in support of God's plan of deliverance, redemption, and reconciliation. "The church must say to men and women," he asserted, "that Good
Friday is a fact of life."[155] With apostolic intensity, he urged believers to live "by
the conviction that through [their] suffering and cross-bearing, the social situation may be redeemed."[156] In other words, the cross is not just some symbol that
the church believes in and cherishes, but, more significantly, is a reality that the
true church lives each day in the context of human struggle and suffering:

> Christianity has always insisted that the cross we bear precedes the
> crown we wear. To be a Christian one must take up the cross, with all
> of its difficulties and agonizing and tension-packed content, and
> carry it until that very cross leaves its marks upon us and redeems us
> to that more excellent way which comes only through suffering.[157]

The idea of "bearing the cross," in King's mind, meant that the church
must always choose the path of sacrificial service and courageous change over

that of serene acceptance, even at the risk of insult, persecution, and martyr-dom.[158] This observation was clearly in line with King's persistent and forceful appeal for radical discipleship on the part of the total church. To the church that dared to pursue the ultimate in self-sacrifice, he offered sage advice, warning that "Before the victory is won, [some] may have to lose jobs, [many] will have to go to jail, [others] will have to face physical death," and still others will be called "rabblerousers, agitators, communists, [and other] bad names."[159]

But the servant church was to rejoice, not despair, King thought, knowing that "God is able to give us the interior resources to confront the trials and dif-ficulties of life."[160] The church could also find strength, he believed, in realizing that the power of the bread and wine in its sacramental life became real to the extent that its believers sacrificed, in the spirit of the Galilean prince, their own bodies and blood in the streets, radically engaging evil.[161] Moreover, King held that the church as cross-bearer, through its struggle and suffering on behalf of humanity, should delight in becoming a redemptive presence, for in this manner it reflected in supreme ways the liberating power of the crucified and risen Christ.[162] King always approached this subject with a fiercely serious mind.

The church's all too pervasive tendency to avoid or surrender the true meaning and demands of the cross disturbed King greatly. Reminding the church of the sheer power of its claim to be "the body of Christ," with some frustration King noted "How we have blemished and scarred that body through social neglect and through fear of being non-conformists."[163] Thus, he con-cluded that Christ, in a real sense, had to be reintroduced to the church, and indeed to the Christian faith.[164]

But King's optimism and strong belief in the ultimate triumph of the moral order kept him from completely losing confidence in the church. In fact, he continued to lift the image of the church as a citadel of hope or, as he himself described it, "a new beacon light of hope."[165] "The church today is challenged," he wrote, "to be the hope of men in all of their complex personal and social problems."[166] Mindful that large segments of the church had tragically surren-dered to a theology of hopelessness, which counseled mere patience in this life in anticipation of salvation in the next,[167] King insisted nonetheless that that institution should prepare persons to look with confident expectation toward the fulfillment on earth of what he variously termed "the beloved community," "the new order," "the New Jerusalem," "the Kingdom of God on Earth," or "the promised land of freedom, justice, and integration." Evidently, images of the Old and New Testaments came together in King's consciousness when he thought of the church as a hopeful community, as a fragmentary and yet visionary pointer to the promised land, or as a bearer and messenger of the hope that "we shall overcome."[168] "We must still face prodigious hilltops of opposition and gigantic mountains of resistance," said King, as he reflected on the challenges ahead, but "Christianity clearly affirms, however, that in the long struggle between good and evil, good eventually will emerge as victor."[169] Turning again to biblical imagery, King further elaborated the point:

> This belief that God is on the side of truth and justice comes down to us from the long tradition of our Christian faith. There is something at the very center of our faith which reminds us that Good Friday may occupy the throne for a day, but ultimately it must give way to the triumphant beat of the drums of Easter. Evil may so shape events that Caesar will occupy a palace and Christ a cross, but one day that same Christ will rise up and split history into A.D. and B.C., and even the life of Caesar must be dated by His name.[170]

Although convinced that hope becomes more accessible, especially to the poor and oppressed, through the church, King was careful to point out that the church is not an end in itself. Rather, it exists within time as a testimony to God's eternal presence in the world and also to the great destiny to which God calls all humanity. In any case, through an examination of King's reflections on the many shapes of the church, one encounters the vital spirit of a man who, by his own admission, deeply loved the church,[171] and who expected no more of it than he was willing to give himself. One also detects a vigorous mind at work, puzzling through the issues in a trenchantly argued and profoundly reasoned way.

From Faith to Praxis: The Church in Action

Living in a time of tumultuous change, Martin Luther King, Jr., spoke and wrote a lot about how the church might best move from ideas to activism, or from faith and proclamation to social praxis, in fulfilling its mission in society.[172] As a committed churchman calling for a fresh ecclesial engagement with social evil in all forms, King could not avoid the obvious but crucial question of the ages: How do we live the true essence of Christianity in practical terms? Leo Tolstoy, the Russian writer and social critic, whom King read and admired, had raised that same question generations earlier. But in answering that question, King did not go as far as Tolstoy, who ultimately concluded that one does not need the church—that one can be a Christian by simply living the Sermon on the Mount in the fifth chapter of the Gospel according to Matthew.[173] King affirmed the indispensability of the church as a force for both personal and social transformation, and he was absolutely convinced that the civil rights movement he led was an extension of Christianity in its most prophetic form.[174] Nothing less could have been expected of one who proclaimed the gospel not simply by words but also by his life, who understood the Christian life in terms of service to both God and humanity, who sought to unmask injustice in its many manifestations, and who brought an ecclesial approach to his work in the civil rights field.

It was at this level of praxis that King seriously engaged the issue of the social and political significance of the church. Ever mindful of the interactions between the political issues of his day and the mission of the church, he insisted on the church's heavy and uncompromising involvements as an arena of political activity and participation. This invariably meant that the church should have some influence on government and public policy in particular and on social life in general. For an example, King determined that the responsibility of persons to register and vote was a legitimate enterprise for the organized church—that it was a proper expression of both Christian stewardship and democratic privilege. Thus, he issued his own call to political activism on the part of the churches in Savannah, Georgia, in 1961, urging "every church in this community to establish a social and political action committee and make it a part of its 1961 church program to have every member in that church registered to vote by the end of this year."[175]

Three years later, as the nation prepared for national elections, King's SCLC proposed the "observance of 'a Civic Responsibility Day' in the nation's churches and synagogues," reporting that the "Main features of the day's observance would be special recognition of all registered voters in each church and synagogue and the organization of car pools by the churches to assure that *ALL* their registered voters get to and from the polls on Tuesday, November 3rd." SCLC went on, in the form of a resolution, to advise "churchmen across the country to express their religious convictions by going to the polls" and "voting in their local, state and national elections for those candidates who will seek to translate into public policy and practice the basic ethical insights of our Judeo-Christian heritage."[176]

When it came to the political function of the church, King was the very embodiment of what Frederick L. Downing calls "the praxis tradition": "that tradition which refuses to separate religious faith and moral considerations from politics, legal matters, and social reformism."[177] Clearly, politics and government at their best, in King's estimation, had to be linked to moral norms. In other words, moral convictions had a legitimate place in public deliberations about issues such as the ballot, legislation, and democratic politics and lawmaking. At the same time, King respected the boundaries separating church and state, and he never said that religious institutions and values should dominate in political life and culture.[178] He was never comfortable with a close alliance between what he labeled "the ecclesiastical power structure" and "the economic and political power structure," or with the thought of the church and government becoming instruments of each other, for he shared the view, strongly advanced by others from Max Weber to Reinhold Niebuhr, that such an arrangement can lead to the compromise of one's ethics, as the lives of too many clergymen in King's day illustrated.[179]

Be that as it may, King's views on the role that the church should assume in negotiating the complex terrains of politics were somewhat reflective of his position on the much broader question of the relationship of the church to culture generally. For King, the church can and does have a leadership role in shaping society and culture. In affirming this, King was not oblivious to the image of the church as just another power structure, often exercising its authority and imposing its teachings and values in ways similar to those employed by civil rulers and institutions. But he believed that the values and actions of the church, despite its shortcomings, should consistently represent a healthy alternative to the manipulative and often immoral policies and practices of the wider political culture of the nation. It was a noble vision for one who was always interested in and at times bewildered by the state of the church in the twentieth century.[180]

Despite assertions to the contrary, King did not simply use the church toward political ends. It is better to say that the church provided for him a base or staging point from which to press moral claims, to promote political mobilization among his people, and to implement action plans aimed at the creation of the beloved community, or the completely integrated society. Perhaps more than any of his contemporaries, King personified the interplay between religion and politics in America, and his activities alone raised the profile of the church as an arena in which political and public policy concerns could be addressed. Moreover, he was able to reconcile his willingness to break laws and to disobey court injunctions, which were used to maintain the status quo, with his love for the church and his profession of the Christian faith. But King's activism in the interest of equal rights and social justice was defined not so much by the norms of the political and ecclesiastical establishments as by the needs of society as a whole. As the civil rights cause was catapulted to the top of the national agenda in the early and mid-1960s, King did not hesitate to inject religion and morality into public affairs and public policy issues, and to employ the power and resources of the church for progressive social ends.[181]

"The nonviolent character of King's protests, his readiness to accept penalties imposed by the very system he was challenging," writes Phillip

E. Hammond, "reflect precisely civility elevated to civil religion."[182] In other words, King became a civil religious figure who judged society critically in light of its own democratic and Judeo-Christian ideals, and who combined religious imagery, political language, and creative social protest to make the nation true to what it professed in its most sacred documents of freedom. Small wonder that King became such an intellectual source and inspiration in the late 1960s for both civil religious theorists and liberation theologians, scholars who were pioneers in their fields of study, and who viewed the civil rights leader as both a model of prophetic Christian activism and a unique representative of the American tradition of creative dissent and protest.[183]

King challenged the church not only with the political method of mass social protests but around the strategy of coalition politics as well. Coalitions designed to promote understanding, goodwill, justice, peace, and community were very much in line with his vision of an ecumenical church, and when intersecting people of various faiths in his crusades, he was at times prone to ask: "How can we collectively put into practice what we as the church are called to be?" Driven by an ethos of inclusion, King as early as 1959 raised the need for the church to work in partnership with organized labor, the federal government, blacks, and liberal white southerners and northerners.[184] In 1964, he envisioned the forging of a "grand alliance of labor, civil rights forces, and intellectual and religious leaders," asserting that "This is the coalition which must continue to grow in depth and breadth if we are to overcome problems which confront us at this juncture in history."[185] King went on, in other speeches, writings, and interviews in 1964, to call for a "biracial committee" to heal racial divisions in St. Augustine, Florida; to advocate "uniting the knowledge and skills of the university with the compassion and wisdom of the church in stimulating community improvement"; and to reiterate his point regarding the need for coalitions that included various elements of society, including the church:

> Now this also means that we recognize that the movement must go all out to build constructive alliances because the Negro does not have political power on his own. He can't get enough political power on his own. He's only representing ten percent of the population so he can't get enough to solve the problem alone. We are seeking to build a grand alliance. The Civil Rights Movement, the labor forces, the religious forces of our nation, intellectuals and liberals must join together. It seems to me that it would be this grand alliance—our working together—that will solve the problems that we face in the days ahead.[186]

King's vision of "a coalition of conscience," based largely in the church, came to fruition during the campaign for voting rights in Selma, Alabama, in early 1965. Highly impressed by what he saw as "the warmest expression of religious unity of Catholic, Protestant, and Jew in the nation's history," King spoke about "the heterogeneity" and "obvious unity" that characterized those who marched during the campaign. "As I stood with them and saw white and Negro, nuns and priests, ministers and rabbis, labor organizers, lawyers, doctors, housemaids and shop-workers brimming with vitality and enjoying a rare comradeship," he recounted soon thereafter, "I knew I was seeing a microcosm of the mankind of the future in this moment of luminous and genuine brotherhood."[187]

Apparently, this "coalition of conscience" evoked images of the beloved community for King, reminding him that approximations of such an ideal are present at times in human experience and history. Nothing could have been more pleasing to one who viewed the church at its best as a coalition of conscience, and who attached great value to community as an integral part of his ethical ideal. Also, that "coalition of conscience" in Selma was very consistent with King's belief in "the interrelated structure of all reality" and especially his conviction that human beings, by virtue of creation, are interrelated and interdependent.[188] The interrelatedness and interdependence of persons in the church's mission, King believed, was illuminated in the Apostle Paul's image of the body of Christ.[189]

By the late 1960s, King sensed that the focus of black political efforts had begun to shift from social protest to electoral politics, thus making it even more essential for his people, as a racial minority, to work though the church and its leadership in forming alliances with persons of other backgrounds and affiliations who shared their interests and vision for the nation. Although convinced that the church should never allow itself to become merely a political coalition,[190] King always held out the possibility of collaborative strategies in church action to rid society of social, political, and economic ills. He reasoned that the church should always be receptive to strategizing on a political level in terms of coalition building. This was the understanding that King brought to his work with organizations such as the Southern Christian Leadership Conference, Clergy and Laity Concerned (CALC), the National Council of Churches (NCC), the National Conference on Religion and Race (NCRR), and the Gandhi Society for Human Rights (GSHR), all of which encouraged interfaith dialogue and cooperation in the interest of justice, peace, and community.[191]

Absorbed into the internal life of the church, King maintained that that institution had a great opportunity to distinguish itself programmatically by becoming a revolutionary vanguard in the struggle to eliminate what he called

"the giant triplets" or "the evil triumvirate"—namely, racism, poverty and economic injustice, and war and human destruction. Knowing that race was the
nation's most wrenching and enduring moral and social dilemma,[192] King
declared that it was "an urgent necessity" for the churches and their theologies
to face the problem of racism while working cooperatively toward a remedy. He
called for "a coalition of conscience on the question of race" and urged "church
leaders to be 'maladjusted' to social injustice." "May the problem of race in
America soon make hearts burn so that prophets will rise up," he proclaimed,
"saying, 'Thus saith the Lord,' and cry out as Amos did, ' . . . let justice roll
down like waters, and righteousness like an ever-flowing stream.'"[193] When it
came to the issue of race, the portrait of the church as Good Samaritan was
most appealing to King, for it mirrored the actions of "a certain man" who,
according to Jesus' parable, looked "beyond the external accidents of race, religion, and nationality" to assist "a wounded man" on the Jericho Road.[194] So
many of King's allusions to New Testament parables such as that of the Good
Samaritan, typically filled with the rhythm and poignancy of language, emphasized the importance of embracing a universal altruism that transcends race or
skin color.

As King reflected on the difficult and often bewildering terrain of the
church's role in race relations, he highlighted that body's inability to come to
terms with human differences and the explosive force of racial upheaval.
"Called to lead men on the highway of brotherhood and to summon them to
rise above the narrow confines of race and class," King wrote, the church "has
often been an active participant in shaping and crystallizing the patterns of the
race-caste system," a posture he found totally unacceptable "in a nation rife
with racial animosity."[195] In King's estimation, the church's failure at the point
of crusading against personal and institutional racism was obviously matched
by its inability to deal effectively with the realities and complexities of enforced
racial segregation. He complained that too many churches were held hostage to
the black-white race paradigm, as evidenced by the fact that "the most segregated hour of Christian America is eleven o'clock on Sunday morning, the
same hour when many are standing to sing, 'In Christ there is no East nor
West.'"[196] "How can segregation exist in the true Body of Christ?," King asked.
"I am told," he continued, "that there is more integration within the entertaining world and other secular agencies than there is in the Christian church.
How appalling this is!"[197] He agonized over the fact that the church remained
"the most segregated major institution in the United States."[198]

King's critique and/or indictment of the church did not ring hollow, in part
because he was always equally willing to offer a vision of new possibilities for
that institution. He actually put forth guidelines for how religious bodies might

move beyond merely a series of pronouncements on race in the form of appeals, petitions, and declarations to constructive, pragmatic activism rooted in nonviolence and other forms of moral coercion, thus arriving at a sustainable solution to the problem. "First, they must make it palpably clear," said King, "that segregation is morally wrong and sinful, and that it stands against all the noble precepts of our Judeo-Christian tradition." A second action "the churches can do," according to King, " is to get to the ideational roots of racial prejudice," thus explaining, "through their channels of religious education," that "the idea of a superior and inferior race is a myth that has been completely refuted by anthropological evidence." King went on to suggest other steps for the churches, such as taking "the lead in social reform," instilling "within their worshippers the spirit of love, penitence, and forgiveness," urging their constituents "to develop a world perspective," and making "it clear that the Negro is not seeking to dominate the nation politically," "to overthrow anything," or "to upset the social structure of the nation," but that "he is merely seeking to create a moral balance within society so that all men can live together as brothers."[199]

King perceptively added to this list of guidelines at various times in his writings, sermons, addresses, and interviews. Those included recommendations for the church to "uplift the dignity and worth of all human personality," to "remove the yoke of segregation from its own body,"[200] to lead in "mitigating the prevailing and irrational fears concerning intermarriage," to "keep men's minds and visions centered on God," and to "urge all followers to go into this new age with understanding goodwill." King also expressed the need for the church "to grapple with the idea that legislation can't solve the problem," for he was certain that only radical changes in the consciousness, minds, and hearts of persons could ultimately lead to the beloved community. In King's view, this made the church's function as "the moral guardian of the community" all the more important.[201] Additionally, he held that the church had to always be in a position to not only discern God's presence in the struggles of those oppressed on grounds of race and color but also to become co-workers with God for their liberation and empowerment. It was in this vein that King challenged the "death of God" theology of his time, while influencing, mostly in positive ways, the critical discourse of civil religious theorists and liberation theologians.[202]

For King, the biblical descriptions of the church as the body of Christ and the people of God underscored its high moral calling "to make the ideal of brotherhood a reality," a conviction he represented in words and spirit. Images of the church as *koinonia*, of the culturally and racially diverse church, of the church as beloved community, and of the church as "a great fellowship of love" shimmered before King as he considered what his egalitarian vision of God and human relations might entail concretely.[203]

Though often displeased with the substance and pace of racial reforms in the society as a whole, King was known to sound a positive note when asked about the church's reassertion of moral leadership in the struggle. "More and more the moral conscience of Christendom is being aroused on the question of race," he stated in response to a strong critic of the church in 1958.[204] In a press conference in July 1963, he offered a more detailed explanation of his point:

> Church groups are now taking the kind of forthright stand that I have
> longed to see as a Minister of the Gospel. The Protestants, or rather
> the National Council of Churches came out, just three weeks ago,
> with a very strong statement calling . . . for its various denominations
> and ministers to participate in demonstrations and direct action
> programs to end segregation. The same thing has developed within
> the Roman Catholic Church, and very strong pronouncements have
> come from the various rabbinical councils. . . . Many of the Rabbis
> have come out, so that I see a new development in the Church which
> is a very significant development, and to my mind, a new beacon
> light of hope. And I think the church now is moving on in the way
> that it should move, and it is making its witness clear.[205]

At first glance, such an assessment seems at odds with King's oft-repeated critique of the church, and it suggests the question: Why did he speak so positively of the churches in some instances, while strongly indicting them at other times for their "pious irrelevancy," their "spiritual paralysis," their proneness "to follow the expedient" rather "than the ethical way," and their record of falling "woefully short of practicing what they preach?"[206] It appeared on the surface that the civil rights leader was grossly inconsistent in his assessment of the church's effectiveness in confronting racial matters. A more plausible explanation may be that King was exercising prudence, realizing that all criticism and no praise always make for bad politics in any effort to appeal to the very best in persons and institutions. Also important is the fact that King was a dialectical thinker who typically spoke to the ambivalent side of the church, stressing both its weaknesses and its redeeming features.

In any event, King spoke in glowing terms of "a hopeful sign" that the church was indeed becoming "sensitized at last to the great toll of human misery that is perpetuated by segregation and discrimination." He said as much and more in his "Appeal to the Churches" as early as 1956, as the success of the Montgomery bus boycott was making headlines around the country. He was unalterably convinced that the church would not always be shackled by what he sometimes called "the superficialities of race and color"—that it would "one day transform the jangling discords of our nation into a beautiful symphony of brotherhood."[207] This conviction alone explained his call for the churches to become sites for profound and effective cross-racial ministries. If by chance the church retreated or failed to move forward in its struggle "for racial justice," King observed, "it will forfeit the loyalty of millions and cause men everywhere to say that it has atrophied its will."[208] In a moment of stern prophecy, he warned that "It will be one of the tragedies of Christian history if future historians record that at the height of the twentieth century the church was one of the greatest bulwarks of white supremacy."[209]

The moral reawakening to which King called the church extended beyond considerations of race and color to include poverty and economic exploitation. Convinced that "God never intended for one group of people to live in superfluous inordinate wealth, while others live in abject poverty," King challenged the church "to make the gospel relevant" to the "economic life of man," while contributing in substantive ways to the improvement of the quality of life for the poor and marginalized:

> Another area in which the influence of the Church is much needed but little felt is that of the economic order. The disadvantages that Negroes suffer in this area are startling indeed. In many fields they cannot get jobs at all; in others they are employed at appallingly low rates. This is a tragic end. It is murder in the first degree. It is strangulation of the moral, physical, and cultural development of the victims. So long as these blatant inequalities exist in the economic order our nation can never come to its full moral, economic, and political maturity. As guardian of the moral and spiritual life of the community the Church cannot look with indifference upon this glaring evil.[210]

Noting that the poor belong to every community of faith, King admonished the church, as a vigorous living organism, to put its enormous wealth and resources to the service of a decent income, food, shelter, health care, quality integrated education, and other "basic necessities of life" for those he commonly referred to as "the least of these":

> "The least of these" are the unemployed. Those not in any way touched by the present federal minimum wage law. They are those who are humiliated by the receipt of welfare when they would much prefer a job at adequate wages. They are the children who have grown up in fatherless homes, because the fathers, unable to find work, often had to leave home so that their families could qualify for Aid to Dependent Children. They are the people within our society who have no stake in that society, and who are daily reminded of that fact

by the humiliation they receive from police, welfare workers, Boards of Education and City Councils.[211]

King declared that the church cannot simultaneously neglect the poor and weak and maintain its foundational commitment to the gospel of Jesus Christ. In other words, faithfulness to the biblical heritage entailed compassionate service to the destitute and the outcast. Indeed, it meant translating the gospel of Jesus Christ into a programmatic agenda for the less fortunate in society. "Whenever the church is true to its genius," King explained, "it recognizes, as Jesus did, that it must preach the gospel to the poor and deliver those who are captives."[212] He related Jesus' understanding of and care for the poor, sick, and handicapped to what he thought should be the church's present concerns with respect to the exploited and downtrodden. "Our New Testament," he asserted, "charges us to be concerned about the hungry, those in prison, the least of these my brethren."[213] Interestingly enough, King used the parables of the New Testament to encourage the church to look at itself and to examine its own values and motivations. He hoped that the Good Samaritan would come alive and live anew in the church. The New Testament image of the shepherd who cares for the sheep was also central to his idea of the mission of the church.[214] Moreover, he breathed new life into the biblical prophets and made their message of judgment and deliverance applicable to issues affecting those "sadly disfigured" by poverty and neglect.[215]

While applauding the launching of anti-poverty programs and the sharing of material goods through the agency of the church, King believed that that institution's stewardship function demanded much more. Identifying "the economic conditions" that afflicted all too many as "not merely a political issue" but "a profound moral issue," he counseled religious institutions to assist in the economic uplift and empowerment of poor and oppressed people through training and the provision of job opportunities on a nondiscriminatory basis:

> This, therefore, becomes a grave challenge to the church and churchmen. To meet it all churches must accept the obligation to create the moral climate in which fair employment practices are viewed positively and accepted willingly. We must utilize the vast resources of the churches and synagogues for the many educational functions they can employ, and for which they have highly developed skills, facilities, and experience. However, to possess resources is worthless without the will to be effective.[216]

In more specific terms, King spoke of the need for the churches to forge common commitments with government in advancing federal contracts that honored "the moral principle of non-discrimination" and that strongly guaranteed equal employment opportunities and "a meaningful, healthful life" for all. "As churchmen we naturally would prefer that men would voluntarily comply with the requirements of such contracts," King explained, "but no one knows better than we do the problems and limitations of maintaining order and moral growth merely by means of persuasion and convincement." Knowing that "Love and persuasion are virtues that are basic and essential," but that "they must forever be complimented by justice and moral coercion," King urged the church to "encourage and stand behind government when it carries out its obligation in refusing or withdrawing federal contracts from those employers who do not in fact live up to the letter and spirit of the non-discrimination clause." He added: "The church must have the courage and the resoluteness to support the government where it determines to make examples of industries in dramatically canceling large contracts where the principle of brotherhood is violated. For in refusing to operate strictly within the framework of the contracts employers violate and degrade human personality—and our most sacred trust."[217]

As King realized increasingly "that economic justice is a much more complex and costlier issue than civil rights," he urged the church not to limit its outreach to cosmetic, reformist activities. In other words, especially in the period from 1966 to 1968, he insisted that true discipleship entailed support for a radical reconstruction of the economic order. "We're called upon . . . to use our resources and our commitment to help the discouraged beggar on life's highway and in life's marketplace," King commented, "but one day we must come to see that an edifice which produces beggars needs re-structuring."[218] He argued that the oppressive economic structures of society had to be replaced with new and more just ones. For the church, this meant attacking the capitalist ethic, which encouraged "cut-throat competition and selfish ambition" and which inspired persons "to be more concerned about making a living than making a life."[219] In failing to critique capitalism, King thought, the church was actually ignoring the source of the impoverishment of the nation's poor and disadvantaged as a whole. The problem was compounded, he believed, by the church's willing participation in and benefits from the capitalistic ethic. In King's assault on capitalism, which dated back to his college years, he in effect challenged the power of the church while proving himself to be not only a courageous and tireless advocate but also a fearless defender of the nation's poor.

Perhaps the strongest evidence of this is seen in King's own efforts to employ the power of the church for the advancement of those living in poverty. Disturbed by what he characterized as "the ravaging effects of the ruthless dehumanization of the urban poor," he spoke in 1966 of using "the forces of the churches" in "our determined crusade to overcome this insidious enemy—the ghetto slum."[220] In early 1968, King expressed pride in the fact that Baptists, Methodists, Presbyterians, Episcopalians, and members of the Church of God in Christ (COGIC) had joined him in Memphis, Tennessee, in supporting sanitation workers, who were involved in street demonstrations and negotiations with city officials concerning wages and union recognition.[221] During the same time, King met with church leaders to consider other actions against poverty and to solicit assistance in the SCLC's plans for a major Poor People's Campaign.[222]

But King was never able to muster the full resources of the churches behind his movement to eliminate poverty and slum conditions. He never ceased to proclaim his hallmark message—namely, that too many churches, owing to an otherworldly gospel, lacked enthusiasm and energy when it came to such concerns.[223] He sadly acknowledged that the church had too often met the anguished cry of people at the margins of life with sheer silence. "And those who have gone to the church to seek the bread of economic justice," King maintained, "have been left in the frustrating midnight of economic privation."[224] Equally disturbing to him was the church's tendency to rationalize its inaction by demonizing the poor. In light of this, King concluded that the church's appropriation of Jesus in worship, prayer, and song was rendered essentially meaningless.

Nothing was more frustrating for King than the church's willingness to align "itself with the privileged classes." The very idea of the church as programs and services rendered for a specific constituency in a particular social context, economic category, and geographical location was an affront to his sense of the "whosoever will, let him come" church. Without hesitation, King declared that "Honesty impels me to admit that the church has often been on the side of the rich, powerful, and prejudiced," and he chided those clergymen who "have often turned to the Bible to find some erroneous justification for the preservation of the old order." Noting that "This, however, is not the whole church," he commented further: "There has been and always will be that section of the church that joins the struggle of the disadvantaged and disinherited peoples of the world. Although they are far too few, there are still those ministers who recognize that the power of the gospel can never be clothed in the garments of a particular class.[225]

Even so, King agonized over the church's tendency to speak the language of power and not the language of compassion. For him, the coldness and lack of conscience of Dives before Lazarus, as portrayed in the New Testament, was a metaphor for the church's neglect of the poor and also for its obsession with power and prestige. King read the parable of the rich young ruler in a similar vein.[226] In too many cases, he contended, the institutional church, with its focus on individualism, materialism, and the privileged classes, had misrepresented Jesus, thus betraying the hopes of those who are poor and exploited. Put another way, the Jesus who had become enshrined in church doctrine, dogma, and ritual had little if any resemblance to the Jesus who was a voice for the voiceless, a friend to the poor and outcast, and a catalyst for change wherever human need was most pronounced.[227]

As one deeply concerned about material prosperity and the oppression caused by the rich and powerful, King clearly extolled a more compassionate vision of the church. He engaged in a vigorous, moral critique of the excesses of churchly power, and of the church's drive for wealth and prestige; and he acknowledged that when it came to the needs of "the least of these," the deficit existed not in human and material resources but in the human will. King also considered how the church might forsake its image as an ally of the privileged and powerful while becoming, once again, a life-giving and community-transforming agency. Knowing that the church had too frequently epitomized the human proclivity to serve idols, he stressed the significance of keeping the focus on people, not materialism. He felt that only a radically transformed or renewed church—a church with a prophetic gospel, a relevant theology, an activist ethic, and a life reshaped by the basic social, economic, and political needs of the poor and downtrodden—could claim legitimacy in his times.[228]

When it came to issues like poverty and economic injustice, King submitted that "the demand is for a new order to be born within the institutions of our democracy," including the church. "It is much more akin to the Christian notion of being 'born again,'" he remarked, "that is this old body politic of ours will be transformed by a new spirit of concern and justice for all humanity."[229] He spoke of this new order in terms of "community," or "the mutually cooperative and voluntary venture of man to assume a semblance of responsibility for his brother."[230] King also used other metaphors to compellingly capture this vision, such as "the promised land" and "the New Jerusalem," which for him translated into "the New Atlanta, the New Chicago, the New New York, and the New America."[231] Here, he was essentially evoking the symbols of an alternate vision of what the church and the nation as a whole could become.

King saw "signs of hope" in the fulfillment of the church's role as Good Samaritan and as "an alliance of conscience." He predicted that this would be the church that would liberate the poor and empower the powerless. He was equally convinced that the harshest judgment would await the church if it failed to conquer what he saw as the last frontier of the civil rights crusade in America—namely, poverty and economic exploitation:

> Seems that I can hear the God of the universe saying that I was
> hungry, and you fed me not. I was naked, and you clothed me not.
> I was sick, and you visited me not. I was in prison, and you didn't

give me consolation. And so get out of my face. You are not ready to enter the Kingdom. This is what the God of the universe is saying.[232]

There is a passion and sense of urgency here that were also strikingly evident whenever King reflected on the church's role in eliminating violence and human destruction. In his mind, the peace-making imperative mandated by the gospel, and especially the Sermon on the Mount, was essential to the identity and purpose of the church. Consequently, King advocated the mobilization of the conscience of the church as a whole to deal with violence and terror in all forms. He was particularly concerned about violence on an interpersonal level; the mob violence he and others encountered in the movement; and the violence that so often accompanied criminal activity, domestic relations, and even capital punishment. In King's estimation, violence in general stood "against the highest expression of love in the nature of God."[233] He repeatedly reminded the church and its leaders: "A mere condemnation of violence is empty without understanding the daily violence which our society inflicts upon many of its members. The violence of poverty and humiliation hurts as intensely as the violence of a club."[234]

The idea that the church should make its witness relevant to issues of war and peace was never really foreign to King. "And the church has a responsibility today, more than ever before," he proclaimed in 1967, "to raise its voice against war."[235] He complained, however, that "In the terrible midnight of war men have knocked on the door of the church to ask for the bread of peace, but the church has often disappointed them."[236] Perhaps even more unfortunate, King thought, the church had "contributed to" much of "the confusion, the hesitation, the bitterness and violence" that haunted humankind. In an interview on the NBC "Today Show" in April 1966, he alluded at some length to his growing disappointment with the church's attitude toward the utility of war, insisting that "There have been too many instances where individual clergymen and the church in general gave a kind of moral sanction to war as if it was a holy venture," and that "it is my strong feeling that we have got to make it clear that war itself is the enemy of mankind, and as President Kennedy said, unless we put an end to war, war will put an end to mankind."[237]

For King, the Vietnam conflict further highlighted the church's refusal to bring anti-war militancy and activism into the field of its moral vision. Although pleased that liberal clergy in certain denominations supported the groundswell of discontent and protest that surfaced in the face of the nation's deepening commitments in Southeast Asia, King was generally displeased with churches and church leaders who found it "expedient not to speak out against the Vietnam War." Declaring that his own public position against the conflict arose out of "the mandates of conscience and the reading of history," King insisted that there was "no excuse for silence."[238] "But I am convinced that the church cannot remain silent," he remarked at another point, "while mankind faces the threat of being plunged into the abyss of nuclear annihilation."[239] King found it even more disgusting that so many churches justified America's military policies and endorsed its misadventure in Vietnam as necessary steps toward defeating communism and ensuring national security. Interestingly enough, Vietnam led him to address issues both timely and age-old about the church and the evils of war. For one who was never really a proponent of war,[240] religious or church-legitimized violence defied logic, let alone high moral standards. It was in his capacity as Vietnam War critic that King, in the minds of many, emerged as the apostle to the church's and the nation's conscience.

The image and traditions of the primitive church provided much of the standard by which King critiqued the church's stance on Vietnam in his own time. In other words, support for the Vietnam War, he believed, signaled a retreat from the nonviolent spirit of Jesus and the ancient Christians, a point he was known to make concerning war in general:

> Never forget the early church. It was a great church. They told Caesar
> they would not fight war. . . . They were persecuted. They were
> thrown into prison. They were taken to the chopping block and they
> were thrown into the dens of lions. They always went there with a
> hymn on their lips, singing about the Glory of God, saying we must
> stick to what we believe is right. And one historian says that
> Christianity won out over all the other religions of the Greco-Roman
> World, because the early Christians were able to out-live, out-think,
> and out-die everybody else.[241]

King saw in the early church the beginnings of a Christian pacifist tradition that stood as a formidable challenge to the church in his day.[242] "The nonviolent resistance of the early Christians shook the Roman Empire," he asserted, as he reminded the contemporary church of its possible influence in the culture.[243] Apparently, the spirit of the Apostolic church largely accounted for King's idea that nonviolence "is nothing more and nothing less than Christianity in action," or "the Christian way of life in solving problems of human relations."[244] Moreover, King held that "Every true Christian is a fighting pacifist," for he "is involved in . . . a spiritual war," struggling, as King so often pointed out, "with Christian methods and Christian weapons."[245] These insights suggested ways by which the church might confront both the proliferation of nuclear weapons and the rising and frightening potential for human self-destruction.

But King knew that a more specific set of priorities and guidelines were needed in order for the church to become a major, positive force in eradicating war and in establishing a culture of peace. First, he suggested the need for the church to reclaim Jesus' image as the prince of peace and also "the sacrificial spirit of the Early Church."[246] Nothing could have been more challenging in a society in which too many congregations had abandoned the ethics of peace in favor of the often misguided war policies of government.

Second, King urged the church not only to question the nation's ever-ready inclination to go to war but also to engage in a more authentic peace-driven ministry. He placed primary responsibility for such an approach squarely on the shoulders of preachers, and especially pastors. "I think the clergyman . . . must in his messages and through his congregation seek to get to the ideational roots of war, so to speak," King argued, "and seek to take a general stand against war itself."[247] Here, King had in mind a revolution of values and priorities sanctioned and supported by the church and geared toward enhancing the possibilities for human survival and welfare on the planet.

Third, King once again encouraged the church as a whole to function as "a coalition" or "an alliance of conscience," using its range of peace-building resources to help create a peacemaking and peacekeeping culture.[248] This essentially meant providing moral, financial, spiritual, and physical support for the peace movement, which blossomed in the late 1960s. King graciously praised churches that became involved in the peace or anti-war movement, for they were among "the catalytic agents" who were radically transforming society through nonviolent means.[249] He never wavered in his view that the spiritual hunger, passion, and curiosity of the church had to be matched by an enduring commitment to peace.

Finally, King concluded that, "If the church is true to its mission it must call for an end to the arms race."[250] "In short," he observed, "we must shift the 'arms race' into 'a peace race.'"[251] Given his passionate paean to nonviolent strategy and his belief in human community, such a recommendation was clearly understandable but not necessarily politically realistic or morally achievable. Even so, it reflected King's conviction that the church should never ally itself with the nation's tendency to stockpile weapons of mass destruction while, at the same time, parading as a significant force for peace, goodwill, and freedom.

Although mindful of the undeniable restlessness and uncertainty that permeated much of church life in the 1950s and 1960s, King never ceased his quest for what he called "the true *ekklesia*."[252] As has been the case with prophets in every age, he spoke forcefully and sympathetically to the failures of present church life, even as he envisioned possibilities for cleansing and reformation.

His leadership and witness brought many questions to the forefront of ecclesi-ological conversation, thus explaining why more books and articles were written on the church in the 1950s and 1960s than perhaps at any previous time in history. Moreover, his faith in the church's capacity for renewal, though frustrated at times, would increasingly find vindication as he turned to the power and resources of his own church tradition in a movement for societal transformation. An account of how and why this happened is provided in the following chapter.

3

A Balm in Gilead

The Black Church as Mission and Movement

Our churches are where we dip our tired bodies in cool springs of
hope, where we retain our wholeness and humanity, despite the
blows of death from the Bosses.

—Richard Wright, *12 Million Black Voices*

In providing a structured social life in which the Negro could give
expression to his deepest feeling and at the same time achieve status
and find meaningful existence, the Negro church provided a refuge
in a hostile white world.

E. Franklin Frazier, *The Negro Church in America*

I am grateful to God that, through the Negro church, the way of
nonviolence became an integral part of our struggle.

—Martin Luther King, Jr., *Why We Can't Wait*

Founded, constituted, and led by African Americans, the Black
church emerged from a people in bondage, who understood the good
news as a liberating message.

—Frances E. Wood

The Negro church was central to Martin Luther King, Jr.'s
understanding and definition of what he called "the body of Christ."[1]
As he analyzed what he considered the main features of that agency,
he came to see it as the nation's best hope for preserving and

extending practical Christianity. Furthermore, King envisioned how the Negro church might play a decisive role in redeeming and renewing the life of the church as a whole. In fact, the movement he led, in and through the Negro church, not only provided the impetus for the redemption and renewal of the American churches but also served, in his own thinking, as a basis for a much broader church initiative in the interest of freedom, justice, peace, and human dignity.[2]

In setting forth his vision for the black church, King was as intentional as Walter Rauschenbusch and Ernst Troeltsch in distinguishing between the church as institution and the church as mission and movement. Knowing that institutions are typically conservative, he clearly had in mind the latter when speaking of the ecclesial ideal. For King, images of the black church as mission and movement took on a special cast within the context of the civil rights struggle. He saw that struggle as a movement of conscience based primarily in the church,[3] and this helps explain why he consistently challenged the black church to explore more creative ways to translate its remarkable spiritual depth and its disciplined devotional life into an active social praxis.

The content of this chapter develops along several lines of discussion. First, King's sense of how the history and struggles of the Negro church had unfolded from slavery times to his generation is treated in some depth. Attention to this subject could not be more important, especially in view of King's belief that social movements in the African American community had always been based in the church and fueled by religion. Second, King's portrait of the civil rights movement as a church-related crusade or a Christian social movement[4] is discussed, with some focus on his assessment of the social change potential of the black church, a concern to which he had given precocious expression in his comments and writings in high school and college. Finally, King's reflections on the ambivalent spirit of the Negro church are highlighted, with some attention to how this was revealed in his conflicts with both the more radical and the more conservative African American religious leaders of his day. The convergence of these various lines of discussion is useful for clarifying the contextual character of the church-based freedom movement of the 1950s and 1960s.

Bound for the Promised Land:
The Black Church in Historical Context

Martin Luther King, Jr., regarded the separate and independent African church movement of the eighteenth and early nineteenth centuries as a critical stage in the beginnings of the black freedom movement in the United States. King felt that Richard Allen, Absalom Jones, Nathaniel Paul, and others who pioneered during the origins and development of the first black churches were compelled to act not only in the interest of religious freedom and ecclesiastical independence but also because of the many abuses visited upon their people in the harsh world of slavery and racial apartheid. Referring to the patterns of white proscription that isolated his African forebears and excluded them from positions of power in the predominantly white churches, King declared that "It is to their everlasting shame that white Christians developed a system of racial segregation within the church, and inflicted so many indignities upon its Negro worshippers that they had to organize their own churches." He said the same regarding the problems that led to the rise of the invisible institution, or what he labeled "secret religious meetings" among the slaves in the antebellum South.[5] King made these points with the understanding that the shared vulnerability of people of African descent throughout the country meant that the efforts to form separate and independent black churches in the North and slave churches in the South constituted essentially the same movement.

Although King knew about the scholarship of W. E. B. DuBois, Melville J. Herskovits, and others on the African-derived religious traditions of the slaves, he did not say a lot about how the African cultural and religious background shaped the early black church and various other elements of black belief, music, and religious practices.[6] King was prone to view the songs created by slaves as they struggled and sacrificed on the plantations not so much as traditions brought from Africa but as products of the black experience in America, and as lenses through which to interpret certain essentials of early Negro church folk culture.[7] As one who studied "songs ranging from the spirituals of the slaves through the folk music of the freedom riders," King held that spirituals such as "Joshua Fit the Battle of Jericho," "Go Down, Moses," "There is a Balm in Gilead," "Nobody Knows the Trouble I See," "All God's Children Got Wings," "Free at Last," "Walk Together, Children, Don't You Get Weary," "Oh Freedom," "Steal Away to Jesus," "I Heard of a City Called Heaven," "Everybody Talkin' 'Bout Heaven," and "Woke Up This Morning with My Mind Stayed on Freedom," spoke volumes about the resiliency of the antebellum black church, North and South, and that they also opened a unique window into its value system, ethos, and worldview.[8]

Frequently acknowledging that such songs gave powerful expression to the tragedies, betrayals, and hopes that marked his ancestors' epic struggle to survive, King was equally mindful of the variety of cultural and political uses to which singing had been put in the slave church.[9] In King's case, it could not have been otherwise, for no African American had had greater exposure to the spirituals in youth than he. Moreover, no one had more appreciation for the heartbreaking pathos and the language of passion and yearning that coursed through slave songs. Thus, it is not surprising that King delighted so much in the artistic genius of Roland Hayes, Marian Anderson, Paul Robeson, and others, who were known for serious renderings of that music in the tradition of the slaves.[10]

The power and appeal that the church held for people in bondage could not have been more evident to King. In an age when enslaved Africans ingeniously merged aspects of their faith and culture, the church, King thought, was not only the stage upon which the folk wrestled with issues of power, identity, and worldview but also a way of making sense of the racial landscape in which they found themselves. Thus, King fully understood that any serious conjuring of black cultural images for the years prior to the Civil War had to include the church and religion at the center. He often said as much and more, noting especially how the faith of the black church provided a shield against the forces of oppression:

> There was a time that in the life of any Negro, religion had a place.
> Go back to the dark days of slavery. Our mothers and fathers knew
> that it was God that would bring them over. . . . Our mothers and
> fathers were able to get over the dark days of slavery and the dark
> days of segregation because religion gave them something within. . . .
> It was the only way that they were able to live with that system.[11]

While cautioning against any tendency to "romanticize slavery," especially since "It was one of the darkest and most evil periods in the history of the world," King nevertheless viewed the pain of that experience as a catalyst for the great artistic outpourings that so often distinguished the antebellum black church from its white counterpart. Knowing that pain and affirmation typically existed side by side in slave songs and in slave art generally, he likened the faith of the slave church, with all of its penetrating vitality and visionary effects, to that of the martyrs of the ancient church:

> Paul at Philippi, incarcerated in a dark and desolate dungeon, his
> body beaten and bloody, his feet chained, and his spirit tired, joyously
> sang the songs of Zion at midnight. The early Christians, facing
> hungry lions in the arena and the excruciating pain of the chopping
> block, rejoiced that they had been deemed worthy to suffer for the
> sake of Christ. Negro slaves, bone-weary in the sizzling heat and the
> marks of whip lashes freshly etched on their backs, sang trium-
> phantly, "By and by I'm Gwin to lay down this heavy load." These are
> living examples of peace that passeth all understanding.[12]

Apparently, biblical images and/or symbols figured prominently in King's sense of the early black church. That body was part of what he had in mind whenever he alluded to "the least of these," "the chosen people," "the Babylonian captivity," "Egyptian bondage," and "the promised land of freedom, justice, and equality." The most persistent single biblical symbol in King's reflections on the history of the black church is that of the Exodus. "This is something of the story of every people struggling for freedom," said he of the accounts of the Exodus in the Old Testament. "It is the first story of man's explicit quest for freedom," he added, "and it demonstrates the stages that seem to inevitably follow the quest for freedom."[13] At other times, King spoke of "the thrilling story" of Moses standing "in Pharaoh's court centuries ago," crying, "'let my people go,'" as "a kind of opening chapter in a continuing story" that included his ancestors' efforts to win both communal emancipation and ecclesiastical independence. "As far back as the early days of slavery," he maintained, "black men heard the story of Moses and learned of this great God who would lead his people to freedom, and so they sang, 'Go Down Moses.'" For King, "this strong biblical tradition" afforded much of the foundation for the protest activities of the historic black church.[14]

Equally significant for King were the ways in which the antebellum black church had used the story of the Exodus and its rich source of language and metaphors to construct a collective memory of the sufferings of Africans in bondage. Put another way, King sensed that the political dimensions of the story were central to the early black church's self-understanding, and that this is why the slaves found it endlessly fascinating, often giving expression to it in songs, sermons, and tales. Also, the slaves wisely noted, King believed, that the exodus of the Israelites from Egyptian bondage contradicted the claims, made frequently by slaveholders and other pro-slavery advocates, that God intended Africans and their descendants to be slaves. To the contrary, King insisted that for his forefathers and foremothers, the Exodus made plain the manner of God's providential dealings with the evils of human bondage, and most especially with both the oppressed and the oppressor. It could hardly have been otherwise for an ecclesial community that was steeped in the Bible, that identified itself as the old Israel or the people of the Exodus, and that laid claim to a mission that was rooted in a powerful sense of providence, racial destiny, and divine vocation.[15]

The black church as old Israel or the Exodus church were not the only images that emerged out of King's reading of both the Old Testament and the history of his forebears in bondage.[16] He spoke with similar vigor and clarity about the alien status of Africans in the evil world of slavery, highlighting their sense of being strangers in a strange land, of being sojourners in Babylon, of being on the margins or the periphery of American life:

> On the Statue of Liberty we read that America is the mother of exiles, but it does not take us long to realize that America has been the mother of its white exiles from Europe. She has not evinced the same maternal care and concern for her black exiles who were brought to this country in chains from Africa, and it is no wonder that our slave worn parents could think about it and they could start singing in a beautiful soul song, in a beautiful sorrow song—"Sometimes I feel like a motherless child." It was this sense of estrangement and rejection that caused our forebears to use such a metaphor.[17]

King perceptively explained why the agony of the alien-exile status became such a powerful theme in slave songs and in black churches, North and South. Despite their untutored state, the slaves understood, as far as he could determine, that the Lord's songs were created not only for Zion but for Babylon (America) as well. Moreover, King found strength in how slaves sang the songs of Zion in good times and bad times. In his estimation, this became the trademark of a people who valued the experience of religion as much as they did the development of their own ecclesiastical structures.[18]

Obviously, King recognized in the antebellum black church a diaspora community that was, for so many of its constituents, an exilic community, or a gathering of resident aliens. The church, he felt, was the place where his ancestors went to make sense of themselves and their condition as an exiled and abused people. In acknowledging such a state of affairs, King was standing in a long tradition of African American thought, for the idea of blacks as an exilic people was deeply rooted in the history of the folk. David Walker, Sojourner Truth, and countless others in the pre-Civil War era had identified their people as captives who languished on foreign and hostile shores. But there was for King another side to the diasporan and pilgrim quality of the early black church. That body, in its struggle to end slavery and to make real the promises of democracy, was embarking on a quest for some end conceived as necessary, noble, and perhaps even sacred. Therefore, King never hesitated to remind black church activists in his time that they were the true, living beneficiaries of their forebears' sacrificial sojourn in this nation.[19]

Although King lived in a period when even the African American scholar E. Franklin Frazier was alleging the predominantly otherworldly character and outlook of the antebellum black church,[20] King never embraced the contention that that institution was essentially uninvolved in its people's struggle for emancipation and empowerment. Instead, he apparently concluded that from its origins, the Negro church, as he called it, understood salvation itself to be personal as well as social, and that that body reinterpreted the gospel in terms of social, political, and economic freedom while also extending a this-worldly call to community action. King was aware of the black church's contributions to the abolitionist movement and the Underground Railroad, and of its important role in challenging the larger culture with a more prophetic and inclusive vision of freedom and democracy.[21] As King saw it, the civil rights interests and activities of black communities in the years before and after the Civil War always paralleled the development and leadership provided by the church.[22] Interestingly enough, this image of the Negro church as a mission and movement-driven church was central to his understanding and interpretation of African American history as a whole.

King knew enough about the history of the early black church to understand that resistance within its ranks took various forms. Frederick Douglass, an active member of the African Methodist Episcopal Zion Church (AMEZ), had represented one side of that church tradition by advocating moral suasion and nonviolent agitation in search of a truly interracial society, an approach that must have greatly intrigued King, who read the works of the nineteenth-century abolitionist and who considered Douglass his idol from the time of his childhood.[23] While questioning the practicality of the violent protests of insurrectionists like Denmark Vesey, the African Methodist layperson, and Nat Turner, the Baptist slave preacher, King graciously acknowledged their "courageous efforts" and undoubtedly attributed much of their spirit of noncooperation with an unjust system to the slave church.[24]

King also alluded at times to the subtle nuances of protest that permeated slave music and folklore, and that found expression in the writings of ex-slaves like Frederick Douglass and free Africans like David Walker.[25] King's knowledge of this history meant that he was not likely to uncritically accept the many easy caricatures of the antebellum black church as advanced in history books,[26] the mass media, and popular culture generally, some of which portrayed that institution as escapist, as otherworldly and compensatory, as an opium of the people, and as a the embodiment of a kind of unenlightened, superficial, bastardized version of the Christian faith.

Convinced that the religious world of his ancestors was much more complex than such caricatures implied, King was far more interested in how the church supported and empowered both their will to free themselves and their daily struggles for survival and meaning.[27] Far from being an instrument of compliance and control, the early black church, he believed, stood as a wellspring of life and renewal, and it also provided a refuge and an ideological framework for bleak and barren times. In King's mind, this was most evident in the church's efforts to develop black personhood and/or personality amid the depersonalizing effects of slavery and white supremacy. He occasionally referred to such efforts as they unfolded in the life of the slave church, or in the invisible institution, noting especially the pivotal role of the slave preacher:

> He didn't know anything about Plato or Aristotle. He never would have understood Einstein's theory of relativity if Einstein had been in existence at that time. But he knew God. And he knew that the God that he had heard about, and read about, was not a God that would subject some of His children, and exalt the others. And he would get there with his broken language. He didn't know how to make his subject and verb agree, you know. He didn't have that. But he knew somehow, that there was an agreement with an eternal power. And he'd look out and say, "You ain't no nigger. You ain't no slave, but you're God's children." And something welled up within them, and they could start singing, even though they didn't have shoes, "I got shoes, you got shoes, all God's children got shoes. When I get to heaven, going to put on my shoes, and I'm just going to walk all over God's heaven." They thought about a chariot swinging low, because they dreamed of a better day. And I would say that we have much to learn from them.[28]

King went on to quote "the words of an old Negro slave preacher [who] spoke words of great symbolic profundity in the form of a prayer: 'Lord, we ain't what we ought to be, we ain't what we want to be, we ain't what we're gonna be, but thank God we ain't what we was.'"[29] Convinced that "Something of the inner spirit of our slave forebears must be pursued today," King insisted that "from the inner depths of our being we must sing with them: 'Before I'll be a slave, I'll be buried in my grave and go home to my Lord and be free.'" "This spirit, this drive, this rugged sense of somebodyness," he continued, "is the first and most vital step that the Negro must take in dealing with his dilemma."[30]

There is no question that King saw the antebellum black church as a structure through which hope was affirmed and maintained. Nothing less could have been expected of one who was known to speak of the entire history of the black church in transcendent terms. King believed that the affirmation of black personhood was part of what made the church such a vital symbol of hope for the slaves.[31] Moreover, he saw the divine at work not only in the spiritual lives of his ancestors but in their material and cultural world as well, and the church as a hopeful community provided what he considered a sound, caring framework for them to cope with tragedy while envisioning the ultimate triumph of good over evil. Declaring that "there is power in hope," King asserted that the church, under the spiritual guidance of the slave preacher, gave the people "something on the inside to stand up amid the difficulties of their days."[32] Pressing the point, he explained how slave songs and sermons, which surged up from the very depths of the soul, transformed tragedy into boundless resilience and hope, while speaking of the Exodus, deliverance, and the promised land. Significantly, this rich and powerful legacy of the early black church figured prominently in King's consciousness whenever he referred to his people's capacity to "keep on keeping on," or "to hope against hope."[33]

The impact of the Civil War and the Emancipation Proclamation on black ecclesiastical life and institutions was never carefully addressed by King. While noting that emancipation left millions of blacks "penniless, illiterate, and standing out in a situation not knowing what to do and where to go,"[34] he never explained how the black church met the challenges resulting from such a catastrophic social crisis, or how it responded to the increasing white hostility toward ex-slaves in the South. He did comment on the leadership of Booker T. Washington in the closing years of the nineteenth century, but made no mention of the extent to which his ethic of "pressureless persuasion" and his program of economic self-uplift were embraced by the church and the African American community as a whole.[35]

King also referred to the feeble attempts to advance citizenship rights for the former slaves through various constitutional amendments and the Civil Rights Bill of 1875, but despite quoting E. Franklin Frazier at points, he said nothing about this black sociologist's discussion of how the political function of the black church unfolded in that particular period. The lack of serious attention to these matters owed much to King's tendency to approach the black church, on the level of ideas, as a sociologist,[36] concerned first and foremost with its significance as a social institution, and not as a historian or one deeply interested in the details of its development in different time frames. In any case, King's view of the black church as "a unique sociological phenomenon" obviously squared with descriptions afforded in the works of Frazier, W. E. B. DuBois, Carter G. Woodson, Benjamin E. Mays, and others, all of whom investigated that institution in the context of social-scientific research.[37]

King's references to the social role of the black church in the early twentieth century are relevant to any discussion of how that agency's approach to racial oppression conflicted with forms of action advocated by leaders like Booker T. Washington, W. E. B. DuBois, and Marcus Garvey. Although aware of the persuasive appeals of these figures to certain elements of the church, King was not in full agreement with their strategies for winning freedom. As suggested earlier, King tended to reduce Washington's advocacy of accommodationism and gradualism to "patient persuasion" or "passive acquiescence," in part because Washington urged his people to surrender their quest for civil rights and political power.[38] DuBois's call for "the talented tenth" to "rise and pull behind it the mass of the race" was equally unacceptable to King, for "there was no role for the whole people," and "it was a tactic for an aristocratic elite who would themselves be benefited while leaving behind the 'untalented' 90 per cent."[39]

Perhaps King's strongest critique was aimed at Garvey's program of African repatriation, which he regarded as unrealistic and impractical, despite the support it received from militant black churchpersons in the North. While recognizing that Garvey's "appeal to the race" after World War I "had the virtue of rejecting concepts of inferiority," that "it touched a truth that had long been dormant in the mind of the Negro," and that it resulted in "a resurgence of race pride" and a movement of "mass dimensions," King concluded nevertheless that Garvey's call for African repatriation "was doomed because an exodus to Africa in the twentieth century by a people who had struck roots for three and a half centuries in the New World did not have the ring of progress."[40] Even so, King felt that the black church could learn much from historic figures like Garvey, who resorted to the language of race and nationality at a time when an immobilizing fear seemed to grip so much of the black community.

Significantly, King found what he considered to be a more viable alternative to the tactics of Washington, DuBois, and Garvey in the legalistic and judicial strategies of the National Association for the Advancement of Colored People (NAACP), and in the Social Gospel tradition that was embraced by what he deemed the most progressive wing of the black church.[41] King said as much and more as he reflected on the events of the half century leading up to the modern civil rights crusade. The NAACP's relentless efforts to win victories in the courts by relying on the Constitution and federal law were most appealing to him—all the more because that civil rights organization, from its origins in 1909, had drawn on the moral and financial resources and support of the church, thus rejecting violence as a tactic.[42]

King categorically rejected the widely held claim that black churches from the turn of the century through the early 1950s were universally apathetic, escapist, and politically dysfunctional. Indeed, the very nature of the black condition, as he saw it, demanded otherwise. At the same time, King knew that the involvement of the church in the freedom struggle over time had been at best ambiguous—that there had almost always been both moderate reformist elements and radical reformist elements in African American congregations. Naturally, he was most interested in that side of the black church that, in the decades prior to the Rosa Parks incident and the Montgomery bus protest, affirmed Social Gospel progressivism and a reform-activist ethic, even in the heart of Dixie:

Throughout the South, for some years prior to Montgomery, the Negro church had emerged with increasing impact in the civil rights struggle. Negro ministers, with a growing awareness that the true witness of a Christian life is the projection of a social gospel, had accepted leadership in the fight for racial justice, had played important roles in a number of NAACP groups, and were making their influence felt throughout the freedom movement.[43]

King went on to suggest that the tradition of Christian nonviolent activism, to which the black church would turn with unparalleled enthusiasm in the 1950s and 1960s, had actually been embraced by the previous generation of black churchpersons under the direction of the preacher:

> The doctrine they preached was a nonviolent doctrine. It was not a doctrine that made their followers yearn for revenge, but one that called upon them to champion change. It was not a doctrine that asked an eye for an eye, but one that summoned men to seek to open the eyes of blind prejudice. The Negro turned his back on force not only because he knew he could not win his freedom through physical force, but also because he believed that through physical force he could lose his soul.[44]

Undoubtedly, King had a historically informed understanding of the significance of the church in African American life and culture. Thus, his sense of how the church might respond to social evil and injustice in his time and in the future owed much to what he knew about its role in the past.[45]

A range of ecclesial images were reaffirmed and reappropriated in the 1950s and 1960s as King considered how the black church might best meet its social and moral responsibility to the nation. One such image was the Negro church as unbroken tradition.[46] More specifically, King felt that the church was the only institution in the Negro community that had historic continuity. Furthermore, he, the great-grandson of a Georgia slave preacher, knew that an eclectic blending of familial and religious influences was the basis of his cultural bond with the antebellum black church.[47] The hope, grace, and promise that are the gifts of that heritage, he believed, had been passed on trans-generationally, and he appealed to values deeply enmeshed in that heritage. Thus, King recognized that his own church-centered activism did not represent an unparalleled departure from the black Christian tradition. To the contrary, he saw that he was merely reinvigorating the black church's longstanding impulse toward radical Christian action.[48] Generally speaking, it was King's knowledge of the entire history of the black church, and especially its prophetic advocacy and tradition of creative protest, that largely accounted for the kind of vision, focus, and drive he brought to his own leadership in the church. He always had this unbroken tradition in mind when he spoke of the many contributions made by the black church to the American society and culture.[49]

The image of the Negro church as old Israel or as the people of the Exodus also resurfaced with renewed vigor within the context of the modern civil rights crusade. As with the slaves generations earlier, the Exodus tradition, rooted deeply in the Old Testament, was lived and relived in the 1960s as blacks confronted the structures of oppression in the streets, at lunch counters, and in jails across the South, thus becoming, in King's own mind, the paradigmatic model of black liberation. Inspired by the Exodus model, King cast the Negro church in the roles of chosen people and suffering servant.[50] Chosen-ness in this case meant that blacks were peculiarly and wonderfully endowed to be God's appeal to a nation and a world drifting rapidly toward violent self-destruction. In other words, King was fully convinced that his people were being used by God as the instrument of a special destiny, and that by embracing nonviolence and taking up the cross of unmerited suffering for a greater good, they were assuming a kind of messianic role in history. This view owed much to King's reading of Arnold Toynbee, who concluded that the Negroes had rediscovered "in Christianity certain original meanings and values" that made them capable of injecting a "new spiritual dynamic" into Western civilization.[51] Be that as it may, the images of the black church as chosen people, as suffering servant, and as a messianic instrument revealed much about how King approached the question of meaning in the black experience.

Also, these images were in tandem with King's affirmation of Henry David Thoreau's claims regarding the value of a creative minority as a progressive, transforming force in society. Consequently, the portrayal of the Negro church as a creative minority, as far as King was concerned, was not to be divorced from its images as chosen people, suffering servant, and messianic presence. Furthermore, this image shared an affinity with the Hebrew prophetic notion of the righteous remnant. Here, the insights of Toynbee and Thoreau congealed in King's consciousness with the values of ancient Hebrew prophecy and the symbolism of the Exodus tradition, especially as King sought to properly define the black church in terms of mission and movement.

King proved equally significant in resurrecting the image of the Negro church as counterculture. Far from being a tool or captive of the state or culture, the black church, King maintained, had always been a disturbing presence in America, subjecting its institutions, values, and practices to sharp critique and indictment. In highlighting the black church's significance as counterculture, or as critic and transformer of culture, King was in effect speaking to its longstanding tendency to resist evil systems while exploring new possibilities for humanity and human community.[52]

King also figured greatly in resuscitating the portrait of the Negro church as "all-comprehending institution." As noted in the first chapter of this work, Carter G. Woodson had explored this image of the black church during King's childhood.[53] Much like Woodson, King fully understood that church life and institutions had always infiltrated virtually every seam of the African American cultural fabric—the social, political, economic, educational, and recreational—thereby functioning as foundational sources of black society. Indeed, this tendency to embrace the whole of black existence, or to intersect with and impact virtually every department of black life, was, in King's thinking, a part of what made the black church such a unique institution in the history of America. Moreover, King knew that this model of the "all-comprehending institution," or the comprehensive community, was reinforced by the fact that the church was so often the only item of property owned by the folk. To be sure, King's concept of the church as the hub of traditional black life would have important implications as far as that agency's role in the civil rights struggle was concerned.[54]

It would be a mistake to establish the antebellum black church as the classical foundation for everything King believed and practiced. Realizing this, Cornel West asserts that King "is a unique figure in Afro-American Christianity in that he represents both a heroic effort to reform and a suicidal effort to revolutionize American society and culture."[55] It is better to say that King brought something old and new to his understanding of the black church and its role in society, and that he sensed that the involvement of that institution in the civil rights cause, under his leadership, signaled both a continuity and a break with its earlier history. There is some truth in Gayraud S. Wilmore's claim that King rescued the Negro church from "a reactionary traditionalism" while projecting "a new image of the church upon the nation and a new awareness of the possibilities inherent in black religion."[56] The contention that King led a movement that resulted in the death of the Negro church and the birth of the black church, made by C. Eric Lincoln and others, is equally persuasive, especially when understood in proper context.[57] All of these reflections suggest that the church was perhaps the most striking image to emerge from the civil rights movement of the 1950s and 1960s.

The movement provided King with much of what both his Atlanta upbringing and his education at Morehouse, Crozer, and Boston had afforded—namely, ways of conceptualizing and building on his black heritage. On the other hand, that heritage empowered the movement for King, much as it had empowered what would have otherwise been powerless liberal thinking for him in the academy. This explains the impelling moral, spiritual, and intellectual power King brought to his church-based civil rights campaigns.

For the Least of These: The Church as Movement Headquarters

It was in Montgomery, Alabama, that King began to think anew and more seriously about the image of the Negro church as mission and movement, especially in the southern context. This was only natural for him, for his return to the South alone spoke to his deep sense of place and of regional responsibility.[58] After accepting the pastorate of the Dexter Avenue Baptist Church in Montgomery in 1954, King turned to the task of reshaping the image of that congregation:

> I was anxious to change the impression in the community that
> Dexter was a sort of silk-stocking church catering only to a certain
> class. Often it was referred to as the "big folks church." Revolting
> against this idea, I was convinced that worship at its best is a social
> experience with people of all levels of life coming together to realize
> their oneness and unity under God. Whenever the church, con-
> sciously or unconsciously, caters to one class it loses the spiritual
> force of the "whosoever will, let him come" doctrine, and is in danger
> of becoming little more than a social club with a thin veneer of
> religiosity.[59]

The family model or family-centered view of the church is what King actually sought to promote in the interior life of Dexter. Additionally, he set out to broaden Dexter's auxiliary program beyond the usual focus on Sunday schools, adult Bible classes, the Baptist Training Union, and the Missionary Society, to include an agenda aimed at the general uplift and empowerment of the larger Montgomery community. With this sense of mission in mind, King recommended "a committee to revitalize education," a "social service committee to channel and invigorate services to the sick and needy," a "social and political action committee," "a committee to raise and administer scholarship funds for high school graduates," and "a cultural committee to give encouragement to promising artists."[60]

From the very beginning of King's pastorate, matters relating to race and to the need for better race relations were routinely discussed at Dexter. A symposium on "The Meaning of Integration for American Society" was held there in March 1955, an event at which clergy and laypersons spoke of the possible impact of integration not only on the Christian church but in the areas of education, politics, and business as well. To further demonstrate its commitments in this

FIGURE 3.1. King as pastor of the Dexter Avenue Baptist Church in Montgomery, a position he held from 1954 to 1959.

area, Dexter opened its door to all races and nations, thus making the biblical call to community a part of both its proclamations and activism.[61] At the encouragement of King, Dexter also consistently expressed an immediate interest in Montgomery's economic life, and particularly in the plight of black laborers or domestic workers. Evidently, the programmatic thrust at Dexter at this time was consistent with King's perception of the Negro church as ultimately involving the entire oppressed community, and not merely worshiping believers. It also showed that King's desire to employ the social-change potential of the black church was finding practical expression months before the Rosa Parks arrest and the events that followed.[62]

Frequently proclaiming that the church is called to demand and inspire change in continuity with the gospel, and that it is required to engage in loving and self-giving service beyond its consecrated walls, King urged every member

of Dexter to "become a registered voter and a member of the NAACP," a challenge he also put before other churches of various denominational affiliations
in Montgomery.[63] Moreover, he considered his own work with the NAACP, the
Citizens Coordinating Committee, the Alabama Council on Human Relations,
and other local civic groups to be an extension of Dexter's ministry and mission
as a congregation.[64] For King, political and social activism of this nature on the
part of the church was to be defined in terms of a calling. At any rate, King's
approach to ministry and mission at Dexter afforded much of the model for
how the Negro church as a whole sought to translate its moral and social vision
into a nonviolent revolution.

King saw in the Montgomery bus boycott a special opportunity for the
black church to establish new credibility and relevance in the annals of human
history and civilization. On December 5, 1955, at the very first mass meeting
held in connection with the Montgomery Improvement Association (MIA), an
organization brought into being to lead the boycott, King, in a rousing speech
at Montgomery's Holt Street Baptist Church, placed the Negro church at the
center of the struggle by invoking the concept of black messianism, a concept
he later articulated at greater length in his *Stride toward Freedom: The Montgom-*
ery Story (1958). He predicted that "Right here in Montgomery, when the history books are written in the future, somebody will have to say, 'There lived a
race of people, a *black* people, fleecy locks and black complexion, a people who
had the moral courage to stand up for their rights,'" thereby injecting "a new
meaning into the veins of history and of civilization." Urging his listeners to
"think of these things [as] we proceed with our program,"[65] King was actually
employing this image of the Negro church as messianic instrument to inspire
and sustain the boycotters.

The exuberance that Montgomery's blacks displayed for Christian-Gandhian principles reinforced King's belief that God was entrusting the Negro
church in America to teach the nation and the world to love and to live in community.[66] The picture of 50,000 black people walking peacefully for freedom,
inspired by moral and spiritual values, could not have been more powerful for
King.[67] In speeches and on paper, he captured the various images of the black
church in the Montgomery bus protest in poignant terms, often accentuating
the positive side of the story. Despite its many shortcomings, King knew that
the Negro church was immensely instrumental in preparing his people to
transform anger at racism and social stratification into a powerful creative force
like nonviolent action.

Perhaps King's most common image was that of the Negro church as a
unifying influence or source of community. According to King, the church was
the key in solidifying what had previously been a divided black community in

Montgomery. The effectiveness of the church in bringing people together, across the pyramid of class, gender, and denominational differences, he often suggested, was most evident in those times when the community faced major setbacks or violent attacks from white racist elements. Such was the case in 1956, when a number of black churches and homes were bombed. "Discouraged, and still revolted by the bombings," and feeling a sense of personal responsibility for what had happened, King had an experience in church that spoke volumes about its significance as both a unifying force and a wellspring of remarkable spiritual depth:

> In this mood I went to the mass meeting on Monday night. There for
> the first time, I broke down in public. I had invited the audience to
> join me in prayer, and had begun by asking God's guidance and
> direction in all our activities. Then, in the grip of an emotion I could
> not control, I said, "Lord, I hope no one will have to die as a result of
> our struggle for freedom in Montgomery. Certainly I don't want to
> die. But if anyone has to die, let it be me." The audience was in an
> uproar. Shouts and cries of "no, no" came from all sides. So intense
> was the reaction, that I could not go on with my prayer. Two of my
> fellow ministers came to the pulpit and suggested that I take a
> seat. For a few minutes I stood with their arms around me, unable
> to move. Finally, with the help of my friends, I sat down. . . .
> Unexpectedly, this episode brought me relief. Many people came
> up to me after the meeting and many called the following day to
> assure me that we were all together until the end.[68]

Here was an occasion when the traditional, public worship experience of the black church served to mobilize an abused and exploited people around a common faith, hope, purpose, and movement for change. Though caught in the web of guilt and emotion, King did not stand alone, for the sense of being a part of a suffering community was indeed overwhelming for all who participated. The experience reminded King of the depth of those qualities of character and faith that led so many of Montgomery's blacks to collectively commit to the boycott despite the risks. The unanimity with which his people declared their refusal to surrender to bus segregation any longer proved both inspiring and instructive for him. Perhaps more than anything else at that point, this spirit of unity and commonality of purpose reaffirmed King's communitarian view of the church, and especially his tendency to see the Negro church and the larger black community as extensions of each other.

The cohesiveness and concerted action on the part of black church leadership could not have been more pleasing to King, especially in view of the persistent efforts of prominent local whites to turn the more established black leaders in Montgomery against him. In King's estimation, the failure of this strategy more than testified to the potential of the Negro church as a builder of community:

> The Negro ministers of the city deserve the highest praise. They have worked indefatiguably and assiduously for the overall cause of freedom. They have been willing to forget denominations, and realize a deep unity of purpose. Above all, those of you who have walked and picked up rides here and there, must have a special place in freedom's hall of fame. There is nothing more majestic and sublime than the quiet testimony of a people willing to sacrifice and suffer together for the cause of freedom.[69]

While well-meaning Christians of both races refused to physically support the boycott, many blacks and a few whites did participate. Thus, Montgomery taught King a lesson about the potential of the church as a whole to live up to its image as the symbol of the beloved community. It was there that he first witnessed the heterogeneity and yet obvious unity of the churches that were actually involved in the movement:

> One of the glories of the Montgomery movement was that Baptists, Methodists, Lutherans, Presbyterians, Episcopalians, and others all came together with a willingness to transcend denominational lines. Although no Catholic priests were actively involved in the protest, many of their parishioners took part. All joined hands in the bond of Christian love. Thus the mass meetings accomplished on Monday and Thursday nights what the Christian church had failed to accomplish on Sunday mornings.[70]

King held that church involvement in the Montgomery bus boycott was closely related to the Social Gospel, which had long been the foundation of the black Christian concern for human community and social justice. "Our church is becoming militant," he observed in 1956, "stressing a social gospel as well as a gospel of personal salvation."[71] He had hoped for a Social Gospel on the part of the churches from the time of his arrival in Montgomery, and as far as he was concerned, the boycott afforded a great opportunity for those institutions to respond affirmatively to the challenge. As King understood it, the Social Gospel was a call to the church to practice discipleship and leadership in ways that were subversive toward the status quo and the entrenched networks of power. This is the message he sought to convey in his sermons, mass-meeting speeches, and protest activities. Clearly, he saw himself and other religious

leaders as interpreters of the Social Gospel for the church community in Montgomery. The demands that that placed on them, he believed, were not to be
trivialized, especially since he encountered all too many blacks who, at least
in principle, reduced the mission of the church to the realm of the personal.
Ultimately, King felt that the church's work in Montgomery then, as in other
contexts, largely involved helping black people to clarify and focus their understanding of the purpose of the church. In his own mind, the boycott became a
force in reshaping the people's conception of the church. Consequently, King
could speak of the rise of "a new Negro" in Montgomery,[72] implying, at least in
some measure, the emergence of a new black church as well.

According to King, the "new Negro" in Montgomery was demonstrating
his new self-esteem and sense of urgency by committing the resources of the
church to the effort to eliminate segregation. This, perhaps more than anything
else, explained the black church's mounting importance as a power base, as
"the headquarters" of the movement, or as a de facto platform for civil rights
activities. More specifically, the church, as King saw it, was providing not only
spiritual and moral support, an eclectic theological heritage, and economic
support but also a refuge, foot soldiers, and space for prayer vigils and mass
meetings. "The meetings rotated from church to church," said King of the
mass meetings, and "The speakers represented the various denominations."[73]
Additionally, King noted that black congregations started a carpool as "a
voluntary 'share-a-ride' plan" for participants in the boycott. "Most of the dispatch stations were located at the Negro churches," he reported. "These
churches cooperated by opening their doors early each morning so that the
waiting passengers could be seated, and many of them provided heat on cold
mornings."[74] This was to be expected in a church culture in which the faithful
had long viewed mission and movement as fundamentally a sharing of themselves with others. Apparently, King was witnessing a reassertion of the black
church's role as "all-comprehending institution." He was delighted that that
institution was reclaiming that part of its essence, while also becoming paradigmatic for addressing social justice issues.

Of equal significance for King was the black church's role in combining
what he termed "the philosophy and method of Mohandas Gandhi with the
Negro's Christian tradition," thereby affording both a philosophical rationale
and practical method by which the people's faith could be translated into a
mass movement.[75] In Montgomery, King routinely encountered ordinary and
proud black church people, but they were also people who had to rediscover
within themselves the capacity to resist social injustice in organized and creative ways. In King's way of thinking, this meant that the richest insights of
Gandhi and the Christian pacifist tradition had to be joined, fashioned into a

coherent philosophy, and practically implemented as part of an overall strategy to achieve a just and peaceful Montgomery.

King saw this happening in the city's black churches. He pointed out that the philosophy and discipline of nonviolence "was disseminated mainly through the regular mass meetings which were held in the various Negro churches of the city." In other words, nonviolent direct action was institutionalized in the Negro church, and that agency furnished the primary arena for the teaching and appropriation of Gandhian-Christian philosophy and methods.[76] Obviously, this was part of that experimental spirit that found expression in the Negro church. For King, the very sight of thousands of ordinary church people totally committed to peaceful means was deeply moving, but not necessarily surprising, for he knew that the ethics of nonviolence and redemptive suffering was as natural an extension of the Negro's religion as the tradition of social protest itself.[77] Convinced that guiding principles are needed in any mass movement or crusade, King also believed that the nonviolent ethic afforded an answer for a people struggling for moral discernment amid complexity and ambiguity in the quest for freedom and justice.[78]

The amazing degree to which the church figured into the successful outcome of the movement in Montgomery could not have been more evident to King. He said as much and more in November 1956, when the Supreme Court upheld a lower court decision banning bus segregation, thus resulting in the cessation of the year-long boycott. King saw the higher court's decision as not only an affirmation of the local protest but also as a challenge to the black church to expand its activities in the civil rights field, especially in the American South. A major step was taken in this direction in January 1957, when King and other church leaders organized the Southern Christian Leadership Conference (SCLC) at the Ebenezer Baptist Church in Atlanta.[79]

As King had envisioned, the SCLC became a network of affiliated organizations rooted in the black church and led by ministers, and it also served as "an institutional framework through which the movement might be extended."[80] Variously referred to as "a church," "a faith operation," "the social action arm of the black church," "the black church writ large," and "an intentional type of religious-political movement," the SCLC, King explained, was designed to "serve as a channel through which local protest organizations in the South could coordinate their protest activities, and to give the total struggle a sense of Christian and disciplined direction."[81] King's choice of the organization's motto—"To redeem the soul of America"—situated the black church in the role of redemptive community.[82] Put another way, the powerful impulse to redeem the moral, social, and political character of the nation tinged the civil rights movement with the crusading righteousness of the church, and freedom marches became "redemptive experiences."[83]

In its capacity as a redemptive force, SCLC took seriously King's vision of the vanguard role that the black church was called to assume in the unfolding history of humankind's redemption. Like the biblical Israel, the Negro church, King thought, had been chosen to be a light to the nations, thereby stirring the embers of a dying faith. King never hesitated to make this claim, for he saw in blackness a powerful symbol of suffering, and he believed that there was something special in the black experience that gave his people not only a deeper insight into the problems of America and the world but also a greater openness to being a liberating and humanizing force. The challenge for the Negro church, then, was to remain at the vanguard of social-justice advocacy. It was in this connection that the various images of the Negro church (i.e., unbroken tradition, chosen people, old Israel or the Exodus church, suffering servant, messianic community, creative minority, counterculture, symbol of hope and community, "all-comprehending institution," etc.) intersected in King's thinking, especially as he invoked the prophetic heritage and "the biblical language of liberation."[84]

The Montgomery protest and the founding of SCLC not only catapulted the southern black church to the center of the freedom struggle but also represented, in King's own estimation, a serious leap in its politicization. With this in mind, King concluded that it was time for the church to strive for the removal of all racial, economic, and psychological barriers that divided and alienated persons. Declaring that "it's not over in Montgomery, and it isn't over in the South," King suggested, in more specific terms, that the Negro churches had much to contribute not only in terms of "economic sharing" and "dedication to nonviolence" but also from the standpoint of interpreting "the role of law in the struggle," fashioning "a unified strategy in the campaign for integrated buses," explaining "the relation of registration and voting to all efforts for justice," and "dealing with violence directed toward the Negro communities."[85] On the political side, King also felt that the church should use some of its resources to help set up voting clinics to assist with the registering of persons and the teaching of voting procedures. Only in this manner, he reasoned, could the Negro church maintain and enhance its own credibility as the social and political base of the movement.[86]

King thought similarly about his own reliability as a chief catalyst in moving people from the affirmation and celebration of faith in the internal life of the church to courageous, life-endangering activism in the streets. He was increasingly frustrated by his inability to reconcile his obligations as a full-time senior pastor at Dexter with his broader commitments as a civil rights leader.[87]

Resolving such a conflict was never easy for King, for he knew that the pastoral role was his tie to the black masses, and that his own commitment to racial justice could be fulfilled only in and through the church. After much thought and prayer, a resolution was achieved. On New Year's Eve in 1959, King surrendered the pastorate at Dexter to become a co-pastor with his father and brother at Atlanta's Ebenezer Baptist Church.[88] Ebenezer was a storytelling symbol in and of itself, and the move there constituted a spiritual homecoming for King. It was not just his home church, but as he himself put it, "a place that has great significance from an historical point of view for our organization."[89] In the 1960s, King would use the pulpit at Ebenezer to challenge bigotry and intolerance, to spotlight the problems of the poor, and to denounce the misuse of political and military power in the United States. In short, Ebenezer would become the iconic image of the church in the modern civil rights era.

With the Ebenezer Church and his SCLC office located roughly a block apart, on Atlanta's Auburn Avenue, King entered the 1960s determined to pursue a much broader civil rights program, a program that, as he described it, would be "centered in the church." As president of the SCLC, he reported, in February 1960, that his organization would "work through the churches" to not only "increase the number of Negro registered voters in the South" but also to spread "the philosophy of nonviolence across the South through workshops and institutes," to "mobilize the masses of our people in the South for the implementation of the noble desegregation decisions that have been rendered in recent years," and to stage "some dramatic campaign at both political conventions in order to mobilize more support for strong civil rights legislation in the future." King insisted at that time on a close alliance between the SCLC, the NAACP, and the church in the pursuit of such initiatives.[90] As the program of the SCLC progressed, King, in May 1961, offered perhaps his most compelling statement on the contribution of the southern black church to the movement, giving some attention to its general significance in black life, culture, and history as well:

> The role of the Negro church in the present struggle of the Negro for
> full citizenship is a unique sociological phenomenon peculiar to the
> Negro community in the south. It should be mentioned that its
> present role is also its past and future role. The record will indicate
> that the civil rights interest and thrust of the Negro community has
> directly paralleled the development and leadership offered by the
> Negro church in every community without exception. This is under-
> standably so, when you consider the social structure of the Negro
> community in the South. . . . The Negro church is his only forum,

owned, operated and controlled by him; it affords the broadest opportunity for social intercourse; it is generally the headquarters of the Negro's struggle for full citizenship; the pastor, traditionally, has been the community leader and champion of the Negro's civil liberties. Most of the protest centers of this present groundswell of civil rights activity, are clergy-led. This is no accident. It is part and parcel of the unique sociological phenomenon mentioned above.[91]

Early in the 1960s, King began to realize that the Negro church, despite its significance up to that point, had to make a number of adjustments and/or readjustments in order to secure its place at the vanguard of the ever-expanding freedom movement. First, he sensed that the church had to find more positive and creative ways of relating to a movement that would be increasingly influenced by youngsters from the ranks of black colleges, some of whom were from the North, were quite militant, considered preachers to be merely Uncle Toms, and felt that the church was hopelessly out of touch with the times. Second, King understood that the church had to further develop its capacity to deal with mounting cycles of white mob violence and terrorism in the South, much of which were directed at the memberships and properties of the churches themselves. Third, he realized that ways of keeping black clergy focused and dedicated to the cause had to be explored continuously, especially since they formed the core of civil rights leadership. Fourth, King knew that the church's role as a refuge, as a powerful source of reaffirmation and reinforcement in the midst of tragedy and grief, had to be redefined and appropriated on a larger scale. Finally, the church had to be prepared, King thought, to put its resources to the service of an expanding civil rights agenda, which included a quest for political power and an assault on poverty, economic injustice, and war and human destruction.[92]

King watched with a combination of pride and exuberance as student participation in the movement reached new levels of intensity with the founding of the Student Nonviolent Coordinating Committee (SNCC) in April 1960, thus presenting a special challenge for the black church and its leadership. He had already witnessed what he labeled "the spirit of self-sacrifice and commitment" on the part of students in Montgomery, who, though faced with expulsion and intimidation from state government, persisted in their demands for justice.[93] As King saw it, the church had to embrace this new militancy as a positive development, even as it remained true to its own values and traditions. But this was easier said than done. Though mindful that church support for the student sit-ins and freedom rides in 1960–61 left much to be desired, King knew that financial and moral backing was provided by the churches, and so was meeting space for the student participants.[94] As the movement extended into Albany, Birmingham, Washington, D.C., and Selma in the early and mid-1960s, King was exposed to the often bitter conflict between his SCLC, which worked through the church, and SNCC, with its emphasis on grassroots organization, but he always embodied the spirit of the church when engaging in participatory initiatives with young activists.[95] He vividly recounted the joy of working with students in the sit-ins and demonstrations in Birmingham in 1963, an experience during which the church served as both an inspiration and rallying point:

> I have stood in a meeting with hundreds of youngsters and joined in
> while they sang "Ain't Gonna Let Nobody Turn Me 'Round." It is not
> just a song; it is a resolve. A few minutes later, I have seen those
> same youngsters refuse to turn around from the onrush of a police
> dog, refuse to turn around before a pugnacious Bull Connor in
> command of men armed with power hoses. These songs bind us
> together, give us courage together, help us to march together.[96]

King was so often torn between the protest agenda of conservative black church leadership and the methods of student protesters. Moreover, many of the students did not share his exuberance for Gandhian principles or for the church as an arena for the dissemination of such principles. Even so, King was increasingly drawn to the type of militancy displayed by the youngsters in SNCC. By the late 1960s, he was breaking with the more moderate church and civil rights leaders on issues like poverty, economic injustice, and the Vietnam War, and allying himself instead with the young militants of SNCC, perhaps hoping that this might further radicalize the Negro church.[97]

But King continued to see in the Negro church what was not so apparent to young militants—namely, a spirit of resilience and resistance that had not been extinguished by even the most intense persecution. He said as much and more in 1962, as he joined a campaign to rebuild churches that had been destroyed by "night-riding arsonists" in Georgia. From the time of his activities in Montgomery, King had witnessed and lamented the burning and bombing of black churches, or of what he called "the church of God," which for him was "not just ordinary property."[98] While participating in the Albany Movement in 1961–62, which amounted to a full-scale, across-the-board offensive against the entire segregated order, he had been brought to tears as he surveyed the shambles of black churches in Georgia.[99] For King, the gracefulness of the Negro church in responding to such terror and lawlessness triggered reminders of the martyrs of the ancient church, who endured suffering and even death because of their faith and vision:

> The role of the Negro church today, by and large, is a glorious
> example in the history of Christendom. For never in Christian
> history, within a Christian country, have Christian churches been
> on the receiving end of such naked brutality and violence as we
> are witnessing here in America today. Not since the days of the
> Christians in the catacombs has God's house, as a symbol,
> weathered such attack as the Negro churches.[100]

King's faith in the power and potential of the black church was significantly enhanced as he observed its willingness to suffer for a noble and righteous cause. He believed that the black church had discovered new meaning in
the death and resurrection of Jesus Christ, and that it was assuming, in impressive ways, the role of a cross-bearing church. Interestingly enough, the cross
was at the very center of King's vision of the messianic role of the black
church.

Equally compelling for King was the black church's proclamation and
application of a gospel of peace in the face of unspeakable violence and terror.
"I am grateful to God that, through the influence of the Negro church, the
dimension of nonviolence entered our struggle," said he in "The Letter from
the Birmingham City Jail" (1963). In the midst of SCLC's Project Confrontation
in Birmingham, which united many of the city's black churches in protesting
segregated lunch counters and discriminatory hiring practices, King elaborated
the point in more specific terms:

> I am happy to say that the nonviolent movement in America has
> come not from secular forces but from the heart of the Negro church.
> The movement has done a great deal to revitalize the Negro church
> and to give its message a relevant and authentic ring. The great
> principles of love and justice which stand at the center of the nonviolent
> movement are deeply rooted in our Judeo-Christian heritage.[101]

King maintained that the many contributions of the black church to nonviolent activism and change essentially proved that much of its leadership was
prepared to practice a creative and dangerous unselfishness. Hence, he categorically rejected the allegation, frequently heard among young militants, that
black preachers were nothing but self-serving Uncle Toms. In King's own
mind, the numerous clergymen arrested during the movements in Montgomery and Albany alone would have put the lie to this generalization.[102] However,
King was concerned, from the time of the Montgomery bus protest, about black
ministers who either refused to support the cause, or gave it only token support. This was to be expected of one who seldom went into a community before

taking time to talk with and to solidify local church leadership. King raised the issue of pastoral support with unbridled passion during the Birmingham campaign: "I pleaded for the projection of strong, firm leadership by the Negro minister, pointing out that he is freer, more independent, than any other person in the community. I asked how the Negro would ever gain his freedom without the guidance, support and inspiration of his spiritual leaders."[103] Apparently, King understood that wholehearted support from black pastors was absolutely essential for the church to maintain center stage in the ever-expanding crusade for civil rights.

King spoke with the same measure of passion and conviction when highlighting the importance of the priestly function of the black church in the struggle. Here, he had in mind the image of the church as a person-affirming agency, or as a source of comfort, reaffirmation, and reinforcement in moments of urgency and times of tragedy and grief. As far as King was concerned, such a role could not have been more critical, especially since far too many of his people were being insulted, injured, and even killed in civil rights campaigns. When four little girls were killed in a blast at Birmingham's Sixteenth Street Baptist Church in September 1963, King experienced first-hand the stirring effects of the church's priestly function as he assured those who wept that "God still has a way of wringing good out of evil," and that "God has a purpose and a will which will transform this tragic moment of our suffering into a magic eternity of redemption."[104] These words, also spoken against the background of those iconic images of water hoses and vicious dogs in Birmingham, revealed King's sense of the vitality of the church in helping people through the grieving process that typically followed the deaths of movement activists. They also demonstrated King's faith in the church as a reenergizing force for those who struggled to make sense of the sacrifices, and who needed the strength and courage to return to the mass meetings and the picket lines after defeats or painful setbacks.

The black church's powers of reaffirmation in the face of those incredibly touched by tragedy greatly impacted King, thus reinforcing his perception of that institution as a refuge and surrogate world for healing. He was ever mindful of how the church had long served as a refuge where the biblical message of deliverance and songs promising the triumph of good over evil were heard. With the bombings in Birmingham, pain surrendered to affirmation, leading King to declare that "Tears came to my eyes that at such a tragic moment, my race still could sing its hope and faith."[105] In a statement that united in pleasant mixture the old and the new, and in which history, culture, and religion came together in one piece, King went on to explain at greater length the rejuvenating power of song in moments of heartbreak and pain:

In a sense the freedom songs are the soul of the movement. They are more than just incantations of clever phrases designed to invigorate a campaign; they are as old as the history of the Negro in America. They are adaptations of the songs the slaves sang—the sorrow songs, the shouts of joy, the battle hymns and the anthems of our movement. I have heard people talk of their beat and rhythm, but we in the movement are as inspired by their words. "Woke Up This Morning with My Mind Stayed on Freedom" is a sentence that needs no music to make its point. We sing the freedom songs today for the same reasons the slaves sang them, because we too are in bondage and the songs add hope to our determination that "We shall overcome, Black and white together, we shall overcome someday."[106]

The spirit of the movement and its indebtedness to long-established traditions in the church loomed large in King's thinking on such occasions. He fully embraced singing and chanting as a vital part of the rituals of civil rights campaigns, as being inseparable from the boycotts, sit-ins, freedom rides, and other techniques of political mobilization. Also, as King witnessed the vital fusion of songs and prayer vigils with courageous acts of civil disobedience, he became even more conscious of that indomitable inner quality that compelled his people to persevere despite persecution and the threat of death. In short, he encountered the soul of a people who had come to view their lives as lived against the background of a cosmic battle between the forces of good and evil.

As the long, arduous struggle against injustice came into clearer focus in the mid-1960s, King suggested the need for a more united and coordinated mission on the church's part for voting rights. To achieve this goal, he and his SCLC worked mostly with small community or neighborhood churches in Alabama, the most important of which was the Brown Chapel African Methodist Episcopal Church (AME) in the town of Selma. To King's delight, the church once again became the focal point of mass meetings, the forum for information and education, the center for the forging of community, and the staging and rallying point for marches and/or street demonstrations; and it also provided funds, staff, demonstrators, food, and lodging for the movement. The uniting of the prayer circle and the picket line left an indelible mark on King's memory, for he saw, as he had on so many occasions, ordinary, dedicated churchgoers who were consumed by the spirit of no surrender.[107] As King pondered the creative fidelity displayed by rank-and-file church members, or by what he saw as the church of the "least of these," the metaphor of movement took on a special meaning. Again, he was compelled to question images of the rural, southern Negro church as merely the creation of a poorly educated and socially marginal people, or as outcasts who simply embraced an exuberant faith as an escape from a painful existence.

King saw in the campaign for the ballot a re-establishment of the political function of the black church. This development could not have been more important for him, for he understood the need to link the political and the religious in this case, and he had no problem with movement business and the worship experience going hand and hand. In fact, King felt that the discipleship model demanded a serious engagement with the *political*, but only to the degree that the church remained prophetic, and as long as the boundaries separating church and state were not transgressed. Therefore, he found pleasure in the fact that the passage of the Voting Rights Act in August 1965, which guaranteed the right to vote, owed much to the pressure exerted by the black church and its leadership in the context of the movement.[108] Moreover, King believed that it was largely what occurred with black churches in the political arena that kept the civil rights cause from losing its spiritual and moral ground.

A significant transition occurred in King's thinking during the last three years of his life, especially as he thought more and more about the need to employ massive civil disobedience as an avenue to a democratic socialist society.[109] As King became increasingly radical in terms of his methods and vision of what constituted the ideal society, or the beloved community, he challenged the black church to take on a more radical posture as well, particularly in addressing the issues of poverty, economic exploitation, and war. In King's mind, this meant attacking the evils of capitalism; promoting the necessity for a radical redistribution of economic power; and lending material, moral, spiritual, and physical support to the peace movement. But King knew that intersecting conservative Negro churches and their leadership into struggles of this kind would not be easy. It was evident to him that all too many in these churches had actually embraced the capitalist ethic uncritically, and that many also, owing to what King called "the whole grain of their natural patriotism," were not comfortable with much of what he said about democratic socialism and the war in Vietnam.[110]

The assault on slum conditions in Chicago, the sanitation strike in Memphis, and the Poor People's Campaign afforded opportunities for King to further observe and reassess the effectiveness of the Negro church as an agent of social change. While involved in the Chicago Freedom Movement in 1966–67, he hoped that nonviolence might also demonstrate its power and effectiveness in application, technique, and discipline in a northern setting.[111] In King's mind, this required strong moral leadership from the church. He dismissed claims, raised by some of his critics, that the black North was entirely different from the black South, culturally speaking, and that support from Chicago's black churches would be less forthcoming than it had been from southern black churches. It was obvious to King that there were churches in both contexts that either supported or opposed his campaigns.

Furthermore, King knew that many of the black church people who supported SCLC's campaign for open and integrated housing in Chicago had roots in the South, and therefore shared much with black Southerners, culturally and in terms of their conviction that racism, segregation, and economic inequality constituted a particularly odious violation of biblical teachings.[112] This explains King's and SCLC's efforts to launch "a multifaceted assault" on Chicago's slums through "a massive nonviolent movement," a movement that would draw on the energy and resources of the church. Interestingly enough, King attributed the ultimate failure of SCLC's efforts not to the lack of support from black churches but primarily to the unwillingness of Mayor Richard J. Daley and the white power structure to uphold their commitments.[113]

Although King challenged the Negro church with a model of self-help and cooperative economics,[114] he also insisted that government had to be pressured to dismantle structures that exploited his people and that denied an equitable distribution of material and immaterial resources. This helps explain both King's plans for a massive Poor People's Campaign and his support for striking garbage workers in Memphis. Plans for SCLC's Poor People's Campaign, which would be based in Washington, D.C., began in 1967, and King's involvement with Memphis sanitation workers occurred in early 1968. In both cases, King appealed to the discipleship model of church service, highlighting the need for leadership on the part of black clergy.

With reference to the Poor People's Campaign, King sought once again to make folk religion and the church the cultural cement in a crusade to dramatize the problem of poverty on a national scale. A powerful inferno of energy was released by his SCLC, but King had problems passing on his own excitement like a holy contagion, in part because of the great uncertainty that some in his own inner circle of ministers had about what such a crusade might achieve.[115] The effort to inject black churches into a national anti-poverty campaign, bringing together people of various racial and ethnic backgrounds, never really materialized during King's lifetime. The situation proved different in Memphis, where black churches fueled the drive for higher wages and union recognition for black sanitation workers.[116] Even so, King saw both the planned Poor People's Campaign and the Memphis Sanitation Strike as a watershed, as signature moments, in his increasing effort to make the church relevant to the struggles and aspirations of the nation's poor.

King also made bold and clearly reasoned calls for black churches to become flashpoints of protest in the national crusade against the Vietnam War, a particularly important and vexing problem in the mid- and late 1960s. Since the Negro church had afforded a model for creative nonviolent dissent and activism from the time of the Montgomery bus boycott, that institution, King felt, could be instrumental in lifting the church as a whole from the stagnant tendency to worship the Prince of Peace while sanctioning war. This was very much in keeping with his vision of the messianic role of the Negro church, and of the Negro church as creative minority.[117] Also, it reflected the biblically informed approach that King brought to the question of the church's role in times of war and human destruction. King took the Sermon on the Mount and Gandhi's ideas and created a strategy for dealing with international conflict. He was inspired as much by the nonviolent example of the early church. His thinking along these lines lends even more credence to the claim that the civil rights movement was to a great extent an advancement of a set of ethical and theological principles grounded in the larger Christian tradition.

It was in the Negro church, with its sense of collective values, that King witnessed his people at their most powerful point in terms of peoplehood. He understood the significance of the church as part of the survival strategy for his people, and as a symbol of both their tragedies and their triumphs. Despite his training, he related to ordinary black churchpersons without feeling alienated and without a sense of theological besiegement and betrayal. Furthermore, King found strength and inspiration in the resourcefulness of these people, who were striving to better themselves and their country under seemingly impossible circumstances. Being under enormous external pressure, he also found courage as he witnessed their devotion to the perpetuation of the values of the movement. This is why King returned again and again to his church heritage, seeking relief through an existential appropriation of black faith.[118] This also explains why he had no problem speaking of the Negro church as a model for the church universal.

Without reference to the Negro church, it is impossible to grasp King's faith in the coming of a new order. He inherited from that church tradition a faith in God's active and ultimately triumphant role in history, leading to the realization of the beloved community.[119] Small wonder that he pressed virtually the same vision and evoked essentially the same symbols that captured the imagination of the earliest pioneers in the black church. Moreover, King himself became for the black church a prophet whose vision of community intuitively answered the deepest longings of his people. Therefore, King, often portrayed in a messianic image by his people, was as important to the black church as the black church was to him.

Equally remarkable is the fact that King consistently reinforced in the Negro church that sense of being on a journey toward the beloved community, or as he so often put it, the promised land. Apparently, the Exodus had meaning for him in terms of the church's struggle against racism, poverty and economic injustice, and war and human destruction.[120] Also, King's vision of the promised land, as suggested earlier, had emotional, spiritual, and physical links to the promised land of biblical history. This, too, spoke to his significance for rank-and-church members, who had come to understand themselves and their world in terms of the images, stories, and conceptual patterns of scripture. More specifically, King employed the metaphor of the promised land to sustain hope in church people who were convinced that the struggles of the ancient Israelites under the old Pharaoh mirrored their own experiences under white oppressors, and who thought in terms of a modern Moses leading them out of bondage.[121] The New Canaan, the New Jerusalem, the Kingdom of God, and other metaphors rooted in the Bible were no less important in this regard. For King, it was difficult to imagine a more remarkable testament to the metaphorical character and power of biblical and/or religious language.

Divided Spirits: Contrasting Images of the Black Church in Mission

Martin Luther King, Jr., occasionally noted that he stood "in the middle of two opposing forces in the Negro community." "One is the force of complacency," he wrote, "made up in part of Negroes" who have "adjusted to segregation" and "have become insensitive to the problems of the masses." "The other force is one of bitterness and hatred," he added, "made up of people [who] have absolutely repudiated Christianity" while coming "perilously close to advocating violence."[122] These different responses to the structures of white supremacy are relevant to any discussion of both King's critique of the Negro church and his conflicts with various elements among its leadership. Evidently, King was challenged by a bewildering array of forces from inside the Negro church, and the ecclesiastical tide in that community was never entirely on his side. This accounted in part for his ambivalent attitude toward the Negro church, or for his tendency to celebrate its redeeming qualities while subjecting its deficiencies to sustained but constructive critique.

King employed essentially two paradigms in his critique of the black church. One was the classic this-worldly vs. otherworldly paradigm,[123] which undoubtedly owed much to King's reading of works by W. E. B. DuBois, Benjamin E. Mays, E. Franklin Frazier, and others. The other was the class paradigm, which King explained extensively in "A Knock at Midnight," a sermon in which he highlighted the church's propensity to abandon the marginalized and out-cast in their most critical hour:

> Two types of Negro churches have failed to provide bread. One burns
> with emotionalism, and the other freezes with classism. The former,
> reducing worship to entertainment, places more emphasis on
> volume than on content and confuses spirituality with muscularity.
> The danger in such a church is that the members may have more
> religion in their hands and feet than in their hearts and souls. At
> midnight this type of church has neither the vitality nor the relevant
> gospel to feed hungry souls. . . . The other type of Negro church that
> feeds no midnight traveler has developed a class system and boasts of
> its dignity, its membership of professional people, and its exclusiveness.
> In such a church the worship service is cold and meaningless, the
> music dull and uninspiring, and the sermon little more than a
> homily on current events. If the pastor says too much about Jesus
> Christ, the members feel that he is robbing the pulpit of dignity. If
> the choir sings a Negro spiritual, the members claim an affront to
> their class status. This type of church tragically fails to recognize that
> worship at its best is a social experience in which people from all
> levels of life come together to affirm their oneness and unity under
> God. At midnight, men are altogether ignored because of their
> limited education, or they are given bread that has been hardened by
> the winter of morbid class consciousness.[124]

From the time King reached Montgomery, he blasted away at the apathy among black churches and their leadership "in the field of civil rights."[125] To his dismay, there were all too many congregations in that city that were not reform-minded or socially active, that equated the kingdom of God with some vague state of the afterlife, and that merely offered an aesthetic of the kind Karl Marx had labeled "an opiate of the people." Convinced that the kingdom of God had to occur both on earth and in heaven, King clearly regarded the other-worldly gospel as well-intentioned but fatally flawed in its outlook on the pur-pose of the church and religion:

> The apparent apathy of the Negro ministers presented a special
> problem. A faithful few had always shown a deep concern for social
> problems, but too many had remained aloof from the area of social
> responsibility. Much of this indifference, it is true, stemmed from a
> sincere feeling that ministers were not supposed to get mixed up in
> such earthly, temporal matters as social and economic improvement;

they were to "preach the gospel," and keep men's minds centered on "the heavenly." But however sincere, this view of religion, I felt, was too confined.[126]

While acknowledging that "otherworldly concerns have a deep and significant place in all religions worthy of the name," King declared that "religion true to its nature must also be concerned about man's social conditions." "Religion deals with both earth and heaven, both time and eternity," and it is therefore "a two-way road,"[127] he maintained. This question of how religion relates to both the proximate and ultimate concerns of humanity is central to any consideration of both King's critique of and critical appropriation of the black church tradition.

Although King knew that the Negro church was never as otherworldly and compensatory as the stereotypes suggested, he lamented the idea that any such institution could be so dynamic in its spiritual thrust toward personal salvation, but static in its social complacency. As far as he was concerned, a myopic view of the kingdom was inexcusable, for it gave Negro churches a false sense of security while sanctioning their inaction and irresponsibility in the face of evil and injustice. Therefore, King was highly determined to expose the superficiality and frivolousness of many of the arguments advanced against a deeper and more responsible social engagement on the part of the church in the world, and he did so in terms that even the most unlearned in the black church could comprehend[128]:

> Now I heard of a big Negro church recently that had its arm out and said, "now we want a pastor who will preach the real gospel of salvation and who will not get involved in these sit-ins and getting involved in going to jail. We want a preacher who will preach the gospel." Now there's somethin' wrong with any church that limits the gospel to talkin' about heaven over yonder. There is something wrong with any minister of the gospel who becomes so otherworldly in his orientation that he forgets about what is happening now. There is something wrong with any church that is so absorbed in the hereafter that it forgets the here. Here where men are trampled over by the iron feet of oppression. Here where thousands of God's children are caught in an air-tight cage. Here where thousands of men and women are depressed and in agony because of their earthly fight. Here where the darkness of life surrounds so many of God's children. . . . It's all right to talk about "silver slippers over yonder," but men need shoes to wear down here. It's all right to talk about streets flowing with "milk and honey" over yonder, but let's get some food to eat for

people down here in Asia and Africa and South America and in our own nation who go to bed hungry at night. It's all right to talk about "mansion in the sky," but I'm thinking about these ghettoes and slums right down here.[129]

In his persistent assault on the largely dysfunctional and unprogressive sides of the Negro church, King never made fundamentalist doctrine or teachings a major issue. While there was some tension between what he believed personally about certain orthodox doctrines and what views he felt obliged to articulate as a black preacher and leader of a popular social movement, he never made a public display of his rejection of traditional concepts such as the virgin birth, hell, and the physical resurrection.[130] Put another way, King refused to flaunt his theological liberalism and his questioning attitude toward doctrinal conformity because he knew that the typical black church was extremely conservative in its view of scripture and tradition, and that it was a place for affirmations of faith and not for open-ended questions, critical thinking, and expressions of doubt. Furthermore, King had absolutely no inclination to confuse or alienate ordinary, devoted church people who were rigidly fundamentalist in their faith but active in the political quest for racial justice. He was also concerned about how his theological liberalism might be used by his critics and adversaries in the church to the detriment of the movement. But what mattered to him most was the integrity of his own leadership and the fact that he never abandoned the spirituality and Christian realism of the Negro church, nor its conviction that the gospel in its most authentic expression demands a persistent and radical engagement with the powers of evil in society.

King was just as intentional about not making denominational affiliation and differences an issue in the movement. He marched with black clergy and laypersons from many different denominations, large and small, and he warned Negro churches and other organizations about "warring against each other with a claim to absolute truth."[131] While acknowledging that churches differed in their denominational identities, doctrinal standards, and systems of polity, King held that this should not obscure their fundamental agreements around social justice matters. Moreover, he never defined church in terms of denominationalism, for he felt that this could only foster competition and disunity. King's plea was for unity and not necessarily uniformity. "There will be inevitable differences of opinion," he declared, "but Negroes can differ and still unite around common goals."[132] In King's opinion, the black church necessarily had to be true to its broad interdenominational tradition of shared involvement in the struggle. The cooperative model of Christian outreach and service was part of what he sought to establish in his work with Negro churches.

But this was easier said than done because of the many opinions about what constituted the identity and mission of the church, especially among black pastors. King was familiar with many ministers who identified the church merely with an uncritical belief in biblical literalism and inerrancy, spirit-enriching messages, unsullied holiness, emotional expression in worship, healing rituals, proselytizing, converting and gaining new recruits in their own ranks, puritanical moral codes, heterosexual absolutism, patriarchial domination, institutional maintenance, political neutrality, and an internal appropriation of the Christian faith. King's concern was to move the Negro church beyond all the routine-ness and the daunting task of "telling the story," to a greater appreciation for the life of radical and sacrificial activism in the interest of the common good.[133]

Black preachers who reduced the church experience to entertainment received the full force of King's indictment. Although he appreciated as much as any of his people the performative character of black preaching and worship, he frowned at the very thought of expressing faith by simply blazing in religious enthusiasm. With the style, clarity, and power that became his trademark, he related one account in which the preaching moment in a Negro church degenerated into charismatic showmanship, thus distorting the very spirit and meaning of the body of Christ:

> And so often we play with the Gospel in order to conform. I was talking
> to a young man not long ago, and he was . . . after the sermon I was
> talking to him, and he was just jumping all over the pulpit and jump-
> ing out and spitting all over everything and screaming with his tune,
> and moaning and groaning, and I said, now I just can't understand
> you, young man, you're getting an education. I can understand that
> there were certain cultural patterns in the past that caused many of the
> older ministers to do this, but I don't understand why you feel you have
> to do this. And he said, "Well, you know, I got to get Aunt Jane," and he
> has reduced the Gospel to showmanship, reduced the Gospel to playing
> in order to get Aunt Jane. I say to you this morning, the Gospel isn't to
> be played with. . . . God is saying, don't play with my Gospel.[134]

With equal facility, King denounced pastors who were obsessed with their personal influence and a gospel of material gain and self-aggrandizement. He knew that the black church had its own share of charlatans and quacks who exploited the resources of the folk and who were literally consumed with middle-class respectability:

> The so-called "Negro Church" must hear the edict of eternity at this
> point. Do you know there are some Negro churches and preachers no

more concerned about the problems that people are facing every day?
And I'm sick and tired of seeing Negro preachers riding around in
big cars and living in big houses and not concerned about the
problems of the people who made it possible for them to get these
things. It seems that I can hear the almighty God say, "Stop preaching
your loud sermons and whooping your irrelevant mess in my face, for
your hands are full of tar for the people I sent you to serve, . . . and
you are doing nothing but being concerned about yourself."[135]

King urged rank-and-file church members to look beyond the self-serving, pristine, otherworldly images that materialistic preachers were so apt to project. He brooded over the fact that such leaders were easy targets for mimics and satirists, especially those who delighted in discrediting the Negro church as a whole. As one who had no compelling interest in becoming wealthy, or famous for that matter, King's critique could not have been more credible and challenging.

But King knew enough about the local realities of black church life and culture in the South to understand the difficulties involved in speaking truth to white power. In those venues of small-town churches, he could see how a narrow, biblical fundamentalism was reinforced by a fear of economic and political reprisals, thereby keeping many Negro churches from serving a proper and radical social function. King realized that the mere act of survival consumed huge amounts of energy on the part of the folk, and that few were prepared to create controversy by moving into the political arena. At the mercy of local white landowners and merchants, on whose properties they lived and from whom they received food, shelter, clothing, and other basic necessities on credit, even good church people reminded King that joining the movement was, at the very least, a difficult judgment call. If this was not telling enough, King discovered that many rural Negro churches were closed to mass meetings, student demonstrations, and other civil rights activities because of the lingering fear of being bombed or burned. Although local pastors dealt daily with the practical problems of their flocks, they, too, functioned largely at the mercy of the white power structures, and often had a stifling effect on their congregations. While in Montgomery, King responded at length to a Mississippi black pastor who feared that he would "be killed or run out of town" if he protested against the Jim Crow system:

> I can well understand the predicament you find yourself in. You have
> at least three choices: First, you can leave Mississippi and go to a
> relatively non-segregated community. Second, you can tacitly accept
> the Jim Crow laws of Mississippi. Third, you can courageously stand

up against them and suffer the consequences. I would not suggest that you accept the first two choices. As a Christian minister and a symbol of the New Negro you have the responsibility to stand up courageously against the Jim Crow laws of your city regardless of the consequences. The fear of physical death and being run out of town should not be your primary concern. Your primary concern should be a devotion to truth, justice, and freedom. Often this means bearing a cross, but like Jesus you must be willing to bear it, realizing that unearned suffering is redemptive. This is hard to do, but it is a sacrifice that we must make if we are to be free.[136]

King encountered what he termed "numerous Negro church reactions" as his SCLC extended nonviolent direct action and civil disobedience campaigns beyond Montgomery. Efforts at black-church mobilization in Birmingham in 1963, as King reported, met with some resistance from black clergy, some of whom felt "pulled into something that they had not helped to organize."[137] King's vision of a unified black church in the struggle was frustrated time and time again, especially as he touched base with pastors in St. Augustine, Selma, and other southern cities who either opposed his strategy and tactics or resented his training, popularity, and achievements. King learned early on that solidarity among black pastors was the key to achieving the kind of broadly based church unity that was required for SCLC to claim meaningful results.

While King never complained openly, he met his strongest challenge from elements in the black church in the North. Ordinary, committed churchgoers in the North generally supported SCLC's civil rights programs, at least in principle,[138] but the real struggle involved securing the unwavering support of black pastors, many of whom were as conservative as some of the pastors King encountered in southern Negro churches. In some parts of the North, King heard from clergymen who were not comfortable with his wedding of faith and politics, who declared that his services were not needed in the North, and who justified their own inactivity and irresponsibility with claims that there were no explicit political echoes in scripture or in Jesus' message concerning the kingdom of God on earth.

In 1964, the Reverend C. Fain Kyle, a black pastor in Richmond, California, who directed the Dedicated Independent Society Committee Against Racial Demonstrations, Inc., actually accused King of working with communists, and he charged that "no minister of God's present day church has ever been called or sent to preach or teach either passive resistance, civil disobedience, integration or segregation." King promptly ignored Kyle's challenge "to a public debate."[139] In Chicago in 1967, King was disappointed to find black pastors who had marched with him in the South, but avoided him in their own territory, mainly because they benefited from the powerful political machine of Mayor Richard Daley.[140] Conflict between King and Adam Clayton Powell, Jr., the progressive black pastor and congressman from New York, occurred at times over the question of leadership style and strategy.[141] Given these and other experiences in the North and South, King was never prone to regard the black church as monolithic or one-dimensional.

To King's displeasure, the clash between the progressive and conservative wings of the Negro church over civil rights strategy and tactics actually came to a head in 1961, when a split in the National Baptist Convention, USA (NBC) resulted in the organization of its rival body, the Progressive National Baptist Convention, Inc. (PNBC), in Cincinnati.[142] The so-called power struggle between progressives who backed King and conservatives who sided with Joseph H. Jackson,[143] the Chicago pastor and president of the NBC, is commonly viewed as the source of the schism. Both King and Jackson had long shared memberships in the NBC, the largest black Baptist organization in the world, but Jackson's theological and political conservatism prompted him to accuse King of exciting racial tensions and creating an atmosphere of confusion and lawlessness. King's determination to lead demonstrations and to pursue acts of civil disobedience conflicted with Jackson's insistence that change could best be effected through exemplary conduct, by employing the politics of cooperation and not confrontation, and through a reliance on the old Booker T. Washington version of gradualism, progressive accommodationism, and economic self-help. Furthermore, King's desire to bring the full resources of the NBC to bear on the civil rights cause put him and other progressive black pastors on a collision course with Jackson and his followers in the NBC.[144]

Although King "had hoped that a split would not take place," he, like his father, Benjamin E. Mays, Samuel Williams, and others who had influenced him immensely, ultimately cast his lot with the PNBC.[145] For King, the conflict actually cast a spotlight on many issues that had to be resolved before the black church could reach its fullest potential as an agent of social change. Also, the conflict must have reinforced King's sense of the duality that was the Negro church—that is, the Negro church as both a bulwark of protest and an agency of accommodation. This was not insignificant for one who had long identified a certain ambivalence in much of the spirit of the Negro church.

King always disagreed vehemently with those militants who insisted that the deficiencies of the Negro church rendered it irrelevant or anachronistic, particularly from the standpoint of its capacity to assume a leadership role in the freedom movement. In the 1950s and 1960s, King defended his church tradition against the attacks of Malcolm X and others in the Nation of Islam

(Black Muslims), who charged that both the Negro church and King represented the old slave attitude of adjustment and submission.[146] As the civil rights movement split into what has been called "two clearly defined operations"—with one side being SNCC, the Congress of Racial Equality (CORE), and black nationalist groups, and the other representatives of the SCLC, the NAACP, and the Urban League[147]—the question of the relevance and/or potential of the black church surfaced perhaps in unprecedented ways. Black nationalists, and particularly the young militants in SNCC, denounced the church while challenging it with attacks on capitalism and calls for black power—a much-needed development in those times, especially since the idealism and commitment of youths, as King recognized, were too often questioned, ignored, or underestimated by black congregations and their leadership.

Convinced that there was "no greater tragedy befalling the Negro than a turn to" the values of "either Communism or Black Nationalism,"[148] King remained steadfast in his belief that the Negro church was the only institution capable of providing the moral, spiritual, and practical guidance his people needed not only to cope with the contradictions and complexities of modern life but also to redeem and transform unjust structures. Obviously, King did not suffer from the dismal plague of pessimism that assailed some of the nationalists, and especially those who felt that King was unfairly imposing upon blacks the burden of being the guardians of America's moral, spiritual, and cultural health.

Although King found some merit in the views and insights that came from even the most radical and anti-church fringe of the freedom movement, he felt that more critics had to come from within the Negro church. Rising "to the level of self-criticism," he maintained, was always "a sign of high maturity."[149] King was not thinking of critics who made little of the sinister side of the black church while highlighting its image as a potential reservoir for the greatest good. He had in mind persons who exposed the church in all of its complexity, even as they loved it, served it, and defended it. More specifically, he believed that integrity demanded that the Negro church be portrayed as an agency both rich in spirituality and culture and mired in contradictions.

As one intimately connected to the structural realities of the Negro church, King never seriously doubted its future as a vital socio-religious phenomenon. However, he insisted that certain adjustments had to be made to ensure the church's continued existence as a flexible and adaptable instrument of black freedom and survival, or as the arena out of which all issues relating to the quality of black life could be addressed. One of those adjustments had to do with the cultivation of well-trained, responsible, unselfish, and charismatic leadership.[150] This could not have been more important, King thought, for such leadership was indispensable if ideas and values were to be made more palatable, visceral, and available for people who needed to grow and prosper, personally and collectively.

King also spoke of the necessity for the Negro church to remain true to its Social Gospel tradition, a tradition that affirms that the Old Testament's prophetic notion of justice and righteousness is as important as the New Testament law of love. King reminded his people that the Negro church, despite its weaknesses, had always practiced cooperative Christianity and an ethic of altruism, and that practical applications of Social Gospel principles had never required a retreat from black-church orthodoxy. There were echoes here of Benjamin Mays, Howard Thurman, George Kelsey, and others who were such a significant part of King's network of personal influences. These men were fixtures in King's life from childhood, and their interpretations of the social context and teachings of Jesus, as stated earlier, constituted much of that essential wellspring from which King drew spiritual, intellectual, and ethical power. Moreover, the faith and praxis of the historic black church were a part of that rich and eclectic theological heritage that King brought to bear on his discussion and critique of the white church and the larger culture. This will be explored to a considerable degree in the next chapter.

4

An Uncertain Sound

The Ambivalent Soul of the White Church

From the beginning, it was the church that put its blessing on slavery and sanctioned a caste system that continues to this day.

—Pierre Berton, *The Comfortable Pew*

The church refuses to follow her Lord into the busy thoroughfares of history, when it talks of love but fails to press for basic justice. . . . , and when it lowers its voice in order to raise its budget.

—Ernest Campbell

Thus, in the realm of morals the role of Christianity has been, at best, ambivalent. . . . It is not too much to say that whoever wishes to become a truly moral human being must first divorce himself from all the prohibitions, crimes, and hypocrises of the Christian church.

—James Baldwin,
The Fire Next Time

The contemporary church is often a weak, ineffectual voice with an uncertain sound.

—Martin Luther King, Jr.,
Why We Can't Wait

Martin Luther King, Jr., lamented the role that race had assumed historically in the complex interactions between black and white churches in America. He spoke to this nexus of race and religion with passion and clarity, declaring that, "ideally there can be no Negro or white church."[1] But King's realism concerning human nature and the church as a human institution made it possible for him to live with racially separate churches while envisioning and struggling for the more inclusive ideal of the church universal, or the church as beloved community. This proved only natural for one who had such an amazing capacity to balance pragmatic and idealistic impulses.

The church was much of what King had in mind when he referred to "this terrible ambivalence in the soul of white America."[2] He literally agonized over what he perceived to be glaring inconsistencies between white churches' professions of faith and their daily practices, or their creeds and their deeds, and his analysis of and efforts to improve the human condition as a pastor inevitably led him into conflict with those institutions. But perhaps more important, King offered suggestions as to how those institutions might overcome their deeply entrenched racial attitudes and behavior while taking on a new life of witness and service. As he saw it, the issue was not simply a matter of rejecting what he often called "any tribal-centered" or "racial-centered ethic,"[3] but the need to struggle for the salvation of the very soul of the church itself. This helps explain King's significance as the premier ecclesiastical thinker and activist of his time.

This chapter treats King's attitude toward the white church and its leadership from several angles. First, his sense of the entire history of the white church in the United States is examined, with some focus on his efforts as a youngster to reconcile the Christian love ethic with that institution's devotion to the values and structures of white supremacy. At this point, the impact of King's academic training is also considered, and so is his emerging critique of the biblicism, theology, and ethics of the white church. Second, considerable attention is given to King's prophetic critique of and challenge to the white church around the issues of race and its corollaries of poverty and economic injustice and war and human destruction. Here, King's differences and conflicts with white fundamentalist and evangelical leaders are explored in some depth, and so is his critical and yet sympathetic engagement of the ambivalent character of the white church. Finally, King's efforts to move the white church toward renewal and a more vital crusade to redeem and transform America are highlighted and assessed, with some attention to his work with liberal white churchpersons in the civil rights and anti-war crusades, and, more generally, in organizations like the National Council of Churches, Clergy and Laity Concerned, and the National Conference on Religion and Race. The flow of the discussion is useful for understanding the range of King's contributions to American life, thought, and culture.

In Pharaoh's Household: The White Church in Historical Context

Images of the white church figured prominently in Martin Luther King, Jr.'s early emotional, spiritual, and intellectual struggle with the problems of social evil and injustice. Growing up with parents who routinely stated that the prevailing social and political order was antithetical to the divine will, King, as early as age six, sensed the odd coupling of the church and white supremacy.[4] He alluded to this in "The Negro and the Constitution" (1944), a speech he gave at age fifteen in Dublin, Georgia, noting particularly the incompatibility between Jim Crow laws and "the central teachings of Jesus." King's questioning attitude toward such matters surfaced in the most profound ways during those early years, as he, while working with other Morehouse College students on a tobacco farm in Simbury, Connecticut, visited white churches in the North without incident. In a letter to his mother, the youngster suggested a distinction between the existence of segregated white churches in the South and what he experienced in the North, where "Negroes and whites go to the same church."[5]

But any illusions King may have had about differences between the North and the South were shattered by 1950, when he and several of his black friends were denied service in a white-owned New Jersey tavern. After that experience, which also involved white witnesses who refused to testify on behalf of King and the others in a civil rights case,[6] King had reason to believe that white institutions across the country, including the church, were essentially the same when it came to the issue of race. Thus, it is not surprising that his most insightful critique of the white church began during his Crozer years (1948–1951), as he struggled intellectually with the moral responsibility of that institution in the face of social evil. It was during this time that King described the white church as "one of the chief exponents of racial bigotry," noting that the average white Christian in the South would "spend thousands of dollars to keep the Negro segregated and discriminated."[7]

Scanning the pages of Christian history with an eagle's eyes, King concluded that the white church had always been a willing partner in the subjection and oppression of people of African descent. He focused with intense interest on the early history of the white church in this country, when the widespread idea of Christian missions went hand in hand with cultural imperialism and colonial conquest, thus creating an atmosphere for the capture and enslavement of Africans. "In colonial Virginia a man could be sent to jail for failing to attend church twice on Sundays," King declared in a sermon in July 1949, "while at the same time the slave trade went on with the sanction of the church and religions."[8] Four years later, while pursuing the Ph.D. at Boston, King reiterated the point, insisting that "Slavery could not have existed in

America for more than two hundred and fifty years if the Church had not sanctioned it."[9] Clearly, the critique he provided as a seminarian and graduate student was indicative of the direction he would take later in terms of his challenge to a whole range of values, traditions, and practices in the white church.

Most of King's comments on the images and roles of the white church from the colonial period up to his own time were made in the context of his own struggle as a pastor and civil rights leader. He focused on that history with telling insight, giving special consideration to what he called "the agonizing and puzzling duality which . . . permeated the race relations posture of the American Christian church all the way back to the colonial epoch." Here, King had in mind the failure of the earliest white churches to take an unwavering and morally consistent stand on the issues of race and on what should be the place of people of African descent in the church and in colonial society generally. In other words, he explained that white churches, from their beginnings in the colonies, had vacillated on the race issue and on whether or not blacks should be evangelized and brought into the Christian fold. From that point on, King asserted, the actions of white Christians would be marked by "continuing ambivalence and vacillation."[10] King went on to identify what he understood to be the source of the problem:

> America was established as a Christian nation which strongly
> believed in religious and political freedom for all mankind. The early
> Protestants who made up the thirteen original colonies were strongly
> influenced by the teaching of John Calvin and soon distorted his
> notions of predestination to justify the presence of slavery. This
> distortion of the faith aids and abets the sinfulness of man and
> society. This is the theological key to our dilemma.[11]

King also devoted major attention to how the earliest white churches had lined up with the establishment to become, in effect, a force for legitimizing rather than subverting the status quo. In too many cases, he thought, the white churches collectively had failed to speak the truth in God's name in response to the critical social issues of the times. As far as King could determine, the problem was not merely the white church's unwillingness to challenge prophetically the prevailing social and political order but, perhaps more important, its failure to respond compassionately to people who were despised, enslaved, persecuted, and exploited. For these and other reasons, the earliest white churches had originated outside of what King regarded as the traditions of the New Testament ekklesia. The white church in cultural captivity, which stood in stark contrast to the New Testament church as counterculture,[12] became one of the most striking images in King's mind, especially as he focused on the issues of power and oppression in the context of the broad reaches of American church history and church history generally.

The white church's complicity in the establishment of the slave trade and the institution of slavery throughout the so-called New World proved to be a recurring theme in King's thought in the period from the Montgomery bus boycott up to the point of his assassination. King believed that the coexistence of Christianity and human bondage presented a serious problem for the church and the society as a whole from the time of the very first settlement at Jamestown:

> We all know the long history of the old order in the United States. It
> had its beginning in 1619, when the first slaves landed on the shores
> of this nation. And unlike the Pilgrim fathers who landed at
> Plymouth a year later, they were brought here against their wills, and
> throughout slavery the Negro was treated as a thing to be used, rather
> than a person to be respected. With the growth of slavery it became
> necessary to give some justification for it. It seems to be a fact of life
> that human beings cannot continue to do wrong without eventually
> reaching out for some thin rationalization to clothe an obvious wrong
> in the beautiful garments of righteousness.[13]

Ever mindful of how race could have survived the American Revolution, the struggle for independence, and that body of egalitarian rhetoric expressed in the Declaration of Independence and the Constitution, King went on to explain how the Bible, Judeo-Christian values, and elements of Aristotelian philosophy were used to legitimize the enslavement of persons of African descent, particularly in the antebellum South, where the institution was more deeply entrenched:

> Even the Bible and religion were used to give slavery moral justifica-
> tion. And, so, from some pulpits it was argued that the Negro was infe-
> rior by nature because of Noah's curse upon the children of Ham.
> The Apostle Paul's dictum became a watchword, "Servants, be
> obedient to your master." And then one of the brethren had probably
> read the logic of Aristotle and he could put his argument in the
> framework of an Aristotelian syllogism. He could say that all men
> were made in the image of God; this was a major premise. Then
> came the minor premise, God as everybody knows is not a Negro.
> Then came the conclusion, therefore the Negro is not a man. He
> could put his argument in that logical framework. . . . This was the
> type of reasoning that prevailed at that time.[14]

The ways in which pro-slavery white churches entered the magic circle of biblical teachings could not have been more perplexing for King, to say nothing of their employment of the Christian faith as a mask for their determination to preserve the structures of white supremacy. With such churches in mind, King addressed this issue, highlighting the misuse of both scripture and science toward evil ends:

> They fell victim to the danger that forever confronts religion and a too literalistic interpretation of the Bible. There is always the danger that religion and the Bible not properly interpreted can be used as forces to crystallize the status quo. This is exactly what happened. . . . There were even pseudo-scientists who sought to prove that in brain size and lung capacity Negroes were inferior to whites.[15]

The dilemma that pro-slavery white churches faced when confronted with the Exodus story must have intrigued King, but he seldom spoke directly to that concern. However, it is clear at points in his writings and speeches that he understood the difference between the white church and the slave church to be largely a matter of how each approached the Exodus and other parts of the Bible. As indicated previously, King understood the biblical account of the Exodus as God working with and through God's people to win deliverance for those in bondage, and this is why he was far more apt to relate this account to the traditions of the slave church than to those of the white church. King was ever mindful of how antebellum white churches had abused scripture while seeking to turn the religion of Jesus and the ancient prophets into a sham. Clearly, the pro-slavery white church is part of what he meant when he referred to "the Pharaohs of the South." In other words, that institution and its unwavering support for slavery were, in King's thinking, simply another chapter in that unfolding story that began with the biblical Pharaoh centuries earlier.[16]

The same might be said of the early white church's role in establishing and crystallizing patterns of segregation, which King regarded as another of its most dreadful blemishes. In King's opinion, the need for segregation rested on assumptions of white cultural superiority, or on the haunting sense of racial difference that pervaded the thinking of white Christians even prior to their arrival in America. King lamented the ways in which the hideous phenomenon of segregation manifested itself in the interior life of the earliest American churches. His perspective on the subject apparently benefited from his reading of the work of Kyle Haselden, who had observed in 1959 that, "Long before the little signs—'White Only' and 'Colored'—appeared in the public utilities they had appeared in the church."[17] King concluded that it was the white churches' refusal to take on an authentic, race-inclusive posture that compelled his ancestors "to organize their own churches." In the South, he held, the unhealthy atmosphere created by segregated white churches forced slaves to "hold secret religious meetings" in which "they gained renewed faith" and an "awareness of being a child of God" despite that wall of assumptions white society sought to impose on them.[18] It was against the background of these developments that King thought of the church as a bulwark of white supremacy.

At the same time, King acknowledged that there were elements in the antebellum white churches that contributed to the rise of the antislavery crusade. Quoting Haselden, he declared that the church had "fathered the abolition movement," an involvement that constituted "one of the few redeeming and gleaming features of professing Christians' dark and drearisome dealings with Negroes in the pre-Civil War days."[19] The white church's role in shaping the overall movement for emancipation simply reminded King that God always has a voice even in Pharaoh's household. This was in line with King's conviction that God often acts in history in strange ways, sometimes confounding even the most righteous and devoted believers. But when King spoke to the larger question of the relationship between the Christian faith and the rise of abolitionist sentiment and activism in antebellum times, he clearly had in mind contributions made by certain factions in both the white and black churches.

For King, the involvements of elements in the white church on both sides of the slavery issue afforded further proof of the ambivalent spirit of that institution. He felt that Haselden, perhaps more than any other white writer of his time, had captured the "schizophrenic, both damning and redeeming, demeanor," that characterized "white Christendom" in that era:

> The author demonstrates vividly the church's quandary as manifested, for example, in the contrasting positions of its divergent sectors regarding the merits of slavery. The writer shows that on the one hand large sectors of American Christendom accepted and accommodated to slavery, utililizing scriptural and pseudo-anthropological writings to prove the sub-human and soul-less character of the blacks; and rationalizing slavery as a Christianizing and uplifting lever for the dark-skinned primitives. On the other hand, the author indicates, other American Christians postulated the inherent worth and dignity for all men, noted the oppressive, dehumanizing and, therefore, unchristian nature of the master-slave relationship, and became the leading opponents against slavery.[20]

The ecclesiastical disputes and schisms over slavery, the Civil War, changes in the social and political condition of newly freed blacks, and the politics of Reconstruction did virtually nothing to sever what King called "the chord of emotional duality that has characterized 'religious' whites as they conceived of and acted upon their conceptions of what was and is the rightful place of the Negro in the societal fabric of this nation."[21] In King's thinking, this disturbing and persistent duality, which undermined the moral authority of the white church as a whole, was reinforced in the postbellum South owing to the growing influence of the Southern Baptist Convention (SBC), an organization formed in 1845, at the height of the debates between the northern and southern wings of the white church over slavery. Even as they prepared for the many challenges of the New South, King thought, white churches seemed trapped in the memories and values of the Old South. "Although Lincoln's decree had brought the Negro nearer to the Red Sea," King noted, "it had not secured his passage through the parted waters and the barrier thrown up by the Pharaohs was that of racial segregation, a new form of slavery disguised by certain niceties of complexity." "The Negro was soon to discover," he added, "that despite the Emancipation Proclamation, the Pharaohs of the South were determined to keep him in bondage."[22] In King's estimation, the unjust and inhuman treatment accorded blacks from the time of Reconstruction up to the turn of the century was as much an indictment against the church as it was against the Ku Klux Klan and other terrorist groups parading in that period.

Far from being a symbol of community, the southern white church emerged, in King's mind, as a sacred shelter for the sustenance and promotion of Jim Crow policies and practices. King knew that Jim Crow, the Black Codes, the "separate but equal" principle, and all of the other developments aimed at the isolation and subjugation of blacks could not have occurred without the backing and blessings of the church. Moreover, King understood the role of the white church in keeping alive the Confederate tradition in the South. The Confederate flag and other symbols of southern regionalism and nationalism, and the general practice of blending Christian rhetoric and imagery with Confederate rhetoric and symbols, were seen by him as part of a strategy to create a separate political culture rooted in a "master race" ethos.[23] This would stand as perhaps King's most pointed indictment against the southern white church and culture for the period extending from the *Plessy v. Ferguson* case (1896) up to *Brown v. the Board of Education* (1954).

King concluded that race had been the chief moral dilemma facing the white church in the period stretching from *Plessy v. Ferguson* up to the civil rights movement. Here, he agreed with W. E. B. DuBois, who wrote about the "Church attitude on Color Lines" in the 1930s.[24] DuBois's reflections on the subject had appeared in *The Atlanta Daily World*, a black newspaper in Georgia when King was just a boy, and they most certainly surfaced in the frank discussions King and his classmates had on race at Morehouse College and in other academic settings.[25] But King would write and say far more than DuBois about race as an ethical question and/or dilemma confronting the white church historically. In fact, when it came to this issue, no scholar or churchman was more vocal than King. Moreover, King was the nation's most analytical and tenacious voice when addressing race as a challenge to the spiritual vitality and moral authority of the white church in twentieth-century America. His comments on the white church's role in lynchings, though not very extensive, reveal the workings of a mind deeply concerned about the continuing vitality of the church as the society's chief spiritual and moral guardian.[26]

Some of King's statements on the white church in the late nineteenth and early twentieth centuries had to do not with specific historical developments but, rather, with emerging trends in theology. This was to be expected of one thoroughly trained in liberal Christian ethics and philosophical theology. When considering the most dominant theological trends, King expressed the least appreciation for Christian fundamentalism, which pervaded the life of both the white and the black churches from the time of Dwight L. Moody through the Great Depression and beyond. Certain expressions of fundamentalism rejected everything from Darwinian evolutionary thought to higher biblical criticism to the study of comparative religions, and they would not gain favor with King, who, heavily trained in liberal thought, believed that the church should be a force in encouraging intellectual openness and critical and analytical thinking. King rejected the virgin birth, the image of hell as eternal damnation, and other points of fundamentalism[27] even as he valued its call for a vital personal relationship between Christ and the believer. Also, King understood that fundamentalism too often discouraged active social involvement in preference for a complacent, laissez-faire approach to life, and that it was related, in ways subtle and not so subtle, to the preservation of longstanding racial arrangements in American life and culture. But while criticizing the ways in which fundamentalism conformed to powerful cultural influences, especially in his native South, King said little specifically about its promotion of the portrait of the passive, self-effacing, long-suffering white Jesus as the symbol and standard for all Christians.[28]

King regarded the Social Gospel movement, personalism, neo-orthodoxy, and Christian realism as highly significant theological trends, and as evidence that the white church had not totally succumbed to moral and theological bankruptcy. He credited the Social Gospel movement, which blossomed chiefly within white Protestantism between 1870 and 1918, with providing "a theological basis for the social concern which had already grown up in me as a result of my early experiences." The Social Gospelism of Walter Rauschenbusch was particularly important for King in this regard, and so was the Boston personalism represented by Edgar S. Brightman and L. Harold DeWolf. Neo-orthodoxy and Christian realism, which emerged as significant movements with Karl Barth, Reinhold Niebuhr, and other white theologians in the 1930s, afforded King critical insights into the superficial optimism of the Social Gospel and other liberal theological trends.[29] Much of the thought of Rauschenbusch, Brightman, DeWolf, Barth, Niebuhr, Paul Tillich, Henry N. Wieman, and others, who identified with various traditions within white Protestantism, either reached King in seminary and graduate-school classrooms or was filtered down to King through black church thinkers such as George D. Kelsey, Benjamin E. Mays, and Howard Thurman.

But even as King identified the strengths and weaknesses in the perspectives of Social Gospelers like Rauschenbusch, critics of personalism such as Tillich and Wieman, neo-Reformed thinkers like Barth, and Christian realists such as Niebuhr, he said, essentially nothing about their failure to take seriously the issue of race and its challenge to the white church in particular and the church in general.[30] This was a bit unusual for one who was not afraid of theological turf battles, and who lived and struggled in a time when parts of the American church were undergoing major theological shifts.

The rise of Christian atheism or "death of God" thought in certain circles of white Protestantism caught King's attention in the 1960s, as he himself affirmed God's activity in the struggle for freedom, human dignity, and equality of opportunity. The influence of Paul Van Buren, Thomas J. J. Altizer, William Hamilton, and other "death of God" theologians was occasionally in the background of King's thinking when he referred to the moral and theological impotence of much of white establishment Christianity in his own time.[31] It was only natural for King to wonder, at least at points during the civil rights crusade, if God was truly alive in the white church and the larger culture. This is undoubtedly what prompted him to raise the question—Who is their God?—a question that pervaded King's consciousness as he observed the "tall church spires and the sprawling brick monuments" that dotted the nation's sacred landscape.[32]

On the basis of his reading of American church history, King determined that white Christians had failed miserably in terms of collective moral achievement. He found it even more disturbing that the white church in his own time, in the North and South, was still "in a quandary about what attitudes to entertain and what conduct to undertake regarding the Negro's continuing quest for justice and opportunity." The best the white church could do to redeem itself in the present, King felt, was to reconcile itself to "a radical refurbishing of the status quo," while joining the crusade against racism, poverty and economic injustice, and war and human destruction. "Thus, the white American churchman, being so responsible for the Negro's plight owing to past and persisting sins of omission and commission," King wrote, "is called upon to leave, on occasion, his traditional and often dormant houses of worship and join the revitalized church which appears in the form of marches, pickets, demonstrations, and sit-ins."[33] King's sense of the various responses of white churches to this challenge is explored in the discussion that follows.

The Forces of Retrogression: The White Church and the Anti-Civil Rights Cause

The Montgomery bus boycott and other civil rights campaigns provided opportunities for Martin Luther King, Jr., to reassess the capacity and potential of the white church as an instrument of social change and/or transformation. He actually expected support in one form or another from the leadership of the white church in Montgomery.[34] While serving as the president of the Montgomery Improvement Association (MIA), he urged white church leaders to be "'maladjusted' to social injustice," a challenge that was not unusual for one who, by this time, had issued an "Appeal to the Churches," and who was addressing issues ranging from the integration of church structures to "The Role of the Church in Mental Health."[35] But King's optimism regarding the participation of the southern white church in the Montgomery bus protest was odd, to say the least, for no one knew better than he that institution's long history of collaboration with the forces of white supremacy. At first glance, it appears that King was being either naïve or prudent—that he was either an unsophisticated idealist and optimist or a shrewd tactician and prudent strategist. The most plausible explanation is that King was consciously being more prudent or diplomatic than realistic, feeling that this was an important part of any strategy geared toward gaining even the least bit of white church support.[36]

Any illusions King may have had about an enduring, functioning alliance between the civil rights movement and the white church were increasingly frustrated as the Montgomery protest reached perhaps its most explosive stage, prompting even some of the city's most prominent white ministers to publicly endorse segregation. King recalled one such figure, the Reverend E. Stanley Frazier, who expressed sentiments that King would hear from white church leaders throughout his career as a civil rights leader, especially as he encountered fundamentalists and evangelicals:

> I remember especially the words of Dr. Frazier—one of the most
> outspoken segregationists in the Methodist Church. Although I had
> heard his name and read his segregationist statements, I had never

been in his presence. Now I saw a tall, distinguished-looking man, the quintessence of dignity. He was, I soon found, articulate and eloquent besides. He talked persuasively about the frailties and weaknesses of human nature. He made it clear that he felt the Negroes were wrong in boycotting the buses; and even the greater wrong, he contended, lay in the fact that the protest was being led by ministers of the gospel. The job of the minister, he averred, is to lead the souls of men to God, not to bring about confusion by getting tangled up in transitory social problems. He moved on to a brief discussion of the Christmas story. In evocative terms he talked of "God's unspeakable gift." He ended by saying that as we moved into the Christmas season, our minds and hearts should be turned toward the babe of Bethlehem; and he urged the Negro ministers to leave the meeting determined to bring this boycott to a close and lead their people instead "to a glorious experience of the Christian faith."[37]

Significant developments occurred in the late 1950s and the 1960s that put King on a seemingly endless collision course with most white churches and their leadership. One such development was King's leadership in the formation of the Southern Christian Leadership Conference (SCLC) in 1957, for that organization supremely symbolized both his expanding role in the civil rights movement and his prophetic challenge to the silence and complacency of the white Christian establishment. In the 1960s, elements in the white church became increasingly uncomfortable and even indignant in response to King's consistent call for more radical methods to eliminate social evil and injustice. As King moved beyond mass meetings, boycotts, prayer vigils, street demonstrations, and sit-ins to advocate the breaking of unjust laws and court injunctions, nonviolent sabotage, and acts of massive civil disobedience, his conflicts with conservative voices in the white church escalated, thus revealing different understandings of the public role of the church and religion.[38]

At the center of King's conflicts with white fundamentalists and evangelicals were a series of questions: What is the proper role of the Christian in society? Is it the church's mission to eliminate unjust social structures, or should its moral responsibility be limited to matters of personal faith and salvation? Are ministers called and commissioned by God to be social and political activists, or to be merely soul-winners? How can one reconcile the Negro's campaign of active nonviolent resistance and civil disobedience with New Testament teachings on obeying duly constituted authorities? What is the nature of the communist challenge to the Christian Church? A careful exploration of the affinities and disaffinities between King's ideas and those of conservative

Christian leaders in the white church, especially in answering these and other questions, reveals not only the tensions and complexities in King's relationship with fundamentalists and evangelicals but also the extent to which people of faith in his time were prone to descend into ecclesial misunderstanding and disagreement. Moreover, such an exploration shows the ways in which King was impacted by the cultural and religious battles of the 1950s and 1960s, and it speaks to his extraordinary ability to frame public debate around matters relative to the nature and purpose of the church.[39]

No where was this more evident than in the case of King's "Letter from the Birmingham City Jail," a document that would become a benchmark for informed discussion on the role of the church and the Christian minister in society. In solitary confinement in April 1963, King wrote the letter in response to eight Alabama clergymen who were not among those who heralded his arrival in Birmingham, who labeled his activities there "unwise and untimely," and who accused him of resorting to "extreme measures" to get attention.[40] But the Birmingham letter was more than simply a rebuttal to this and other challenges to King's right to protest in a particular southern city. It was in effect a letter from a pastor to other pastors, or from one churchman to other churchmen, about what should have been major pastoral and ecclesial concerns.[41] Determined to inspire moral commitment to the struggle, King constructively analyzed the meaning, coherence, and implications of Judeo-Christian and democratic claims in a historical framework, offered a provocative Christian assessment of what was wrong with society's values and institutions, and issued a resounding call for a new way of viewing and being the church. King also provided a well-reasoned defense of the minister's role as an agent of social change. His dissatisfaction with the white church and its clergy up to that point, stated sharply, was broadly in line with his sense of the entire biblical and prophetic tradition:

> I have been so greatly disappointed with the white church and its
> leadership. Of course, there are some notable exceptions. I am not
> unmindful of the fact that each of you has taken some significant stands
> on the issue. I commend you, Reverend Stallings, for your Christian
> stand on this past Sunday, in welcoming Negroes to your worship service
> on a nonsegregated basis. I commend the Catholic leaders of this state
> for integrating Spring Hill College several years ago. . . . But despite
> these notable exceptions, I must honestly reiterate that I have been
> disappointed with the church. I do not say this as one of those negative
> critics who can always find something wrong with the church. I say this
> as a minister of the gospel, who loves the church; who was nurtured in

its bosom; who has been sustained by its spiritual blessings and who will remain true to it as long as the cord of life shall lengthen. . . . When I was suddenly catapulted into the leadership of the bus protest in Montgomery, Alabama, a few years ago, I felt we would be supported by the white church. I felt that the white ministers, priests and rabbis of the South would be among our strongest allies. Instead, some have been outright opponents, refusing to understand the freedom movement and misrepresenting its leaders; all too many others have been more cautious than courageous and have remained silent behind the anesthetizing security of stained-glass windows. . . . In spite of my shattered dreams, I came to Birmingham with the hope that the white religious leadership of this community would see the justice of our cause and, with deep moral concern, would serve as the channel through which our just grievances could reach the power structure. I had hoped that each of you would understand. But again I have been disappointed.[42]

King went on, in his "Letter from the Birmingham City Jail," to advance his critique of the white church and its leadership to another level, noting particularly their unwillingness to be unwavering, prophetic witnesses and activists in the crusade for justice and equal opportunity:

I have heard numerous southern religious leaders admonish their worshipers to comply with a desegregation decision because it is the law, but I have longed to hear white ministers declare: "Follow this decree because integration is morally right and because the Negro is your brother." In the midst of blatant injustices inflicted upon the Negro, I have watched white churchmen stand on the sideline and mouth pious irrelevancies and sanctimonious trivialities. In the midst of a mighty struggle to rid our nation of racial and economic injustice, I have heard many ministers say: "Those are social issues, with which the gospel has no real concern." And I have watched many churches commit themselves to a completely otherworldly religion which makes a strange un-Biblical distinction between body and soul, between the sacred and the secular.[43]

King and the white pastors to whom he responded were obviously driven by different contextual readings of scripture and history. King challenged the clergymen on the very ground that they claimed to hold most sacred—namely, Judeo-Christian and democratic values and traditions. As far as King was concerned, these pastors, who called him "an outsider" and "a trouble-maker," and who urged blacks to abandon protest and to rest their hopes on the force of civil law, were undermining the very values and traditions that had characterized the early church[44] and that had freed America from British colonial domination. Also, King knew that the idea of working through the court system, which frequently came from white preachers, seemed much like appealing to Pharaoh or to Caesar to resolve civil rights violations.

King's passionate and informed critique of the white church was virtually impossible to ignore, especially since his Birmingham letter was written with a rare combination of warmth, passion, and grace. The power-laden words, the carefully crafted theological argumentation, the impeccability of the logic, the stridently liberal tone of the rhetoric, and the thinly veiled message of hope helped make the "Letter from the Birmingham City Jail" the iconic document of the modern civil rights era. That document also became the most stirring example of King's ability to silence his ideological foes in the white church,[45] some of whom seemed deeply wedded to the conservative Darwinist idea that progress would inevitably be gradually achieved.

King found himself surrounded by three general categories of clergy from the white church. First, there were the old-line fundamentalists like Bob Jones, Sr. and Jr. and Jerry Falwell, who believed in preaching the word of God and keeping their congregations' attention centered on the heavenly; who denounced the Social Gospel as pure socialism or communism; and who avoided civil rights activities, which they considered secular and political. Second, there were establishment evangelicals such as Billy Graham, who declared that the Christian faith, like politics, should affirm the status quo; who viewed individual conversion experiences as the most important step in transforming the society and culture; and who tolerated civil rights protests as long as they did not amount to what they regarded as extreme acts of civil disobedience. Finally, there were the religious liberals, who were represented by Protestants, Catholics, and Jews; who embraced King's concept of the Social Gospel; and who routinely participated in civil rights demonstrations.[46] This last group will be highlighted in the final section of this chapter.

The old-line fundamentalists in the white church presented perhaps the strongest challenge for King, mainly because they opposed both his vision of the beloved community and his methods for actualizing that vision. Many in this group were based in the South, they affiliated with either the Baptist or Methodist churches, and they commonly invoked the Bible and conservative theology to justify and even sanction segregation and the existing racial order. Bob Jones, Sr. and Jr., whose names were synonymous with hard-line fundamentalist Christianity and who presided over Bob Jones University in

Greenville, South, Carolina, simply disliked Martin Luther King, Jr., and they insisted that social justice should never define the mission of the church.[47] The same can be said of Jerry Falwell, who pastored the Thomas Road Baptist Church in Lynchburg, Virginia, and who consistently declared that the church was called to "Preach the Word," not to "reform the externals" or "to wage wars against bootleggers, liquor stores, gamblers, murderers, prostitutes, racketeers, prejudiced persons and institutions, or any other existing evil as such." Furthermore, Falwell and the Joneses shared the view that the civil rights "demonstrations and marches have done more to damage race relations and to engender hate than to help!" King was all too familiar with the ideas of figures like the Joneses and Falwell, but he never dignified their proclamations with any careful, extensive responses.[48]

Fundamentalist leaders in the Southern Baptist Convention were known to attack the civil rights cause and King himself with the ferocity of lions. Throughout the 1950s and 1960s, Southern Baptist preachers like Henry L. Lyons, Jr., of Montgomery;[49] Carey Daniel and Wallie A. Criswell of Dallas, Texas; Noel Smith and John R. Rice of Tennessee; and Ferrell Griswold of Birmingham offered biblical defenses of segregation while promoting the myth of harmonious race relations in the South. Disturbed by what they saw as the increasing worldliness of the church, these and other Southern Baptist preachers consistently sought to undermine and discredit King's leadership, variously charging that King was driven by an insatiable appetite for power and recognition; that he meddled too much in temporal affairs; that he was using the rhetoric of Christianity, civil rights, and racial integrationism for personal glory and self-gain; that he was a tool of communists and socialists; that he was straying from biblical orthodoxy; that his protest methods fostered social and political anarchy; that he was trying to turn the gospel of Jesus Christ into a revolutionary ideology; and that his liberal views on scripture, the virgin birth, hell, and other fundamental dogmas made him an apostate and an enemy of true Christianity.[50]

King was hardly surprised because he knew that the South was the region with a history of demonizing those who seemed to threaten its way of life, a history extending as far back as the abolition movement. He also understood the neurotic sensitivity to outsiders and white southern hostility toward outside interference. But the baseless allegations and the deliberate and vicious efforts to tarnish King's image, which increased among SBC leaders as the civil rights leader reached the zenith of his personal popularity, were strange indeed, especially in a region where people were also commonly identified with social virtues such as hospitality and kindness to strangers.[51] In any case, King, who often endured slander and assault on his person, and who was known for a calmness of spirit, remained undeterred by the mean-spirited condemnations of virtually everything he believed and stood for, but he was always rankled by the charge that his tactics precipitated violence. "Well, isn't this like condemning Jesus because his unique God-consciousness and his commitment to truth caused the men who were misguided to bring upon him the evil act of crucifixion?," King asked.[52]

King boldly defended his nonviolent activism and civil disobedience against the claim, made by one Southern Baptist clergyman after the appearance of the "Letter from the Birmingham City Jail," that there was no precedent for such methods in the New Testament and the traditions of the early church.[53] The civil rights leader also insisted that the positions of his critics as a whole were not informed by Christian understanding, compassion, reasonableness, and goodwill.[54] He saw the hostility and scorn he received from clergy in the Southern Baptist Convention as a natural part of the contested terrain on which he lived and functioned. With his own situation in mind, King reminded his followers that "The same religious community which produced the prophets also produced the conservative religious forces which stoned the prophets to death."[55]

While acknowledging that "The nation is looking to the white ministers of the South for much of this leadership"[56] in the crusade for a more just, inclusive, and democratic America, King had reasons to seriously doubt that such an expectation would find fulfillment. He felt that the physical and material resources were there, especially with the SBC, the largest Protestant body in the South and in the nation, but he found that too many of its leaders lacked the will. In September 1964, King said in a press conference in London "that the Negroes received less support from Southern Baptists than from any other denomination," a problem that "grieved him as a Baptist minister."[57] At that time, he was still viewing the SBC as the prime example of how religion was used to inhibit urgently needed social change. Even so, King's realism regarding that body's impotence and indifference in a time of racial upheaval never degenerated into outright cynicism.

King came to see that there was a strong relationship between fundamentalist Christian beliefs and the advancement of white supremacy in America. This is part of what made the white church so agonizingly complicated for him. Moreover, this explained both that agency's lack of progress in race relations and its failure to confront its own racism head-on. As far as King could determine, the white church in the South was as guilty as any other southern institution when it came to the employment of the artificial binary of "black" and "white" to establish the social, economic, political, and legal structures of Jim Crow. The white church in the North, in which there were too often subtle practices of exclusion based on race, was, in King's estimation, no less irresponsible and grotesque, for it too undermined the gospel's thrust and divided the body of Christ.[58] King often wondered how the white church could be so adamant in sanctioning a culture of racial hatred and intolerance while proclaiming, at the same time, that Christian morality should be the ruling ethos of the country.

In his critiques of the white church's preoccupation with the color line, King complained most often about the Southern Baptist Convention. Here, he found what he considered the most tenacious defenders of white supremacy.[59] He also regarded the SBC as the primary source of much of the biblicism and theology invoked in defense of the legal and state-sponsored systems of segregation. "Pressed for a religious vindication for their conviction," King wrote, "they will even argue that God was the first segregationist."[60] King was probably thinking at this point of the Reverend Carey Daniel, the pastor of the First Baptist Church of West Dallas, Texas, who, drawing on the antebellum myth of Ham (Genesis 10:32), delivered a sermon entitled, "God the Original Segregator."[61] While noting that "many of our white brothers have moved away now from the argument that the Negro is inferior by nature because of Noah's curse upon the children of Ham," King could see that many pro-segregationist thinkers in the SBC were as determined as pro-slavery thinkers in antebellum times to use this and other passages of scripture to justify their views on biblical and theological grounds. He wrote passionately about "the passages of scripture that the segregationists use in an attempt to justify their position":

> One argument that they used is that the Negro is inferior by nature because of Noah's curse upon the children of Ham. As you well know, this is a misrepresentation of an incident that is recorded in the Book of Genesis. The 17th Chapter and 26th Verse of the Book of Acts is used also. It is the last part of this verse that is used which states "and hath determined the times before appointed, and the bounds of their habitation." You may read this whole passage and see it is a glaring misrepresentation of what the Scripture teaches. These are but two of the many arguments that are used.[62]

King was never able to reconcile the South's lofty image as the Bible Belt with the segregated practices of its most powerful white denomination. Referring to segregation in the internal life of the SBC, he observed that "If a black man went into the average southern Baptist Church, they'd kick him out."[63] On another occasion, he noted that despite being "a Baptist minister" and the "pastor of a big Baptist Church in Atlanta, Georgia, . . . my church could never join the Southern Baptist Convention, because it's an all-white convention."[64]

Far from being a haven of toleration and free, critical thinking, the SBC, King thought, had produced segregation's most devoted Christian apologists.

Evidently, King had the SBC in focus whenever he thought of the church as the anti-Christ, or the church as "one of the greatest bulwarks of white supremacy."[65] He found it most unsettling that general exhortations about love, brotherhood, kindness, and other Christian virtues were accepted by Southern Baptists so long as they did not target specific cases like racism and integration. King also scoffed at the Southern Baptists' tendency toward the easy rationalization of their sins and shortcomings in the sphere of race relations. When addressing such matters, King spoke objectively and with virtually no trace of condescension toward segregationists in the church. And even as he attacked the SBC's enslavement to the poisonous horror of southern racism, he believed, as he stated in 1964, that "many Southern Baptists now had a nagging conscience about the fact that the church [is] the most segregated institution in the USA and 11 o'clock on Sunday morning the most segregated hour of the week."[66] King hoped this would be an important step in what could possibly and ultimately be the SBC's public witness to the unity of the body of Christ.

King's experiences with white evangelicals like Billy Graham were generally more positive than those he had with fundamentalists, and especially leading figures in the SBC. It is no less accurate to say that King found establishment evangelicals in the white church to be both similar to and different from the fundamentalists. He was mindful that Graham shared much of the conservative theology of the fundamentalists, and that he was equally devoted to evangelism, missionary activity, doctrinal conformity, and defending and preserving orthodoxy against certain growing intellectual trends in the culture—matters that were not of the utmost importance for King. But Graham was different from white fundamentalists in that he had some association with King, and he also occasionally expressed support for the values of the civil rights movement.[67] Furthermore, Graham never engaged in a merciless assault on King's personality and religious integrity, even when he found King's tactics questionable. This apparently did not go unnoticed on King's part, and King initially viewed Graham as living proof that the white church was not beyond redemption.

As early as February 1957, King was approached with the possibility that Graham "may be able to be an ally in this struggle."[68] That possibility loomed larger five months later, when King delivered the opening prayer during Graham's evangelistic campaign at Madison Square Garden, in New York City. Reports of "a Graham-and-King crusade that would convert racially mixed audiences first in the North, then in the border states, and finally in the Deep South," were heard in some church circles.[69] King himself wrote Graham in August 1957, explaining how he might be a highly effective and vital supportive force in the civil rights cause:

I am deeply grateful to you for the stand which you have taken in the area of race relations. You have courageously brought the Christian gospel to bear on the question of race in all of its urgent dimensions. I am sure you will continue this emphasis in all of your preaching, for you, above any other preacher in America can open the eyes of many persons on this question. Your tremendous popularity, your extensive influence and your powerful message give you an opportunity in the area of human rights above almost any other person that we can point to. Your message in this area has additional weight because you are a native southerner. I am delighted to know that you will be conducting a crusade in Charlotte, North Carolina on a non-segregated basis. This is certainly a great step. I hope you will see your way clear to conduct an evangelistic crusade in one of the hard-core states in the deep south, even if it is not on as large a scale as most of your crusades. The impact of such a crusade would be immeasurably great.[70]

In 1959, King spoke in a similar vein, noting that Graham had "in recent years" taken "a very strong stand against segregation." "There was a time when he would even preach before segregated audiences," King added, "But now he refuses to preach to any audience that is segregated, which, I think, is a marvelous step."[71] A year later, King declared that "Had it not been for the ministry of my good friend, Dr. Billy Graham, my own work in the civil rights movement would not have been as successful as it has been."[72] The suggestion that King was "practicing flattery" in much of his praise for Graham, "as preachers tend to do for one another,"[73] is quite convincing, but King was also driven in part by the need to nurture and maintain the best possible relationship with the leading clerical voice of the white church in America.

But King soon discovered that there was a disturbing credibility gap between much of what Graham said and what he did when it came to the issues of race. In 1958, Graham rejected King's advice and appeared on the platform at one of his crusades in San Antonio with Texas Governor Price Daniel, a rabid segregationist. Though not entirely surprised, King was bitterly disappointed, for he had warned Graham that such a joint appearance would carry "political overtones designed to humiliate the Negro citizenry of Texas and the South"; that it would "be interpreted as your endorsement of racial segregation and discrimination"; that it could "have a damaging effect on the struggle of Negro Americans for human dignity"; and that it would "greatly reduce the importance of your message to them as a Christian minister who believes in the fatherhood of God and the brotherhood of man."[74] To be sure, Graham's

FIGURE 4.1. King and America's evangelist pose for a picture after King delivered a prayer at a Graham crusade in 1957.

actions virtually dashed any hopes of a public partnership between him and King to address the race problem.[75] Furthermore, Graham's behavior was for King yet another reminder of the ambivalent character of the white church, and this undoubtedly crossed King's mind a few years later when he alluded to his disappointment with the white church and its leadership in his celebrated "Letter from the Birmingham City Jail" (1963).

Graham's association with Price Daniel in San Antonio, which clearly contributed to the success of the governor's reelection bid, brought into sharp relief major differences between the popular evangelist and King, thus rendering absurd the claim that King was "a Billy Graham of civil rights."[76] The key point of contention for Graham was King's tactics in the streets, which at times took the form of civil disobedience. Graham was always concerned about King's operating within the boundaries of the laws and court injunctions, and he was never comfortable with King's belief that allegiance to a higher moral law required the breaking of such laws and injunctions in cases where they upheld segregation. When King and other activists turned to marches, sit-ins, and acts of civil disobedience in Birmingham in 1963, Graham advised King to "put the brakes on a bit."[77] During King's campaign for voting rights in Selma, Alabama, in 1965, Graham expressed concern that the forces of extremism would take over in both King's SCLC and the Student Nonviolent Co-ordinating Committee (SNCC). The evangelist believed then, as he would later, that "the permanent answer" to "racial troubles" was "in the gospel—not in the action of extremists on either side."[78] In 1966, Graham told the delegates at the general assembly of the National Council of Churches that "concern with social issues was an intrinsic part of religious conversion," but he went on to imply that the role of the minister was primarily "one of bringing people into the church."[79] King was seldom if ever moved by such evangelical proclamations because he clearly had a different understanding of how the church and its leadership could best witness to the Lordship of Christ.

It is also evident that Graham lacked the creative imagination King had when it came to specific ways in which the church could support the movement of the oppressed in the streets, at lunch counters, and in other arenas in which artificial racial barriers unjustifiably separated people. From all indications, Graham did not share King's depth of commitment to the actualization of the beloved community.[80] Moreover, Graham never really understood that the oppressed had to, in King's words, constantly "plague Pharaoh" in order to get justice.[81] This explains to some degree Graham's absolute refusal to participate in the mass meetings, the prayer vigils, the sit-ins, the street marches and demonstrations, and the other civil rights activities. King knew that Graham walked a tightrope, and this is why he urged the evangelist "to keep doing what" he "was doing—preaching the Gospel to integrated audiences and supporting his goals by example—and not to join him in the streets."[82] Ordinarily, King would have insisted that Graham combine his evangelistic activity with active participation in the civil rights crusade, a challenge he constantly put before black clergymen, but King could see that Graham was not free enough, so to speak, to make such a courageous and sacrificial move. In other words, King understood that Graham had to routinely make compromises where race was concerned in order to maintain his broad evangelical base in the white church, to keep his standing in the seductive halls of power, and to remain the de facto chaplain for Washington's elite.[83] By King's standards, then, Graham was merely a preacher, an evangelist, a revivalist—the high priest of conservative white Christians in America—and not in any real sense a prophet, or one who spoke truth to power even at the risk of life itself.[84]

King identified the fear of being nonconformists as perhaps the greatest sin of leaders in the white church. He felt that the problem was not confined to major evangelists like Graham, because all about him he saw even young white ministers who casually tiptoed around social evil and injustice while bowing to what he called "the enticing cult of conformity." King recalled an experience in 1966 that reminded him of the sheer depths of the problem:

> Not long ago, I spoke at Duke University in North Carolina. Most of the people in the audience were white. I talked about the mandate of the gospel, and at the end of the speech a young white theological student said: "You know, Dr. King, I agree with everything you said. I believe in it even more since I've come into theological school and studied the meaning of the gospel." On all of these issues, he said, "I just wish I could do something about it. But you know, I'm the pastor of a white church about 80 miles away from here and if I said anything like this, if I even talked about brotherhood from my pulpit, they would kick me out."[85]

King insisted that it was a myopic Christian orthodoxy that too often led some of the most prestigious white churches to be indifferent to struggles for social uplift, to proclaim that revivalism and getting people saved were the panacea for the nation's ills, and to seek pastors who were entirely safe on social and political questions. King remembered such a church in early 1963, which "sent out a statement" suggesting that its pulpit was not open to ministers who perpetuated models of Christian social activism:

> The other day a church was looking for a pastor. It was one of the big, downtown . . . white churches in one of the major cities of our country. And they set up some of the major qualifications and the first qualification for the new minister was this: he must be able to preach the true gospel and not talk about social issues. The true gospel according to that church didn't deal with social issues. . . . Whenever a church gets like that, it will stand in the midst of the injustices of life and yet refuse to say anything about them. Whenever a church gets like that it will refuse to hear Amos cry out, "Let justice roll down like waters and righteousness like a mighty stream." Whenever a church gets like that it will fail to hear Micah: "What does the Lord require of thee but to do justice, to love mercy, and to walk humbly with thy God."[86]

King acknowledged with regret that vast sectors of white middle-class America readily turned to self-styled evangelical churches, which typically induced a laissez-faire attitude toward life and existence, and which did not challenge their social and political values. "And who are the popular preachers today?," King asked, as he critiqued this kind of church culture. "They are so often preachers who can preach nice little soothing sermons on how to relax . . . , how to be happy . . . , and how to keep your blood pressure down." King further explained that such preachers are "seduced by the success symbols of the world," and they avoid saying anything from the pulpit "which might disturb the respectable views of the comfortable members" of their churches.[87]

Most white evangelicals essentially ignored King's critique of and challenge to their churches. In this respect, they were much like white fundamentalists, who felt that King's liberal theology rendered his vision for the church basically un-Christian and thus meaningless. Doubts about King's orthodoxy were occasionally expressed on both sides, in part because King brought to his ecclesial vision a healthy respect for non-Christian sources. For example, some white Christian conservatives undoubtedly had serious problems with King's tendency to draw on the images and insights of figures like Karl Marx and Mohandas K. Gandhi in presenting his challenge to the church. Of particular concern for them was King's suggestion that the church had much to learn from Marx about the evils of traditional capitalism, about "Jesus' concern for 'the least of these,'" and about the need to champion "the cause of the poor, the exploited, and the disinherited."[88] For the vast majority of white fundamentalists and evangelicals, the very thought of Marx as a source of enlightenment for the church was, at the very least, nauseating, especially since Marx was an atheist. This helps explain in some measure the charge, made by the fundamentalist preacher Gerald L. K. Smith, and heard most often in the so-called Bible Belt, that King was a Marxist or that his movement was being controlled, manipulated, and secretly directed by Communist Party insurgents.[89]

King's openness to the Marxist critique of class consciousness and differences was known among certain conservative leaders in the white church, and this most likely influenced their opposition to the civil rights leader's call for a radical redistribution of economic power. In response to such opposition, King denounced the capitalistic version of the Christian faith as advanced by white fundamentalists and evangelicals, insisting that the church must "never condone evil" in its "economic dimensions"—that it "must forever stand in judgment upon every economic system."[90] Drawing on scripture, King likened the typical rich Christian to Dives, or to "the American capitalist who never seeks to bridge the economic gulf between himself and the laborer, because he feels that it is natural for some to live in inordinate luxury while others live in abject poverty."[91] King went on to suggest that the white church's selective moral indignation and immobilizing complacency in the face of issues confronting the poor was an obscenity, and he declared that the exploitation of what he labeled "the have-nots" was spiraling the church as a whole deeper and deeper into moral bankruptcy. In light of these and other glaring realities, King must have found it strange and ironic that highly affluent leaders like Bob Jones, Sr., and Billy Graham were so quick to identify the anti-Christ with communism.

King believed that the failure of the white church to take an unflinching public stance on blatant inequalities in the economic order, and more specifically on issues such as decent wages, fair employment practices, universal health care, and quality housing for the poor, was attributable to a range of factors, aside from a distorted biblicism, a deep callousness toward human misery, and a lack of ecclesiastical will. Too many white congregations, King thought, lacked a clear sense of the vibrancy of the prophetic tradition and its condemnation of structural injustice and the abuse and misuse of both material and immaterial power. Others were confined by an intense institutional pride and egoism, which translated into an excessive concern with their own traditions, numbers, and influence. White Christians in this category, King felt, had become deeply enmeshed in dusty symbols, an unchanging code of absolutes, and the labyrinth of myth and dogma, and were more dedicated to the institutional church than they were to the Lord of the church. Still others were immobilized by what King called a "fear of social, political, and economic reprisals,"[92] or the feeling that their comfortable ways of life and of practicing religion would be upset. Be that as it may, King maintained that the white church could not remain relevant while ignoring the dynamic intersections of race and economics.

When it came to the question of the economic uplift and advancement of the poor generally, the white church was, in King's estimation, a sleeping giant that needed to be aroused and revitalized. Convinced that the church at its best is not an internal service institution, King highlighted the need for white churches to promote a more social-justice-oriented expression of Christianity, to commit their vast resources to much needed economic change, and to adjust to new economic realities.[93] Instead of leaving the disinherited and exploited stranded on life's Jericho Road, he reasoned, the white church was compelled by the gospel to take on the image of the Good Samaritan, or to become that presence that counters the satanic powers of economic injustice. Here, King moved beyond a constructive critique of the white church to offer a profile of the type of church that meets human need. As stated previously, this was part of the genius of one who employed biblical language, concepts, and metaphors to define the mission of the church, and who helped shape the identity and theological outlook of the church in his times.

For many clergymen in the white church, King's fascination with Mohandas Gandhi was as problematic as his appropriation of certain elements of the

Marxist critique of capitalism. After all, Gandhi was not only a Hindu and a staunch critic of Western Christianity but also a major source to which King turned to explain both his devotion to the poor and his use of the methods of nonviolence and civil disobedience. Having a strong and unwavering belief in the exclusivity of salvation based on the Christian faith, conservatives in the white church were prone to include Gandhi among the unsaved, and some openly questioned how King could be both a follower of Christ and a proponent of Gandhian ideas and methods. Bob Spencer, a fundamentalist Baptist pastor in Alabama, accused King of rejecting "the cardinal tenets of Biblical Christianity for the heathen philosophy of Mahatma Gandhi."[94] When King joined a distinguished group of lawyers in 1962 in forming the Gandhi Society, an educational foundation designed "to serve as a crucible for new ideas and nonviolent direct action," even some progressive-minded white clergymen wondered if the civil rights leader was "forsaking the Christian church in order to turn to a new kind of American sectarianism." Surprised and annoyed, King chided those clergymen for their "religious intolerance," and he boldly stated that God had worked through Gandhi, and that Gandhi reflected the spirit of Jesus Christ.[95] Apparently, King was not confined to the traditional Western understanding of the church, which was too frequently associated with a community of persons who made public professions of faith. More important, church for him meant being true to the spirit and example of Jesus Christ.

King concluded that the white church had long violated this spirit and example in its approaches to the problem of violence and human destruction. He agonized over the fact that so few in the white churches openly and actively embraced the redemptive and reconciliatory aspects of nonviolence. He was even more disturbed that certain elements in these institutions had not only adjusted to the brutality of mob rule in the South but also were actually participants in the unspeakable acts of savagery aimed at the oppressed:

> Go to your lynching mobs. So often Negroes in Mississippi and
> Alabama and Georgia and other places have been taken to that tree
> that bears strange fruit. And do you know that folk who are lynching
> them are often big deacons in Baptist churches and stewards in
> Methodist churches, feeling that by killing and murdering and
> lynching another human being they are doing the will of the
> almighty God? The most vicious oppressors of the Negro today are
> probably in church. Ross Barnett teaches Sunday school in a
> Methodist church in Mississippi. Mr. Wallace of Alabama taught
> Sunday school for years. One white Sunday school teacher down in
> Mississippi said not long ago that God was a charter member of the

White Citizens Council—using God to sanction their prejudice. . . . It isn't enough to go to church. It isn't enough to engage in worship. It is necessary to gain the real tenets of religion and live the ethical life of religion. Because if we fail to do this we will allow the ceremonial demands of Sunday to become a substitute for the ethical demands of Monday.[96]

As one who modeled his own life after the man from Galilee, King wondered how religious whites could be so callous toward people who presented them with no threat, but only proffers of friendship. He could think of nothing "more pagan" than the fact that J. W. Milan and Roy Bryant, the men who lynched Emmett Till, "are church members."[97] White churchpersons who turned to violence to preserve the old order were, in King's mind, no different from the Ku Klux Klan and the White Citizens Council, both of which hijacked Christian discourse and belief to justify their acts of violence and terrorism. The same applied in the case of white churches that always stood with those who sowed seeds of division and hatred, and that were so often silent when spasms of violence victimized black protestors. King maintained that it was shameful that so many white Christians displayed moral indignation when blacks demonstrated, but not when civil rights activists were murdered by racist mobs.[98] For King, the path of discipleship demanded something far more positive and noble.

But King knew that this was yet another example of the striking and seemingly unending ambivalence in the soul of the white church. His feelings along these lines were vindicated again and again, as leaders in the white churches publicly praised him for being nonviolent while refusing to strongly condemn the verbal and physical assaults on his own person. Strangely enough, there would be few official gestures of mourning even after King was assassinated, and fundamentalists at Bob Jones University and evangelicals at the Los Angeles Bible College actually greeted the civil rights leader's death with cheers. Clearly, such extreme reactions revealed what was a lingering animosity between conservative white churches and the King-led civil rights campaigns.[99]

War was another of those most vital and contentious issues that put King at odds with much of the white religious establishment. For King, U.S. involvement in Vietnam served as a clarion call for faithful and radical discipleship in the interest of peace, and he declared in prophetic tones that the white church should be one arena in which ethical questions about war should be seriously pondered and addressed.[100] The highest possible standard had already been set by the early church, which was for King a masterful frame of reference for understanding how devotees to the faith should respond to violent conflict on all levels.[101] As mentioned earlier, the refusal of the ancient Christians to go to war under any circumstances was for King the greatest expression of love and discipleship. Hence, he challenged the white church to embrace that model by devoting less time to enshrining Jesus in doctrine, dogma, and ritual, and more energy to translating his love ethic into a means of resolving conflicts between persons, groups, and nations.[102]

But King failed once again to awaken the often still voice of conscience in most of the white church community. As his position against the Vietnam conflict became more widely known in the late 1960s, he grew even more controversial in American church circles. For many white Christian conservatives, King's historic antiwar speech, "A Time to Break Silence," delivered at the Riverside Church in New York on 4 April 1967, was added proof that the civil rights leader was not only tied to Communist front groups and causes but also had begun to parrot their slogans and to advance their anti-American objectives.[103] The common view among many white fundamentalists and evangelicals was that King's activities embodied the seeds of his own destruction.

Perhaps the strongest opposition to King's stance on the war in Vietnam came from "the Radical Right," which, according to him, included political conservatives in the Republican Party and die-hard segregationists from the South. When King spoke of "the fanaticism of the Right," this is much of what he had in mind.[104] Figuring prominently in this equation were many white Christian conservatives, who viewed King, and the peace movement as a whole, as unpatriotic and anti-American. The Southern Baptist Convention, which King felt epitomized virtually all that had gone wrong with the white church, denounced what it saw as the excesses of antiwar protesters.[105] Many whites, and especially those in the southern churches, were infuriated when King advised draft-age men to file as conscientious objectors, to say nothing of his stated belief that such persons should also be accorded the same respect as war heroes. Even white moderates in the South, who had previously provided financial and moral support for King's "program of Christian nonviolence," broke ranks with the civil rights leader over these issues.[106]

King wondered how such Christians, whom he viewed as uncritical lovers of the church, could speak soberly and piously about the Prince of Peace while, at the same time, supporting the Vietnam War and failing to denounce its abuses and excesses. King was also perplexed that the same whites who "applauded me when I told Negroes" to be nonviolent in Montgomery, Albany, and Birmingham, in the freedom rides and sit-ins, and toward racist officials like Bull Connor and Jim Clark, were now "damning me when I tell people that they ought to be nonviolent toward little brown children in Vietnam."[107] King could only conclude that such critics had somehow missed the real challenge of Jesus' words in the Sermon on the Mount and were thus unfaithful to the biblical reality that brought the church into existence. In other words, they had, perhaps unconsciously, surrendered to a Christless Christianity and to counterfeit images of what the church should be about. Such an indictment could not have been more perceptive, coming, as it did, from one who always felt the need to remind white Christians that the New Testament is a work about both Christ and the church.

The confusion King detected in the pulpits and congregations of much of white America was painfully evident when it came to the question of New Testament teachings regarding the relationship of the Christian to the state. From the time of the Montgomery bus boycott, King was compelled to explain again and again why the Christian must never render to the state a reverence due to God alone. In 1957, King received a letter from a white Christian who asked: "How do you reconcile Paul's statements on obeying duly constituted authorities, Romans 13:1–7, with the Negro's campaign of passive resistance in the South?" King's response reflected, on the deepest possible level, his conviction that the spirit of the times demanded a more critical and flexible attitude on the part of the church toward the state:

> Like many Biblical affirmations, the words of the Apostle Paul must be interpreted in terms of the historical setting and psychological mood of the age in which they were written. The Apostle Paul—along with all of the early Christians—believed that the world was coming to an end in a few days. Feeling that the time was not long, the Apostle Paul urged men to concentrate on preparing themselves for the new age rather than changing external conditions. It was this belief in the coming new age and the second coming of Christ which conditioned a great deal of Paul's thinking. Early Christianity was far from accepting the existing social order as satisfactory, but it was conscious of no mission to change it for the better. It taught its adherents neither to conform to the external framework of their time, nor to seek directly to alter it, but to live within it a life rooted in a totally different order. Today we live in a new age with a different theological emphasis; consequently we have both a moral and religious justification for passively resisting evil conditions within the social order.[108]

This is one among many of King's statements that suggested that his own civil faith and civic-religious creed differed substantially from that of his critics in the white church. Unlike many of them, King did not give divine sanction to the governmental authorities in America, and he chided those white churches that were "the ready lackeys of state governments."[109] Clearly, he viewed "the authority of God as superior to the authority of the state," and this was one of the cardinal principles upon which the civil rights movement was based.[110]

King spoke of an America uniquely blessed by God, but he differed with white Christian conservatives who called America a Godly nation, who subscribed uncritically to messianic myths about the nation, and who insisted that its government existed by divine command. To the contrary, King consistently referred to America as a nation under God, or as a nation subject to divine judgment and wrath owing to its history of evil and injustice toward "the least of these."[111] Although he made "tactical use of civil religious rhetoric as a means of communication with White America,"[112] he was far more prone to appeal to the Hebrew-Christian prophetic tradition when challenging state authority and denouncing the nation's social ills and moral failures. King never accepted conservative white Christians' almost rigid insistence on conformity to the authority of the state when it came to civil rights protests, for he knew that they themselves were prone to take action and to make political and religious judgments that challenged such authority, especially when advancing their own interests.

The evidence of this was most abundant in the South, where white Christians had long led the resistance to federal mandates that challenged Jim Crow practices. This speaks to much of the difficulty in identifying King with the traditions of southern civil religion.[113] In contrast to white Christians in the South, King never thought of the southern way of life, and especially its white supremacist political and governmental structures, in sacred terms, and he categorically rejected the identification of Christian principles with southern regional patriotism and/or chauvinism. Piety, honor, sacrifice, virtue, morality, and other notions that echoed through the general faith of white southerners had a different meaning for King. Furthermore, King never embraced the white South's sanitized and romanticized versions of the Old South and the Confederate tradition, its reverence for Confederate heroes, the respect it attached to the symbolism of the Confederate flag and the singing of "Dixie," and its tendency to use scripture and Christian rhetoric to justify and even sanction the existing social, political, and economic order. To the contrary, King tended to identify all of this with a master-race ethos.[114]

King's civic-religious faith was clearly more prophetic than that of the vast majority of white southern Christians, in this and in other respects. Even as King spoke of God being at work in the South, using the region as a proving ground for the triumph of American democracy, he rejected the messianic symbolism and mythology that all too many white Christians associated with the region and its history.[115] Also, King readily acknowledged the deep ties of common songs and symbols that southern white and black Christians shared in a religio-mystical context, despite the vicious myth of white supremacy and the rigid Jim Crow structures, but he was always mindful of all that distinguished southern white churches from Negro churches as well.

For King, the civil rights movement was the moment of decision as to where the white church stood on a range of social justice issues. Obviously, he was always disappointed with the level of support he received from that institution as a whole, even when he put the best possible face on the situation, but he knew that the white church was not monolithic or one-dimensional. Not surprisingly, King found hope in the fact that liberal white religious leaders would rank among his strongest allies from the time of the Montgomery bus protest. But, strangely enough, his faith in the possibilities for the redemption of the white church would not be limited to these voices of progression, which were isolated and small in number, for he also hinted, especially during those early years of his public life, that even the most vicious racist could be converted under the dynamics of the Christian faith: "I want to tell you this evening that I believe that Senator Engelhardt's heart can be changed. I believe that Senator Eastland's heart can be changed. I believe that the Ku Klux Klan can be transformed into a clan for God's kingdom. I believe that the White Citizens Council can be transformed into a Right Citizens Council! I believe that. That's the essence of the Gospel."[116] This faith, rooted in King's strong belief in the power of God and the assurance of God's grace, was renewed again and again as King witnessed the sacrifices of committed white Christians in the context of both the civil rights and anti-war crusades.

Voices of Progression: Pro-Civil Rights Forces in the White Church

From the time of his arrival in Montgomery in 1954, Martin Luther King, Jr., demonstrated a ferocious desire to work with representatives from the white church for the improvement of race relations, locally and regionally. He soon joined the Montgomery Chapter of the Council on Human Relations (ACHR), an interracial group that employed education, research, and practical action in search of "equal opportunity for all the people of Alabama."[117] Several white clergymen were also involved with the group, among whom were Ray Wadley, the Methodist minister and president of the council, the Episcopal Rector Thomas P. Thrasher, and the Lutheran minister Robert S. Graetz. For perhaps the first time in his life, King, who quickly emerged as the council's vice president,[118] worked closely with white pastors who essentially shared his progressive social vision in a southern context. His experiences with the ACHR would prove beneficial during and after the Montgomery bus boycott, especially as he made appeals to churches across racial and denominational lines.

King included Wadley, Thrasher, Graetz, Robert E. Hughes, and Glenn Smiley among that chorus of distinguished voices that made the movement in Montgomery possible. According to King, Wadley was later moved to a small, rural community after his all-white St. Mark's Methodist Church bitterly complained about his activities for better race relations.[119] King was most impressed with Thrasher, who, at a critical stage in the Montgomery protest, joined the white Methodist pastor Robert E. Hughes in helping to arrange an important meeting of the city fathers, the bus company, and the Montgomery Improvement Association (MIA), the organization that King headed, and that launched the boycott. Because of Thrasher's refusal to stop addressing racial issues from his pulpit, and his rebuke of his white congregation for hiring a guard to prevent blacks from attending services, he eventually met virtually the same fate as Wadley. King witnessed the same in the case of Hughes, who also served the ACHR as director, who defended the Supreme Court's decision in *Brown v. the Board of Education* (1954), and who was forced out of Alabama after being harassed by the Klan and white supremacists in Alabama's judicial system.[120]

King's relationships with Graetz and Smiley seem to have been much more personal and extensive than his ties with Wadley, Thrasher, and Hughes. Graetz served on the executive committee of the MIA, participated in the carpool set up for boycotters, prayed and read scripture at mass meetings, and tried desperately and unsuccessfully to secure the support of Montgomery's white ministerial alliance for the boycott. Inspired by the calm and charitable spirit Graetz displayed in the face of verbal insults, threatening telephone calls, and the bombing of his home, King wrote: "This boyish-looking white minister of the Negro Trinity Lutheran Church was a constant reminder to us in the trying months of the protest that many white people as well as Negroes were applying the 'love-thy-neighbor-as-thyself' teachings of Christianity in their daily lives."[121] Much the same could have been said about Glenn Smiley, a southern-born white clergyman and activist in the Fellowship of Reconciliation (FOR), who earned the respect and admiration of both Graetz and King, mainly owing to his unflagging commitment to nonviolence despite persecution. Smiley was most helpful to King as King sorted out the practical dimensions of nonviolent resistance in Montgomery, and he was also King's seatmate when the two rode the very first integrated bus in the city.[122] Whenever King spoke of the need for a more prophetic witness and posture on the part of the white church as a whole, he was thinking of the kind of example provided by Smiley, and by exemplary figures like Wadley, Thrasher, Hughes, and Graetz.

FIGURE 4.2. Robert S. Graetz (1928–), one of the few white pastors who worked with King during the Montgomery bus boycott.

Montgomery reminded King that there were white Christians in the South who were genuinely interested in both the freedom of blacks and the creation of an interracial community. King rejoiced in the fact that even some white Christians who seemed comfortable with segregation "could not stomach the excesses performed in its name." He made special mention of the "Several white ministers" who "denounced the bombing" of black churches and homes in Montgomery "as unchristian and uncivilized," and whose "statement was repeated all through the day by the distinguished minister of First Presbyterian Church, the Rev. Merle Patterson."[123] This was one source of the optimism that informed King's vision of a "New South."[124]

In December 1956, on the eve of the successful outcome of the bus boycott, King made a special appeal to southern white churches and their leaders for support in the expanding crusade for civil rights across the region, urging them "to see beyond the narrow concepts of the past."[125] As had been the case up to that point, few white clergymen responded favorably. When King and almost a hundred other ministers met in Atlanta in January 1957, and voted to form the SCLC, Will D. Campbell, a Southern Baptist, was the only white clergyman present.[126] But King seemed convinced that there were numerous progressive visionary leaders in the white church in the South who would in time witness to the legitimacy of the freedom cause. He said as much and more during a "Conference on the Christian Faith and Human Relations" in Nashville, Tennessee, in April 1957:

> I am not unmindful of the fact that many white ministers in the South have already acted. Many such ministers are here today. I have nothing but praise for those ministers of the gospel who have stood unflinchingly amid threats and intimidation, inconvenience and unpopularity, and even at times amid sheer physical danger. There is nothing, to my mind, more majestic and sublime than the deter-mined courage of an individual willing to suffer and sacrifice for truth. For such noble servants of God there is the consolation of the words of Jesus: "Blessed are ye when men shall revile you and persecute and say all manner of evil against you, falsely, for my sake; rejoice and be exceedingly glad; for so persecuted they the prophets which were before you."[127]

In 1958, King acknowledged with pleasure those "white ministers of Atlanta, Richmond, Dallas, and other cities" who spoke out against racists who broke and evaded the law by encouraging violence and heightened animosity between blacks and whites. King was particularly impressed with the actions of some of the white church leaders in his own city, noting that "High tribute and appreciation is due the ninety ministers of Atlanta, Georgia, who so coura-geously signed the noble statement calling for compliance with the law and a reopening of the channels of communication between the races." "All of these things are admirable," King quickly added, "But we must admit that these cou-rageous stands from the church are still far too few."[128]

Much of King's optimism about assistance from the white church had faded when he joined the Albany Movement, his second major attempt at social protest, in 1961, but he was still lavishing much praise on those white cler-gymen who provided physical, moral, and financial support for the cause. But his was praise tempered perhaps with some apprehension. When seventy-five white ministers and rabbis appeared and offered their support to what was essentially an across-the-board, full-scale assault on segregation in Albany, King graciously received them and was inspired by their willingness to accept the harshest penalties for their resistance. With that campaign in view, King would later thank God "that some noble souls from the ranks of organized religion have broken loose from the paralyzing chains of conformity and joined us as active partners in the struggle":

> They have left their secure congregations and walked the streets of
> Albany, Georgia with us. They have gone down the highways of the
> South on tortuous rides for freedom. Yes, they have gone to jail with
> us. Some have been dismissed from their churches, have lost the
> support of their bishops and fellow ministers. But they have acted in
> the faith that right defeated is stronger than evil triumphant. Their
> witness has been the spiritual salt that has preserved the true
> meaning of the gospel in these troubled times. They have carved a
> tunnel of hope through the dark mountain of disappointment.[129]

White church support for SCLC's Project C (Confrontation) in Birmingham in 1963 came primarily through financial contributions and expressions of moral support. This accounted for much of the tone of King's "Letter from the Birmingham City Jail." Although King expressed disappointment with the white church as a whole, he acknowledged that some among the eight white clergymen who criticized his activities in Birmingham, and who inspired him to write the Birmingham letter, had taken important positions on the race issue. He commended the Reverend Earl Stallings for welcoming blacks to worship services at his all-white First Baptist Church, and he praised Catholic leaders in Alabama for having integrated Spring Hill College some years earlier. In other writings, King also spoke highly of Eugene Carson Blake, the national head of the United Presbyterian Church, and other nationally renowned Protestant leaders, Catholic priests, and rabbis who participated in demonstrations in Birmingham after the publication of the Birmingham letter, and who also ended up in jail cells.[130]

King was especially gracious when assessing the level of support provided by white churches for the march on Washington in 1963, a campaign designed to unite civil rights leadership and to dramatize civil rights issues before the entire nation. King wrote:

> One significant element of the march was the participation of white
> churches. Never before had they been so fully, so enthusiastically, so
> directly involved. One writer observed that the march "brought the
> country's three major religious faiths closer than any other issue in
> the nation's peacetime history." I venture to say that no single factor
> which emerged in the summer of 1963 gave so much momentum to

the on-rushing revolution and to its aim of touching the conscience of the nation as the decision of the religious leaders of this country to defy tradition and become an integral part of the quest of the Negro for his rights.[131]

A year later, King reported that "I have never seen white clergymen as active in civil rights as they are now and as they have been since the march on Washington."[132] He went on to assert that even "many Southern Baptists now had a nagging conscience about" racial discrimination in ecclesial circles. On an optimistic note, King further affirmed that "There had been real progress in the last year" with Southern Baptists, and that "more churches and ministers were coming to the aid of the Negroes."[133]

In King's estimation, the 1965 campaign for voting rights in Selma, Alabama, exceeded even the march on Washington in terms of the levels of support from white religious communities. Four hundred white clergymen from various denominations and faith traditions appeared in Selma, contributing to what King described as "the greatest and warmest expression of religious unity of Catholic, Protestant and Jew in our nation's history."[134] Unable to hold back the torrents of pride and joy swelling within him on that occasion, King saw in this iconic moment, in this checkered mix of religious personalities, a real testimony to the powerful image of the church as a coalition of conscience. He also sensed what might be labeled an approximation of the ethical ideal of the beloved community, for he himself said, turning to theological language, that "I was sure that this alliance of conscience could only be a sign of the coming of the Kingdom."[135] This was only natural for one who viewed all of his campaigns as essentially crucial spiritual strides toward reconciliation and community.

Perhaps more than any other civil rights campaign, the one in Selma produced what King called "martyrs of faith,"[136] among whom were white churchpersons such as James Reeb, Viola Liuzzo, and Jonathan Daniels. Reeb, a Unitarian minister from Boston, died after a severe beating. Liuzzo, a devoted Catholic and housewife from Detroit, was gunned down during the Selma to Montgomery march. Shortly thereafter, Daniels, an Episcopal seminarian from New Hampshire, was brutally murdered. The price paid by these figures came together in King's consciousness with the sacrifices of Michael Schwerner and Andrew Goodman, two Jewish students who had given their lives in the struggle in 1964, a year earlier.[137] These images literally permeated King's sense of the sacrificial church, or the church as the suffering servant. He spoke directly about the meaning of Reeb's death for the church and the society as a whole:

> His death comes as a great loss to the church community, the nation and
> all of the ideals to which he passionately devoted his life. He now joins

the ranks of those martyred heroes who have died in the struggle for freedom and human dignity. . . . This racist murder has so revolted the conscience of America that the forces of Church and State can quickly and creatively move to bring positive change to our segregated society.[138]

Throughout the 1960s, King continued to speak of figures like Reeb, Liuzzo, and Daniels as noble examples for the church universal of his day. King praised such figures with all of the tenacity of his struggle for freedom, viewing them as evidence that the white church was "reasserting moral leadership" on some levels.[139] They accounted largely for King's tendency to highlight the well-intentioned white church, or that church which was fostering a progressive social vision in a religious culture known for sacrificing moral and social responsibility on the altar of a narrow spirituality.

Knowing that the compelling ideal of interracial church unity with equality would remain an unacceptable scenario for many white Christians, King always appreciated even those ordinary, unheralded white clergymen who labored to keep the integrationist model of ecclesiastical life before the highest councils of American church leadership. King was equally appreciative of those predominantly white church organizations and agencies that rejected the confrontational model embraced by many white Christian fundamentalists and that embodied and pursued the fullness of the beloved community ideal in various ways. Included among these were the American Baptist Convention (ABC), the National Council of the Churches of Christ (NCC), the National Conference on Religion and Race (NCRR), the Episcopal Society for Cultural and Racial Unity (ESCRU), the National Student Christian Federation (NSCF), the Student Interracial Ministry Committee (SIMC), the General Synod of the United Church of Christ (UCC), Clergy and Laity Concerned (CALC), the Synagogue Council of America (SCA), and the numerous other local, regional, and national groups with which King worked and associated in making the church a vital force in the struggle.[140]

Strangely enough, King's relationship to the American Baptist Convention began on the most serious note at roughly the same time as he was experiencing difficulties and conflicts with Joseph H. Jackson and other conservative elements in the traditionally black National Baptist Convention, USA(NBC). In January 1962, the members of Atlanta's Ebenezer Baptist Church, at which King served as co-pastor with his father and brother, "unanimously voted to have our church affiliate with the American Baptist Convention." "This decision was made," King continued, "because of our awareness of the great work your Convention is doing for Kingdom building, and our strong convictions concerning an integrated church." While King understood that the white church as a whole was ill-prepared to engage the black church on a deep level of understanding and cooperation, he was convinced that "our association with the American Baptist Convention" could provide a context in which blacks and whites might engage each other in a common Christian fellowship, and that it "could strengthen immeasurably our position on this issue."[141]

These words could not have been more meaningful, coming, as they did, from one who had long encouraged the presence of whites at both Montgomery's Dexter Avenue Baptist Church and Ebenezer Baptist in Atlanta,[142] and who was always mindful of how his movement affected blacks in mostly white denominations. King's affiliation with both the American Baptist Convention and the Progressive National Baptist Convention (PNBC), a predominantly black body, after 1962, was symbolic of his desire to bring the white church and the black church together in a joint effort for much-needed social change.[143] This was a critical part of his creative determination and overall effort to heal a nation he considered not only bitterly divided but also wounded and in search of a soul.

King knew that the National Council of the Churches of Christ had been involved in civil rights from the time of his activities in Montgomery, and perhaps even before. NCC leaders like Eugene Carson Blake, who headed the organization, had provided moral and financial assistance for the bus boycott. In 1958, King reported that "The National Council of Churches has condemned segregation over and over again, and has requested its constituent denominations to do likewise." "Most of the denominations have endorsed that action," he added.[144] In the early and late 1960s, King repeatedly singled out the NCC for commendation, mainly for encouraging its ministers and churches to participate in demonstrations and a range of other direct action programs to end discrimination.[145]

When the NCC threw the weight of its support behind a National Conference on Religion and Race in 1962–63, King applauded the move and agreed to serve on the Steering Committee of the NCRR. He actually attended the conference in January 1963, and presented a paper entitled "A Challenge to the Churches and Synagogues." White religious leaders such as Will Campbell and Rabbi Abraham J. Heschel were also heavily involved, and inclusivity was highlighted as the great theme of the gospel and the biblical revelation. King, who never ceased to sound the trumpet for love and community, called the NCRR, which united in formal cooperation the National Council of Churches, the Synagogue Council of America, and the National Catholic Welfare Conference, "one of the most significant and historic conferences that has ever been held in this nation."[146] Concerning the details of the conference, King recounted the following:

There were signs of hope this week. Several of my co-workers from the South and I spent the early part of this week in Chicago, Illinois, attending the National Conference on Religion and Race. It was an assemblage of the most imposing array of theologians, pastors, and church leaders from all over the nation representing three major faith groups, Protestant, Catholic and Jewish. It marked the first time in the history of our nation that representatives from these bodies had come together in dialogue for any reason. . . . The mere fact that they came together to grapple with America's number one domestic ill is a hopeful sign that our nation has become sensitized at last to the great toll of human misery that is perpetuated by segregation and discrimination. . . . For these four days, in common fellowship, we shared a spiritual catharsis—confessing our sins of race and color prejudice—and then in a Declaration of Conscience, reaffirmed our commitment to our Hebraic-Christian traditions. It is my sincere hope that this confrontation with our own ineptness as it relates to race will give us the courage to take up the prophetic task of seeing to it that "justice rolls down like waters and righteousness as a mighty stream" in our nation.[147]

King frequently acknowledged other predominantly white ecclesiastical and religious associations and agencies for their positive contributions to the struggle against racism and segregation. He delighted in the financial and moral support he received from white clergymen in groups such as the Episcopal Society for Cultural and Racial Unity and the General Synod of the United Church of Christ. In July 1965, King wrote the UCC expressing hope that it would continue to finance the work of ministers in the SCLC "as a concrete tie between our organizations." Such support could not have been more important to King "because the major salaries of our movement are provided by churches" and because this "firmly exemplifies the religious character of the movement."[148]

King's supported agencies like the National Student Christian Federation and the Student Interracial Ministry Committee because of the need to prepare both white and black seminarians for participation in integrated church situations. His SCLC was a co-sponsor of the seminarian summer project of 1961, which developed under the auspices of both groups; and King, referring to the project, insisted that "The prospect of dedicated young men, Negro and white, entering parishes of the deep South to serve as 'ministerial internees' is a bold and creative venture in human relations." King was particularly supportive of white seminarians having "the opportunity to live and work within the framework of a Negro church community [for] a period of 10–12 weeks," declaring that they needed to know blacks "intimately, sense their hopes and fears, their joys and sorrows." He further explained that "This will aid inestimably in preparing them to serve the church and to give clear Christian witness."[149] King was most pleased that elements in the white church were willing to support such a project, but he suggested that it should be an ongoing and far more serious effort.

As King turned increasingly to economic justice and international peace issues in the late-1960s, supporters in the white church became smaller and smaller in number. His critique of the capitalist ethic and call for a radical redistribution of economic power were simply too controversial for all but the most liberal voices in the white church community, among whom were a few Jewish leaders and activists in groups like the American Baptist Convention and the National Council of Churches. King's attack on the escalated war in Vietnam gained support from essentially the same liberal faction. He thanked God that the "National Council of Churches [was speaking out] in a beautiful way, criticizing our foreign policy and the present war, and criticizing war in general."[150] Eugene Carson Blake of the NCC and Harry Emerson Fosdick, the pastor of New York's Riverside Church and an intellectual source of King's, joined King in opposing U.S. involvement in Vietnam and in encouraging conscientious objectors. A few dedicated religious leaders sided with King in the peace movement and in denouncing the war effort through Clergy and Laity Concerned About Vietnam, chief among whom were Rabbi Abraham Heschel, of the Jewish Theological Seminary of America; Father John McKenzie, a professor at the University of Chicago Divinity School; and John C. Bennett, the president of New York's Union Theological Seminary. Reinhold Niebuhr, who had a decisive influence on King's Christian realism, actually wrote the foreword to a collection of King's speeches on Vietnam, a collection published by CALC.[151]

It is difficult to exaggerate the profundity and complexity of King's challenge to the white church in the 1950s and 1960s. King and the movement he led constituted a necessary step toward the maturation of the white church. Even white fundamentalists and evangelicals learned valuable lessons from the civil rights leader, as they later came to terms with the whole question of the proper role of religion and the church in the public arena. Moreover, King's challenge, as the next chapter shows, inspired the American churches to move beyond sectional loyalties to more fully engage a world torn between chaos and community.

5

Unrestricted Freedom

The Church and the World House

The Kingdom of God is not confined within the limits of the Church
and its activities.

—Walter Rauschenbusch,
A Theology of the Social Gospel

If the Church abides by the spirit of Jesus, there is room in her for
every form of Christian piety, even for that which claims unrestricted
freedom.

—Albert Schweitzer,
Out of My Life and Thought: An Autobiography

The Church must come out of its stagnation. We must move out
again into the open air of intellectual discussion with the world, and
risk saying controversial things, if we are to get down to the serious
problems of life.

—Dietrich Bonhoeffer,
Letters and Papers from Prison

However deeply American Negroes are caught in the struggle to be at
last at home in our homeland of the United States, we cannot ignore
the larger world house in which we are dwellers.

—Martin Luther King, Jr.,
Where Do We Go from Here: Chaos or Community?

Martin Luther King, Jr., viewed himself "as a citizen of the world,"[1] and he refused to isolate the civil rights struggle in the United States from the struggles of the oppressed and exploited worldwide. This was evident from the time of his earliest attempts at social protest, when he, in May 1956, spoke of the Montgomery bus boycott as "part of this overall movement in the world in which oppressed people are revolting against the imperialism and colonialism that have too long existed."[2] King's insistence on identifying with oppressed humanity irrespective of color, creed, and nationality must be considered in any serious discussion of how he understood the spiritual role and moral responsibility of the church in an international context.[3]

This chapter analyzes King's thinking on the ministry and mission of the Christian church on a global scale. First, his views on how the American churches, black and white, should do evangelism and missions abroad are covered in some detail. Here, King's tendency to stress practical or applied Christianity over doctrinal or missionary Christianity in the traditional sense is highlighted. Second, King's ideas on how the church universal could best contribute to the elimination of racism, poverty and economic injustice, and war and human destruction as world problems are examined. Finally, attention is devoted to King's thoughts on how the church might contribute to a positive pluralism by promoting a healthy ecumenism, by developing models of participative leadership, and by respectfully and effectively engaging other major religions worldwide.

The World as a Parish: The American Churches and Foreign Missions

Martin Luther King, Jr., said as much as any other religious leader of his times about how the American churches should relate to a world in which people are unduly separated in ideology, culture, and interests. In his messages throughout the country, he frequently highlighted the need for the churches to instill within their constituents "the world perspective."[4] For King, this was particularly important in the case of children because, as he saw it, "the new order that is embracing the world needs the strength of the young."[5] Here, he opted for a global ethic rather than a nationalistic approach,[6] for he was convinced that a myopia exists whenever the church limits its mission priorities to a particular geographical or cultural context. With this in mind, King challenged every Christian in the United States to "become an effective disciple in the world of men" or "to live with Christ in the midst of a world in revolution."[7] Apparently, he never lost that sense of the church as one and universal, even as he worked from the Negro church as a base.

King's challenge to the church in America was consistent with his belief that Christianity in its most authentic expression had something special to offer the world, especially in the realm of values. This in why he agreed in principle with "the Great Commission" as advanced in St. Matthew 28:19–20. From the very beginning of his pastorate at the Dexter Avenue Baptist Church in Montgomery, King affirmed that congregation's covenant as it related to missionary outreach, or to the un-churched at home and abroad. Dexter's covenant not only supported "a faithful and evangelical message among us" but also called for "the spread of the Gospel throughout the world."[8] As King himself put it, "when Jesus says to his disciples 'go ye into all the world and preach my gospel,' he is saying in effect, propagandize my word, spread it, disseminate it, push it into every nook and crack of the universe."[9] At other points, King explained that this involved "efforts to bring the world to Christ," a mission he identified with the whole history of the Christian church:

> Ever since the dawn of the Christian era, Christians have considered it a serious part of their basic responsibility to carry the gospel of Jesus Christ into all the world and to every creature. This is one of the things that distinguishes Christianity from the other great religions of the world. Most of the other great religions have had profound admiration for their founders, but they do not consider it a serious part of their responsibility to carry the message of their founders into all the world. Christianity has never been content to wrap itself up in the garments of any particular society. If there is any one word that characterizes our creed it is *go*. It started with Jesus and continued with Paul. Go ye into all the world. Now this demand to carry the gospel to every creature has long since been known as missionary work. From the beginning Christians have been considered missionaries.[10]

The potential power of such "missionary zeal" was never lost in King's consciousness, for he occasionally believed that "The fact that we are living in a world of revolution is in large measure attributable to the preaching of the Gospel, and the work of missionaries around the world."[11] Here, King meant the proclamation of the ethics of Jesus and not the values of Western Christianity, a distinction also made by Mohandas K. Gandhi and Howard Thurman, two of his most important intellectual sources. "If we take Christ to the world, we will turn it upside down," said King while still at Crozer, "but the tragedy is that we too often take Christianity."[12] This sense of missionary activity at its best coursed through many of King's sermons on the relationship of the church to the world, among which are his "Is the Church the Hope of the World?,"

"The Vision of a World Made New," and "Redirecting Our Missionary Zeal."[13] In each sermon, mission is defined in terms of the practical power and application of the Christian faith.

King held that "the only serious rival" to the spread of Christianity in its most genuine form throughout the globe was communism, a claim he made as far back as his seminary days.[14] "If I lived in a Communist country today where certain principles dear to the Christian faith are suppressed," he declared in 1963, "I believe I would openly advocate disobeying these anti-religious laws."[15] There was obviously a challenge here for missionaries who insisted on embodying and advancing the power of the gospel on foreign shores. King went on to note with pride that, owing to the power of a crusading and uncompromising missionary spirit, the church was a growing phenomenon even in the Soviet Union, where the government desperately sought to extinguish the glowing flame of its witness:

> Visitors to Soviet Russia, whose official policy is atheistic, report that the churches in that nation are not only crowded, but that attendance continues to grow. Harrison Salisbury, in an article in *The New York Times*, states that Communist officials are disturbed that so many young people express a growing interest in the church and religion. After forty years of the most vigorous efforts to suppress religion, the hierarchy of the Communist party now faces the inescapable fact that millions of people are knocking on the door of the church.[16]

King related a similar account regarding the spread of Christianity in East Berlin, where communist officials were equally devoted to destroying not only Christian influences, but all forms of religion:

> But I also met another people called to be the conscience of a God-less society, a society which has attempted to strip itself of every vestige of religion. These are the Christians of East Berlin. Most of the young people here have grown up under Communism. They have attended Communist schools, belonged to Communist youth organizations, and been trained for Communist jobs, but they still maintain their faith in God and continue to practice their faith, even though it may cause them a great deal of conflict with the authorities. In spite of all efforts of a Communist government in East Germany, the Church continues to flourish. This has caused a great deal of concern in the Communist hierarchy, but finally even they are beginning to relent and to appropriate funds for the building and repair of churches.[17]

This heightened interest in the faith behind the so-called Iron Curtain and in East Germany could not have been more meaningful for King, for it reminded him of the prophetic, crusading zeal of the early church and also of the need for new and more creative models of mission on the part of the American churches. In a strange way, this mounting devotion to Christianity in Russia and East Germany also testified to the impact of King's own moral leadership on the church universal. In any case, the civil rights leader was convinced that American missionaries had much to learn from people who remained devoted to the Christian faith despite the kind of abuses they suffered under communist rule.

But King did not feel that organized Christian missions should be the primary focus in his country's relationship to other lands. He never displayed a lot of interest in overseas missions as understood in the Western world, and he, unlike Billy Graham and so many others, never summoned the American churches to assume a leadership role in the Christianization of the world. To be sure, King's distrust of missionary efforts grew out of a skepticism about the appropriateness of white Americans conveying the Christian gospel to the darker segments of humanity, whom they had long abused and exploited. Like Gandhi, King knew that so much of missionary Christianity was also imperial Christianity, and that foreign missionary efforts too often amounted to merely cultural imperialism. He was especially critical of those white Christians who talked glibly about what the church must do to reach the world and who, acting on questionable motives, poured their resources into missionary work on the African continent:

> Think of the millions of dollars raised by many of the white churches
> in the South and all over America sent to Africa for the missionary
> effort because of a humanitarian love. And yet if the Africans who got
> that money came into their churches to worship on Sunday morning
> they would kick them out. They love humanity in general, but they
> don't love Africans in particular. There is always this danger in
> humanitarian love—that it will not quite get there.[18]

King's strongest critique was aimed at the Southern Baptists, who viewed the church as exclusively a soul-saving headquarters, who were more concerned about pious superficiality and cliché-ridden moralisms than about justice and humanity, and whose enthusiasm for world missions existed in the most bellicose form. For King, the very idea of the Southern Baptists constituting a missional church engaged in planting congregations throughout the globe was alarming, especially in view of their segregated practices. In 1967, he offered a specific example of how the missionary function of the Southern Baptist Convention was mired in white supremacy:

> Now it's denominational, and a lot of money. . . . They send millions
> of dollars to Africa for the cause of missions. But do you know, an
> African student was studying at Mercer University in Georgia, and
> the First Baptist Church, white, of Macon, Georgia, where Mercer
> University is located, sponsored and gave him a scholarship to
> Mercer. And the young man, when he got here, decided that he
> wanted to go to that church, and he wanted to sing in the choir. The
> pastor was for it, the assistant pastor, the choir director, but do you
> know the members of that church refused to allow him to sing in the
> choir, and they voted the preacher, the assistant pastor, and the choir
> director out because they wanted him to sing in the choir. And
> if a Negro went in many of those churches today, he would be
> kicked out.[19]

In King's mind, the incident with the African student from Mercer University brought into sharp focus the fragilities of the kind of missionary Christianity that Southern Baptists had sought to advance worldwide for more than a century. In other words, it was a clear indication of how white Christians not only engaged in a half-hearted Christianity but also how they bowed to roles assigned by the ecclesiastical status quo and the surrounding cultural milieu, thus undermining their own moral authority abroad. Clearly, King had a different view of what it meant to follow Christ and to be his body in the world. He opted for a more globally responsible image of and vision for the church.[20]

King advanced certain ideas about how the foreign missionary enterprise of the American churches could become more credible and perhaps more consistent with the mandate of the Great Commission. He alluded to the need for white Christians to be more intentional in terms of identifying and empathizing with those peoples of color in various lands who were the focus of their missionary outreach. "The missionary movement would be better off if the missionary sat where the natives sat," King observed, as he reflected on the efforts to convert peoples in Africa and India to Christianity.[21] He also called upon the churches to redirect their missionary zeal inwardly, and especially among white Americans themselves, many of whom had a long history of worshiping the church while rejecting the Lord of the church:

> All that I am saying leads to this—along with our work on the foreign
> field we must begin to do missionary work right here. Each of us
> must do this. And we must begin with the white man. He is pagan in
> his conceptions. What is more pagan than. . . . Milan and Bryant are
> church members. The paradox of it all is that the white man
> considers himself the supreme missionary. He sends millions of

dollars to the foreign field. And in the midst of that he tramples over the Negro. . . . No wonder Mahatma Gandhi said to someone that the greatest enemy that Christ has in India is Christianity.[22]

King believed that it was only natural and right for the American churches to share what he termed "the principles of Christ"[23] with other nations and peoples, but he did not embrace the idea of the exclusivity of salvation based on Christianity. He lamented the fact that foreign mission efforts were typically rooted in the dogmatic claim that Christians alone are the bearers of truth and that an eternal hell awaited all who rejected conversion to their point of view. This is why King was never comfortable with the missionary ethos of Western Christianity. In his estimation, such an ethos was both false and dangerous, especially in a world of religious pluralism and competing ideologies.[24]

The concept of foreign missions as proselytism, especially as understood by groups like the Southern Baptists, appeared to King to be a narrow sectarianism and a kind of religious bigotry and intolerance that no moral and rational person could accept. In other words, proselytism in these terms was essentially no different from the advancement of an ethic of white supremacy throughout the globe. King had absolutely no interest in parading as a soul-saving evangelist, in proselytism as a means of revitalizing a declining institutional Christianity, or in the expansion of a global church infrastructure. In letters he exchanged with leaders from various faith traditions, he clearly separated himself from those fundamentalist and evangelical Christians who understood the call "to go and make disciples" as a mandate to challenge the legitimacy of other world religions and cultures.[25]

Strangely enough, King functioned in a black church culture in which many not only accepted uncritically the Western stereotypes of the so-called non-Western and non-Christian religions, cultures, and societies but also shared Western Christianity's sense of missionary urgency and compassion. Even in the National Baptist Convention, USA (NBC), of which King was a part for much of his life, there were pastors and congregations that supported foreign missions as a way of fulfilling the mandate of the Great Commission. Despite feelings of identification with peoples in the so-called Third World, who also suffered on grounds of race and economics, some in the black churches became willing partners with white American churches in the spread of imperial Christianity in Africa, Asia, and other foreign lands.[26] Always guided by prudence and a sense of pragmatism, King never made an issue of the expansionist missionary sentiment and activities supported by certain Negro churches, because he knew that this resulted largely from an acculturation and socialization process that could in time be reversed. With this in mind, he desperately sought to encourage alternative ways of viewing the Negro church's relationship to the world. Seeing no need to reorient his own perception of the church and how it might best witness to the world, King drew a sharp distinction between foreign missions as proselytizing ventures and foreign missions as service to humanity. It was the latter that he sought to encourage in American church circles, and most especially in Negro churches.

King called upon the Negro churches in America to become a force not in the Christianization of the world but, rather, in its humanization. It was in this connection that he lifted the image of the Negro church as a messianic community and instrument. From the very beginning of the Montgomery bus boycott in 1955, King raised the possibility that the Negro church would become "God's instrument" for the actualization of a higher human and ethical ideal. Quoting from Arnold Toynbee's A Study of History (1946), King held that "This is a great hour for the Negro [to] become the instruments of a great idea," or "to give the new spiritual dynamic to Western civilization that it so desperately needs to survive":

> I hope this is possible. The spiritual power that the Negro can
> radiate to the world comes from love, understanding, goodwill, and
> nonviolence. It may even be possible for the Negro, through
> adherence to nonviolence, so to challenge the nations of the world
> that they will seriously seek an alternative to war and destruction. In
> a day when Sputniks and Explorers dash through outer space and
> guided ballistic missiles are carving highways of death through the
> stratosphere, nobody can win a war. Today the choice is no longer
> between violence and nonviolence. It is either nonviolence or
> nonexistence. The Negro may be God's appeal to this age—an age
> drifting rapidly to its doom.[27]

King later made the same point more confidently, noting that "I am now convinced that if the Negro holds fast to the spirit of nonviolence, our struggle and example will challenge and help redeem not only America but the world."[28] It was thus apparent that whenever King considered how the Negro church might effectively do witness and mission in an international context, a range of images, aside from that of the messianic community and instrument, surfaced in his mind, chief among which were the black church as the chosen people of God, as suffering servant, as creative minority, as redemptive community, as a symbol of hope, and as a fragmentary but reliable pointer to the promised land.

Significantly, King's view of the spiritual and moral power of the Negro church as God's gift to all humanity was strengthened as he traveled and spoke

in different parts of the world, where his people's "tenacious struggle and sacrifices had won the admiration of all freedom-loving people."[29] In Germany in
1964, the enthusiastic crowds that appeared to hear King speak at the "largest
cathedrals in Berlin" were so enormous that the civil rights leader would later
make the following report as he visited Negro churches: "These people were
not there just to hear me speak. They were there to hear me tell your story. This
interest confirms my belief that the Negro is now in a position to lead the world.
As the Negro goes, so goes the world. We are the conscience of the Western
World. We represent the problems of democracy, not just the problems of the
Negro."[30]

In setting forth his vision of the Negro church as a humanizing force in the
world, King was standing in a tradition as old as David Walker and as recent as
W. E. B. DuBois. He was actually echoing DuBois's claim that "Negro blood has
a message for the world": that black people's experience of oppression in America, and the creative insights they brought to their interpretations of that experience, could be instructive for the whole of humankind.[31] In a real sense, King
could not have been more perceptive, especially since black Americans, through
art, spiritual values, and the movement itself, were already having perhaps a
greater impact on the world than any other single group of people in Western
society.[32]

For King, added proof of this came in 1964 when he received the Nobel
Peace Prize, an award that, in his own thinking, meant that the Negro struggle
had achieved world recognition and approval. King used the occasion to reflect
on the ways in which black Christians had transformed their suffering into a
creative and redemptive force for the benefit of all humanity. "Peace in this
nation and in the world is due in large measure to the willingness of Negro
Americans to suffer injustice and persecution, and their ability to respond
to their oppressors with love," King averred. "This may be the most significant
fact in the world today," he concluded, "that God has entrusted his black
children in America to teach the world to love, and to live together in brotherhood."[33]

The Nobel Prize was for King "a more profound recognition that the nonviolent way, the American Negro's way, is the answer to the crucial political and
moral questions of our time; the need for man to overcome oppression and
violence without resorting to violence and oppression."[34] He marveled at how
"my people in the agonizing struggles of recent years have taken suffering
upon themselves instead of inflicting it on others." As far as King was concerned, "many guns are muzzled and whips are useless, chiefly because the
Negro's creative use of nonviolence has made them arms of dubious value."[35]
The lessons gained from the church-centered Negro struggle, King continued,

had shown that "the philosophy and strategy of nonviolence" should "become immediately a subject for study and serious experimentation in every field of human conflict, including relations between nations." King acknowledged that he was being highly idealistic, but also deeply pragmatic: "This is not, I believe, an unrealistic suggestion. World peace through nonviolent means is neither absurd nor unattainable. All other methods have failed. Thus we must begin anew. Nonviolence is a good starting point."[36]

The very thought of black Americans collaborating with the white Western world in the kind of missionary outreach that ignored or reinforced the subjugation and oppression of peoples of color abroad was literally nauseating for King, especially in view of his sense of the messianic role of the Negro church. He said as much and more in 1967, as he assessed the price his people had to pay to ensure strong moral leadership in the world. Leadership of this kind, King maintained, had to categorically reject any missionary ethos rooted in cultural biases and in the temptation to do violence to other peoples and cultures. "I do feel that the Negro people, because of their peculiar experiences with oppression through the use of physical violence," King wrote, "have a particular responsibility to not participate in inflicting oppressive violence on another people." "This is not a privilege but an exceptional moral responsibility," he added, "the weight of which is far from a happy burden."[37] As King saw it, the Negro, in his proper role as missionary on the world stage, could serve best by using his many moral, spiritual, and material resources to help free those tormented most by the subversive impact of racism, colonialism, and neo-colonialism. He was convinced that "The hard cold facts today indicate that the hope of the people of color in the world may well rest on the American Negro and his ability to reform the structure of racist imperialism from within and thereby turn the technology and wealth of the West to the task of liberating the world from want."[38]

While often disappointed and frustrated, King never abandoned the hope that the American churches would be instrumental in bringing about "a new world order" or what he, in theological terms, envisioned as "the Kingdom of God on earth."[39] Clearly, he believed that the Negro church was better suited than the white church to assume a vanguard role in the ongoing struggle to enlarge the reach of the human endeavor, but he also understood that the sacrifices and contributions of both institutions were essential to the creation of a world free of bigotry, intolerance, and oppression. Success in this regard could occur, King felt, only if the white church as a whole abandoned concepts of mission that arrogantly asserted the need to Christianize and civilize peoples in foreign lands, and especially in non-Western cultures. Put another way, white Christians had to transform themselves before becoming a key element in the transformation of the world. King hoped that the white church would, as part of an effort to fulfill this need, seek to reach the world through positive and creative means, and especially by taking to the streets and giving practical lessons in the power of the Christian ethic and of inclusive, participatory democracy.[40] But King knew that this was easier said than done. As far as he could determine, instilling within the white church an ethic of service to the global community would be most difficult, for too many of its constituents had a tragically limited worldview and a distorted sense of mission, to say nothing of its long history of being on the wrong side of world revolutions.

Even so, King constantly reminded the churches in the United States that great advances in science and technology meant that the problems of the world had become America's problems and that traditional approaches to mission had become anachronistic. In other words, he realized that what was occurring on the small canvas of America had ramifications in an ethical dimension for the church and humanity everywhere. Consequently, as outwardly religious as America continued to appear, King thought, its churches could not justifiably continue to pursue evangelism and soul-winning missions while resisting the burden of true moral leadership, especially considering the sheer magnitude of both the human condition and their spiritual and material resources. King also saw that, in a much broader sense, this burden of moral leadership ultimately rested with the church universal. To be sure, the civil rights leader was enormously important in bringing the church to a greater sense of the world as the locus of its mission, and to the idea of mission as not so much saving souls but saving humanity.[41] His tendency to equate missionary activity at its best with strategies for human uplift and empowerment proved to be one of his most original and creative contributions to the definition of the church.

Toward World Liberation and Community: A Challenge for the Church Universal

Martin Luther King, Jr., learned a lot about Christian churches in different nations as he traveled the world and studied the vast landscape of humanity. While he had much to say about churches abroad that was commendable, he also came to see that they shared a great deal with the American churches when it came to the question of their relationship to culture and the status quo. This could not have been more evident to King than in 1957, when he went to London and stood before the structures of ecclesiastical power in the Church of England, a body that had absolutely refused to condemn the British Empire's occupation and domination of much of Australia, Canada, China, Africa, and India:

> Then I remember, we went on over to Westminster Abbey. And I thought about several things when we went into this great church, this great cathedral, the center of the Church of England. We walked around and went to the tombs of kings and queens buried there. Most of the kings and queens of England are buried right there in Westminster Abbey. And I walked around. On the one hand I enjoyed and appreciated the great gothic architecture of that massive cathedral. I stood there in awe thinking about the greatness of God and man's feeble attempt to reach up to God. . . . All of these things came to my mind, when I stood there in Westminster Abbey with all of its beauty, and I thought about all of the beautiful hymns and anthems that the people would go in there to sing. And yet the Church of England never took a stand against this system. The Church of England sanctioned it. The Church of England gave it moral stature. All of the exploitation perpetuated by the British Empire was sanctioned by the Church of England.[42]

King pointed to yet another form of this kind of distorted and misguided discipleship, offering some sense of how he viewed the function of the church in Eastern Europe. He noted how the Greek Church in Russia had virtually lost "its power and its soul," in part because it "allied itself with the status quo," becoming "so inextricably bound to the despotic czarist regime that it became impossible to be rid of the corrupt political and social system without being rid of the church." King went on to explain that "Such is the fate of every ecclesiastical organization that allies itself with things-as-they-are."[43]

Owing in part to a deep distrust for the status quo church and the image it projected to the world, King preferred the American principle of the separation of church and state over the state-church tradition so prevalent in England and much of Europe. He lamented the very thought of a state church, of a partnership between the church and the status quo, or of the intrusion of government into church affairs. But King must have found it interesting, and certainly disturbing, that despite the constitutional arrangement of church-state separation in the United States, the American churches were as apt to become tools or servants of the state as the churches anywhere else in the world. This had been demonstrated throughout American history, and certainly in King's experiences with churches in the context of the civil rights movement.[44]

In his own times, King repeatedly spoke in the most critical terms about the alliance between the Dutch Reformed Protestant Church and the racist government of the Union of South Africa. Here, he saw what he considered to be "The classic example of organized and institutionalized racism," a system in which "14 million black men and women, boys, and girls" were "segregated on two percent of their land," having "to use passes to walk the streets." Such "vicious, inhuman apartheid practices are sanctioned, and to a large extent, set up by the Dutch Reformed Protestant Church," King reported. "Over and over again Chief Luthuli, that great black leading Christian, has knocked on the door of the church of South Africa," he added, "but the response has been, 'Get away from this door. We don't have time to bother with you. We're busy reciting our creedal system.'"[45]

Noting that the Dutch Reformed Protestant Church was more concerned about converted souls than with saving or liberating people, King declared in 1967: "Do you know that if you go to South Africa today the churches are full?" And, further on, King chided the church for collaborating with the state in subduing those black South Africans who dared to take a stand for justice:

> And even if they rise up to protest against the oppressions that they face, they are shot down. Their leaders are placed in jail without a trial; some have been in for life. A Christian like Chief Luthuli is a house prisoner, can't even go out to address a meeting. Stay around there long enough and you will discover that the whole segregated system of South Africa came into being with the sanction of the Protestant Church. Daniel Malone, one of the great leaders that brought apartheid into being, was a Dutch Reformed Protestant preacher. He worshipped Christ emotionally, but not morally.[46]

King often spoke of the Dutch Reformed Protestant Church in South Africa, the Church of England in India, and the Southern Baptist Convention in the United States in the same vein, highlighting the inconsistencies and ethical problems that attended their definitions of the body of Christ.[47] Always mindful of how oppression in one nation reinforced oppression elsewhere, King saw the problems in these various contexts not as entirely separate and different from each other but, rather, as manifestations of the same structure of evil. This sense of the broader dynamics of the human struggle was, as he viewed it, something that the church had to grasp before Christianity could become an effective instrument for humanizing the world.

In March 1957, while still involved in the struggle in Montgomery, King took his first major trip abroad, appearing at the independence celebration of Ghana at the invitation of Prime Minister Kwame Nkrumah. There, King met with Michael Scott, an Anglican priest who had worked with unwanted lepers in South Africa, "who symbolized in the past decade the best of the church working for justice against colonialism" and who shared King's nonviolent philosophy. King and Scott began a dialogue on how the church might best fulfill its moral obligation in addressing world problems, particularly as they related to issues like racism and colonialism and their impact on Africa.[48] That dialogue continued over time as the two men explored ways of forging a coalition of conscience within the universal church, and also of isolating and ultimately dismantling South Africa's apartheid regime.[49] As King saw it, Scott was a courageous and empowering voice for the outcast and unheard in the world, a role that was not to be trivialized, especially since "Millions of Africans, patiently knocking on the door of the Christian church where they seek the bread of social justice, have either been altogether ignored or told to wait until later, which almost always means never." In 1959, King stated that "While Christianity has been timid in too much of Africa, I am glad that Michael Scott—a clergyman—for more than a decade has represented the Herero people of South West Africa when South Africa refused to allow their representatives to appear before the U.N."[50]

In July 1957, almost four months after the meeting with Scott in Ghana, King met at the Community Church in New York with Ambrose Reeves, the Anglican bishop of Johannesburg, South Africa. Again, the discussion turned specifically to South African apartheid, and more generally to racism as a global phenomenon. Reeves, who had "defied his Government's new legislation ordering segregation in Church attendance," stressed the "tremendous role of the churches 'in improving race relations,'" a view King embraced wholeheartedly. The two leaders also discussed "the similarities in the racial problems and tensions in their respective countries," and noted that "Our duty is to keep life on a nonviolent road if we can possibly do it."[51] Apparently, King and Reeves were determined to advance the struggles against Jim Crow and apartheid into the world spotlight. At the same time, they hoped that the church would develop alternative ways of viewing the world and the human condition, that it would eradicate racism from its own ranks, and that it would be a mediating force between the races in both the United States and South Africa. The meeting with Reeves, as with Scott earlier, could not have been more significant for King, for no one was more interested than he in the question of the Negro church's relationship to African Christians, and in placing the civil rights movement in the larger context of the church universal and of international relations.

King's involvement with the worldwide Declaration of Conscience in 1957, which advocated condemnation of South African apartheid, afforded the opportunity for him to act on his conviction that the problems of the world demanded unified action on the part of the church universal. The Declaration was cosponsored by King, Eleanor Roosevelt, and the Episcopal Bishop James A. Pike, under the auspices of the American Committee on Africa (ACOA). King saw the Declaration, which was signed by more than a hundred world leaders, many of whom were church leaders and theologians, as an important step in the advancement of the image of the church as a universal coalition of conscience. Many of the signatories of the Declaration, such as Michael Scott, Ambrose Reeves, and Reinhold Niebuhr, were clergymen and theologians who shared King's vision of a global church that spoke with a united voice in promoting both civil and human rights.[52]

Support for the Declaration also came from the Episcopal bishop of West Virginia and from groups such as the Young Men's Christian Association of Colombo (Ceylon), the Olympia (Washington) Council of Churches, the Council of Churches of Greater Kansas City, and the Christian Council of Nigeria.[53] King received a check and an interesting letter from a member of the Norwegian Lutheran Church, who reported that, "due to disagreement with the dogmas I left the church many years ago, and had not been inside one for many years until I heard you in the Wentworth Lutheran Church in Chicago, Illinois, some two years ago."[54] King's national and international profile rose rapidly as Christian activists around the world were inspired by his vision for the church, and by his efforts to make the church relevant to the struggles of the abused and marginalized in all corners of the earth. As responses to the Declaration began to subside, King reminded the Christian church once again of its responsibility to the international community. "The church," said he, "should teach a worldview, make it clear that racial segregation is morally evil, expose the roots of segregation in thought and life, open channels of communication between races, develop better programs for racial justice and other social causes, and remove the yoke of segregation from its own body."[55] In other words, King set forth essentially the same agenda for both the American churches and the church universal.

Evidently, King never subscribed to the notion that the churches in America had everything to teach and nothing to learn from churches in other parts of the world. While in England in 1964, he was part of a conversation on this very subject, and it was decided that "Baptists the world over" were in a position to "encourage the Southern Baptist Convention" in the United States "to come out on the side of integration and condemn segregation both in word and practice."[56] Here, the portrait of the church as Good Samaritan was evoked as King and others struggled with what it meant to, in the spirit of Christ, bear the cross for the redemption of the world. It is no exaggeration to claim that King was among that small and unique cadre of church leaders who brought a new dimension to human rights discourse in global Christianity in the 1950s and 1960s.

The American Committee on Africa's Appeal for Action Against Apartheid, initiated in 1962, was yet another effort that united King in spirit and outlook with Christians throughout the world. The initial sponsors of this worldwide Appeal were King and the black South African Albert John Luthuli, who was also the Zulu chief, the president-general of the African National Congress (ANC), a Methodist lay preacher, and a 1960 Nobel Peace Prize recipient.[57] The Appeal, which was "in the nature of a follow-up on" the ACOA's "1957 Declaration of Conscience," urged churches, unions, clubs, lodges, and heads of governments to not only designate December 10, 1962, as a day of protest against South Africa's apartheid system but to also support economic sanctions against the South African government, to push for the "international isolation of South Africa," and to avoid trading and investing in that country.[58] Some twenty church and/or religious leaders from various countries signed the Appeal, among whom were Michael Scott, Bishop Ambrose Reeves, theologians Paul Tillich and Reinhold Niebuhr, Harry Emerson Fosdick of New York's monumental Riverside Church, Martin Niemoller of the Evangelical Church in Germany, and Bishop Trevor Huddleston of Tanganyika.[59] Though separated by geography and culture, these figures were united with King and Luthuli by their sense of the church as a worldwide coalition of conscience and, more specifically, by their belief that the church and religion had to be a force in overcoming apartheid and establishing human community.

King regarded this campaign as one among many hopeful signs that the church universal was beginning to speak louder and more forthrightly on issues that mattered most to the international community. He rejoiced in the fact that Catholics the world over were expressing a growing concern for social-justice issues, and he actually met with a group of American bishops at the Ecumenical Council in Rome in 1964 to talk about the global impact of racial injustice.[60] After visiting the Vatican, King wrote approvingly about how the pope, as "one so endowed with influence and moral power," voiced unwavering support for what he often called "my humble attempt to bring the clear insight of our Christian faith to bear on the difficult problem of racial injustice in our nation and the world."[61]

King was equally touched by the increasing support of the World Council of Churches (WCC), an ecumenical body that he, as early as 1957, had predicted would "hound every Christian layman everywhere with a nagging conscience."[62] The WCC's advocacy of racial justice and inclusiveness would reach its greatest expression as King and other activists throughout the globe were occasionally invited to address the body. Although King never found the time to honor such invitations, a recording of one of his sermons, played before the delegates at the WCC meeting in Geneva in 1966, received an "excellent and effective" reception.

Although the civil rights leader always appreciated the interest that the WCC had in him as a figure of universal reach and resonance, he attached far more importance to the willingness of that body to consistently raise its voice in the interest of freedom, justice, and human dignity.[63]

Having a growing sensitivity to the world's injustices and imbalances, King maintained that the Christian church should devote more attention to the larger global dynamics that figured into the "perennial allies"[64] of racism and economic injustice. In his *Trumpet of Conscience* (1967), one of his last books, he "saw the next step as a global nonviolent movement using escalating acts of massive civil disobedience to disrupt the entire international order and block economic and political exploitation across borders."[65] In this continuing, global march toward freedom, King insisted on the active engagement of the church in a sustained effort to eradicate world poverty. He held that it was morally inconsistent to worship the biblical God and remain unconcerned with the ravaging and debilitating effects of a globalized capitalism, which left millions in "lands and villages all over the world" poverty-stricken or "undernourished, ill-housed and shabbily clad."[66]

While devoted to the poor generally, King expressed a special concern for nations in Africa,[67] Asia, and Latin America, which evoked scenes of unimaginable suffering. He urged the church to become "a fountainhead of a better social order,"[68] declaring that, as one of the world's richest institutions, it had the resources "to help the discouraged beggar on life's highway and in life's marketplace," and also to begin to change the economic structures and behaviors in this fragile world. But having the resources, King argued, meant nothing if there was a deficit in the human will.[69] Even so, King believed that the failure of the church to effectively address such concerns over time would completely stymie its mission to the world. This stress on the church's responsibility toward the poor was part of King's "call for a worldwide fellowship that lifts neighborly concern beyond one's tribe, race, class, and nation" to "an all-embracing and unconditional love for all men."[70]

As King saw it, the ways in which India and the Scandinavian countries responded to "the least of these" could be instructive for the church and humanity as a whole, a recognition that was especially challenging for the United States, a nation that claimed to be the moral leader of the world and that drew so much of its power and influence from its global economic strength and the export of its own ideas. Noting that the Indian government had made "the discrimination of untouchability" a "violation of the law" and "punishable by imprisonment," and that it had upheld "the view that there is a deep ethical responsibility of the whole people toward the untouchables," King went on to observe: "I submit to you that while India may have to learn much in technology from us, we can learn much of moral attitude from her."[71] During a visit to Sweden in 1964, King, alluding to the need to eliminate oppressive economic structures altogether, struck a similar note: "We feel we have much to learn from Scandinavia's democratic socialist traditions, and especially from the manner in which you have overcome so many of the problems of poverty, housing, unemployment, and medical care"—problems that "still plague far more powerful and affluent nations."[72] Such acknowledgments on King's part could not have been more meaningful, especially considering his efforts to convince the Christian church that the capitalistic ethic, in which it fully participated, was antithetical to the gospel mandate regarding the poor and outcast.

King had reason to believe that the church could become a major asset and indeed an indispensable vehicle in the global war on poverty and economic injustice. While entering Norway in 1964, he "was greatly encouraged" to hear of "Pope Paul VI's powerful message on poverty issued after his visit to India, where he witnessed poverty in its most abject form." "In his plea for a 'peaceful battle'," said King, the pontiff "called upon nations to cease the armament race and devote their resources and energies to assisting those throughout the world who lack food, clothing, shelter and medical care." King cast a special spotlight on the pope's remarks, knowing that he represented millions of Christians worldwide, and he insisted that "We must implement this plea here in the United States, where the budget for the war on poverty is less than one percent of the military budget."[73]

There were other encouraging signs from Eugene Carson Blake and other leading figures in the World Council of Churches, who offered to join King's campaign against poverty and slum conditions in Chicago in 1966. In a letter to King, Blake and others in the WCC spoke of the tensions "between rich and poor, between East and West," and "between developing and developed nations" as issues to be seriously considered as they wrestled "on a global scale with the task of Christians in a revolutionary age." They went on to assure King that "We are eager to learn from the work of the civil rights movement in Chicago, for many countries are struggling with similar problems."[74] Such expressions of support and encouragement were most inspiring to King as he prepared to confront the issue of poverty and economic injustice with greater force in 1967–1968, particularly in terms of his involvement with the Poor People's Campaign and with sanitation workers in Memphis, Tennessee.

Convinced of the interconnectedness of economic-justice concerns and issues of war and peace, King was no less concerned about how the church universal might offer new and different paradigms for ministry and mission in an increasingly hostile and violent world.[75] The WCC and other global church agencies, he concluded, were the ideal settings in which to explore and resolve ethical questions concerning war, a problem on which King's heart and mind spoke with one voice. While viewing the United Nations (U.N.) as "a gesture in the direction of nonviolence on a world scale," this, as far as King was concerned, in no way released the church from its role as a universal voice and agent of peace. Against the escalating danger and lure of nuclear warfare and catastrophe, King admonished the church to assume a legitimate and enduring role in the shift from "the arms race" to "the peace race."[76] Actually, the globalization of the agape love ethic is what he had in mind, or, in more pragmatic terms, the application of "the Gandhian method of nonviolent direct action" in "international affairs."[77]

Two major developments significantly impacted King's perspective on the peace-making role and potential of the church in an international context. One was his reception of the Nobel Peace Prize in 1964, an honor that intensified his stance on and concern for world problems.[78] The other was the United States' involvement in the Vietnam War, which King viewed as ill-advised, senseless, and unjust.[79] King held that Vietnam signaled the need for churches to recapture the radical spirit of the Sermon on the Mount and to become truly a global power in extricating the nation "from this nightmarish conflict," and in moving the world along the trajectory of peace and community. "Meanwhile we in the churches and synagogues have a continuing task as we urge our government to disengage itself from a disgraceful commitment," King maintained.[80]

This sense of urgency could not have been greater for the church as a whole, King thought, especially since his country had "cooperated in the" slaughter of women and children, and also in "the crushing of" the "unified Buddhist church," Vietnam's "only non-Communist revolutionary political force." Convinced that those who remained silent on Vietnam were guilty, at the very least, of contributory negligence, King encouraged "all ministers of draft age to give up their ministerial exemptions and seek status as conscientious objectors."[81] By taking a stand on the unpopular side of the Vietnam conflict, King showed that he was more concerned about the church's functioning as a force for world peace than he was about maintaining a certain character profile in the media and in the powerful circles of government.[82]

King delighted in the fact that there were increasing numbers in the church universal in the 1960s who publicly opposed the Vietnam War and who shared his vision of a world in which human life is not maimed and destroyed, but protected, nurtured, and sustained. In 1964, he eagerly reported that "The World Council of Churches has made it very clear through recent proclamations and resolutions that war is immoral and that some alternative to it must be found." "The same thing is true of the Roman Catholic Church and other religious bodies," he added.[83] In 1966, King pointed out that Pope Paul VI had "come out in very vocal and forthright terms," calling "for the recognition of Red China in order to ease tensions in Southeast Asia, calling for the cessation of the bombings in the north, and other things that are vitally necessary I think to bring about peace in that very turbulent situation." "The pope revealed again that we must beat our swords into plowshares and spears into pruning hooks," said King on another occasion.[84] In 1967, King was pleased to announce "the largest coalition of religious, civic and public leaders so far organized in protest against U.S. escalation in Vietnam."[85] As far as he could surmise, the primacy of peace over war and human destruction was being vindicated, largely because of prophetic voices in the worldwide church.

As previously indicated, King never separated the mission of the church in the black American community from the mission of the church worldwide. For him, that mission was essentially one and the same, especially since, as he put it, "race is not the only issue which confronts our world and Negroes are not the only Christians who are in need of justice."[86] As one who truly understood the interconnections between systems of oppression and injustice worldwide, King challenged the church to embrace a liberation model in which neither the oppressed nor the oppressor could be redeemed without each other. His sense of "the interrelated structure of reality" clearly grounded his belief that "Equality with whites" in America would "not solve the problems of either whites or Negroes if it" meant "equality in a world stricken by poverty and in a universe doomed to extinction by war."[87]

King's globally responsible ethic of community meant that the Christian church had to be as committed to the problems of the world's white people as it was to peoples of color. This is why he appealed to "the same world opinion" that condemned South Africa's treatment of black Christians to also keep "the communists from running over Christians behind the iron curtain."[88] In 1964, while speaking in Berlin, King admonished the church to break down the walls between East and West Germany, proclaiming that "on either side of the wall are God's children and no man-made barrier can obliterate that fact."[89] Before the European Baptist Assembly in Amsterdam, Holland, in 1964, and during his European tour in 1966, King reiterated his conviction that the barriers that separated European Christians should be quickly and permanently eliminated.[90] Here, he left no doubt about his perception of the role of the church within the broader cultures of East and West.

There is some question about whether or not King considered a globalized beloved community achievable in human history, for he never abandoned the Niebuhrian idea of the depth and prevalence of sin at all levels of human existence.[91] However, what may be more important was King's belief that the beloved community should remain a regulative ideal for both the church and the world. Instead of impeding the pilgrimage toward authentic human community, then, both, King explained, had an obligation to push toward new horizons of understanding, goodwill, and cooperation. He really believed that the church and the world could be true to themselves while responsibly engaging each other around issues of unity and diversity. Out of this kind of collaboration, King felt, personal dignity and a humanizing solidarity would flourish.

King concluded that the world would not be won for Christ through traditional expressions of missionary Christianity. As stated previously, a healthier alternative for him was practical or applied Christianity, which, in his estimation, offered better possibilities for the kind of globalized and humanitarian world that he envisioned in his metaphorical use of "the world house."[92] His belief in the moral universe and his expectation of an utter reversal in the world's socioeconomic and political order not only underscored the radicalism of his vision but also shed light on both the appeal of his message to the world's outcast and the threat he posed to established ecclesiastical and political elites.

In Search of a Positive Pluralism: The Church, Other World Religions, and Inter-religious Dialogue

The following questions should figure into any discussion of Martin Luther King, Jr.'s thoughts on how the church might view and relate to the other great world religions: What are the major points of conflict between the Christian church and other great faiths, and how can they be resolved? What values and traditions do the church share with the other major world religions, and how might these serve as a basis for inter-religious dialogue and cooperation? What can the church give to Judaism, Islam, Buddhism, Hinduism, and other faith traditions, and what can it learn and receive from those traditions? What is inter-religious dialogue, and what form should it take in the contemporary world? King approached such questions with an open, analytical, and critical mind, always mindful that the peaceful coexistence of the world's religions required not mutual toleration but equal and innate respect.

Three points must be established at the outset in treating King's attitude toward religious diversity and/or pluralism. First, he categorically rejected the claim, made in churches internationally, that Christianity constitutes the only path to truth, and he affirmed that more truth inheres in all the world's religions combined than in any one religion alone. Second, he insisted that for Christians, other religions embodied rich resources and opportunities for learning, especially in the realm of values. In other words, King was convinced that the church could be positively transformed by encounters with various religious traditions, despite the fact that there was not a strong resonance in the ecclesial community as a whole for this idea.[93] Finally, King encouraged the church to promote inter-religious or pan-religious dialogue as a matter of both conversation and cooperative, concrete action,[94] and also as a means of breaking down some of the greatest barriers to world peace and community. This could be accomplished in part, King felt, through spoken dialogue, the arts, shared religious observances, and other means. At the levels of both theory and praxis, King did much to advance the posture of the church as a catalyst for pan-religious dialogue and cooperation, and as a worldwide coalition of conscience.

Interestingly enough, King understood the entire history of the church largely in terms of its encounter with religious pluralism. "The Greco-Roman world in which the early church developed was one of diverse religions," he wrote, while still a student at Crozer Theological Seminary. And, further on, he stated: "The conditions of that era made it possible for these religions to sweep like a tidal wave over the ancient world. The people of that age were eager and zealous in their search for religious experience. The existence of this atmosphere was vitally important in the development and eventual triumph of Christianity."[95] King made essentially this same point in some of his academic papers at Boston University.[96] Undoubtedly, he was always receptive to the multi-religious character of the world, and he felt that religious diversity was a healthy and much-needed challenge to the church universal.

But this does not mean that King went as far as Mohandas K. Gandhi in embracing "the *Sarva dharma sambava*," or "the equality of all religions," especially during those early years.[97] While King's training at Crozer and Boston helped him see the profound and eternal truths in all the great world religions, he still had a tendency to attach more validity to Christianity as a source of divine revelation, a tendency that reflected the influence of his cultural upbringing and that also undermined any claim that he always rejected Western notions of the superiority of Christianity over other religions. While serving as pastor of the Dexter Avenue Church in Montgomery in 1958, King illustrated the point in his answer to a questioner, who wanted to know if "Christianity, as a religion, [is] more valid than the tribal religions practiced at one time by Africans":

> I believe that God reveals Himself in all religions. Wherever we find truth we find the revelation of God, and there is some element of truth in all religions. This does not mean, however, that God reveals Himself equally in all religions. Christianity is an expression of the highest revelation of God. It is the synthesis of the best in all

religions. In this sense Christianity is more valid than the tribal religions practiced by our African ancestors. This does not mean that these tribal religions are totally devoid of truth. It simply means that Christianity, while flowing through the stream of history, has incorporated the truths of all other religions and brought them together into a meaningful and coherent system. Moreover, at the center of Christianity stands the Christ who is now and ever shall be the highest revelation of God. He, more than any other person that has ever lived in history, reveals the true nature of God. Through his life, death, and resurrection the power of eternity broke forth into time.[98]

In a letter to the editor of *The Christian Century* in 1962, King reiterated the point, claiming, "God reveals himself more completely and uniquely in Christianity than in any other religion."[99] This attitude grounded King's perception of the church as "the voice of moral and spiritual authority on earth."[100] It invariably meant that the church at its best had a message to share with all religions about the need to pursue unequivocally the highest human and ethical ideals. Much of that message had to do with the dignity and worth of all human personality, a lesson King felt was particularly important in a world in which some religions marginalized and subordinated women. "One of the great contributions that Christianity has made to the world is that of lifting the status of womanhood from that of an insignificant child-bearer to a position of dignity and honor and respect," King maintained. "Women must be respected as human beings and not be treated as mere means."[101] While this statement reflected what might be viewed as a glaring insensitivity to patriarchal structures and sexism in the Christian church, it was equally evident of King's early tendency to distinguish Christianity from the other major religions of the world.

As he studied the ecclesiastical landscape through the prism of history, King must have questioned the capacity of the church worldwide to function comfortably in a multi-religious and multicultural world. But to those who questioned the church's significance as a possible force for good in a religiously diverse world, King offered a direct rejoinder:

Do you really believe in this thing called Christianity? Do you believe that herein lies the solution to the world's problems? Do you believe that Christianity has the power to give new meaning to life? Well, tell the world about it. Tell your colleagues about it, your workers, your fraternity brothers, your playmates. And don't be afraid to defend the Church where necessary. Certainly the Church is not perfect. It has often stood in the way of social and scientific progress, and . . . I am often ashamed of the Church, but in spite of its errors I would hate to see what the world would be like without it.[102]

Evidently, King's critique of the church was matched by a deep faith in its potential as a liberating and redemptive force in an international context. But the church for him amounted to one of many avenues to the kingdom of God on earth. Like L. Harold DeWolf, his former professor at Boston University, King bemoaned the self-righteous and narrow-minded view that the church equates with "the whole kingdom of God."[103] For him, nothing could have been more problematic in a world of competing faiths and values.

The tone of some of King's remarks about the power of Christianity in the context of a pluralistic world sometimes evoked expressions of concern from practitioners of other religions. Although generally respectful of King and his efforts, there were Muslims who resented his suggestion that the Christian ethic afforded the best path to the moral high ground in the struggle for a just and peaceful society and world. In 1961, when a member of the Jewish faith questioned King's comments about "America becoming a Christian nation," the civil rights leader was compelled to respond in the most apologetic fashion, while also repeating claims he always made when challenged on the issue of religious diversity:

> I was not referring to Christianity as an organized institutional religion. I was referring more to the principles of Christ, which I think are sound and valid for any nation and civilization. I have never been a victim of religious bigotry. I have never condemned any of the great religions of the world, for it is my sincere conviction that no religion has a monopoly on truth and that God has revealed Himself in all of the religions of mankind. So let me assure you that when I speak of America rising to the heights of a Democratic and Christian nation, I am referring to the need of rising to the heights of noble ethical and moral principles. I am sure that you are aware of the fact that many people, Christians and non-Christians, theists and humanists, have found within the Sermon on the Mount and other insights of Jesus Christ, great ethical principles that they can adhere to even though they would not accept institutionalized Christianity.[104]

"I am very sorry that you are so offended by the word *Christian*," said King in ending his reply. "Maybe it is due to the fact that we Christians have not always been Christian in our dealing with people of other religions, and sometimes in our dealings with people of our own religion."[105] Mindful of the history of anti-Semitism as both a racist movement and an expression of religious intolerance in the history of the Christian church, King never hesitated to denounce the tragic state of affairs that pitted "religions against religions."[106] He characterized anti-Semitism as "wrong" and as "immoral and self-destructive," and he challenged it in the black community and wherever else he found it.[107] King offered the following response to one black person who voiced his dislike for Jews, but expressed a desire to "overcome this feeling":

> It is very unfortunate that you dislike Jews. This is a problem which you need to solve immediately, because it is no different from the attitude that many whites have concerning the whole Negro race. In order to deal with this problem, you must get at the roots of your dislike for the Jews. Most hate is rooted in fear, ignorance and pride. You must be sure that all of these factors are removed from your personality where the Jews are concerned. The word prejudice means literally to prejudge, that is, to pass judgment before you have all of the facts. You have probably prejudged the Jewish community by an experience you had with one or more Jews or by some half-truths or distorted ideas that you have heard circulated concerning Jews. You can only remove this by knowing the truth and realizing that no one shortcoming can characterize a whole race. I would suggest that you seek real personal fellowship with Jews and you will discover that some of the finest persons in our nation are members of the Jewish community. Through this type of personal fellowship, you will come to know them and love them and thereby transcend the bounds of bigotry.[108]

For King, the story of the Good Samaritan in Luke 10:29–37 was meaningful and instructive for the church in its encounter not only with Judaism but other religions as well. According to King, the Samaritan who stopped to help a wounded Jew on the Jericho Road was a reminder of how Christians might "remove the cataracts of provincialism from our spiritual eyes" and look beyond "the eternal accidents of religion" to see people as people. "If the Samaritan had considered the wounded man as a Jew first, he would not have stopped," King wrote, "for the Jews and the Samaritans had no dealings. He saw him as a human being first, who was a Jew only by accident."[109] This sense of the church as Good Samaritan weighed heavily in King's thinking as he spoke of the need to engage different religious traditions experientially and cognitively. And this helps explain why he, as early as his student days at Boston University, stated approvingly that the doors of the Ebenezer Baptist Church in Atlanta, his home church, were "opened to peoples of all races, all nationalities, and all religious backgrounds."[110]

Religious bigotry and intolerance was at the core of some of King's conflicts with evangelical Christians in the United States. He encountered the problem in the early 1960s after participating in the formation of the Gandhi Society, an educational foundation designed to assist nonviolent activists in their quest for civil and human rights. Confused by King's involvement, editors from *The Christian Century* reported that he was abandoning the Christian faith for a new type of sectarianism. Needless to say, King was highly alarmed, and he chided the editors for what he termed "a narrow sectarianism and a degree of religious intolerance that cause me real concern." King went on to explain:

> I cannot make myself believe that God did not reveal himself in other religions. I believe that in some marvelous way, God worked through Gandhi, and the spirit of Jesus Christ saturated his life. It is ironic, yet inescapably true that the greatest Christian of the modern world was a man who never embraced Christianity. This is not an indictment on Christ but a tribute to Him—a tribute to his universality and His Lordship. When I think of Gandhi, I think of the Master's way in the words of the fourth gospel: "I have other sheep that are not of this fold."[111]

The church's intolerance toward truth in other religious traditions was for King the epitome of arrogance and self-righteousness, to say nothing of its tendency to demonize other religions. He outright rejected the notion that an appreciation for religious pluralism necessarily slighted the power and distinctiveness of Christianity, especially since, in his own mind, religious traditions were not to be viewed as neatly separate or mutually exclusive. King consistently condemned the ignorance and stereotypes that too often marred relationships between Christians and representatives of other faiths, and he admonished the church to learn from other religions and cultures so that it could see that its reality is not the only legitimate way of understanding God and the world.[112] This was one of many reasons white Christian conservatives were so inhospitable to King's version of the social gospel.

But King's thought on other major religions was not, as some fundamentalists and evangelicals might have suggested, devoid of an analytical and critical focus. In fact, he could be as critical of other religions as he was of Christianity, particularly if they lacked an emphasis on the social dimensions of life. In one of his earliest critiques of religion, King highlighted what he considered to be glaring weaknesses in Brahmanism, which embodied the religious beliefs and practices of ancient India as reflected in the Vedas:

Brahmanism has often been too tolerant. It has tolerated magic and
all manner of superstitions. Far from attempting to reform the cruel
social injustices of the caste system, it has found a moral justification
for them. The religion has founded no church; it has developed no
social activities; it has cared little to serve humanity. Salvation is to be
won by inner meditation by oneself. One is taught to conceive
himself in an intellectual manner to be identified with one's neighbor
and love him as oneself, but little motivation is afforded to incite one
to go actively to a neighbor's material assistance in any manner.[113]

Obviously, King did not go as far as those Christian fundamentalists who
equated other religions with primitivism or heathenism, and who suggested
that world salvation hinged on the spreading of the gospel and the subjugation,
if not elimination, of all rival faiths.[114] King never hesitated to refute such attitudes and ideas, always averring that the church had nothing to fear from other
world religions. As far as he was concerned, "Such great world religions as
Judaism, Buddhism, Hinduism, and Mohammedanism are possible alterna-
tives to Christianity, but no one conversant with the hard facts of the modern
world will deny that Communism is Christianity's most formidable rival."[115]

Although King did not discuss religious bigotry and intolerance as one of
the major barriers to world peace and community in his book, *Where Do We Go
from Here: Chaos or Community?* (1967), it is clear that the problem was antithetical to his idealization of what he called "the world house" or "the worldwide neighborhood." In the final chapter of that book, King employed these
metaphors in promoting his vision of a world in which all artificial human
barriers, including religion, would be transcended in the interest of understanding, goodwill, and cooperation between humans:

This is the great new problem of mankind. We have inherited a large
house, a great "world house" in which we have to live together—
black and white, Easterner and Westerner, Gentile and Jew, Catholic
and Protestant, Moslem and Hindu—a family unduly separated in
ideas, culture and interest, who, because we can never again live
apart, must learn somehow to live with each other in peace. . . . All
inhabitants of the globe are now neighbors. This worldwide
neighborhood has been brought into being largely as a result of the
modern scientific and technological revolutions.[116]

This sense of "the world house" or "the world-wide neighborhood" was at
the root of King's interest in and support for inter-religious dialogue. But unlike
many in the Christian church who advocated inter-religious dialogue, King

did not have in mind merely academic and ecclesiastical models of conversation or the sharing of ideas. For him, inter-religious dialogue at its best had to have some practical resonance, which means that its fullest and most authentic expression could occur only through cooperative, concrete action on the part of representatives of the different religions. In more specific terms, inter-religious dialogue for King had to involve a collective commitment to the alleviation of human suffering and the achievement of social justice.[117] He actually called for a new model of pan-religious dialogue grounded in Christian-Jewish-Muslim-Hindu-Buddhist solidarity against structures of exclusion and oppression.

King felt that the church had to do more in terms of transcending the sectarian and parochial boundaries within its own ranks before becoming an effective promoter of inter-religious or pan-religious dialogue. He was most familiar with the ways in which sectarian and denominational loyalties impeded the ecumenical witness of the church. Moreover, King had little patience with Christians who defined themselves as the true church and who denounced any ecclesiastical or religious model that differed from their own. Always concerned about the gospel and its implications for ecumenical and/or interfaith cooperation, he was unyielding in his insistence that the church should more actively pursue the goals of Christian unity and pan-religious understanding.[118] Here, he had in mind a revitalized church, a community aware not only of its theological commitments and ecumenical mission but of its pan-religious function and social responsibilities as well. Only in this manner, King held, could the work of transforming society and the world be more effectively achieved.

Perhaps more than any other church leader of his time, King "brought ecumenism into the public square" and proved instrumental in making the civil rights movement an expression of "vital ecumenical activity."[119] Under his leadership, the church became not only an ecumenical venture through which Protestants and Catholics affirmed their essential unity as the body of Christ but also a base from which to promote interfaith cooperation in the interest of freedom and justice.[120] In other words, King intersected Protestants, Catholics, and Jews in the movement, and he was open to contributions and influences from representatives of all major religions. Cooperative church and interfaith activism became his rallying cry, taking precedence over any creeds, labels, or traditions that divided those involved. This was most evident in the voting rights campaign of 1965, which brought together Protestants, Catholics, and Jews in a common struggle for full participatory democracy. King called this crusade "the greatest ecumenical council that this world has known," and he was "sorry to have to say that [it] took place in the little town of Selma," and "not at Rome."[121] On a practical level, then, King brought a unifying vision to the church, and the images of the ecumenical or world church and the church as an alliance and voice of conscience came together for him while assuming new meaning and relevance in the context of struggle.[122]

With equal facility, King demonstrated how the church should function in the emerging global community of many faiths and cultures. He played a significant role in intersecting Christians and other people of faith from various parts of the world in an assault on South African apartheid, colonialism in Africa, and other world problems. This was King's way of bringing some practical application to his conviction that the church "must forever offer to the world a dynamic positive."[123] In more precise terms, he advanced a richer vision of the essential catholicity of the church, a vision in which Christians could realize a greater sense of unity with Christ, with one another, and with other faith traditions. Furthermore, King, with fervency and urgency, engaged the World Council of Churches, the World Convention of Churches of Christ, and other Christian communities around the world, challenging them to "first discern what God is calling" them "to do in the presence of international conflict" and to make their "witness known, not merely through pronouncements but by the submission of their bodies as a living witness to the truth of Christ."[124]

The civil rights movement had much to do with King's faith in the potential of the church as a catalyst for inter-religious or pan-religious dialogue. He was never concerned about merely blazing some fresh pathway to religious tolerance. The movement he led created the basis and context for not only meaningful dialogue between Christians and Jews but also for a growing appreciation for religious pluralism. King worked with Jews as early as the Montgomery bus protest,[125] and he forged bonds with them that would extend through virtually all of the civil rights campaigns of the 1950s and 1960s. King led a crusade in which Christians and Jews marched, sang, prayed, wept, bled, and died together in a quest for what both considered the beloved community.[126] Consequently, the civil rights leader became a part of a long tradition in the African American encounter with Jews and Judaism,[127] a tradition that preceded the founding of the National Association for the Advancement of Colored People (NAACP) in 1909. But King built significantly on that tradition by making the church a pivotal presence in that encounter.

The Jerusalem Post suggested that King's "Jewish associations," especially through the American Jewish Congress (AJC), constituted perhaps the most critical moment of inter-religious cooperation during the civil rights era.[128] In Montgomery in 1958, King and Dr. Israel Goldstein of the AJC collaborated as major speakers at a Joint Legislative Conference around the theme "Where are We Going: Human Rights in 1958." Topics such as "Civil Liberties to Release the Free Spirit of Man," "Civil Rights to Forge Human Rights," and "Religion,

State and Freedom" were addressed at length in the panel workshops that followed.[129] In subsequent years, such collaboration would assume added significance and gain more media attention as King worked with a number of Jewish
organizations, chief among which were the AJC and the Synagogue Council of
America (SCA). It was out of this kind of collaboration that King's sense of
inter-religious or pan-religious dialogue as both conversation and praxis was
strengthened.

Most of these joint efforts occurred in the 1960s, as King presented a
stronger challenge to what he called "the giant triplets" or "the evil triumvirate"[130]—
namely, racism, poverty, and war. Of particular importance was King's appearance with Rabbi Abraham J. Heschel at a major Conference on Religion and
Race in Chicago in 1963, a conference at which King issued "A Challenge to the
Churches and Synagogues."[131] King also delivered a stirring speech before the
Synagogue Council of America in 1965, reaffirming links with the Jewish community in a common cause for the benefit of the church and all humanity.[132]
Jewish rabbis were among the four hundred white religious leaders who
strongly supported SCLC's campaign in Selma in that same year, thus contributing to King's image of the church as a coalition of conscience.[133] Later, King,
reflecting on the inter-religious character of the movement, spoke of the "deep
need for the partnership, fellowship and courage of our Jewish brother," and he
ebulliently reported, with figures like Rabbis Goldstein and Heschel in his
thoughts, the presence of "Hebrew prophets among us today"—prophetic
voices "from which the passion for justice and compassion for man is still
heard."[134] King's awareness of how the prophetic spirit moved across religious
traditions, especially Jewish and Christian traditions, could not have been more
evident on this occasion.

Jewish rabbis and theologians joined King and other Christian leaders
from the United States and abroad in heavily supporting a number of worldwide declarations, petitions, and appeals in the interest of human rights in the
1950s and 1960s. Rabbi Israel Goldstein and Martin Buber were among the
signatories of the Declaration of Conscience in 1957, an international effort on
behalf of South African freedom, co-sponsored by King, Bishop James Pike,
and Eleanor Roosevelt.[135] Rabbi Roland B. Gittelsohn of Boston and Irving M.
Engel, past president of the American Jewish Committee, joined King and
other Christian ministers and theologians in supporting that same cause
through a petition circulated by the Americans for Democratic Action in
1960.[136] Rabbi Goldstein, Buber, Rabbi Abba Hillel Silver, and Dr. Samuel
Hugo Bergman of Israel signed the Appeal for Action Against Apartheid in
1962, an initiative co-sponsored by King and Albert Luthuli in connection with
the American Committee on Africa.[137] The fact that representatives from some

of the traditional religions of Africa and Asia also supported these efforts is further testimony to the inter-religious character of King's efforts to realize the beloved community on a global scale. These joint involvements must have heightened his sense of how the turbulent waters of inter-religious or pan-religious dialogue and cooperation might be more effectively navigated under the auspices of the church.

The plight of Jews worldwide figured heavily in the encounter between the Jewish and African American communities in the sixties, and no one symbolized the positive side of this more than King. In the face of black nationalists who consistently attacked Israel for its treatment of the Palestinians, and for occupying what they considered to be "a dark people's territory," King defended "Israel's right to exist as a state in security" as "incontestable" while at the same time insisting that "the great powers have the obligation to recognize that the Arab world is in a state of imposed poverty and backwardness that must threaten peace and harmony."[138] King also joined some twenty-five Jewish organizations in an attempt to awaken the conscience of the world concerning the condition of 3 million Jews in the Soviet Union in the late 1960s. "Nothing concerns me more than the continued religious and personal persecution of Jews in the Soviet Union," said King in a letter to Rabbi Seymour J. Cohen in September 1965.[139]

In other cases where Jews felt that they were victims of discrimination by various nations, King's advice and insight were often solicited and generously offered.[140] Because of his longstanding advocacy of Jewish causes, the Synagogue Council of America made him the recipient of the Judaism and World Peace Award in 1965. King responded with delight, while also praising Jews for their contributions to civil rights for blacks. "I must say that of all the ethnic groups that have supported our struggle, I find none more consistent and unswerving in that support than the Jewish community," he wrote. "I am sure that a large part of this grows out of the deep sense of justice that stands at the center of the prophetic tradition of Judaism."[141]

King brought this same notion of the prophetic to his witness against the Vietnam War, using the church as a center from which to draw support from adherents of both Western and Eastern religions. Christian and Jewish leaders worked with him in Clergy and Laity Concerned About Vietnam and in other forums, highlighting the dangers of the nuclear threat and affirming the higher values of world peace and community. As plans for the escalation of the conflict in Vietnam surfaced, King announced the organization of what he believed to be the largest coalition of religious, civic, and public leaders to protest U.S. war policy.[142] Christians, Jews, Muslims, and even skeptics stood with him, signaling a significant link, at least in spirit, between the civil rights struggle and the peace movement. In 1967, King participated in a joint interview in Louisville, Kentucky, with Muhammad Ali, the heavyweight boxing champion and member of the Nation of Islam, and both expressed solidarity in opposition to the Vietnam War. In the course of the interview, King noted that he and Ali were driven by shared interests that transcended religious boundaries. "Even though we may have different religious beliefs," King observed, "this is not at all a thing about difference in terms of our concern." He went on to affirm his solidarity with Ali and peoples of all faiths who opposed U.S. aggression in Vietnam, asserting that "we are all victims of the same system of oppression."[143]

The same sentiments surrounded the collaborative efforts between King and Thich Nhat Hanh, the South Vietnamese Buddhist monk, both of whom criticized the American venture in Vietnam on spiritual and moral grounds. The two religious leaders met in Chicago in 1966, and in the truest spirit of pan-religious dialogue, they shared their convictions and acknowledged their common struggle in a joint statement:

> We believe that Buddhists who have sacrificed themselves, like the martyrs of the civil rights movement, do not aim at the injury of the oppressors but only at changing their policies. The enemies of those struggling for freedom and democracy are not man. They are discrimination, dictatorship, greed, hatred and violence, which lie with the heart of man. These are the real enemies of man—not man himself. . . . We believe that the struggles for equality and freedom in Birmingham, Selma and Chicago, as in Hue, Danang and Saigon, are aimed not at the domination of one people by another. They are aimed at self-determination, peaceful social change, and a better life for all human beings. And we believe that only in a world of peace can the work of construction, of building good societies everywhere, go forward.[144]

Hahn would go on to assert that "warfare respects no man, woman or child, whether he be Catholic, Protestant or Buddhist,"[145] a point with which King obviously agreed. King's insistence that "Buddhism is parallel with the struggle for civil rights here" left a lasting impression with Hahn.[146] In 1967, King, a Nobel Peace Prize recipient himself, actually nominated Hanh for the honor. The two figures developed similar concepts of religious understanding and world unity, as was described in King's *Where Do We Go from Here: Chaos or Community* (1967) and later in Hanh's *Living Buddha, Living Christ* (1995).[147] King's relationship to Hanh, at a time when Buddhism was labeled "an alien religion" in the United States, offered important lessons in interfaith or pan-religious dialogue as service to humanity.

FIGURE 5.1. King visits Gandhi's gravesite during a trip to India in 1959.

Mindful of the impact of different religious and moral values on the civil rights movement, and more specifically on King, John Thatamanil contends that the encounter between the African American community and Gandhi represents "perhaps the most important moment of interfaith dialogue in recent history."[148] Thatamanil highlights King's admission that "Christ furnished the spirit and motivation" and Gandhi "the method" for the civil rights crusade, and also Gandhi's appreciation for the lessons of the black struggle as revealed in the Negro spirituals. The essential point is that King and Gandhi, a Christian and a Hindu, are symbolic of how certain kinds of values and traditions move across different religions. King's and Gandhi's common emphasis on love as expressed through redemptive suffering and on the ethic of nonviolent direct action is instructive in making such a claim. Thatamanil's suggestion that "There was a real reciprosity and a deep spiritual kinship that joined" the "communities and movements" of King and Gandhi "together" is persuasive, and there is implicit here a model for how pan-religious dialogue at its best might find expression in any age.[149]

As one who valued community as the highest human and ethical ideal, King was far more interested in what the religions of the world shared than what they did not share, for it was his belief that "God has intended through all religions to keep intact the brotherhood of man."[150] Discounting the notion that his crusade was rooted only in Christian values, King wrote:

> When I speak of love, I am speaking of that force which all the great religions have seen as the supreme unifying principle of life. Love is the key that unlocks the door which leads to ultimate reality. This Hindu-Moslem-Christian-Jewish-Buddhist belief about ultimate reality is beautifully summed up in the First Epistle of Saint John: "Let us love one another; for love is of God; and everyone that loveth is born of God, and knoweth God. He that loveth not knoweth not God; for God is love. . . . If we love one another, God dwelleth in us, and his love is perfected in us."[151]

In an interview in 1964, King addressed this issue at greater length, focusing especially on the collective and often unrealized potential of the world's religions as a force for creating world peace and human community:

> Religion at its best has always sought to promote peace and good will among men. This is true of all the great religions of the world. In their ethical systems, we find the love ethic standing at the center. This is true of Judaism, this is true of Christianity, this is true of Islam, of Hinduism and Buddhism, and if we go right through all the great religions of the world we find this central message of love and this idea of the need for peace, the need for understanding, and the need for good will among men. Now the problem has been that these noble creeds and ethical insights of the great religions have not been followed by the adherents of the particular religions, and we must face the shameful fact that all too many religious people have been religious in their creeds but not enough in their deeds. I have felt all along that if religion—and that includes all religions—would take a real stand against war and go all-out for peace and brotherhood, then we would be further along the way in making these into reality. . . . If religious institutions had really been true to their creeds all along, to the demand for justice, the demand for peace, then we would have peace and justice.[152]

But King never surrendered to the diagnoses of incurable pessimists, who casually dismissed the potential for inter-faith or pan-religious cooperation as a global effort, and who routinely insisted that the church and religion in general would continue to be a barrier rather than a healthy contributor to international peace and community. King's own diagnoses was much more positive and optimistic:

Now even though there has been a great deal of negligence and even though the religions of the world have not done enough to inspire their followers to work passionately and unrelentingly for peace, I think that in the present and the future religion can play a great role. If brotherhood is to become a reality, religion must somehow get into the thick of the battle for peace and reaffirm the fact that, as the Old Testament says, men must beat their swords into plowshares and their spears into pruning hooks, and nations must not rise up against nations; neither must they study war any more. If we are to have a just and lasting peace, religion will have to do more to influence the minds of men and women to be true to their ethical insights.[153]

For King, "the beloved community," "the world house," and "the world-wide neighborhood" amounted to a sort of overarching telos that embraced all of the major religions as valid pointers to God. This was for him one of the keys to inter-religious dialogue in its most authentic and fruitful manifestations. With a deep sense of urgency, King encouraged the religions of the world to learn how to coexist peacefully, to pursue a path of humility and of openness to the fullness of truth, and to move beyond a restricted and dangerous mono-logue to a rich and productive dialogue:

But I am sure that if the religions of the world are to bring about the peace that I am talking about and create the climate for it, they've got to rise to the level of not fighting among themselves. Some of the most tragic wars in the world have been religious wars. There is a need for individual religions to realize that God has revealed Himself to all religions and there is some truth in all. And no religion should permit itself to be so arrogant that it fails to see that God has not left Himself without a witness, even though it may be in another religion.[154]

The fact that King borrowed ideas, concepts, and practices from different religions affords additional proof of his belief in and commitment to inter-reli-gious or pan-religious dialogue as both conversation and activism. He took ideas from Hinduism, Buddhism, Judaism, Islam, and atheism, and he synthe-sized them with insights from the Christian traditions, thus forging from this a philosophy and methods that were useful in the assault on a multitude of social evils.[155] No one has made this claim more perceptively than Roy Money, who suggests that King recognized "a fundamental congruence between his own Christian beliefs and Buddhist concepts he was becoming familiar with," particularly after associating with Thich Nhat Hanh. Money places special emphasis on King's stress on "the interrelated structure of all reality," noting that there is "a strong congruence" here with "a central Buddhist concept variously known as 'dependent origination,' 'interdependent arising,' or 'interbeing.'"[156] Hence, when King spoke of humans as "caught in an inescapable network of mutuality, tied in a single garment of destiny,"[157] he was giving voice to essentially the same communitarian ideal that coursed through the thought of not only Hanh but also Gandhi, the Hebrew Prophets, Jesus, and the great sages of Islam. It is clear, then, that King's moral and spiritual arguments "extended way beyond people who were coming from a Christian perspective."[158]

King's views on religion and inter-faith dialogue were never simply about asserting the worth of religious pluralism and pan-religious cooperation. Generally speaking, they constituted further proof of the catholicity of his concern for humanity. He never wavered in his conviction that there is a universal path to God's Kingdom that intersects with people of all faith claims and cultures. Speaking in concrete terms in 1967, a year before his death, King, in language that recalled the great Leo Tolstoy, declared, "The kingdom of God is not yet a universal phenomenon, and it may not come in history as a universal phenomenon, but the kingdom is here in the sense that it is in you."[159] At other times, he appeared more optimistic, asserting, "In a dark confused world the Kingdom of God may yet reign in the hearts of men."[160] This became his legacy of hope to the generations he knew would follow him.

Perhaps more than any other Christian leader in his time, King envisioned the future church's encounter with globalization. This explained in part his call for a richer vision of the church's universality in an interrelated and interdependent world. In an increasingly globalized world, he knew the dangers inherent in the church's Manichean division of the world into *us* and *them*. Thus, he sought to globalize an ethical ideal, the beloved community, and was therefore a precursor of much of the kind of thinking currently associated with globalization. This, too, should be accounted as a fundamental aspect of King's legacy. The next chapter, the final one in this volume, examines at greater length the meaning of that legacy for the contemporary church and world.

6

To Be Maladjusted

A Kingian Model for Church Renewal

It may be that the salvation of the world lies in the hands of the maladjusted.

—Martin Luther King, Jr.

We must ask ourselves, earnestly and prayerfully, whether *we* are still the church. If we discover that God has turned to other vehicles, it is not because he has left his people, but because the people have left God.

—Will D. Campbell

The challenge to the church in general is for a renewed commitment to biblical egalitarianism, which promotes the dignity and integrity of both men and women.

—Vashti M. McKenzie, *Not Without a Struggle: Leadership Development for African American Women in Ministry*

The brothers on the street have skills and resources that the church needs. They have been written off by the larger society and, unfortunately, by many churches.

—Jawanza Kunjufu, *Adam! Where are You? Why Most Black Men Don't Go to Church*

The assassination of Martin Luther King, Jr., closed an important and unique chapter in the history of the Christian church and its relationship to struggles for justice, peace, and human dignity. The tragedy, occurring in Memphis, Tennessee, on April 4, 1968, during the Easter season, had a kind of redemptive significance for the church everywhere, for no one had done more than King to restore the public credibility of that institution. Reactions to King's death in the American churches covered the spectrum, from deep outrage and intense grief to pure silence to wild applause and obvious delight.[1] Crucifixion metaphors filtered through many of the tributes and expressions of condolence shared and heard in ecclesial circles worldwide. For the Reverend Joseph Barndt, who would later serve as co-director of Crossroads, a ministry devoted to dismantling racism and creating a multicultural church, the images of Holy week and Jesus being crucified, and of King being assassinated, became essentially one picture.[2] In a similar vein, Pope Paul VI identified King's murder with "the tragic story of the passion of Christ," and similar sentiments echoed through the memorial services held by churches and church organizations as varied as the Spanish Evangelical Church, the Christian Council of Kenya, the United Evangelical Center of Mexico City, the World Council of Churches, and Protestant and Catholic groups in parts of France, England, Germany, and South Africa.[3]

King's death and enduring legacy afford the background from which the content of this final chapter flows. The approach is threefold. First, the ways in which the ministry and mission of the Christian church have unfolded in the decades since King's death are discussed, with a particular focus on the changing face of that institution and the emerging definitional crisis surrounding it. Second, several broad, intertwining images from King's thought—the church as "the least of these," as creative minority, as conscience of the state, as symbol of the beloved community, as prophetic witness and activism, and as sacrificial lamb—are identified and cast onto a hermeneutical grid that critiques existing church forms and, more especially, the contemporary prosperity mega churches.[4] Finally, this chapter establishes the need for the church to reclaim King's prophetic model of ministry and praxis, especially in these times, when the ecclesial landscape is shifting rapidly and when ecclesial communities are yearning for a voice of wisdom that is clear, certain, engaging, provocative, and persuasive. Thus, any effort on the part of the church to historicize King, or to confine him to the civil rights era of the 1950s and 1960s, is virtually impossible to sustain on pragmatic grounds.

Beyond Civil Rights: The Changing Face of the Church in the
Post-King Age

Martin Luther King, Jr.'s death signaled the beginnings of a decisive shift on
the part of the churches away from the mass social-protest phase of the civil
rights crusade that marked the 1950s and 1960s. By the 1970s, many black
churches had retreated into the same sort of "reactionary traditionalism" that
had characterized them before the rise of King, and there were fewer challenges to the structures of white supremacy.[5] Carlyle F. Stewart, III, explains
how black churches succumbed to "the disillusionment of a post-civil rights
malaise," thus abandoning a strong sense of the prophetic.[6] Robert C. Smith
concludes that by the 1990s, the civil rights movement had "been almost wholly
encapsulated into mainstream institutions, coopted, and marginalized," and
that its leadership, based substantially in the church, had "become largely irrelevant in the development of organizations, strategies, and programs that would
address the multifaceted problems of race in the post-civil rights era."[7]

The politicization of the church has been among the ecclesiastical trends
that have emerged in the decades since King's death. In the 1970s and 1980s,
black churches, which had once been the centers of mass meetings and the
rallying points for demonstrators, became arenas for voting clinics and proving
grounds for black political leadership, even as many of them retreated into
enclaves of conservative, revivalistic Christianity. For the first time since Reconstruction, the church assumed much of the burden of moral and financial support as African Americans voted in considerable numbers, entered the sphere
of electoral politics, and occupied public office in various parts of the South. In
the 1980s, Jesse Jackson, a former aide to King, worked from the black church
as a base while pursuing the presidency of the United States, thus forging
intertwining links between "religion, politics, and the quest for racial justice."[8]
The trend extended through the 1990s into the early years of the new century, as Al Sharpton made a similar bid for the highest office in the land. For
Jackson, Sharpton, and many others in public and/or political life, who were
inspired by King's leadership and legacy, the church continued to serve as the
black community's greatest source of refuge and empowerment.[9]

These trends in the black church were matched by the resurgence of fundamentalist and evangelical forms in white churches in the 1970s and 1980s, along
with their increasing incursion into American political life. The animosity that
had existed between white conservative churches and the civil rights movement
had faded to some degree, as some fundamentalist and numerous evangelical
leaders also shifted to a more politicized interpretation of Christian responsibility.

Jerry Falwell, Wallie A. Criswell, and other conservative clergy, who had once castigated King for his involvement in social and political activities, now turned to activities of this nature themselves, focusing mostly on selective moral issues such as abortion, pornography, and homosexuality. This politicization of white fundamentalist and evangelical churches crystallized in the eighties as Falwell, Criswell, Pat Robertson, James Robison, and "other politically oriented preachers and programs of the electronic church" united with Ronald Reagan, Strom Thurmond, Jesse Helms, and others on the political Right to restore what they perceived to be the biblical and moral foundations of American life and culture.[10]

This alliance between the so-called Christian Right and the political Right became an immensely powerful force as national religio-political organizations like the Moral Majority, Christian Voice, and Religious Roundtable emerged, along with hard-line pro-life groups, anti-homosexuality movements, pro-family groups, and "anti-sex education, anti-ERA, pro-prayer in public schools, and anti-pornography constituencies."[11] Although some of these religio-political and hard-line groups had faded from the scene by the end of the twentieth century, new alliances between the religious and political Right, involving both white and black churches, emerged as George W. Bush and the conservative forces in the Republican Party assumed control of American governmental life. With these developments, the image of the church in America changed radically, thus becoming a serious challenge to what Martin Luther King, Jr., had envisioned for that institution.

The ambivalent approach to King's legacy on the part of certain elements in the American churches became painfully evident in the two decades after his death. Black churches honored King as a religious hero while abandoning his call for the church to remain a force in combining mass social protest with electoral politics.[12] In a different vein, Christian conservatives in white churches denounced the civil rights leader for the worst of all sins and moral failures, while also claiming him when he proved useful in the promotion of their own ideas, causes, and agenda. In 1989, Curtis W. Caine, a Southern Baptist minister from Jackson, Mississippi, attacked King's communitarian vision for the church and society, labeling him "a fraud"; and other white fundamentalists and evangelicals pointed to allegations regarding King's alleged sexual escapades in attempts to trivialize and even deny his contributions to the church and to civil and human rights.[13] At the same time, King became an authoritative source when some of these same Christian conservatives sought to launch their assault on public policy that seemed to favor women, blacks, and other marginalized groups over white males in the society.

This ambivalent but positive recourse to King's legacy was probably more evident with high-profile figures on the so-called religious Right. Rejecting his previous stance on the role of the church in public affairs, which was glaringly evident during the civil rights movement, Jerry Falwell insisted in 1981, "I feel that what King was doing is exactly what we are doing."[14] Rabbi Yehuda Levin and others in the so-called pro-life movement declared in the early 1990s that "their protests," which included acts that violated civil law under the claims of a higher moral law, "follow in the tradition of Martin Luther King, Jr.'s civil rights movement."[15] Newt Gingrich, Dick Armey, Clint Bolick, and other rabid advocates of anti-affirmative action, in both government and the church, quoted King's speeches in defense of their positions, and especially King's insistence that persons be judged on the basis of character rather than skin color.[16] By the beginning of the twenty-first century, prominent political conservatives in both races were "proclaiming that Rev. Martin Luther King, Jr. was a Republican," and that "It is time for conservatives to lay claim to" his legacy. King's "core beliefs, such as the power and necessity of faith-based association and self-government based on absolute truth and moral law, are profoundly conservative," declared one such source in 2006.[17]

Such white and black voices from the Right are contributing to mass public confusion about who King was and what he might expect of the church in these times of acquiescence. Conservatives suggest that King was a harmless, gentle preacher who viewed the status quo church, or the church that serves the interests of the state, as the ideal, and liberals contend that King was an uncompromising voice of the prophetic church, or that body that consistently proclaims God's judgment upon America owing to its idolatry, racism, militarism, and mistreatment of the poor. Thus, "the profound sense of national amnesia" that currently surrounds annual celebrations of King's birth is probably more evident in the church than anywhere else.[18] Disagreements over King's legacy are translating into different definitions and expectations of the church, and nowhere is this more evident than in the recent debates about the fiery and controversial proclamations of the Reverend Jeremiah Wright and whether or not he stands in the same prophetic tradition that produced King.[19] Clearly, Wright's proclamations concerning God's judgment upon the evils and arrogance of America, and especially its white supremacist practices and aggression against other nations, fueled renewed public debate about the legacy of King and his vision for the church.[20]

The competing images of King's identity and mission as a churchman are not surprising, for they are the product of a religious culture dominated by politically charged and status-quo-oriented televangelists, the rise and popularity of the mega churches, and mega-church gurus. Before being rocked by a series of scandals in the mid- and late-1980s, the charismatic Southern Baptist Pat Roberston, the Independent Baptist Jerry Falwell, the Assemblies of God ministers Jim Bakker and Jimmy Swaggart, the Reformed Church of America's Robert Schuller, and other highly successful televangelists and media ministries had already prepared the ground for not only the conservative Christian resurgence but also the high-profile, super-churches that have little resemblance to the churches that inspired and nurtured King and the crusade for civil rights.[21] Boasting an average weekly attendance of at least two thousand each, with their very large and imposing structures, these mega churches grew in number to 250 by 1990 and to almost 800 by 2000. Needless to say, the size of their budgets and the magnitude of their influence have led to new conceptions of ministry and mission. Black and white suburbanites, and especially young families, flock to these churches in droves, lending credence to the idea of the crowd drawing the crowd.[22]

The mega church has remained largely a southern phenomenon, thus making the question of its relationship to King's legacy all the more interesting.[23] Although hewing to a strict biblical line, the mega churches, which cluster in urban centers, and which range from the denominational and independent to the charismatic and evangelical, mirror the corporate structure in their organization, management, and outreach. They are in fact corporations with enormous financial resources, with ministers operating as CEOs, with dozens of clerical staff, and with satellite facilities and networks, television airtime, daily talk shows, music studios, publishing houses, computer graphic design suites, computer Web sites, and an entrepreneurial approach to matters of an economic and business nature. Mega-church pastors such as Joel Osteen of Lakewood Church in Houston; Jerry Falwell of Thomas Road Baptist Church in Lynchburg, Virginia; Creflo Dollar of World Changers in College Park, Georgia; Bishop T. D. Jakes of The Potter's House in Dallas; Bishop Eddie Long of the New Birth Missionary Baptist Church in Dekalb County, Georgia; and Rick Warren of Saddleback Valley Community Church in Lake Forrest, California, have emerged as national celebrities while assuming center stage in the culture.[24] Clearly, with the emergence of the highly visible and popular mega churches and their leaders, the new faces of both the white church and the black church have become increasingly evident. Also, the conversation concerning the role of religious convictions in politics, public service, and public policymaking—a conversation triggered decades ago by the church-centered social movement King led—has gained tremendous traction in the contemporary church and the larger American society.[25]

The mega churches constitute a mix of politics and spirituality that King would undoubtedly find strange and counterproductive, and these churches are preoccupied with prosperity, praise, and personal enrichment themes. They are massive arenas in which church management and marketing strategies are immensely important. Spirit-enriching sermons are tailored to a base of Christian evangelicals, and the spiritualizing proclivity and converting people are greatly emphasized. Much stress is placed on the therapeutic model of ecclesial life, which majors in a feel-good-about-yourself spirituality. Hence, if one refuses to wave one's hands, throw handkerchiefs, speak in tongues, stand in healing lines, run up and down church aisles, and drive a Cadillac, then one is not considered "spiritual."[26] Interestingly enough, the prosperity mega preachers themselves view their models of the church in the most positive light, and they deny that their work betrays the King legacy and the unfinished agenda of the civil rights movement.

Both white and black mega-church leaders claim without hesitation that, through their activities on behalf of the church and society, they are standing in the very best tradition of King and other Christian martyrs. As suggested previously, Jerry Falwell and other white, right-wing, politically active clergymen have been making this claim for almost three decades.[27] Rick Warren, who has said much in recent times about the significance of "the purpose-driven church" in "the purpose-driven life," literally delights in being identified with the country's long tradition of "pastors" like King, who were at the forefront of "every major movement" for freedom in this country.[28] T. D. Jakes has been included among the inheritors of King's mantle,[29] and Eddie Long, who pastors a membership of roughly 25,000, has made perhaps a greater claim than anyone else to the mantle of King's leadership, especially since he was supposedly anointed for that purpose by members of the King family in 2004.[30] Creflo Dollar, who pastors some 23,000, is among a "new generation of televangelists" and "mega church preachers" who insist that they are "extending King's ministry by emphasizing issues such as economic empowerment." "Dr. King stood for the freedom of all people, and I believe that deliverance from debt is an integral part of that freedom," Dollar maintains. "When a man is out of debt," he adds, "he is better able to accomplish God's divine purpose for his life by being a blessing to others."[31] Bishop Paul Morton, senior pastor of Greater St. Stephens Full Gospel Church in New Orleans, another mega church, completely agrees, claiming that "teaching black people better money management is the 'next dimension' of King's ministry."[32]

This view of the social and/or service-oriented side of mega-church ministries is also advanced by Jakes and Long, and by Warren and other white mega-church leaders as well. With figures like Jakes, Long, and Dollar in mind, Robert M. Franklin acknowledges that "today's mega churches are products of the traditional black church," and that they "are beginning to expand and redefine that tradition"—points quite significant for understanding the mega-church phenomenon in relation to King's legacy. Franklin goes on to note, however, that while "Congregations with thousands of members have social, political, and economic power that is unprecedented in black church history," it is obvious that "a cleavage between the tradition and these innovators has emerged."[33]

In promoting the values of economic self-help, which are deeply rooted in the black church tradition,[34] mega churches are honoring an important dimension of King's vision and ministry. To a considerable extent, these bodies have assumed some of the functions of government through nonprofit organizations and faith-based initiatives, and they are creating new opportunities for ministry in the fields of social welfare, health care, and education.[35] After the Hurricane Katrina crisis in 2005, mega churches mobilized to help thousands of "Gulf Coast residents, providing meals and housing."[36] By sponsoring homeless shelters, health-care screenings, food banks, soup kitchens, counseling services, educational initiatives, and other social services and charitable good works, with varying degrees of vigor and success, these churches actually affirm some of the moral obligations of the church as a whole toward what King called "the least of these."

Even as they claim a connection to the legacies of King and the civil rights movement, mega-church preachers are not consciously seeking to duplicate his churchmanship and style of ministry. T. D. Jakes, the "CEO and spiritual savant of the 30,000-member Dallas-based Potter's House Ministries," readily admits, "mega-ministers are not the civil-rights preachers that traditionally populated our pulpits in the past." "People often ask me if I [am] the next Martin Luther King," Jakes observed. "God does not make the next anything. We are all originals and because we are originals, we contribute in our communities in different ways."[37] In another statement in 2008, Jakes commented further: "I'm not against marching, but in the 60s, the challenge of the black church was to march. And there are times now perhaps that we may need to march. But there's more facing us than social justice. There's personal responsibility, motivating and equipping people to live the best lives that they can."[38]

The rise of the mega-church phenomenon is contemporaneous with yet another trend that is changing the image of the church in this post-King age— namely, the increasing decline of the neighborhood church. As the mega churches grow and expand in the nation's suburbs, smaller churches are moving out of neighborhoods, including the inner cities where the fear of crime is epidemic, and seeking a safer existence elsewhere. Consequently, there are growing numbers of people in the neighborhoods and inner cities of America, especially youth, who have never been to church, who know nothing about that institution, and who have not the slightest respect for what it proclaims and practices. In too many cases, urban dwellers, with their different values and pluralistic lifestyles, no longer have ready access to the church, a body that afforded a refuge, a comprehensive community, and a surrogate world for many in King's times.[39]

As the foregoing discussion suggests, the definition of the church is in such a crisis today, and is being rewritten. The very idea of church in this post-King era is an illusive phenomenon that, more often than not, defies definition and precise explication. This definitional and/or identity crisis, as already established, is attributable to a range of factors, among which are the politicization of fundamentalism and evangelicalism, the wedding of the religious and political Right, the emergence of new church models, and differing conceptions of how the church might best advance the unfinished agenda of King's sacred crusade.[40] The crisis is also evident in the increasing divisions and manifold organizational forms, and in the church's vastly diverse and ever-changing constituencies. Much is being written about the electronic church, the public or politicized church, the mega church, the small neighborhood church, the multicultural or multiethnic church, the gay church, the nondenominational church, and other ecclesial forms, and the extent of the diversity alone has increased the Christian church's uncertainty about its own identity and purpose.

As the debates between the so-called conservative and liberal wings of society continue, even the churches themselves are likely to become far more divided over what constitutes the true *ekklesia*. King viewed the church as a refuge, as a voice for the voiceless, as the conscience of the state, and as the chief symbol of the beloved community, but how have these images changed in the minds of people, and especially the ecclesial community? What does it mean to speak of the church today in these terms? Where are the reformist voices in the church? Can the church lead the way in this new century and millennium? Can it become a place glistening with new ideas and energy, or will it continue to allow religious and social conservatives to dominate the faith and politics debate? Can the church develop a new identity, vision, and sense of mission and movement? How might King's vision for the church be reclaimed and implemented for the good of all humanity?[41] Questions like this precipitate the need for fresh and ongoing evaluations, definitions, and redefinitions of the church, and King remains a critical resource in such an endeavor.

Critiquing Contemporary Church Forms:
King as a Resource for Ecclesial Rationale

Martin Luther King, Jr., always had serious misgivings about Americans who stood on the extreme right of the religious and political spectrum. His fear that powerful elements in the church would capitulate to the agenda of what he labeled "the Radical Right"[42] was always real, and by the 1980s, it had become more than justified as Christian conservatives devoted their spiritual energy and political clout to the service of the status quo. While it is true that the so-called Christian Right of the 1970s and 1980s was similar to King in its attempts to "bring religiously affiliated ideas into politics," or to relate faith to matters of public consequence, it evidently differed sharply from King when faced with the question of how the church should be used in this arena. Writing in 1982, Daniel C. Maguire explained the contrast in visions in graphic terms:

> There is all the difference imaginable between what Martin Luther
> King, Jr., brought to the political order and what the Falwells and
> LaHayes bring. When King left his pulpit and ceased his political
> activism, many who had lacked rights before had come to possess
> those rights. People were voting who could not vote before, were
> getting hired and educated who would have known only rejection,
> and were finding decent housing who could not before. In short,
> King's interventions in politics were *enabling* and *empowering*.
> However, when the Falwells of the New Right leave their pulpits and
> end their political activism, inasmuch as they are successful, people
> who had rights would have lost them. Their interventions are
> *disabling* and *disempowering*. Also, depending on their success, the
> most wholesome elements of the American dream will have been
> undermined.[43]

Maguire goes on to state, quite convincingly, that King, unlike right-wing Christian conservatives in the white church, "did not preach a privatized religion," that he "went from pulpit to polling booth," and that he "took the ideals that were bred in evangelical piety and made them the basis of a movement that eventually yielded civil rights legislation and affirmative action executive orders."[44] Furthermore, the Christian Right of the seventies and eighties, as Maguire argues, did not embrace King's interest in eliminating the problems of racism, poverty and economic injustice, and war and human destruction, and its most vocal spokespersons supported government cutbacks in aid for the poor while agreeing with the massive military budgets of the Reagan-Bush years. "The Hebrew and Christian scriptures from which King drank are obsessed with the needs of the poor and the powerless in society," continued Maguire. "How the New Right can read those scriptures and support elitist monopolies, weaken civil rights enforcement, and cut back on aid to poor children is an epic of hypocrisy that must be called by its name."[45]

By choosing the rich and the powerful over the poor and marginalized, the right-wing church essentially abandoned King's vision while setting the stage for what would occur on a larger scale with the mega churches in the 1990s and beyond. The very idea of a mega church, with its gospel of prosperity positivism and materialism, and billions raised through media ministries and the mail, is antithetical to King's images of the church as "the least of these" and the church as creative minority. Mega churches routinely equate success with numbers, the breadth of their appeals, the availability of their resources, and a kind of holy materialism. King always said that mission is larger than simply extending the ranks of the church, and he found it impossible to identify "bigness," an entrepreneurial spirit, a gospel of material prosperity, lavish lifestyles, and popularity and/or social acceptability with the gospel of Jesus Christ and radical, costly discipleship. Much of King's critique of the church targeted its preoccupation with size, wealth, and influence. "We worship that which is big—big buildings, big cars, big houses, big corporations," he once complained. "We find our great security in bigness."[46] In another remark, King challenged the very premise on which many mega churches and their leadership today claim legitimacy, power, and success:

> This numerical growth should not be overemphasized. We must not
> be tempted to confuse spiritual power and large numbers.
> Jumboism, as someone has called it, is an utterly fallacious standard
> for measuring positive power. An increase in quantity does not
> automatically bring an increase in quality. A larger membership does
> not necessarily represent a correspondingly increased commitment
> to Christ. Almost always the creative, dedicated minority has made
> the world better.[47]

While maintaining, "Jesus never made a universal indictment against all wealth," King felt nonetheless that an obsession with the capitalist ethic and materialistic ingredients could only result in the spiritual death of the church as the body of Christ and as a prophetic voice in society.[48] He consistently cautioned the church against a narrow, self-serving mission, and most especially against a preoccupation with its own institutional maintenance and advancement. Convinced that the church as "the least of these" and the church as creative minority constituted the ecclesial ideal, King held that a seemingly insatiable appetite for materialistic gain was central to the church's inability to break the yoke of its middle- and upper-class captivity. From this standpoint, his views are quite useful as a lens through which to constructively critique the contemporary mega-church phenomenon. After all, King reminded us that no church model should go unexamined and unchallenged, no matter how powerful and popular.

The same might be said of King in relationship to the leadership model exemplified by today's most celebrated television preachers and mega-church pastors, who, through a commodification of the gospel, have not only found ways to connect with and sway large numbers of people on a spiritual and emotional level but also to become filthy rich. Drawing enormous salaries, living in multi-million-dollar homes, and driving expensive cars, these media and mega ministers, unlike the Jesus whom King followed,[49] cannot even identify with the poor, let alone serve them adequately. Relishing in extravagant lifestyles and in an abundance of life biblicism and theology, some are consummate showpersons who promote a puritanical moral code; who revel in showering their congregants with pristine, otherworldly images; who boast of their vast power and networks of personal influence; who promote a consumerism devoid of authentic discipleship; and who scoff at any concept of the church as suffering servant or sacrificial lamb.[50] The fact that some of these figures pastor churches that are beginning to exhibit the authoritarian features of a cult, of movements associated in earlier times with the likes of Father Divine and Sweet Daddy Grace, is all the more cause for concern, especially for those who see the need to reclaim King's ecclesial vision in this new century.

Knowing the role that charlatans and opportunists had played historically in creating religious experience for both blacks and whites, King was never comfortable with pastors who, as he put it, "are more concerned about the size of the wheel base on their automobiles and the honorariums that come with their anniversaries than they are about saving souls of men."[51] He called for leaders who not only "avoid the extremes of 'hot-headedness' and 'Uncle Tomism,'" but also who exercise "wise judgment and sound integrity," who are "not in love with money but in love with justice," who are "not in love with publicity, but in love with humanity," and who "can subject their particular egos to the greatness of the cause." Furthermore, King consciously avoided the lure of materialism himself, observing on one occasion, "If I have any weaknesses, they are not in the area of coveting wealth."[52] The prostitution of the faith for personal profit and institutional gain was never an option for him, for he took seriously Jesus' proclamation that "it is easier for a camel to go through the eye of a needle, than for a rich man to enter into the kingdom of God" (Matthew 19:24).

Needless to say, King identified greed on the part of clergy with the most sinister side of the church, or as an affront to the images of the church as "the least of these," creative minority, and sacrificial presence. He maintained that greatness is determined not by wealth and influence but by service, and his own grandeur arose out of his commitment to a cause he considered noble, not from what he owned.[53] Moreover, King believed that high moral leadership, especially in the church, demanded a different set of values and priorities from those of pimps and drug dealers, who are also known for their fine homes, big cars, expensive clothes, and exotic jewelry. Thus, King has much to say to the church when it comes to demanding new levels of accountability for televangelists and mega-church preachers in the financial and ethical areas of life. But can his message be heard in an age in which holy materialism and prosperity have become "the theological doctrine of American culture," and in which "the battle between the prophetic and prosperity ministers" is being won by what one critic calls "the Rev. Ikes?"[54]

The stress on the values of individualism is another area in which the contemporary mega churches deviate from King's ecclesial model. King vehemently attacked the ethics of individualism, with its tendencies toward selfish ambition and cutthroat competition, and he literally cherished the communitarian and Social Gospel values that so characterized the church tradition that shaped his life, vision, and sense of mission. This explained King's emphasis on the idea of the church as the chief symbol of the beloved community. A different set of values is implicit in the message of the typical mega church today. Its "gospel of personal piety focuses on individual transformation," on "delivering people from sin, debt and dysfunctional relationships," and it proclaims that "Individuals must be saved before the world can be saved." "'Rather than focus on what's wrong with our society, we choose to focus on sharing the gospel of Jesus Christ with every person we possibly can,'" says Creflo Dollar. "'If people would make a decision to live their lives by the principles of the Word of God, all of the social ills in our society would cease to exist.'"[55]

King never relegated following Christ to the private, spiritual realm, or to the arenas of personal piety. Also, the conviction that one can change society by merely converting individuals, which courses through much of the history of evangelical Christianity, was never taken seriously by King, for he considered it nothing more than a half-truth. It was King's unwavering belief that the quests for individual salvation and social salvation had to occur simultaneously; that the experience of rebirth for individuals does not necessarily translate into just institutions, structures, and laws.[56] For King, the church at its best always addresses both concerns, thus justifying its existence as both the conscience of the state and the greatest symbol of the beloved community.

The emphasis on materialism and individualism stands as perhaps the strongest evidence of how black mega churches are absorbing the values of the larger culture, and especially white-establishment Christianity. But there are also other examples of this movement away from the Kingian model of the church, or of this willingness and often eagerness to conform to the standards and expectations of the dominant culture. Black mega churches and their leadership are increasingly capitulating to the agenda of the so-called Religious Right in the white church, a situation in which faith claims, morality, patriotism, and even the name of God are being manipulated for political ends.[57] As they move inside the world of right-wing Christian conservatism, black mega churches are typically displaying, on an unprecedented level, a selective moral outrage, targeting issues like abortion, the Equal Rights Amendment (ERA), school prayer, pornography, quotas, and homosexuality, while ignoring racism, economic injustice, war, and other issues that King deemed far more important, especially as he thought in terms of the church of "the least of these."[58]

Mega-church pastors such as Dollar, Eddie Long, T. D. Jakes, Bishop Paul Morton, Bishop Charles Blake, and Bishop Harry R. Jackson, Jr., have been included among "a new breed of leaders" who are traveling the country promoting a "'Black Contract With America on Moral Values,'" expressing strong opposition to abortion, affirmative action, and same-sex marriage.[59] Interestingly enough, they claim a devotion to King's legacy while following in the footsteps of Southern Baptists, who constitute almost a fourth of the nation's mega churches, who are zealously seeking to overturn the 1973 Roe V. Wade Supreme Court decision, who are unrelenting in their assault on governmental initiatives for the poor and oppressed, who vehemently oppose female pastors, and who devoted 2003 to what they call "their fight against the 'homosexual agenda' on several fronts."[60] Although the media ministers and mega-church pastors are not likely to admit it, the goal is to disempower and disenable women, people of color, and gays and lesbians. By avoiding those social evils that victimize and marginalize the most vulnerable elements in society, black mega churches are guilty, at the very least, of contributory negligence. Moreover, they bear some responsibility for making the church a willing partner in the great arsenal of human oppression, a development that King felt could only destroy the power and credibility of that institution.

The mission King envisioned for the black church as a whole, especially in terms of its messianic role, is getting lost in the efforts of Dollar, Long, Jakes, Morton, Blake, Jackson, and others to create an alternative black church. In ways uncharacteristic of this "new generation of televangelists," King, as explained in the previous chapter of this work, saw the black church as a potential vanguard in the struggle to enlarge the stretch of human freedom and dignity. On a more practical level, King drew on the resources of the church with the goal of extending people's rights, but the mega ministers use the church as a platform from which to limit a woman's right to chose and to deny the rights of gays and lesbians to self-determination and the pursuit of happiness. The image of King marching with gay activists such as Bayard Rustin and James Baldwin for better wages, income, health care, and housing for the poor stands in stark contrast to pictures of Eddie Long and Bernice A. King, King's youngest daughter, leading some 10,000 in support of a ban on same-sex marriage.[61] The "growing tug of war between those ministers who still preach a gospel of social justice in the tradition of Martin Luther King, Jr." and those who "mirror the gospel of their white counterparts such as Pat Robertson and Jerry Falwell"[62] is too evident to be overlooked and too unnerving to go unchallenged.

A number of other concerns should be raised in any discussion of the black mega church and its increasing surrender to the right-wing values of conservative white Christians. In the first place, the so-called Christian Right has displayed strong tendencies toward a kind of ethical extremism[63] that can only deprive black churches, to a much greater degree than ever before, of the moral authority that they have claimed and cherished throughout much of their history, and especially during the King years. That extremism is evident with Christian conservatives who go to any lengths, however unethical, to sanction and preserve the structures of power,[64] who insist that God is a Republican, who advocate the murder of abortion doctors,[65] who call for the assassination of certain heads of state,[66] and who consistently quote scripture while screaming that "God hates fags."[67] This is not what King had in mind when he, in the "Letter from the Birmingham City Jail" (1963), called the church to a healthy "extremism" in the interest of the common good.[68] Even in his own times, he lamented what he termed "the fanaticism of the Right."[69] In King's estimation, misguided extremism in support of the status quo essentially made the church the servant of the state, not its conscience or chief moral guardian. There are useful lessons here for the contemporary church, particularly in view of the excessively close and often unhealthy relationship between right-wing Christian conservatism, the Republican Party, and government.

Much of the force behind right-wing political activity in contemporary America comes from the predominantly black and white mega churches. These institutions have "become a centerpiece of Republican Black outreach," and of the far right's efforts "to create an 'alternative Black leadership.'"[70] The year 2000 was a watershed in a new and more organized campaign to attract more blacks into the Republican Party and to the religious Right's moral mandate for America. After George W. Bush's second inauguration in 2004, Eddie Long, T. D. Jakes, Harry Jackson, Kirbyjohn Caldwell, and other "hand-picked," conservative black preachers were invited to the White House to discuss how the administration's brand of "compassionate conservatism" might best benefit blacks and other Americans. Interestingly enough, the meeting lasted for more than an hour, considerably longer than President Bush's meeting with the Congressional Black Caucus a day later.[71] Jesse Jackson, Joseph E. Lowery, C. T. Vivian, and other ministers who worked with Martin Luther King, Jr., and who best symbolize a continuation of King's devotion to the church of "the least of these" and the church as the conscience of the state, were not invited to what was dubbed "the most public illustration yet of the raised political stakes in the battle for the soul of the Black church and its leaders."[72]

The 2004 meeting convinced some black journalists that "Black mega church ministers" had "'sold out' to the Bush administration and its faith-based" strategy, which was designed to "help churches and other religious groups obtain millions of social service dollars with few strings attached."[73] Bishop T. D. Jakes dismissed criticisms of the meeting as "political gamesmanship without merit," noting, "just because I have lunched with the president does not" necessarily amount to "an endorsement."[74] Bishop Eddie Long, also referring to the meeting with Bush, echoed Jakes's thoughts in much stronger language. "Just because we went to his house does not mean we had intercourse," he bellowed. Long went on to note: "And somebody has to go to the house. We cannot be afraid to understand that we are now revaluating our destiny and direction. By meeting with Bush at the White House, if we do need to pick up the phone and call them, we now have access."[75] Ready access to the halls of government may appear on the surface to be very positive indeed, but as King often said, it can lead to compromise and acquiescence on the part of the church, even when circumstances suggest the need to speak truth to power.

In 2005, Bishop Harry Jackson, pastor of the Hope Christian Church of Lanham, Maryland, downplayed claims of a newfound love between black mega-church pastors and the leadership of the Republican Party, suggesting instead that the relationship is motivated not by greed or the need to co-opt black pastors, but by a genuine concern on both sides to elevate the African American community. "I believe that in the day of the mega church there is a new Black church," he observed. "There has to be a reconstruction of the Black family, and there has to be a coming together with the broader Evangelical community in order for us to make a change." Jackson further explained, "There aren't enough of us to make all the politicians bow down and say, 'Black people, we love you.'"[76]

Be that as it may, it is difficult to avoid the conclusion that the far Right is using the black mega churches to impose a certain moral and political agenda on African Americans. Bush's faith-based strategy seemed to be part of a larger plan to subsidize the black church, thus assuring that it never produces another black messiah like Martin Luther King, Jr., and that it will never again take on the caring and protest posture for which it was known in the 1950s and 1960s. Today's mega-church pastors are unquestioned allies of the established order,[77] and their "preaching has become increasingly indistinguishable from the preaching found within cultures of privilege."[78] They are not the Jeremiah Wrights, who make the power elite uncomfortable. They are the Eddie Longs, who urge blacks to "forget racism because they have already reached the promised land"; the Creflo Dollars, who suggests that Jesus Christ was a rich man with no special identification with the poor; the Bishop Alfred Owenses, who unapologetically refer to gays as faggots and sissies; and a host of conservative preachers, who proclaim that God cannot call women to be preachers and pastors.[79] Obviously, there is a repudiation here of King's sense of the church as "the least of these" and as an alliance of conscience.

This is why the black mega-church pastors were so accepted in the centers of power during the Bush years, having full access to the president and others in the administration. This was not the case with King, who, after attacking the capitalistic system and the U.S.'s role in Vietnam, was no longer welcome at the White House. But King knew the price of healthy, prophetic dissent and creative nonviolent protest, for he had skillfully addressed this in his "Letter from the Birmingham City Jail," in which he actually highlighted the tension between an image of the church that blesses the status quo and a model of the church that challenges the principalities and powers and evil in high places. The television and mega ministers, especially those known for flag-waving, patriotic rhetoric, are representative of the church as the archdefender of the status quo, whereas King epitomized the concept of the church as the conscience of the state.[80]

This contrast is most apparent when one considers King's prophetic social witness against poverty and America's aggression in Vietnam over against the failure of television and mega-church ministers to challenge the economic and physical costs of the government's policies in Iraq. Charity ministries aimed at the needy and helpless are to be commended, but they do not eliminate the need to challenge the imperialistic structures, the capitalistic ethos, and the systemic injustices that make and keep people poor and destitute in the first place. King not only struggled to provide for the spiritual and material needs of the poor, the sick, the uneducated, and the lost, he also attacked institutions and structures of injustice that exploited and marginalized people, economically and otherwise. "Philanthropy is commendable," King conceded, "but it must not cause the philanthropist to overlook the circumstances of economic injustice which makes philanthropy necessary." Here, King was making an important distinction between those who become preoccupied with single individual effects, and those interested in curing "injustice at the causal source."[81]

King's witness against the Vietnam War in particular and war in general was in the very best tradition of the prophetic church, or the church as the conscience of the state. The standard he set around these issues has not been maintained in the prosperity mega churches. Long, Jakes, Jackson, Dollar, Kirbyjohn Caldwell, Joel Osteen, Rick Warren, and other highly popular clergymen have never seriously questioned the moral legitimacy of the wars in Iraq and Afghanistan. They are constantly seen and heard in the public arena, but when it comes to these and other issues of a controversial nature, they are among the silenced voices of the present age.[82] In this respect, there is no essential difference between them and figures like John Hagee, Pat Robertson, and James Dobson, all of whom act as if America's wars are holy crusades. This country's aggression in and occupation of Iraq and Afghanistan remain stunning examples of contemporary social evil, and any attempt to use the Prince of Peace, the most anti-imperialist figure in the ancient world, to support this policy is foreign to everything for which King stood.[83] Undoubtedly, America's hyper-military foreign policy conveys the need for the church to reclaim its image as both an alliance of conscience and peacemaker.

King's legacy stands as a reminder to mega churches that being a prophet has nothing to do with patriarchal domination, heterosexual absolutism, and apolitical neutrality in the face of structural evil and injustice. King held that whenever the actions of governmental authorities conflict with the explicitly stated commands of God, and with the highest standards of morality, the real prophet boldly speaks truth to power despite the risks involved. Being a prophet, then, is not for the weak and faint of heart. What one sees with today's mega churches is not an affirmation and practice of prophetic social witness and activism but, rather, "the perversion of public religion."[84] By amassing wealth and prestige, they invariably become a part of the very structures that the Hebrew prophets and Jesus condemned. This does not square with the church tradition proudly embraced by King, whose activities in the social-justice field actually helped prepare the atmosphere for the rise of the mega-church phenomenon.

Despite their obvious preference for the prosperity church model over that of the prophetic church, there are mega-church pastors who concede that there is much to gain from looking to King for the postmodernist quagmire of church vision and utility. This became quite evident during a television program on the fortieth anniversary of the King assassination, in April 2008, when Bishops Eddie Long and Harry Jackson joined the Reverends Joseph E. Lowery and Bernice A. King on the Trinity Broadcasting Network (TBN), the world's largest religious broadcasting network, in a frank and lively discussion of King's relevance for the contemporary church. The coming together of two controversial mega-church pastors with King's former aide and youngest daughter seemed more symbolic than substantive. In any case, Long called for "the same spirit that guided King" to be reclaimed in the Christian church. Insisting that "the same problems King faced in the Birmingham Jail are still here," Jackson challenged white and black Christians to "desegregate the church," to "bear some of the burden for the creation of racial reconciliation," and to "break down the cultural-racial divide." Lowery evoked images of the church as a coalition of conscience, and Bernice King raised the issues of racism, poverty, and war, while calling for a revival of "the kind of spiritual wildfire" that broke out in Montgomery with her father and others in 1955. The four clergypersons agreed on the need for "not just one prophetic voice" but "a prophetic army" that will spearhead "a new justice movement,"[85] thus advancing King's vision for the church and the human struggle to the next level.

Perhaps the most telling moment came when Bishop Long implied that the prophetic mantle had been passed to Bishop Jackson, that in Jackson God had raised up a prophetic voice that was sounding the trumpet forty years after King's death. This is yet another indication of how King has become a useful symbol in a protracted campaign by mega churches to promote a conservative moral and political platform. While not always so obvious, there are efforts to package King so that his image will stand acceptably in both the ecclesiastical establishment and the halls of government.[86] This is not entirely surprising, since King's legacy has been manipulated to fit the purposes and agenda of many different groups in this country, including right-wing politicians. But those clergypersons and politicians who use King as a kind of sacred aura for their political ends cannot honestly deny the depth of his prophetic critique of and challenge to the church and the nation, and nor can they overlook his willingness to pursue radical discipleship to the point of martyrdom.

Fear of the cross may account, perhaps more than anything else, for the failure of televangelists and mega preachers to fully embrace King's model of radical, prophetic ministry. King always said that the true prophet inevitably bears a cross, and the standard he set remains a challenge to the church that finds value in the spirit of sacrifice and in the redemptive possibilities of unearned suffering. "The cross may mean the death of your popularity," said King some fifty years ago. King went on to press the point in terms that are instructive for today's media ministers and mega-church pastors: "It may mean the death of your bridge to the White House. It may mean the death of a foundation grant. It may cut your budget down a little, but take up your cross and just bear it. And that is the way I have decided to go. Come what may, it doesn't matter now.[87]

The risks of martyrdom mean that few in today's churches, black and white, are willing and ready to create controversy by becoming uncompromisingly prophetic voices in society. Too many American churches are now afflicted with the virus of an anti-prophetic passion, and must therefore find ways to reclaim relevance and accountability. From all indications, the cross-bearing church, or image of the church as sacrificial lamb, died with King and the social-protest phase of the freedom movement. This could not be more unfortunate at a time when mega churches and their pastors are touching and speaking to far more people in this society and worldwide than King ever dreamed of addressing in his own time. Having such access and outreach appears at first glance to be a sign of divine favor, but the churches, in their new forms of corporate existence, are currently not equipped to transform a suffering and divided world, in part because their own infrastructures shield them from the cross.

Revisioning the Church: King as a Model for Reflection

The challenges confronting the Christian Church as a whole today are greater and more complex than at any other point in history, including the period during which Martin Luther King, Jr., lived and struggled. Some of these challenges are frighteningly evident in the internal life of the church itself, ranging from pedophilia among clergy and other issues of sexual abuse and integrity to differences over evangelism and pedagogy to the decline of mainline denominationalism. Other challenges are reflected in the larger sphere of the church's relationship to a world in which intolerance, injustice, violence, and human oppression still exist in alarming and growing proportions. Thus, there is a real need for the church to undergo a process of continuous renewal that is linked to a strong emphasis on the prophetic function.[88] King has much to say to the church in this regard, all the more because he was at heart a churchman and a faithful witness to the prophetic dimensions of the gospel. Moreover, so many of the problems with which he struggled remain in full force with the church today, and at a time when questions about the meaning of that institution and its proper role in the world still have tremendous traction.

The prophetic tradition of the ancient Hebrews, Jesus, and the Apostolic church lived anew for King as he set forth an alternative vision for the church in an age of peril and promise. He found echoes of this tradition in the black church, the Social Gospel, and personal idealism, intellectual sources that informed his challenge to the church around the problem of social evil. King interpreted, reinterpreted, and built on that prophetic tradition as he, in and through the church, applied its critical insights to the prevailing institutions, structures, values, priorities, and practices in order to expose their tendencies toward evil and injustice.[89]

King's model of prophetic witness and mission, not the entrepreneurial spirituality of today's mega preachers, holds the key to an authentically renewed and revitalized church in the twenty-first century. The mega-church phenomenon is elitist, capitalistic, and materialistic, whereas King offered a powerful alternative model for envisioning what constitutes the prophetic church. The need to reclaim that model could not be more important for the church as a whole, especially as it confronts both a crisis of values and serious questions about its relevance and reliability for today and tomorrow. This point of view is more carefully advanced in the subsequent paragraphs, which explain how King's prophetic vision and activism can be useful in not only reawakening and reforming the church but also, and perhaps more importantly, in making it a vital vehicle in creating and sustaining a culture of life, of openness and enlargement, of radical democracy, of peace and nonviolence, of sacrificial servant-hood, and of constructive self-criticism. These categories are not King's, but they are based on what has been learned from King and the movement he led.

King's thoughts on how the Christian faith might best speak to and ensure a culture of life are most essential for the church as that institution struggles for some consensus as to what this actually means. For many on the conservative wing of the church, it means fierce opposition to *Roe v. Wade* and any other effort aimed at sustaining both abortion rights and embryonic stem cell research. For many liberal Christians, a culture of life involves environmental stewardship, joining the fight against HIV AIDS, and meeting the basic necessities of the undernourished, ill-housed, and shabbily-clad, a mission priority also embraced by some progressive evangelicals today. King spoke to and acted on some of these concerns in prophetic ways in the 1950s and 1960s.[90] He took seriously the significance of Jesus Christ for the experience of the abundant life, and he clearly understood the life-giving power and resources of the church in these terms.[91] Also, he stressed the problem of ecclesiastical structures that produce unhealthy environments and people, and he had much to say for church traditions that affirm the dignity and worth of life, and that lift a vision of true humanity characterized by the beloved community. Hence, King's call for the church to respect life while caring for people in healthy, life-giving ways is instructive for Christians as they explore angles for addressing the global AIDS crisis, environmental protection concerns, post-Cold War ethnic cleansings, terrorism, genocide, public health, the needs of the handicapped, and issues of social, political, and economic justice.

Furthermore, pro-life Christian conservatives have much to learn from King about achieving moral consistency around the question of reverence for life. Strangely enough, through a political hijacking and manipulation of scripture and theological language, these fundamentalists and evangelicals oppose abortion and embryonic stem cell research while simultaneously sanctioning capital punishment and war,[92] thereby supporting King's oft-repeated assertion that even the church is susceptible to a tragic ambivalence in its soul, or to a schizophrenic personality. Also, many of the so-called pro-life Christians have eagerly supported government policies that lower pollution standards and ignore global environmental policies, especially during the George W. Bush administration. Unlike anti-abortionists or the so-called pro-lifers on the far right of the church, King's concern extended beyond the beginnings of life to embrace the complete continuum of life's issues. His strong opposition to the death penalty, war, and the taking of life generally can never be casually dismissed because it obviously squares with core and age-old church teachings, particularly as they relate to the *imago dei* principle and to an understanding of the communion of human lives equally precious before God.[93] King's pro-life position is also consistent with the Jesus tradition and the ethics of the early church—sources the church universal claims to accept as foundational and authoritative.

It is around the need for a culture of openness and enlargement that King's legacy continues to challenge the contemporary church on so many levels. King exhibited an amazing openness and receptivity to human differences, and not simply tolerance. To be sure, a culture of openness and enlargement was quite consistent with his understanding of the prophetic heritage, and also with his social and ethical personalism. Unfortunately, intolerance and loveless-ness have become metaphors for virtually all that has gone awry in the church since King's death. Much of this spirit is evident in the lingering, antiquated thinking about race and ethnicity, and in the personal and institutionalized racism that continues to fragment the social and political landscape on a national and global scale. Although more blacks and other persons of color are exposed to white ministries because of the pull of the media and the electronic church,[94] the Christian church as a whole is still essentially too European American in its structures, doctrines, mission outreach, and symbolism, and it remains one of the bastions of white supremacy in America. Moreover, multiracial and multiethnic churches that stand at the vanguard of prophetic-social justice advocacy are surprisingly few in number. King's sermons, mass meeting speeches, and writings, along with his superb record of social activism, are still among the most valuable resources for the church if it is to provide moral leadership in conquering the subtleties and complexities of racial and ethnic bigotry and intolerance.

It is also clear that when it comes to race and ethnicity as underlying and perennial issues, the church today faces challenges that were not as conspicuous and explosive during the King years. Because of immigration patterns, the cities of this country are becoming increasingly colored but not black, and this is leading to a resurfacing of white supremacist attitudes, anti-immigrant fears and biases in white and black communities, and new trends in the polarization and tensions that exist between the growing ethnic populations in the central cities of America's metropolitan areas.[95] The phenomenon of the racialized others becomes more apparent when issues like poverty, crime, and the overarching incarceration rates of African Americans and Hispanics are seriously considered.

This still unresolved effort to come to terms with the realities of race, and with issues of racial and ethnic diversity, is also reflected in an international context, forcing the United Nations in recent years to hold world conferences on racism.[96] King had deep concerns in his own time about the global impact of racism, and especially white supremacy, and he addressed the problem forthrightly through his prophetic witness and outreach, giving priority to an ethic of openness and enlargement.[97] Urgency demands that the contemporary church function likewise, even as it struggles to adjust to cultural shifts in communities, and even as it moves beyond King in reframing the dialogue on race, far beyond but not neglecting issues of black-white relations. The election of Barack Hussein Obama as the first African American president of the United States, in November 2008, does not mean that we now live in a postracial society and world. It may indeed result in a more powerful resurgence of raw racism and ethnic rivalries, thus reinforcing the need for moral leadership on the part of the church. Undoubtedly, efforts to broaden the dialogue on race and ethnicity would yield more possibilities for the creation of what King envisioned as a truly inclusive church.

Establishing a culture of openness and enlargement must also entail lifting a vision of a church and society without sexism and female subordination. This, too, is in conformity with King's legacy, for he spoke of raising "the status of womanhood" to positions "of dignity and honor and respect."[98] But gender discrimination continues to permeate the social, economic, and political fabric of America and of other countries, and it is still glaringly evident in the subtle and not so subtle ways in which the church worldwide continues to silence women.[99] Pastoral leadership remains largely a forbidden church role for women, and when it comes to female clergy in any capacity, routine-ness is still the great liability of the church, a problem evident in matters ranging from its unwillingness to alter unpopular teachings to its determination to maintain patriarchal structures. The dis-fellowshiping of congregations that approve women for ministry is common in some church communities, such as the Southern Baptist Convention. The role that the church and church structures play in the psychological and sexual abuse of women merely compounds the problem.

Although King was unable to transcend much of the cultural conditioning that validates male power and authority over women, he never accepted patriarchy as a divine ontological decree, at least in principle, and his model of the church was ultimately one of female inclusion. This was clearly consistent with his understanding of the church as the chief symbol of the beloved community. In defense of a unified body of Christ, or a body of believers that look beyond human differences, even gender, King turned to the Apostle Paul's assertion that "there is neither Jew nor Greek, there is neither slave nor free, there is neither male nor female, for you are all one in Jesus Christ" (Galatians 3:28).[100] Having witnessed firsthand the unique perspectives, gifts, and talents that women brought to the church and the human struggle in his times, King also established his defense on practical grounds.[101] His idea of opening the church to the strength of its own diversity is antithetical to the very concept of the patriarchal church, and it suggests the need to talk about the church universal in a way that is not only gender inclusive, but also biblically responsible.[102]

Undoubtedly, homosexuality and same-sex marriage constitute the greatest challenge facing any church that pursues a culture of openness and enlargement. Same-sex marriage is now perhaps the most compelling issue driving those on the right side of the religious and political spectrum, and homophobia is apparent in much of the internal life and critical discourse of religious institutions in the United States and abroad. Voices in churches of all denominations view pro-gay and lesbian activists as immoral and godless.[103] These issues are actually unfolding worldwide, as homophobia is becoming as much an emerging problem for the churches in Africa, Asia, Latin America, England, and Eastern Europe as it is for racist extremists in the United States, Germany, and Russia.[104] Some critics view the Christian churches as "the single greatest source" of the oppression of "lesbian, gay, bisexual, and transgender people."[105] Pierre Berton's description of the homosexual as the modern equivalent of "the leper in Biblical times,"[106] offered in 1965, is even more accurate today, thus undermining the image of the church as a refuge for "the least of these," or for the despised and rejected.

King was not a homophobe or an anti-gay bigot,[107] and his vision of a world completely free of hatred, intolerance, and oppression remains relevant for the church universal as it constructively confronts and addresses the contemporary moral quagmire surrounding sexual ethics and the broader issues of human sexuality. The ethicist Victor Anderson raises the central question for those who admire Martin Luther King, Jr.: "In the context of culture wars over sexuality and marriage, will the church be an advocate for the status quo or a moral institution of provocation, advocacy and celebration of difference?"[108] A careful study of King's own association with gays in the civil rights movement constitutes a real challenge for churches that refuse to honor the dignity and worth of such persons, and that see no need to reexamine their long-held assumptions about sex and sexuality. Clearly, issues involving lesbian, gay, bisexual, and transgender people cannot be legitimately ignored when considering what it means today to speak of King's enduring vision of the church as the symbol of the beloved community, a vision that defines all forms of bigotry and intolerance as equally problematic.

A culture of openness and enlargement also means that the church must be receptive to different worldviews, especially since it is functioning in an increasingly multicultural and multifaith world. This is consistent with King's growing sense of a globalized world, and of his use of the metaphors of "the world house" and "the world-wide neighborhood," in which people expand their understanding of what it means to live in a culturally, religiously, and ideologically diverse world.[109] The church universal has not yet learned how to nurture and sustain religious diversity in positive and meaningful ways, or how to witness and do mission in a world that also includes Judaism, Islam, Buddhism, Hinduism, and other faiths. This accounts in large measure for its troubled and uneasy relationship with different world cultures, philosophies, and religions, and, more specifically, for its insecurity in the face of atheism and secularism, for its inability to transcend an anti-Islamic, anti-Arab sensibility, for its lack of success in diagnosing and addressing the root causes of anti-Americanism in the Islamic world, and for its failure to deal creatively and in preventive ways with the dangers that lurk within various forms of religious terrorism.

King often suggested that the greatest barrier to understanding stems from Christians who assume that the truths they happen to affirm are universal ones, and he was always clear in maintaining that learning from different peoples and cultures is helpful in seeing that there are other legitimate and valuable ways of viewing the world and life itself. King believed that the growing pluralization of the society demanded a movement away from viewing diversity as a weakness to legitimizing it as a source of strength. Moreover, King, as stated previously, called for cooperation between people of different faiths, cultural backgrounds, and political persuasions so that the work of fashioning what he called "a new kind of man" could prosper, a course that would ultimately involve a mingling of the highest human values of peoples from every part of the globe."[110]

The last chapter of King's book *Where Do We Go from Here: Chaos or Community?* (1967) offers not only an exciting blueprint for church unity and

activism, but also a model for the type on pan-religious and inter-cultural dialogue that embraces justice, dignity, and human rights for all.[111] To be sure,
King challenged the church with a richer vision of its own universality, while
reminding it of the open-mindedness of the early Christians, who "believed
Christ to be at work in other faiths."[112] This could not be more relevant in a
world in which human-rights discourse is an emerging category for ideologues
with every kind of agenda, and in virtually every religious, cultural, and political
community. Serious reflections on King's legacy in this post-9/11 world, in
which there are deep tensions between the Christianity of America and the
West and the Islam of the East,[113] point to the need for not only the truly ecumenical church but also the church with a decisively pan-religious outlook and
agenda.

Although seldom noted, the church has an equally important role to play
in the shaping of a culture of radical democracy. The reference here is to the
type of democracy that King had in mind—namely, that which encourages the
mobilization and empowerment of local communities, participative leadership,
mass mobilization and movement, and prophetic possibilities for the expansion of rights and human enlargement. King held that the church could be an
important instrument in swaying the workings of democracy in the direction of
greater rights and privileges. Much of what has happened in recent years with
the church's involvement in politics is not a healthy leveling of this kind of
democracy. The interjection of the right-wing church view of Bible-based values
into American civic and political life led to an erosion of constitutional protections for everyone during the presidency of George W. Bush.[114] Since 9/11, the
most conservative side of the church has desperately sought to become a force
in forging an imperial America that subverts what most freedom-loving Americans cherish about their democratic life and values.[115] For the Christian Right,
including the mega churches, democracy serves the interests of the elite, not
what King called "the least of these."[116] This outlook is not prophetic, and it is
inconsistent with the very nature of a church supposedly committed to strength-
ening the spectrum of human rights and freedoms everywhere.

King viewed freedom as the most inestimable gift of God conferred on
humanity, and the goal of his crusade was the overturning of the prevailing
order of injustice and inequality while building in its place a democracy that
serves the interests of a broader justice and equality, and also the promise of
civil and political liberties. This is why King stands as a model for how the
church talks, envisions, and practices democracy. Furthermore, King demonstrated that prophetic advocacy is germane to the processes of true democracy, and one of the most monumental achievements of his movement is that
it taught citizens in the United States and abroad that even acts of civil

disobedience are morally justified as a protest against the denial and/or erosion of basic constitutional guarantees and protections. Perhaps more important, King made the church an instrument of this endeavor.[117]

As the nation struggles with the increasingly illusive concepts of liberty
and equality, which are contributing to a political current more uncertain than
ever before, the church needs to be empowered by a new democratic vision. It
needs a more perceptive and healthy view of how to reconcile faith with our
modern, pluralistic democracy; and King, who had a keen recollection of the
saddening silence from the church when basic civil liberties and personal pri-
vacy were imperiled by McCarthyism,[118] has much to offer in terms of insight
and example. It was his conviction that in a culture of radical democracy, dis-
senting voices and beliefs must always be treated with respect, a point too often
ignored by the most dogmatic and self-righteous in the churches today.

Another major challenge for the Christian church lies in the harnessing of
its commitment and energy in pursuit of a culture of peace and nonviolence,[119]
especially in this age of relentless and often violent change. The church has
tolerated violence for so long that it easily lives with it, and it is often morally
insensitive to those who are victims of physical, sexual, and psychological violence, some of which can be blamed on segments of the church itself and its
leadership.[120] The problem looms in larger and more disturbing proportions
on a global scale, as evidenced by sectarian warfare in Iraq, organized torture
and terrorism, ethnic cleansings, genocide, religiously based violence, political
assassinations, and the cycles of violence, repression, and reprisal that continue unabated in the Middle East.[121] The mounting cycles of violence at the
interpersonal, inter-group, and international levels further underscore the need
to revisit so much of what King said about the church as peacemaker.

In church cultures in which King's birthday is celebrated annually, nationally and internationally, the hard questions are inescapable: What would King
think of the many forms of violence?[122] In light of King's legacy of peace and
nonviolence, what should be the message of the church to the United States, a
nation known for its high rates of criminal violence, its hyper-military foreign
policy, its aggression against other nations, and its image as the prime culprit
in a frightening spectacle of world nuclear proliferation? What should the
church say to political leaders who ignore the Geneva Accords and other global
restraints, who disregard the world's system of justice, and who disavow longstanding international agreements relative to the control of nuclear, biological,
and chemical weapons? What should be the church's stand on global terrorism? Can the church morally justify its deafening silence in response to the
persecution, suffering, and death in Darfur and on other parts of the African
continent? The best answers to these questions will undoubtedly come from

ecclesial communities that are not tuned to a provincial myopia, but to a Kingian concept of peaceful coexistence for all humanity.

King's call for the church to "direct her concern toward the question of world peace," and to choose "the peace race" over "the arms race,"[123] is perhaps more urgent and necessary today than it was a half century ago. It is a call for the church to explore new paradigms for the ethics of war and peace. Too many in the churches are still framing war as a moral crusade, and few publicly embrace King's idea that peace is both an end in itself and a means to that end.[124] In highlighting peace as both a theological principle and an ethical priority, the church would do well to recall the normative authority of the early church, which was the prime motivation for King's peace advocacy in an ecclesial context. A potent and effective peace witness spearheaded by the church is what he wanted to see ultimately. Often quoting the Prophet Isaiah, he envisioned a day when "Men will beat their swords into plowshares, and their spears into pruning hooks, and nation shall not rise up against nation, and neither shall they study war anymore" (Isaiah 2:4).[125] By appropriating and re-appropriating King's teachings and model of nonviolent coexistence, the church could assume much-needed leadership in creating venues for peace talks, negotiations, and nonviolent resolution of conflict at all levels of human life. That institution must become a more willing and giving partner in God's mission of peacemaking and compassionate service. As King so often pointed out, the church cannot follow the Prince of Peace while sanctioning or remaining silent in the face of violence and human destruction.

There remains a real need for the church as a whole to reclaim King's legacy of an active faith by committing itself to a culture of sacrificial servant-hood.[126] King found a workable model for the church in Jesus' sacrifice on the cross, and he scolded the church for proudly displaying the symbol of the cross while refusing to bear it in all of its agonizing intensity. For King, radical, costly discipleship was about the ultimate calling of the church to share fully in the sacrificial life of Christ himself. This is part of what he was thinking when he challenged the church to turn to the gospel mandate in a suffering world. By sacrificing himself in the service of the poor, oppressed, and outcast, King, like Jesus and the Apostolic church, transformed undeserved suffering into a creative force,[127] and highlighted the need for a fundamental redirection of the church's attitude and resources. Furthermore, King exposed the superficiality and frivolousness of arguments made against radical, sacrificial discipleship, while calling, at the same time, for a dangerous, universal, and excessive altruism.[128]

Strangely, King's concept of the committed and sacrificial life[129] is being overshadowed by the mega preachers' emphasis on the abundant and prosperous life. Here, sacrificial servant-hood is too often equated with certain charity and social outreach ministries, and never with a persistent, prophetic assault on the structures of power and of social, economic, and political injustice. King's own life and eventual martyrdom mirrored profound images of the sacrificial church, of the cross-bearing church, and the church as suffering servant.[130] To be sure, his prophetic advocacy, social activism, and willingness to die for the highest ethical ideal are a much-needed corrective for those Christians who construct edifices to shield themselves from any form of crucifixion, and who ignore the biblical connection between personal faith, a dangerous unselfishness, and sacrificial service. Restoring the church's image as sacrificial servant, as the chief symbol of redemptive suffering, is perhaps the most powerful way for that institution to take King's values into the twenty-first century. African American theologians, such as Delores S. Williams, Anthony B. Pinn, and others find this concept of the cross to be very problematic,[131] but for King, a theologian himself, there was no Christianity or Christian social witness without the cross.[132]

Equally significant is the need to reassert the church's role in promoting a culture of constructive self-criticism. By word and example, King demonstrated that there is no necessary inconsistency between being an ardent defender of the faith, an astute and constructive critic of the church, and a courageous and persistent advocate for ecclesial reform. By viewing itself from a new satirical perspective, for example, the church could perhaps better understand why so much of the world considers it irrelevant and even anachronistic. This may be necessary in a culture in which there is a larger distrust for institutions as a whole, including the church. A satirical look at the contemporary church scene could make the institutional church more receptive to the need for change in its identity, programs, and activity. A truly prophetic self-evaluation, in the Kingian mode, holds even greater possibilities for ecclesial reformation.[133]

King personified this capacity for self-criticism, for he was as critical of himself as he was of the Christian church. Like the ancient Hebrew prophets, he turned his critique inward to keep himself true to his calling and purpose, for he knew that he, too, was under the judgment of what he proclaimed.[134] Also in ways reminiscent of the prophets, he experienced one failure after another, was often unpopular, and died before accomplishing his goals, but he was sustained by the conviction that though he had been unsuccessful at times, God would not ultimately fail. Here, King's humility in confronting his own personal failures was clearly matched by the courage with which he criticized the institutional church. In compassionate and compelling terms, he spoke to the crisis in the church in an age of uncertainty and hope, a crisis compounded by that body's failure to embark upon a painful journey of self-critique and examination. Moreover, King echoed the same concerns as the prophets as he attacked the church's racism, its idolatry, and its neglect of the poor and help-less. He saw in the church an institution that appeared healthy in all of its external ways, but rotten to the core. This is why he frequently quoted Amos 5:24: "But let justice roll down like waters, and righteousness as an ever-flowing stream."[135] The message King proclaimed so eloquently to the church was at once simple and endlessly prophetic. That message was also twofold. First, that God would not continue to allow devoted people not to practice what they affirmed in creeds and ceremonies, because there has to be continuity between what is affirmed and celebrated in worship and what is practiced in daily life. Second, that the church should seek God and not evil in the face of the coming judgment.[136]

King maintained that constructive critics had to come from within the church, and no one fulfilled that role better than he, even as he loved, served, defended, and used the church as a social and political base for his civil and human rights activities. The call to constructive self-criticism was clearly apart of King's vision for ecclesial renewal.[137] The dominant model of the church today is not conducive to an intense, internal critique of its structures and lead-ership, and, in that regard, it falls short of King's more critical and holistic approach. This explains in part why the contemporary church is in danger of losing a sense of itself and what it was called to be in the world. In the face of this crisis, King's concept of a church that avails itself to the same kind of pro-phetic critique that it so freely visits upon bars, nightclubs, and gambling estab-lishments obviously has some pedagogical value.[138]

How might the church benefit from King's prophetic critique of ecclesial structures and exiting forms of church life? Is it really possible for the contem-porary church to forge the collective ecclesial will to address constructively and prophetically its own weaknesses and failures? Much of this study rests on the thesis that a lot of what King said remains a relevant commentary on the limi-tations and failures of the church, and that the church has the power and resources to experience a rebirth, or to reinvent itself in conformity with King's more radical view of the biblical-prophetic tradition, and with the demands of a vibrant culture of constructive self-criticism. However, this will require a number of important steps on the part of the church, aside from producing constructive critics within its own ranks.

First, the church must discover new ways of interpreting, applying, and putting into practice what it affirms and celebrates in its liturgical and/or sac-ramental life.[139] The whole history of the church reveals an ongoing tension between attempts to preserve traditional teachings, values, and styles of wor-ship and the mandate to be Christ to the world, or to deal sufficiently and in highly practical ways with fresh challenges, changing cultural realities, and an ever-declining human condition. For the sake of moral consistency, the church must bring its creedal, ceremonial, and celebrational life more in line with mission priorities that meet human needs, hopes, and aspirations. This is what King had in mind when he spoke of the need for the church to refocus its power, genius, and resources in broader directions. As King so often suggested, the church should not do or say any more on Sunday morning than it is willing to suffer and die for during the rest of the week.[140]

Second, the church needs to rethink and reshape its relationship to the state and the body politic. When the state subsidizes the church, through faith-based initiatives and other government programs, it is impossible for the church to be prophetic in any real sense. This explains the unhealthy alliance that existed in recent years between the conservative side of the church, including the mega-church phenomenon, and the U.S. government, an issue that should be seriously considered in any call for a culture of constructive self-criticism in the internal life of the church. At points in American and world history, the state has too often dictated, even in subtle ways, church affairs and initiatives, and the idea of a federal law that would prevent church involvement in political activities altogether is disturbing but not necessarily beyond the realm of the possibility.[141] One can only imagine what would have happened had such a federal mandate existed in King's time, when the politicization of the church occurred perhaps on an unprecedented scale.

In a culture in which church involvement in political affairs and in public policy initiatives has become a part of mainstream development discourse, the church, in being true to itself and its calling, must cease being the embodiment of a type of civil religion that serves the interests of the state, and that validates or sanctions the status quo.[142] This is King's enduring challenge to the church of today and tomorrow. Lines between Christian conservatives and the Republican Party should be more clearly drawn and detectable, and self-serving politicians should not be allowed to use the church as a platform for the advancement of a narrow moral reform agenda, and as a convenient place for photo opportunities. Also, the prophetic and protest possibilities of the church need to be restored and more fully actualized, especially if it is to intervene creatively and productively in public affairs and in the kind of public policy-making that truly benefit what King labeled "the least of these." Developments in this vein would help restore the idea of the church as a workable model for radical, prophetic social service and transformation, a model King established and drew on substantially. King's metaphors of the nonconformist church, the church as conscience of the state, or the church as a maladjusted presence,[143] which grew out of his reading of the ancient church, is what must become more real and visible in these times.

Third, the church should develop better and more practical ways of employing its material power for the common good, and not merely for self-serving mega preachers and other church leaders, an issue King raised on some occasions.[144] The church is one of the richest and most influential institutions in the world, but its power is too often misused and abused. Pedophilia, sexism, and homophobia have become metaphors for the general abuse of power in the contemporary church, a problem aggravated by the church's reluctance to be decisively self-critical and self-transforming. The answer, as King so often said, is never in defending the rigidity of present ecclesial patterns and structures, but in revolutionizing them and putting them to the service of human liberation and empowerment on the broadest scale possible. In other words, ecclesial communities must cease being impervious to the echoes of King's impassioned calls for a church that generously uses its vast resources to address human need on life's Jericho Road.[145]

A fourth necessary step on the part of the church involves a turning toward a more biblical conception of what it means to be genuinely prophetic. Merely claiming the Bible as an authoritative source and guide in matters of faith, doctrine, morality, and practice is not enough, as King consistently noted. Scripture has to be read as a divine command to not only speak truth to power but also to critique and ultimately eliminate evil and unjust structures, laws, and institutions. This is how King understood the meaning and significance of the prophetic church.[146] Today there is a need to take back the scriptures from the so-called Christian Right, which is distorting them in support of an accommodationist rather than a prophetic ethic, and which is using them to defend the rich and powerful and to demonize the poor and marginalized. King's sermons suggest possibilities for constructive thought and reflection around the question of how the ancient Hebrew prophets, and the biblical-prophetic tradition as a whole, can be made relevant for the church in this venture and in every age.[147]

The church has reached a watershed moment in its history, a period during which it is affected by a vast and complex array of forces that King never fully envisioned. A deep restlessness and uncertainty permeate much of contemporary church life, and few of the faithful are actually talking about breathing new life into the church's moribund structures, or moving into an intentional mode of co-creating the future church with God. Moreover, more questions are being raised about the ability of the church to remain a living, vigorous organism, and, more specifically, about its capacity to spearhead purposeful Christian witness and praxis in the world in this new century and millennium.

Apparently, there is a need for a new Pentecost breaking out in the church, or an experience of discovering God's will anew; and King, who remains in some ways the soul and conscience of the church, has something to say to that institution about this. King often told us that the church is a provisional entity that requires continuing renewal in light of changing social realities. He also taught that the mission of the church begins in the hearts and minds of committed human beings, and he modeled a path to ecclesial involvement that Christians in the contemporary world can proudly follow. But King's role was only to lead the church across the Red Sea into the wilderness, not into the Promised Land. He hinted at this in a speech on the last night of his life, when he, in a moment of epiphany, declared that he had reached the mountaintop.[148] King also suggested that the church, and perhaps all humanity, would ultimately reach the land of promise, even if he himself failed to get there with them. At that particular point, and indeed throughout his life, the future ideal of the church was the real church for him; the church of the not yet, or that church that was and still is in a state of becoming.[149]

Afterword

When Martin Luther King, Jr., was shot in Memphis, Tennessee, on April 4, 1968, news of the terror spread. For many people, news of the assassination provoked profound anger—a black liberator had been gunned down by some white-faced bigot. There were explosive race riots in sixty cities. For others, perhaps because of the season, King's death seemed a reiteration of the cross; they read King as a Christian martyr. Gradually, most of us citizens realized that Martin's death was the most powerful event in the history of twentieth-century America. The pattern of his life and death reshaped our nation. Now we celebrate King, on his birthday each January, with sermons and speeches, marching and spirituals. A Christian martyr has become a national holiday.

In the process, however, something has happened to the national memory. Most Americans now celebrate King as a social leader—the "Reverend" in front of his name has all but disappeared. We forget that he was a minister, that his social vision was shaped by scripture, and that all of his life he was a child of the church. Lewis V. Baldwin's book is a grand gift because we can once more remember Martin Luther King, Jr.'s life as a churchperson, and we can recover the theological wisdom from which he viewed both church and culture.

A Catholic friend once observed, "Instead of Apostolic Succession, you Protestants have family trees." Maybe that is the case. King's father was a preacher, and his great-grandfather, grandfather, uncles, and brother as well. His mother was a trained Christian musician. As a child, King knew what it meant to live from Sunday to

Sunday. What's more, his ministerial descent was wonderfully defined; for his grandfather and father, both pastors in Atlanta, were actively involved in the pursuit of social justice. Their sermons resonated beyond the stained-glass windows and walls of the church. We honor King's birthday, locating him on a day in our annual calendar, without realizing that by birth he entered a family that was itself a ministry. Baldwin helps us to recover this astonishing heritage, reminding us that King was involved with the church all his life.

But now, having read the pages of this volume, we know that Martin did not celebrate the institutional church uncritically. He believed that churches were called not only to save souls one by one but also to champion Isaiah's vision of God's new social order, a world in which the brokenhearted would be healed, the imprisoned released, and the oppressed set free in the freedom of God. So King had harsh words for churches with ministries that lacked a social dimension, or that preached nothing more than inward renewal for a people victimized by racism, poverty, and cruel, psychotic public policy. The church needs a challenge of this nature today.

Baldwin has devoted much of his academic life to studying the figure of Martin Luther King, Jr. Baldwin is an ace historian, perceptive and meticulous— good heavens, even his endnotes are good reading. Most of us are familiar with his two-volume work, *There is a Balm in Gilead: The Cultural Roots of Martin Luther King, Jr.* (1991) and *To Make the Wounded Whole: The Cultural Legacy of Martin Luther King, Jr.* (1992), but his research has continued with several studies since, relating King's influence to troubled South Africa, and examining the Muslim and Christian perspectives of Malcolm and Martin, as well as an important volume surveying issues of law, politics, and religion as necessary and related ingredients in the context of King's struggle for social justice. But the volume you have in hand paints a picture of King's life and contributions as a churchman, and it may come closer to portraying the essence of the man himself than anything else you will have read. Baldwin, himself an active churchman and fine theologian in the black church, and one who has known the struggle for social justice first hand, is superbly equipped to understand the complex image that is Martin Luther King, Jr.

Were you moved by reading this book? I most certainly was. I found myself moved and, in a way, rededicated. Oh, Lewis V. Baldwin would never be preachy; but somehow the bold portrait he has provided of King should encourage any minister, any churchgoer, any Christian, to live free in a wider way in God's massive human world, for the church at its best cannot be confined by any artificial human barriers.

Having given us a profound picture of Martin Luther King, Jr., in a last chapter, Baldwin leads us into the midst of our own troubled time and place. We now live in an America in which mega churches have direct phone lines to the White House, where a rising right-wing seems intent on splitting the image of the "beloved community" into contending sides, and where "the word of God" is often something swiped from old Internet sermons or locked up in the rote of a weekly lectionary. The prophet Amos, whose powerful words coursed through King's proclamations, seems prescient nowadays. Once Amos described a people who "wander from sea to sea," and who "run to and fro, seeking the word of God," but were unable to find it anywhere in the land. There are echoes of this today. Today theology has disappeared from public thought in America, so that people are left to make up their minds from political commitments, patriotic hoopla, or stock market prosperity. They wander. Amos's brutal diagnosis highlighted a famine of the word of God, and so does Baldwin's portrayal of the church in the post-King world. Perhaps more important, Baldwin, after locating us in our strained and violent contemporary world, asks the church to learn from a fallen Christian leader, Martin Luther King, Jr. He reminds us that King was not simply a civil rights professional, but also a dedicated churchman whose theological smarts guided every move he made, let alone his vision for the future. As Baldwin notes, King obviously heard "the word of the Lord," and so must the church in our times.

Reading Lewis V. Baldwin's book will deepen any reader's faith in the living God and in the divine mandate for the church. In many churches, one gets the feeling that a once-upon-a-time God comes to us from a big Bible-book designed for the therapy of individual souls. As Baldwin says over and over, this image of the church must not ultimately prevail, especially if King's legacy is to be taken seriously. King, though surely shaped by a biblical heritage, always seemed to have an eye on the future of God. He saw the coming kingdom of God not as some cushioned hereafter but as a new social order, or a world-size "beloved community." Small wonder that in his last years, he turned to the broad issues of poverty and peace, thus setting a new standard for church-based social activism. As Baldwin points out repeatedly, there are lessons here for the contemporary church.

One cannot honestly study King's thought, label it "social gospel," and then discard it as outmoded, or as something left over from the 1920s, or even the 1950s and 1960s, for that matter. No, King's "social gospel" was Gospel, *the Gospel*, which is surely why his bold words, which transformed the land in which we live, also remain as a challenge to the church today and tomorrow.

Page after page, Baldwin has written a wonderful book, a gift for us all.

David G. Buttrick
Drucilla Moore Buffington Professor of
Homiletics and Liturgics, Emeritus
Divinity School, Vanderbilt University

Notes

INTRODUCTION

1. Vivian Green, *A New History of Christianity* (New York: Continuum, 1996), 372; Lewis V. Baldwin, *To Make the Wounded Whole: The Cultural Legacy of Martin Luther King, Jr.* (Minneapolis: Fortress Press, 1992), 84; Peter J. Paris, "The Religious World of African Americans," in Jacob Neusner, ed., *World Religions in America: An Introduction* (Louisville: Westminster John Knox Press, 2000), 54; and Ronald S. Flowers, *Religion in Strange Times: The 1960s and 1970s* (Macon: Mercer University Press, 1984), 187. For similar and more extensive assessments of King in relation to African American religion, history, and culture, see Lewis V. Baldwin, *There Is a Balm in Gilead: The Cultural Roots of Martin Luther King, Jr.* (Minneapolis: Fortress Press, 1991), 1–14; James H. Cone, *Martin & Malcolm & America: A Dream or a Nightmare* (Maryknoll, N.Y.: Orbis Books, 1991), 19–37; Gayraud S. Wilmore, *Last Things First* (Philadelphia: Westminster Press, 1982), 89–90; Gayraud S. Wilmore and Choan-Seng Song, *Asians and Blacks: Joseph Cook Memorial Lectures*, Sixth Series (Spring 1972), 64–75; and Gayraud S. Wilmore, *Black Religion and Black Radicalism: An Interpretation of the Religious History of African Americans*, Third Edition (Maryknoll, N.Y.: Orbis Books, 1998), 204–213.

2. See William G. McLoughlin and Robert N. Bellah, eds., *Religion in America* (Boston: Beacon Press, 1970), 376; Martin E. Marty, *Pilgrims in Their Own Land: 500 Years of Religion in America* (New York: Penguin Books, 1986), 444; Amanda Porterfield, *The Transformation of American Religion: The Story of a Late Twentieth Century Awakening* (New York: Oxford University Press, 2001), 97–98; and Jay Tolson, "The New Old-Time Religion: Evangelicals Defy Easy Labels," *U. S. News & World Report*, 135, no.20 (8 December 2003),

41. According to some scholars in the field, King was "probably the foremost Christian personality in America in the twentieth century." Thus, it is very unfortunate that American church historians, especially those who specialize in developments in the South, have given so little attention to King. See Ronald C. White, Jr. et al., eds., *American Christianity: A Case Approach* (Grand Rapids, Mich.: William B. Eerdmans, 1986), 138.

3. See Porterfield, *The Transformation of American Religion*, 105; Charles R. Wilson, *Judgment & Grace in Dixie: Southern Faiths from Faulkner to Elvis* (Athens: University of Georgia Press, 1995), 31–32 and 162; Andrew M. Manis, *Southern Civil Religions in Conflict: Civil Rights and the Culture Wars* (Macon, Ga.: Mercer University Press, 2002), 4 and 9; Robert N. Bellah and Phillip E. Hammond, *Varieties of Civil Religion* (San Francisco: Harper & Row, 1980), 15 and 194; John D. Elder, "Martin Luther King and American Civil Religion," *Harvard Divinity Bulletin*, New Series, 1, no.3 (Spring 1968), 17–18; David Howard Pitney, *The Afro-American Jeremiad: Appeals for Justice in America* (Philadelphia: Temple University Press, 1990), 142–143; and Andrew Shanks, *Civil Society, Civil Religion* (Cambridge, Mass.: Blackwell Publishers, 1995), 6. Charles R. Wilson's claim that King used the rhetoric of southern civil religion, and most especially the language of the late-nineteenth-century "lost cause," is strongly critiqued in Lewis V. Baldwin et al., *The Legacy of Martin Luther King, Jr.: The Boundaries of Law, Politics, and Religion* (Notre Dame, Ind.: University of Notre Dame Press, 2002), 42–51.

4. For a work that compares King and Bonhoeffer on the concepts of radical discipleship and authentic churchmanship, see J. Deotis Roberts, *Bonhoeffer & King: Speaking Truth to Power* ((Louisville: Westminster John Knox, 2005), 3–130. Swift is correct in referring to King's efforts as "applied Christianity," or as "an appeal to essential Christianity." See Donald C. Swift, *Religion and the American Experience: A Social and Cultural History, 1765–1997* (New York: M. E. Sharpe, 1998), 171.

5. Among the unpublished theses on the subject, one might consider Phillip A. Rahming, "The Church and the Civil Rights Movement in the Thought of Martin Luther King, Jr." unpublished M.Th. thesis, Southern Baptist Theological Seminary, Louisville, Kentucky (July 1971); Randall G. Anderson, "The Beloved Community: A Contemporary Model for the Mission of the Church in America." unpublished D.Min. dissertation, the Claremont School of Theology, Claremont, California (May 1978); and John M. Thompson, "Martin Luther King, Jr. and Christian Witness: An Interpretation of King Based on a Theological Model of Prophetic Witness," unpublished Ph.D. dissertation, Fordham University, New York (1981).

6. Of particular importance are Martin Luther King, Jr., "An Autobiography of Religious Development," in Clayborne Carson et al., eds., *The Papers of Martin Luther King, Jr., Volume I: Called to Serve, January 1929–June 1951* (Berkeley: University of California Press, 1992), 359–362; Martin Luther King, Jr., *Stride Toward Freedom: The Montgomery Story* (New York: Harper & Row, 1958), 9–224; Martin Luther King, Sr., *Daddy King: An Autobiography*, with Clayton Riley (New York: William Morrow, 1980), 13–214; Clayborne Carson, ed., *The Autobiography of Martin Luther King, Jr.* (New York: Warner Books, 1998), 1–366; and Coretta Scott King, *My Life with Martin Luther King, Jr.* (New York: Henry Holt, 1993), 1–315.

7. Miller is quite right in concluding that "King's thought is not rigorously systematic," and so is Smith, who declares that "there were unresolved tensions in King's thought up to the time of his assassination." See William R. Miller, "Gandhi and King," *Fellowship*, January 1969, 7; and Kenneth L. Smith, "Foreword" to Lewis V. Baldwin, *Toward the Beloved Community: Martin Luther King, Jr. and South Africa* (Cleveland: Pilgrim Press, 1995), x.

8. See Henry Bettenson and Chris Maunder, eds., *Documents of the Christian Church*, Third Edition (New York: Oxford University Press, 1999), 375.

9. Peter J. Ling, *Martin Luther King* (New York: Routledge, 2000), 11–14.

10. Carson et al., eds., *King Papers*, I, 363.

11. Baldwin, *Balm*, 124–126 and 166–168.

12. Carson et al., eds., *King Papers*, I, 361.

13. Richard Lischer, *The Preacher King: Martin Luther King, Jr. and the Word that Moved America* (New York: Oxford University Press, 1995), 5–6. One might go beyond Lischer's claim to suggest that it was the black church community as a whole in Atlanta, irrespective of denominational differences, that nurtured and shaped young King, spiritually, morally, intellectually, and otherwise. To limit that influence to the black Baptist Church in Atlanta is to suggest, quite unconvincingly, that denominationalism posed major barriers or perhaps insurmountable boundaries between black churches in King's childhood environment. To the contrary, the Big Bethel African Methodist Episcopal Church (AME) on Auburn Avenue in Atlanta had as much impact on forging the church culture and world to which King was introduced quite early in life as did the Ebenezer and Wheat Street Baptist Churches. All three of these churches existed in close proximity to each other on Auburn Avenue. See Baldwin, *Balm*, 159–228; Carson et al., eds., *King Papers*, I, 9; and Michael G. Long, *Against Us, But for Us: Martin Luther King, Jr. and the State* (Macon, Ga.: Mercer University Press, 2002), 15–20.

14. See "Hugh Downs Interview with Martin Luther King, Jr.," NBC "Today Show" (18 April 1966), unpublished document, The Library and Archives of the Martin Luther King, Jr., Center for Nonviolent Social Change (KCLA), Atlanta, Georgia, 1–2; Martin Luther King, Jr., "Address at a Conference of Religious Leaders," Sheraton Hotel, Washington, D.C. (11 May 1959), unpublished document, KCLA, 4; Martin Luther King, Jr., "America's Chief Moral Dilemma," an address delivered at the General Synod of the United Church of Christ, Palmer House, Chicago (6 July 1965), KCLA, 2; Martin Luther King, Jr., "The Mission to Social Frontiers," a speech (n.d.), unpublished document, KCLA, 5; and Walter E. Fluker, *They Looked for a City: A Comparative Analysis of the Ideal of Community in the Thought of Howard Thurman and Martin Luther King, Jr.* (Lanham, Md.: University Press of America, 1989), 150.

15. Martin Luther King, Jr., *Why We Can't Wait* (New York: New American Library, 1964), 89–90.

16. John J. Ansbro, *Martin Luther King, Jr.: Nonviolent Strategies and Tactics for Social Change* (Lanham, Md.: Madison Books, 2000), 111.

17. See William D. Watley, *Roots of Resistance: The Nonviolent Ethic of Martin Luther King, Jr.* (Valley Forge, Pa.: Judson Press, 1985), 17; Baldwin, *Balm*, 183–206; and Adam Fairclough, *To Redeem the Soul of America: The Southern Christian Leadership*

Conference and Martin Luther King, Jr. (Athens, Ga.: University of Georgia Press, 1987), 1–3. Ahlstrom has in mind, first and foremost, the preaching tradition and spiritual songs that extend deep into the history and traditions of the black church. See Sydney E. Ahlstrom, *A Religious History of the American People* (New Haven: Yale University Press, 1972), 1076.

18. Baldwin, *Balm*, 181–182; and John Hope Franklin, "The Forerunners," in *American Visions*, 1, no.1 (January-February 1986), 26–35.

19. See Timothy L. Lake, "A Certain Democracy: The Political Philosophies of Martin Luther King, Jr. and Cornel West." unpublished Ph.D. dissertation, Bowling Green State University, Bowling Green, Ohio (May 2004), xi–xii (Preface); Fairclough, *To Redeem*, 4–7; and Brian Ward and Tony Badger, eds., *The Making of Martin Luther King, Jr. and the Civil Rights Movement* (New York: New York University Press, 1996), 1. One scholar underscores "the mood among recent scholars of the American Civil Rights Movement, who have been trying to escape what might be termed 'King-centric' studies for more than a decade." See Ling, *King*, 1.

20. Rufus Burrow has also stated the point well. "The question," he submits, "is not whether or not the person was more important or influential than the movement or the counter-movement, but the extent to which each impacted the development of the other." Burrow continues: "Indeed, without the person(al) factor, i.e., King, any movement or counter-movement would be different from what they were. In this case there was a movement and counter-movement precisely because there was a Martin Luther King, Jr. at that precise time in American History." Rufus Burrow, Jr., to Lewis V. Baldwin (24 March 2005), 1.

21. See Wilmore, *Black Religion*, 204; Baldwin, *Balm*, 227–328 and 334; and C. Eric Lincoln, "The Black Church and a Decade of Change," Part II, *Tuesday at Home*, March 1976, 7.

22. See Flowers, *Religion*, 187. C. Eric Lincoln was probably the first scholar to forcefully make this point. "The Black Church is not the Negro Church radicalized," he wrote in the early 1970s; "rather, it is a conscious departure from the critical norms which made the Negro Church what it was." Lincoln added: "The Negro Church died in the moral and ethical holocaust of the Black struggle for self documentation because the call to Christian responsibility is in fact first and foremost a call to human dignity and therefore logically inconsistent with the limitations of Negro-ness." Lincoln's claim that the black church emerged as the product of the conflict between "conscienceless power" and "powerless conscience" is difficult to refute. See C. Eric Lincoln, *The Black Church Since Frazier* (New York: Schocken Books, 1974), 106–110.

23. See Wilmore, *Black Religion*, 204; Ward and Badger, eds., *The Making of Martin*, 1–12.

24. See Flowers, *Religion*, 180, 185, and 187.

25. Peter W. Williams, *America's Religions: Traditions and Cultures* (New York: MacMillan, 1990), 396.

26. Perhaps King's most perceptive and measured critique of the white church is afforded in his "Letter from the Birmingham City Jail" (1963). See King, *Can't Wait*, 89–90.

27. Scholars are exploring these issues increasingly as they focus on various dimensions of the civil rights and peace movements of the fifties and sixties. See Michael B. Friedland, *Lift Up Your Voice Like a Trumpet: White Clergy and the Civil Rights and Antiwar Movements* (Chapel Hill: University of North Carolina Press, 1998), 78–80, 114–131, 182–183, and 202–204; Andrew M. Manis, "'Dying from the Neck Up': Southern Baptist Resistance to the Civil Rights Movement," *Baptist History and Heritage*, 34, no.1 (Winter 1999), 33–48; Bill J. Leonard, "A Theology for Racism: Southern Fundamentalists and the Civil Rights Movement," *Baptist History and Heritage*, 34, no.1 (Winter 1999), 49–68; and Baldwin et al., *Legacy*, 81–123.

28. Ronald J. Sider, ed., *Evangelicals and Development: Toward a Theology of Social Change* (Philadelphia: Westminster Press, 1981), 48. King would have agreed with Flynt's contention that "Like white Baptist defenders of slavery a century earlier, southern racism fed off biblical literalism." See J. Wayne Flynt, *Alabama Baptists: Southern Baptists in the Heart of Dixie* (Tuscaloosa: University of Alabama Press, 1998), 458.

29. See Martin Luther King, Jr., "Who is Their God?" *Nation*, 195 (13 October 1962), 209–210; King, *Can't Wait*, 89–91; and S. Jonathan Bass, *Blessed Are the Peacemakers: Martin Luther King, Jr., Eight White Religious Leaders, and the "Letter from Birmingham Jail"* (Baton Rouge: Louisiana State University Press, 2001), 1–258.

30. Baldwin, *Balm*, 229–272.

31. See Martin Luther King, Jr., *Where Do We Go from Here: Chaos or Community?* (Boston: Beacon Press, 1968), 167–168.

32. Martin Luther King, Jr., to Dr. Harold E. Fey (23 June 1962), KCLA, 1–3; and Lewis V. Baldwin and Amiri YaSin Al-Hadid, *Between Cross and Crescent: Christian and Muslim Perspectives on Malcolm and Martin* (Gainesville: University Press of Florida, 2002), 120–121.

33. This subject is examined to some degree in Baldwin and Al-Hadid, *Cross and Crescent*, 3 and 115–127.

34. This point is strongly advanced in Lewis V. Baldwin, "Revisioning the Church: Martin Luther King, Jr. as a Model for Reflection," in *Theology Today*, 65, no.1 (April 2008), 26–40.

35. Baldwin, "Revisioning," 26–27.

36. Lewis V. Baldwin, "The Perversion of Public Religion," *Orbis*, 5, no.7 (April 2006), 12–13 and 18; and Dale P. Andrews, "Global Conflict and the Preaching Tradition of Martin Luther King, Jr.," in *The Review of Faith & International Affairs*, 6, no.1 (Spring 2008), 61–63.

CHAPTER 1

1. Lewis V. Baldwin, *There Is a Balm in Gilead: The Cultural Roots of Martin Luther King, Jr.* (Minneapolis: Fortress Press, 1991), 30–44 and 159–228; Lewis V. Baldwin, "Understanding Martin Luther King, Jr. within the Context of Southern Black Religious History," *Journal of Religious Studies*, 13, no.2 (Fall 1987), 1–26; and Lewis V.

Baldwin et al., *The Legacy of Martin Luther King, Jr.: The Boundaries of Law, Politics, and Religion* (Notre Dame, Ind.: University of Notre Dame Press, 2002), 1–51.

2. King's church experiences during his student days in Chester, Pennsylvania, and Boston, Massachusetts, have not been treated seriously by scholars. For some attention to the subject, see Baldwin, *Balm*, 125–127 and 167.

3. One might also speak of "the Ebenezer ethos" or what Richard Lischer terms the "Ebenezer Gospel." From the perspective of this author, the "Ebenezer tradition" encompasses both. The "Ebenezer tradition" refers to the ways in which Atlanta's Ebenezer Baptist Church has historically combined a biblically and theologically conservative message of personal salvation with a political demand for justice and equality of opportunity. Lischer seems to suggest that the "Ebenezer Gospel" should be associated with King, Jr., only. That concept, and the larger phenomenon of the "Ebenezer tradition," should extend to A. D. Williams and King, Sr., as well. See Richard Lischer, *The Preacher King: Martin Luther King, Jr. and the Word that Moved America* (New York: Oxford University Press, 1995), 221–242.

4. "An Historical Overview," in *Ebenezer Baptist Church: The Centennial Celebration, 1886–1986: A Program Booklet* (Atlanta: Colton Communications, 1986), 1; Martin Luther King, Sr., *Daddy King: An Autobiography*, with Clayton Riley (New York: William Morrow, 1980), 68–102; and Coretta Scott King, *My Life with Martin Luther King, Jr.*, Third Edition (New York: Henry Holt, 1993), 14–16 and 304–306.

5. G. S. Ellington, "A Short Sketch of the Life and Work of Rev. A. D. Williams, D. D.," in *Programme of the Thirtieth Anniversary of the Pastorate of Rev. A. D. Williams of Ebenezer Baptist Church* (16 March 1924), 1–2; Bruce A. Calhoun, "The Family Background of Martin Luther King, Jr.: 1810–1893," King Project Seminar Paper, 1987, Library and Archives of the Martin Luther King, Jr. Center for Nonviolent Social Change, Inc. (KCLA), Atlanta, Georgia, 1–5; "Rev. A. D. Williams," *Atlanta Independent* (4 April 1904); King, *Daddy King*, 82–87; Clayborne Carson et al., eds., *The Papers of Martin Luther King, Jr., Volume I: Called to Serve, January 1929-June 1951* (Berkeley: University of California Press, 1992), 1–57; "Dr. M. L. King, Jr.'s Church Designated National Landmark," *Atlanta Daily World*, 5 July 1974, 1; "Daddy King Dies," *Atlanta Daily World*, 13 November 1984, 1 and 6; "Some Highlights in Rev. King, Sr.'s Career," *Atlanta Daily World*, 15 November 1984, 1; and Keith D. Miller, "The Roots of the Dream," *New York Times Book Review*, 15 March 1992, 13–14.

6. "Mrs. Jennie C. Williams Dies Suddenly: Funeral Will be Conducted Wednesday," *Atlanta Daily World*, 19 May 1941, 1; "Last Respects are Paid to Mrs. Williams: Hundreds Crowd Ebenezer Church for Final Rites," *Atlanta Daily World*, 22 May 1941, 1 and 5; "Mrs. M. L. King, Sr. Taught Only Love," *Atlanta Daily World*, 2 July 1974, 1; and "Mrs. King Called Mother to Some and Friend to All," *Atlanta Daily World*, 5 July 1974, 1.

7. Eugene D. Genovese, "Pilgrim's Progress," *New Republic*, 11 May 1992, 34; Clayborne Carson, ed., *The Autobiography of Martin Luther King, Jr.* (New York: Warner Books, 1998), 6; and Baldwin, *Balm*, 159–174.

8. Carson et al., eds., *King Papers*, I, 361; and Carson, ed., *King Autobiography*, 6.

9. Carson et al., eds., *King Papers*, I, 30 and 102–107; and Carson, ed., *King Autobiography*, 6.

10. Carson et al., eds., *King Papers*, I, 1–74 and 359–363; Carson, ed., *King Autobiography*, 1–12; King, *My Life*, 4–5, 8–9, and 75–78; King, *Daddy King*, 108–109 and 127; Baldwin, *Balm*, 17–21 and 103–126; and Genovese, "Pilgrim's Progress," 34. Apparently, King, Jr.'s church and home came together in his consciousness when he spoke of the kind of moral and spiritual discipline he received as a child. He noted:

> Well, I guess it was a relatively strict—coming up in a minister's home I faced the discipline that you would face in the very—a fervent religious background. However, I don't think it was over strict to the point that I developed any personality conflicts—conflicts as a result of my early childhood, but it was strict enough for me to develop certain disciplinary principles as I came up.

See John Freeman, "Face to Face: BBC Interview with Martin Luther King, Jr.," U.K. London, England, transcribed from a TV telediphone recording (29 October 1961), unpublished document, KCLA, 2.

11. Carson, ed., *King Autobiography*, 6; Carson et al., eds., *King Papers*, I, 361; Baldwin, *Balm*, 165–166; Keith D. Miller, *Voice of Deliverance: The Language of Martin Luther King, Jr. and Its Sources* (New York: Free Press, 1992), 39–40; and James J. Bacik, *Contemporary Theologians—Martin Luther King, Jr.: Struggling for Freedom* (Chicago: Thomas More Association, 1988), no. 18, 1–2.

12. Carson, ed., *King Autobiography*, 15–16; and Zelia S. Evans and J. T. Alexander, eds., *The Dexter Avenue Baptist Church, 1877–1977* (Montgomery: Dexter Avenue Baptist Church, 1978), 69.

13. Evans and Alexander, eds., *Dexter Avenue*, 69; John Hope Franklin, ed., *The Souls of Black Folk in Three Negro Classics* (New York: Avon Books, 1965), 338–339; private interview with the Reverend Ralph David Abernathy, Atlanta, Georgia (7 May 1987); and Baldwin, *Balm*, 31.

14. See E. Franklin Frazier, *The Negro Church in America* (New York: Schocken Books, 1963), 45; Martin Luther King, Jr., *Stride toward Freedom: The Montgomery Story* (New York: Harper & Row, 1958), 177–178; and Baldwin, *Balm*, 191–192. For a remarkably interesting essay that is quite useful for understanding this dimension of black church life, see Cheryl Townsend Gilkes, "The Black Church as a Therapeutic Community: Suggested Areas for Research into the Black Religious Experience," *Journal of the Interdenominational Theological Center*, 8, no.1 (Fall 1980), 29–44.

15. While King, Jr., lamented what he saw as excessive emotionalism in the black church, there is no evidence that he thought any differently about white fundamentalist and evangelical churches in Atlanta and across the South, for they, too, were known for such excesses. Being barred from white churches would not have shielded him from a knowledge of this, especially since the subject received wide commentary from critics of southern life and culture like H. L. Mencken. Mencken referred to the South as "a religious funny farm," and "In the minds of most Americans the twentieth century South" was "a curious mixture of earnest, toothy Evangelicals and briar-hopping, Bible-thumping, snake-handling zealots." See David E.

Harrell, Jr., ed., *Varieties of Southern Evangelicalism* (Macon, Ga.: Mercer University Press, 1981), 45.

16. King, *Daddy King*, 127.

17. Carson et al., eds., *King Papers*, I, 1, 30, and 107; and King, *Daddy King*, 109 and 127.

18. For important references to the black church as "a place of refuge," and the extent to which King cherished this image, see Bacik, *Contemporary Theologians*, 2.

19. King, *Daddy King*, 85; and "Atlanta is Swept by Raging Mobs Due to Assaults on White Women: 16 Negroes Reported to be Dead," *Atlanta Constitution*, 23 September 1906, 1–2.

20. Carson et al., eds., *King Papers*, I, 21.

21. Martin Luther King, Jr., to the Reverend Jerry M. Chance (9 May 1961), unpublished document, Martin Luther King, Jr. Papers, Special Collections, Mugar Memorial Library, Boston University, Boston, Massachusetts, 1; Martin Luther King, Jr., "Discerning the Signs of History," a sermon delivered at Ebenezer Baptist Church, Atlanta (15 November 1964), unpublished document, KCLA, 4–5; and Baldwin, *Balm*, 224–227.

22. Carson, ed., *King Autobiography*, 6; Carson et al., eds., *King Papers*, I, 361; Baldwin, *Balm*, 159–174; and Walter E. Fluker, *They Looked for a City: A Comparative Analysis of the Ideal of Community in the Thought of Howard Thurman and Martin Luther King, Jr.* (Lanham, Md.: University Press of America, 1989), 81–86.

23. The sheer power of this image registers when one considers the fact that members of Ebenezer were present when King, Jr., was born and baptized, during his graduation celebrations and wedding, when he was licensed and ordained, when he was installed as pastor at Dexter Avenue Baptist in Montgomery and as co-pastor at Ebenezer, when his four children were born, at the time he was awarded the Nobel Peace Prize in 1964, and during his funeral in April 1968. See Carson, ed., *King Autobiography*, 6–7; Carson et al., eds., *King Papers*, I, 360–363; King, *Daddy King*, 141, 169, 183, and 191; and King, *My Life*, 4, 9, 14–15, 50, 62–64, 69, 72, 75, 77, 87, 93, 140, 181, 201, 206, 225–226, 232, 288, 292, 300, and 314–315.

24. Apparently, this extended family network was just as powerful in the King home, which was occupied at one time by three generations in the King family: A. D. and Jennie C. Parks Williams, Martin, Sr., and Alberta Williams King, and Martin, Jr., his sister Christine, and his brother A. D. Daddy King has stated that "What some people now call the extended family was very much a part of Negro life in those days, and Reverend and Mrs. Williams had always kept their home filled with aunts, cousins, friends of the family, boarders—anyone who required a place to live in solid Christian harmony." See King, *Daddy King*, 72 and 81.

25. Carson, ed., *King Autobiography*, 6–7; Carson et al., eds., *King Papers*, I, 360–363; Lewis V. Baldwin, "The Making of a Dreamer: The Georgia Roots of Martin Luther King, Jr.—A Review Essay," in *Georgia Historical Quarterly*, 76, no.3 (Fall 1992), 639–646; Baldwin, *Balm*, 91–127 and 159–206; and Fluker, *Looked for a City*, 81–92.

26. See Hart M. Nelsen et al., eds., *The Black Church in America* (New York: Basic Books, 1971), 29–43 and 77–99; W. E. B. DuBois, *The Negro Church: A Social Study Done Under the Auspices of Atlanta University* (Atlanta, Ga.: Atlanta University Press,

1903), 1–208; Carter G. Woodson, *The History of the Negro Church* (Washington, D.C.: Associated Publishers, 1921), 242–260; and Benjamin E. Mays and Joseph W. Nicholson, *The Negro's Church* (New York: Russell & Russell, 1933), 1–19, 154–167, and 278–294.

27. King, *Daddy King*, 71, 82, 85, and 89; and Baldwin, *Balm*, 95.

28. King, *Daddy King*, 81–86, 89, and 91–194; Carson et al., eds., *King Papers*, I, 26, 30, and 34; "Last Respects Paid to Mrs. Williams," 1; King, *My Life*, 75; and Michael G. Long, *Against Us, But for Us: Martin Luther King, Jr. and the State* (Macon, Ga.: Mercer University Press, 2002), 7–15.

29. Baldwin, *Balm*, 95; King, *Daddy King*, 81–86 and 89; and Carson et al., eds., *King Papers*, I, 10–26. Interestingly enough, A. D. Williams is either completely ignored or rarely mentioned in major studies of African Americans and the Social Gospel movement. See, for examples, Ronald C. White, Jr., *Liberty and Justice for All: Racial Reform and the Social Gospel* (San Francisco: Harper and Row, 1990), 77–265; Ralph E. Luker, *The Social Gospel in Black & White: American Racial Reform, 1885–1912* (Chapel Hill: University of North Carolina Press, 1991), 14 and 177; and Calvin S. Morris, *Reverdy C. Ransom: Black Advocate of the Social Gospel* (Lanham, Md.: University of America Press, 1990), 1–171. For support for the claim that Williams stood in the same tradition as black Social Gospelers such as Reverdy C. Ransom, see Ransom's piece on "The Race Problem in a Christian State" (1906) in Milton C. Sernett, ed., *African American Religious History: A Documentary Witness* (Durham, N.C.: Duke University Press, 1999), 337–346.

30. King, *Daddy King*, 82–85; "Noted Atlanta Divine Dies Suddenly: Sudden Death of Reverend A. D. Williams Shocks Entire Nation," in *Georgia Baptist* (10 April 1931), 1; Lizzie Hunnicut, "In Memoriam," *Georgia Baptist* (25 August 1931), 1–3; *Program for Rev. Adam Daniel Williams' Funeral Service* (24 March 1931), Christine King Farris Personal Collection, Atlanta, Georgia; King, *Daddy King*, 82, 85, and 90; Carson et al., eds., *King Papers*, I, 10–26; *Atlanta Constitution*, 22 March 1931, 16A; and Baldwin, *Balm*, 95.

31. See Gayraud S. Wilmore, *Black Religion and Black Radicalism: An Interpretation of the Religious History of African Americans* (Maryknoll, N.Y.: Orbis Books, 1998), 170–174 and 190–191.

32. King, *Daddy King*, 89.

33. A. D. Williams, "Address at the National Convention of the NAACP," Cleveland, Ohio (26 June 1919), unpublished document, 1–3. This document was provided by Clayborne Carson, the Senior Editor of the Martin Luther King, Jr. Papers Project at Stanford University, Stanford, California.

34. King, *Daddy King*, 82.

35. Williams, "Address at the National Convention," 1–3; and King, *Daddy King*, 81–90.

36. One King scholar has noted that "A. D. Williams, Daddy King's father-in-law and predecessor at Ebenezer Baptist, was a major impetus behind Daddy King's involvement in politics." See Long, *Against Us*, 11.

37. One source views Williams as "a pioneering advocate of a distinctive African-American version of the social gospel, endorsing a strategy that combined

elements of Washington's emphasis on black business development and
W. E. B. DuBois's call for civil rights activism." See Carson et al., eds., *King Papers*,
I, 10 and 26; Rufus Burrow, Jr., *God and Human Dignity: The Personalism, Theology,
and Ethics of Martin Luther King, Jr.*, unpublished manuscript (2004), 1–200; and
Clayborne Carson, "Martin Luther King, Jr., and the African American Social
Gospel," in Timothy E. Fulop and Albert J. Raboteau, eds., *African-American
Religion: Interpretive Essays in History and Culture* (New York: Routledge, 1997),
341–364.

38. Long, *Against Us*, 9–10; King, *Daddy King*, 103–106; Baldwin, *Balm*, 120–121;
and Carson et al., eds., *King Papers*, I, 33–34.

39. Speaking of his father's interest in civil rights on one occasion, King, Jr.,
recounted:

> Well, he's quite interested, actually. He has had an actual interest in civil
> rights, across the years. He is a pastor of a large church in Atlanta, Georgia,
> and, incidentally, I'm co-pastor of the church, and he has had a strong
> interest in civil rights. He has been president of the National Association for
> the Advancement of Colored People in Atlanta, and he has always stood out
> in social reform.

See Freeman, "Face to Face," 1; and King, *Stride*, 20.

40. Minutes of the Thirty-Sixth Annual Session of the Atlanta Missionary Baptist
Association, Inc., Mt. Zion Baptist Church, Cartersville, Georgia (October 15–17, 1940),
18. Carson et al., eds., *King Papers*, I, 34; and Long, *Against Us*, 10.

41. See Gayraud S. Wilmore, *Black Religion and Black Radicalism: An
Interpretation of the Religious History of African Americans* (Maryknoll, N.Y.: Orbis
Books, 1998), 163–195.

42. Minutes of the Thirty-Sixth Annual Session, 18. Also see King, Sr.'s speech
in Minutes of the Thirty-Ninth Annual Session of the Atlanta Missionary Baptist
Association, Inc., Zion Hill Baptist Church, Atlanta, Georgia (12–14 October 1943),
12–14.

43. Concerning the church as "all-comprehending institution," Woodson wrote
the following:

> The Negro church touches almost every ramification of the life of the Negro.
> As stated elsewhere, the Negro church, in the absence of other agencies to
> assume such responsibilities, has had to do more than its duty in taking care
> of the general interests of the race. A definitive history of the Negro church,
> therefore, would leave practically no phase of the history of the Negro in
> America untouched. All efforts of the Negro in things economic, educational
> and political have branched out of or connected in some way with the rise
> and development of the Negro church.

See Carter G. Woodson, "The Negro Church, an All-Comprehending Institution," in
The Negro History Bulletin, 3, no.1 (October 1939), 7; Lewis V. Baldwin, "Revisiting the
'All-Comprehending Institution': Historical Reflections on the Public Roles of Black
Churches," in R. Drew Smith, ed., *New Day Begun: African American Churches and*

Civic Culture in Post-Civil Rights America (Durham, N.C.: Duke University Press, 2003), 15–38; and Milton C. Sernett, *Black Religion and American Evangelicalism: White Protestantism, Plantation Missions, and the Flowering of Negro Christianity, 1787–1865* (Metuchen, N.J.: Scarecrow Press, and American Theological Library Association, 1975), 19 and 175 n.3.

44. Early in life, King, Jr., himself wrote: "Even though I have never had an abrupt conversion experience, religion has been real to me and closely knitted to life. In fact the two cannot be separated; religion for me is life." See Carson et al., eds., *King Papers*, I, 363.

45. Robert M. Franklin, "Awesome Music, Great Preaching, and Revolutionary Action: The Mind of Martin Luther King, Jr.," *Princeton Seminary Bulletin*, 23, no.4 (New Series 2002), 176; Baldwin, *Balm*, 159–228; and Noel Leo Erskine, *King Among the Theologians* (Cleveland: Pilgrim Press, 1994), 1–10.

46. Carson, ed., *King Autobiography*, 9–11; Carson et al., eds., *King Papers*, I, 108–111 and 362; and Long, *Against Us*, 3–7.

47. Lewis V. Baldwin and Amiri YaSin Al-Hadid, *Between Cross and Crescent: Christian and Muslim Perspectives on Malcolm and Martin* (Gainesville: University Press of Florida, 2002), 24 and 366 n.53; "M. L. King Contributes to Sociology Digest," *Atlanta Daily World*, 29 June 1948, 1; Carson, ed., *King Autobiography*, 15; and Carson et al., eds., *King Papers*, I, 121.

48. A. D. Williams' influence on King, Jr., has not received sufficient attention from scholars, and even less attention has been given to the ways in which Jennie C. Parks Williams and Alberta Williams King impacted King, Jr.'s thinking and life of Christian service. One of the most interesting treatments of A. D. Williams's and Daddy King's influence on King, Jr., is afforded in Long, *Against Us*, 7–15.

49. At the time of her death, Mrs. Williams was eulogized in glowing terms and was variously referred to as "a prominent church worker," as a women "prominent in city and state church affairs," as "a missionary worker," as "a splendid wife and a good church worker," as one who "gave the church' her "loyal and untiring service," and as a "beloved Baptist leader who, during her husband's lifetime, helped him build the edifice in which she was funeralized." See "Mrs. Jennie C. Williams Dies Suddenly," 1; "Last Respects are Paid to Mrs. Williams," 1 and 5; "Funeral Notices," *Atlanta Daily World*, 19 May 1941, 6; "Funeral Wednesday," *Atlanta Daily World*, 20 May 1941, 1; "Mrs. Williams to be Funeralized this Afternoon," *Atlanta Daily World*, 21 May 1941, 1; "Funeral Notices," *Atlanta Daily World*, 21 May 1941, 6; *Atlanta Daily World*, 22 May 1941, 1 and 5; Carson, ed., *King Autobiography*, 1; and Carson et al., eds., *King Papers*, I, 29 and 359. For an interesting and insightful analysis of Big Mama Jennie's influence on the faith development of King, Jr., see Frederick L. Downing, *To See the Promised Land: The Faith Pilgrimage of Martin Luther King, Jr.* (Macon, Ga.: Mercer University Press, 1986), 97–120.

50. Carson et al., eds., *King Papers*, I, 359; Downing, *Promised Land*, 97–120; and Baldwin, *Balm*, 34, 94, 101–102, and 107–111.

51. "Mrs. M. L. King, Sr.," 1; "Mrs. King Called Mother," 1; "Mrs. M. L. King, Sr., Deacon are Fatally Shot in Church: Suspect Allegedly was Gunning for Rev.

King–Gunman's Third Victim Recovering at Grady," *Atlanta Daily World*, 2 July 1974, 1; "'How Much More Can a Man Take?'—Dr. King," *Atlanta Daily World*, 2 July 1974, 1; "Atlantans Urge End to Protests During Mourning for Mrs. King," *Atlanta Daily World*, 4 July 1974, 1; "Thousands Mourn Mrs. King's Death: FBI Probes Conspiracy Possibility," *Atlanta Daily World*, 4 July 1974, 1; "Death Pace Emphasized by King Rites," *Atlanta Daily World*, 4 July 1974, 5; "NEA Regrets Death of Mrs. King," *Atlanta Daily World*, 7 July 1974, 2; "Ebenezer Baptist Moves on Inspite [sic] of Tragedy," *Atlanta Daily World*, 9 July 1974, 1; "Seek Motives in King Death, Jordan Asks," *Atlanta Daily World*, 9 July 1974, 3; "Mrs. King's Accused Killer Indicted; Asks Sanity Exam—Judge Refuses to Delay Indictment," *Atlanta Daily World*, 11 July 1974, 1; and Carson et al., eds., *King Papers*, I, 360 and 362. King once stated that "I owe a special debt to my mother and father, whose deep commitment to the Christian faith and unswerving devotion to its timeless principles have given me an inspiring example of the strength to love." See Martin Luther King, Jr., "An Address at the Recognition Dinner in Celebration of the Nobel Peace Prize," Dinkler Plaza Hotel, Atlanta (27 January 1965), unpublished document, KCLA, 3. King, Jr.'s tendency to avoid violence during his childhood owed much to Alberta's influence, for he recalled:

> Well, I think probably it was a combination of two things. I hadn't thought of nonviolence at that early age, as a system of thought, or as a practical technique. I think a great part of it was that I just didn't think; I wouldn't dare retaliate or hit back when a white person was involved, and I think some of it was a part of my native structure so to speak; that is, I have never been one to hit back too much.

See Freeman, "Face to Face," 5.

52. King, *Stride*, 19; Carson et al., eds., *King Papers*, I, 362–363; and Christine King Farris, "The Young Martin: From Childhood through College," *Ebony*, 41, no.3 (January 1986), 57. The claim that King, Jr., "despised the white race" during his childhood is a bit too harsh and is certainly open to debate. King, Jr., himself spoke at points of coming "perilously close to resenting all white people," and at other times of feeling "determined to hate every white person," but it is highly doubtful that he actually hated whites, for that was not typical among black children in a religious culture that constantly highlighted the danger of returning hatred for hatred. See Michael G. Long, *Martin Luther King, Jr. on Creative Living* (St. Louis, Mo.: Chalice Press, 2004), 47–48 n.33; King, *Stride*, 90; and Carson et al., eds., *King Papers*, I, 362–363.

53. Freeman, "Face to Face," 3; Carson et al., eds., *King Papers*, I, 32 n.101 and 359–363; and King, *Daddy King*, 130.

54. One King scholar offers brilliant insights which are useful for understanding Ebenezer's role in the shaping of King, Jr.'s sense of self:

> The effort to develop personality is one of the reasons that recognition is such an important aspect of black church life. Anyone who is part of the

black church or who has attended black church functions will note the amount of time spent in calling the names of people and recognizing the various services and contributions rendered by the membership. Everyone from the cooks in the kitchen, the person who typed the program, to the larger contributors, is recognized. It is true that many persons consider these acts of recognition immature and a waste of time. However, one must recognize that this is one of the black church's many ways of building a sense of personal worth in those who must survive in a system which depersonalizes them every day of the week.

See William D. Watley, *Roots of Resistance: The Nonviolent Ethic of Martin Luther King, Jr.* (Valley Forge, Pa.: Judson Press, 1985), 35.

55. Carson et al., eds., *King Papers*, I, 30 and 79. It is reported that King, Jr., "had a performer's voice as well as a performer's ear," and that Alberta "nurtured his musicality. By the 1940s, her annual church choir concerts attracted overflowing crowds." See Peter Ling, *King* (New York: Routledge, 2002), 14. King, Jr., spoke of having accompanied his mother "on two or three occasions" as she served as organist for the Women's Auxiliary of the National Baptist Convention when that group met on the campus of the Southern Baptist Theological Seminary in Louisville, Kentucky. See Martin Luther King, Jr., "The Church on the Frontier of Racial Tension: An Address Given as One of the Gay Lectures," Southern Baptist Theological Seminary, Louisville, Kentucky (19 April 1961), unpublished document, KCLA, 1.

56. Carson et al., eds., *King Papers*, I, 28.

57. King, *Stride*, 19–21; and Baldwin, *Balm*, 121–124. When only six years old, King, Jr., heard his father speak in strikingly similar terms in an Atlanta shoe store after being told to sit in the colored section before being served. "I still remember walking down the street beside him," King, Jr., recounted of his father years later, "as he muttered, 'I don't care how long I have to live with this system, I will never accept it.'" One source captures Daddy King as one "relentless in his pursuit of justice," and as one who "was an inspiration to his children, who carried on his outstanding tradition." Another source noted that from "the seeds" of Daddy King's "body blossomed the flower that liberated a people and touched the soul of a nation." See "An Historical Overview," 1; and D. Michael Cheers and Moneta Sleet, Jr., "Dignitaries Eulogize 'Daddy' King During Final Atlanta Rites," *Jet*, 67, no.13 (3 December 1984), 12. King once remarked that "My home influenced me because my father, as a minister, was always interested in civil rights and helping people who had been treated unjustly or unfairly." See "An Interview with Martin Luther King, Jr.," George A. Towns Elementary School, Atlanta (11 March 1964), unpublished document, KCLA, 1; Dora Byron to Martin Luther King, Jr. (4 April 1964), unpublished document, KCLA, 1; "Profile Series: The Script for a Taped Interview with Martin Luther King, Jr.," Emory University and Station WAII-TV (Channel 11), Atlanta (9 April 1964), unpublished document, KLCA, 3; and Donald M. Schwartz, "The Making of an Integration Leader," *Chicago Sun-Times*, 21 January 1963, 16 and 29.

58. Carson et al., eds., *King Papers*, I, 53–54; Miller, *Voice*, 29–40; Freeman, "Face to Face," 1.

59. Carson et al., eds., *King Papers*, I, 363; and Baldwin, *Balm*, 277–279. Interestingly enough, King, Jr., stated in a 1964 interview that "I always wanted to be a minister. My father is a minister, as you know. My grandfather was a minister and my great grandfather (so I'm told) was a minister also." On another occasion, King, Jr., observed: "Because of the influence of my mother and father, I guess I always had a deep urge to serve humanity, but I didn't start out with an interest to enter the ministry. I thought I could probably do it better as a lawyer or doctor." See "King Interview," George A. Towns, 1; Martin Luther King, Jr., "Early Days," unpublished excerpts from "Thou Fool," a sermon delivered at the Mt. Pisgah Missionary Baptist Church, Chicago (27 August 1967), KCLA, 1; Freeman, "Face to Face,"1; and Carson, ed., *King Autobiography*, 14.

60. Baldwin, *Balm*, 160–206 and 224–225. Peter J. Ling contends that "Martin Luther King would inherit and expand upon his family's oratorical gifts," especially as revealed in the sermonic styles of A. D. Williams and King, Sr., and the storytelling ability of Jennie C. Parks Williams. Keith D. Miller most likely had this in mind when he commented that King "enlarged" or "expanded folk preaching in significant ways," taking it beyond "any political effort black America had previously mounted." It is virtually impossible to think of King, Jr.'s oratorical gifts apart from those of King, Sr., and of A. D. Williams, who was described as "a forceful and impressive speaker." See Ling, *King*, 14; Miller, *Voice*, 140; Carson et al., eds., *King Papers*, I, 15; and "Adam Daniel Williams," in A. B. Caldwell, ed., *History of the American Negro and His Institutions: Georgia Edition* (Atlanta: A. B. Caldwell, 1917), 214.

61. Evans and Alexander, eds., *Dexter Avenue*, 69; and Genovese, "Pilgrim's Progress," 34.

62. Miller, *Voice*, 29. Also see Baldwin, *Balm*, 273–310.

63. King, *My Life*, 83.

64. "Newsmakers: An Interview with Martin Luther King, Jr.," transcript of a program on Channel 2, KNXT-TV, Los Angeles (10 July 1965), unpublished document, KCLA, 5; and "Certificate of Ordination to the Gospel Ministry for Martin Luther King, Jr.," Ebenezer Baptist Church, Atlanta (25 February 1948), unpublished document, KCLA, 1.

65. Freeman, "Face to Face," 2; and "Transcript of an Interview with Martin Luther King, Jr. and Harry Belafonte," "Merv Griffin Show," New York (6 July 1967), KCLA, 2. In the church culture in which King, Jr., grew up in the South, very young men who claimed to have received "the call to preach" were at times required to preach their trial sermons from the floor, not the pulpit. The idea was that the candidate had to grow and prove himself in the eyes of the elders before ascending to the pulpit.

66. King, *My Life*, 5; and Keith D. Miller, "Martin Luther King, Jr. and the Black Folk Pulpit," in *Journal of American History*, 78, no.1 (June 1991), 121.

67. King, Sr., offered the following reflections on King, Jr.'s increasing maturity as a young preacher at Ebenezer:

Listening to the fine sermons that combined so many of the Bible's truths with wisdom of the modern world, I marveled at how all was interwoven into a most compelling, stirring oratory. M. L. was still a son of the Baptist South; there'd never be any doubt about that. But there was a deeper, considerably more resonant quality in his preaching, and on the Sundays he relieved me in the pulpit, I grew increasingly more moved by his growth, the probing quality of his mind, the urgency, the fire that makes for brilliance in every theological setting.

See King, *Daddy King*, 147.

68. Carson et al., eds., *King Papers*, I, 108–111 and 121.

69. "King Interview," George A. Towns, 1; Freeman, "Face to Face," 1–2; King, "Address at Recognition Dinner," 3; Schwartz, "The Making of an Integration Leader,"16 and 29; Byron to King (4 April 1964); "Profile Series," 3; King, "Thou Fool," 1; King, *Stride*, 18–22; and King, *My Life*, 62.

70. Surprisingly, this larger church community has received little attention even from the most celebrated King scholars. Some attention is given to the subject in Baldwin, *Balm*, 125, 167, and 282–287.

71. Carson et al., eds., *King Papers*, I, 9 and 16; and Long, *Against Us*, 15–16.

72. Fluker, *Looked for a City*, 85; and Long, *Against Us*, 1–38.

73. One of the best sources for understanding this culture is King, *Daddy King*, 14–139.

74. Carson et al., eds., *King Papers*, I, 360; and Carson, ed., *King Autobiography*, 2.

75. Carson et al., eds., *King Papers*, I, 9, 10, 13, 14n, 16, 18, 25, 28, and 85; King, *Daddy King*, 155 and 157; and Long, *Against Us*, 15–20.

76. "NAACP Plans Big Meeting Sunday," *Atlanta World*, 27 January 1932, 1; and Carson et al., eds., *King Papers*, I, 16.

77. Genovese, "Pilgrim's Progress," 34; and Long, *Against Us*, 7–20.

78. "Mrs. Williams to be Funeralized," 1.

79. "Western Union Telefax from Martin Luther King, Jr. to Mrs. Julia P. Borders" (28 September 1965), unpublished document, KCLA, 1; and Martin Luther King, Jr., "Statement Regarding the Death of Mrs. Julia P. Borders" (24 October 1965), unpublished document, KCLA, 1.

80. Lewis V. Baldwin, private interview with the Reverend Ralph David Abernathy, Atlanta (17 March 1987), unpublished, the author's files; and Baldwin, *Balm*, 276. It has been reported that "a bitter rivalry of sorts developed between Daddy King and Borders," but neither King, Sr., nor King, Jr., made reference to this. See Long, *Against Us*, 16.

81. For two of the most interesting works on Borders's life and ministry, see James W. English, *The Prophet of Wheat Street: The Story of William Holmes Borders—A Man Who Refused to Fail* (Elgin, Ill.: David C. Cook, 1973), 3–205; and James W. English, *Handyman of the Lord: The Life and Ministry of the Reverend William Holmes Borders* (New York: Meredith Press, 1967), 3–177. Also see Long, *Against Us*, 15–20.

82. Carson et al., eds., *King Papers*, I, 14–18, 81, 83, 78, 85, and 89.

83. King, Jr.'s tendency not to attach a lot of significance to church labels and denominational differences was apparently one quality that heavily influenced the attitude toward the church held by the young lady, Coretta Scott, who was a member of

the African Methodist Episcopal Zion Church and who would become his wife. See King, *My Life*, 50–51, 57, and 72.

84. In a brilliant essay, Lawrence Jones reminds us that the quest for the beloved community among African Americans began long before King, Jr., made this the goal of his life. See Lawrence N. Jones, "Black Christians in Antebellum America: In Quest of the Beloved Community," in *Journal of Religious Thought*, 38, no.1 (Spring-Summer 1981), 12–19. Also see Baldwin, *Balm*, 172–173.

85. Carson et al., eds., *King Papers*, I, 121.

86. King, *Daddy King*, 127, 141, and 144; King, *My Life*, 63; "Cultural League Meets Tonight," *Atlanta Daily World*, 1 June 1948, 3; "Cultural League Meets Tonight," *Atlanta Daily World*, 15 June 1948, 1; "Rev. M. L. King, Jr. to Preach Sunday at Ebenezer," *Atlanta Daily World*, 24 July 1948, 3; "Rev. M. L. King, Jr. to Fill Pulpit at Ebenezer Sunday," *Atlanta Daily World*, 21 August 1948, 2; Carson, ed., *King Autobiography*, 15; Baldwin and Al-Hadid, *Cross and Crescent*, 23–24 and 366–367 n.53; and Baldwin, *Balm*, 32.

87. *Atlanta: A City of the Modern South*, compiled under the auspices of The Writer's Program of The Works Projects Administration in the State of Georgia (New York: Smith and Durrell, 1942), 132–133; Farris, "The Young Martin," 56; and Baldwin, *Balm*, 163–164.

88. Andrew P. Watson makes an important distinction between shouting and sacred dance, one which is useful for this discussion of the spiritual and artistic side of African American church life in King, Jr.'s early years. Watson writes:

> Shouting as described here is not to be confused with the "holy dance." Such of these dances as have been observed are group affairs and have specified places in the ceremony. In most cases, there are instruments, and the dancers move and sway to the music and singing. Shouting, on the other hand, is a spontaneous act, and may happen any time the individual feels the spirit.

See Clifton H. Johnson, ed., *God Struck Me Dead: Voices of Ex-Slaves* (Cleveland: Pilgrim Press, 1993), 12.

89. This term is taken from Lawrence W. Levine, *Black Culture and Black Consciousness: Afro-American Folk Thought from Slavery to Freedom* (New York: Oxford University Press, 1978), ix (Preface).

90. Evans and Alexander, eds., *Dexter Avenue*, 69; Carson, ed., *King Autobiography*, 6 and 15–16; Lee E. Dirks, "'The Essence is Love': The Theology of Martin Luther King, Jr.," *National Observer*, 30 December 1963, 1 and 12; Miller, *Voice*, 39–40; and King, *My Life*, 57 and 83.

91. Baldwin, *Balm*, 24–25; Baldwin and Al-Hadid, *Cross and Crescent*, 26–28; and Long, *Against Us*, xi–xxi and 1–229.

92. Fluker, *Looked for a City*, 156–158; and Baldwin, *Balm*, 16–36.

93. Carson, ed., *King Autobiography*, 6 and 15–16; Carson et al., eds., *King Papers*, I, 361–363; and King, *My Life*, 12–13 and 57.

94. King, *Daddy King*, 71.

95. Carson et al., eds., *King Papers*, I, 38. Also see King, *My Life*, 12–13.

96. Ling, *King*, 21. Eugene Genovese says that at Morehouse, King, Jr., "was rather prone to partying" and "was not yet an especially dedicated student." See Genovese, "Pilgrim's Progress," 33.

97. Baldwin and Al-Hadid, *Cross and Crescent*, 16–17; Ling, *King*, 21; and Carson et al., eds., *King Papers*, I, 38.

98. See, for an example, "Heads Look Over Corruption in Church, Says Dr. Woodson," *Atlanta World*, 2 December 1931, 2; and Baldwin and Al-Hadid, *Cross and Crescent*, 14.

99. "King Interview," George A. Towns, 1; Dereck J. Rovaris, Sr., *Mays and Morehouse: How Benjamin E. Mays Developed Morehouse College, 1940–1967* (Silver Spring, Md.: Beckham House, n.d.), 3; Lawrence E. Carter, Sr., ed., *Walking Integrity: Benjamin E. Mays, Mentor to Martin Luther King, Jr.* (Macon, Ga.: Mercer University Press, 1998), 197–214; Long, *Against Us*, 23–28 and 30–31; and Carson et al., eds., *King Papers*, I, 37–38, 40–46, 142, 145, 152–153, and 155 n.451.

100. See George D. Kelsey, "Protestantism and Democratic Intergroup Living," *Phylon*, 8, no.1 (1947), 81; Mays and Nicholson, *Negro's Church*, 1–292; Benjamin E. Mays, *The Negro's God as Reflected in His Literature* (New York: Atheneum, 1968), 1–255; and Long, *Against Us*, 23–28 and 30–31.

101. Carson et al., eds., *King Papers*, I, 42; and Long, *Against Us*, 23–31. King, Jr., actually quoted from George Kelsey's seminal work, *Racism and the Christian Understanding of Man* (1965) in Martin Luther King, Jr., *Where Do We Go from Here: Chaos or Community?* (Boston: Beacon Press, 1968), 69. For an excellent treatment of Benjamin Mays's views on the church and race, see Mark L. Chapman, *Christianity on Trial: African American Religious Thought Before and After Black Power* (Maryknoll, N.Y.: Orbis Books, 1996), 15–41.

102. Carson et al., eds., *King Papers*, I, 37; Carson, ed., *King Autobiography*, 13–16; Baldwin, *Balm*, 166; and Baldwin, Abernathy Interview (17 March 1987). Michael Long convincingly argues that "the social gospel tradition preached by Benjamin Mays" was a significant influence on King, Jr. See Long, *Creative Living*, 13 n.14; and Long, *Against Us*, 29. Anthony Pinn associates this Social Gospel tradition with the earliest black churches in the United States. See Anthony B. Pinn, *The Black Church in the Post-Civil Rights Era* (Maryknoll, N.Y.: Orbis Books, 2002), 13.

103. Carson, ed., *King Autobiography*, 16; Carson et al., eds., *King Papers*, I, 44; and "King Interview," George A. Towns, 1.

104. Carson, ed., *King Autobiography*, 16; Martin Luther King, Jr., "Call to Preach," a statement before The American Baptist Convention (7 August 1959), KCLA, 1; Carson et al., eds., *King Papers*, I, 43–44; and Baldwin, *Balm*, 25 and 280. King, Jr.'s urge and determination "to serve God and humanity" were very much in line with the Morehouse College credo, which stated: "Whatever you do in this hostile world, be the best." See Linda Williams, "Molding Men: At Morehouse College, Middle Class Blacks are Taught to Lead," *Wall Street Journal*, 5 May 1987, 1 and 25.

105. Carson, ed., *The Autobiography of Martin Luther King, Jr.*, 16. King, Jr., spoke of this "urge" as "inescapable," and George D. Kelsey, his Morehouse professor, noted that the young man impressed him "as being quite serious about the ministry and as having a call

rather than a professional urge." This kind of spirit was very much in conformity with the values and traditions of the black church. See Carson et al., eds., *King Papers*, I, 155.

106. For much of this idea, I am indebted to Genovese, "Pilgrim's Progress," 40. Lucius M. Tobin and George D. Kelsey were among those ministers and intellectuals at Morehouse who did see in King great potential as far as ministry and service to humanity were concerned. See Carson et al., eds., *King Papers*, I, 151 and 155.

107. King, *Stride*, 91; and Baldwin et al., *Legacy*, 78–79.

108. See "Understanding Mahatma Gandhi," *Atlanta World*, 13 December 1931, 7.

109. See Benjamin E. Mays, *Born to Rebel: An Autobiography* (New York: Charles Scribner's Sons, 1971), 155–156. Gandhi was assassinated in January 1948, toward the end of King, Jr.'s senior year at Morehouse. Undoubtedly, Mays had something to say about this to the Morehouse family, most likely during a Tuesday morning chapel address. Even King, Jr., indicated, perhaps with his Morehouse experience in mind, that "Like most people, I had heard of Gandhi, but I had never studied him seriously." See Carson, ed., *King Autobiography*, 23. But the Morehouse connection to Gandhi and the independence struggle in India predated both Mays and King. See Sudarshan Kapur, *Raising Up the African-American Encounter with Gandhi* (Boston: Beacon Press, 1992), 12–15 and 145–147.

110. Richard Lischer reminds us that "Any number of Mays's favorite poems turn up in King's sermons and speeches." See Lischer, *Preacher King*, 43–45.

111. Keith D. Miller convincingly argues that Morehouse "was an extension" of King, Jr.'s "church and family." See Miller, *Voice*, 39. Also See Lischer, *Preacher King*, 51.

112. Carson, ed., *King Autobiography*, 13.

113. Miller, *Voice*, 11, 39, and 44; and "Certificate of Ordination," 1.

114. See Eugene D. Genovese, *The Southern Front: History and Politics in the Cultural War* (Columbia: University of Missouri Press, 1995), 157–191; and Baldwin, *Balm*, 1–44.

115. Larry G. Murphy et al., eds., *Encyclopedia of African American Religions* (New York: Garland Publishing, 1993), 69; and Carson et al., eds., *King Papers*, I, 47 and 125.

116. Carson et al., eds., *King Papers*, I, 47, 125, and 161.

117. Barbour was variously referred to in his time as "a laudable example of religious leadership," "a forthright representative of Negro Baptists in national and international assemblies," "an influential leader in behalf of racial uplift and community welfare," and "the most prominent theological spokesman of his generation for the National Baptist Convention." See "Helen Hunt Reports: Shaw Confers Doctorate Upon Noted Local Cleric," *Chester (Pa.) Times*, 10 June 1949, 10; G. Elaine Smith, ed., *The Centennial Yearbook of the Calvary Baptist Church, Chester, Pennsylvania, 1879–1979* (Chester, Pa.: Linder Printing Company, 1979), 18–26; and Carson et al., eds., *King Papers*, I, 125 n.1.

118. Smith, ed., *Centennial Yearbook*, 12 and 25; Baldwin, *Balm*, 37–38, 125, and 282; Lewis V. Baldwin, private interview with Sara Richardson, Chester, Pennsylvania (29 May 1987); and Lewis V. Baldwin, private interview with Emma Anderson (29 May 1987).

119. Dr. Lawrence Reddick, one of King, Jr.'s earliest biographers, reported, at Barbour's funeral in 1974, that "Dr. King credited J. Pius Barbour as being one of the single most influential forces in his life." With this and other evidence in mind, it is difficult to explain why some King scholars totally ignore Barbour while stressing King's indebtedness to figures like George Kelsey, Benjamin E. Mays, and William H. Borders. See Smith, ed., *Centennial Yearbook*, 25; Baldwin, Richardson interview (29 May 1987); Baldwin, Anderson interview (29 May 1987); Baldwin, *Balm*, 282; and Long, *Against Us*, 15–34. There were other "sons of Calvary" who would also make their marks in the area of civil rights, among them Samuel DeWitt Proctor and William A. Jones.

120. Carson et al., eds., *King Papers*, I, 47 and 161; Baldwin, *Balm*, 36–37, 125, and 282; Baldwin, Richardson interview (29 May 1987); Baldwin, Anderson interview (29 May 1987); and Miller, *Voice*, 44.

121. Baldwin, Anderson interview (29 May 1987); and Baldwin, Richardson interview (29 May 1987).

122. Baldwin, Anderson interview (29 May 1987); and Baldwin, *Balm*, 38.

123. Smith, ed., *Centennial Yearbook*, 25; and Baldwin, *Balm*, 37.

124. See Ling, *King*, 21–22; Baldwin, *Balm*, 36–37 and 125; Carson et al., eds., *King Papers*, I, 47; and Miller, *Voice*, 44.

125. Baldwin, Richardson interview (29 May 1978); Baldwin, Anderson interview (29 May 1987); and Baldwin, *Balm*, 282.

126. Baldwin, Anderson interview (29 May 1978); and Baldwin, Richardson interview (29 May 1987).

127. *One Hundred and Five Years by Faith: A History of the Twelfth Baptist Church, 1840–1945* (Boston: Twelfth Baptist Church, 1946), 9–24; and *Three-Fold Celebration Year: The Souvenir Journal of Twelfth Baptist Church* (Boston: Twelfth Baptist Church, 1985), 18.

128. *Three-Fold Celebration*, 18–19; Lewis V. Baldwin, private interview with Reverend Michael E. Haynes, Twelfth Baptist Church, Boston, Massachusetts (25 June 1987); and Baldwin, *Balm*, 39, 125, and 282–283.

129. King, Jr., is said to have "joined the legacy of Twelfth Baptist preachers as a 'drum major for justice' and freedom throughout the world." See *Three-Fold Celebration*, 19; Baldwin, Haynes interview (25 June 1987); and Baldwin, *Balm*, 39, 125, and 282–283.

130. Clayborne Carson et al., eds., *The Papers of Martin Luther King, Jr., Volume II: Rediscovering Precious Values, July 1951-November 1955* (Berkeley: University of California Press, 1994), 11; and King, *Daddy King*, 147–149. William Hester was known widely as "one of the great black preachers of his time" and as the preacher who had "the longest pastoral era in the history of the historic Twelfth Baptist Church," and his congregation celebrated him for "his encouragement of young ministers" and for the fact that "the promotion of Christian education was a marked characteristic of his work." See *Three-Fold Celebration*, 19.

131. Carson et al., eds., *King Papers*, II, 11, 43, 298, 305, 309, and 316; and Baldwin, *Balm*, 283. The Reverend Michael Haynes remembered that "Twelfth Baptist became Martin's preaching station, his fellowship station, and feeding trough." Haynes added:

"This was his home away from home." Haynes also recounted that because of the influence of Twelfth Baptist, King, Jr., really "wanted to look at working with young black people." "And had he not been forced into the movement," Haynes observes, "I think he would have spent some time with a special focus on youth." Baldwin, Haynes interview (25 June 1987).

132. King, *Daddy King*, 147.

133. Baldwin, Haynes interview (25 June 1987).

134. King, *My Life*, 86; Baldwin, Haynes interview (25 June 1987); King, *Daddy King*, 147–149; and Carson et al., eds., *King Papers*, II, 11 and 43.

135. Mary Powell, who was related to Mays by marriage, actually set up the first meeting between King, Jr., and Coretta Scott in Boston. Scott admitted that at that time she thought of ministers as unenlightened and overly pious, and the Baptist Church as too fundamentalist, excessively emotional, and misguided in its baptismal practices. However, Coretta eventually abandoned such thoughts and actually joined Atlanta's Ebenezer Baptist Church one Sunday after King, Jr., preached. See King, *My Life*, 18–19, 50–51, 57, and 72; Baldwin, *Balm*, 127–129; and Carson et al., eds., *King Papers*, II, 19.

136. King, *My Life*, 57, 60, 64, 67–72, and 87.

137. Carson, ed., *King Autobiography*, 35–37; King, *My Life*, 18–21; and Baldwin, *Balm*, 41 and 127–158.

138. King, *My Life*, 85–87.

139. Lewis V. Baldwin, private interview with Phillip Lenud, Nashville, Tennessee (7 April 1987). Lenud associated with King, Jr., at Morehouse and in Boston, and he illumined aspects of King's life and activities in those settings that only an intimate friend would know.

140. Baldwin, *Balm*, 175; and King, *My Life*, 90–91.

141. King, *My Life*, 58.

142. Carson et al., eds., *King Papers*, II, 1.

143. King, Jr., went on to say: "My studies had made me skeptical, and I could not see how many of the facts of science could be squared with religion." See Carson et al., eds., *King Papers*, I, 361–363; and Carson, ed., *King Autobiography*, 15–16.

144. Carson, ed., *King Autobiography*, 6 and 14; and Carson et al., eds., *King Papers*, I, 43 n.135.

145. Miller, *Voice*, 40; and "Certificate of Ordination," 1. King, Jr., never accepted the traditional Christian view of the virgin birth, and he would later declare that "the traditional issues of theology—sin and salvation, the divinity of Christ, His virgin birth, His bodily resurrection are peripheral" and not "central" to the Christian faith. One of his interviewers reported in 1963: "But Dr. King rejects the virgin birth of Christ as a literal fact. The early Christians, he says, had noticed the moral uniqueness of Jesus; to make this uniqueness appear plausible, they devised a mythological story of Jesus' biological uniqueness." See Dirks, "Essence," 1 and 12.

146. Miller, *Voice*, 40; "Certificate of Ordination," 1; and Lewis V. Baldwin, "Anchored in the Word: King, the Bible, and Black Church Traditions," unpublished paper, author's files (Fall 2003), 7–8.

147. It was during his studies at Crozer that King, Jr., wrote his "An Autobiography of Religious Development," which affords fascinating forays into the early spiritual and intellectual life of this phenomenal figure." See Carson et al., eds., *King Papers*, I, 359–363.

148. Carson, ed., *King Autobiography*, 17–29; and Carson et al., eds., *King Papers*, I, 363.

149. Peter J. Ling reminds us that "Young Martin's doubts about what he regarded as his father's outmoded religious outlook included matters of doctrine as well as prescribed social practices," and it also involved political ideology. Coretta King attributes King, Jr.'s differences with his father and with many of the traditional church teachings to "his normal youthful rebellion against tradition." See Ling, *King*, 21; King, *My Life*, 81; King, *Daddy King*, 147; Carson et al., eds., *King Papers*, I, 34 and 38; and Carson et al., eds., *King Papers*, II, 2.

150. Lischer, *Preacher King*, 52–53.

151. King, Jr.'s comment must be seriously considered in light of the Reverend William E. Gardner's claim that "King may have become somewhat estranged from his Ebenezer roots." See Carson et al., eds., *King Papers*, I, 53 and 363.

152. Ling, *King*, 12 and 21; Sydney E. Ahlstrom, *A Religious History of the American People* (New Haven: Yale University Press, 1974), 1076; and Jay Tolson, "The New-Old Time Religion: Evangelicals Defy Easy Labels," *U. S. News & World Report*, 135, no.20 (8 December 2003), 41.

153. Carson, ed., *King Autobiography*, 14–16; Carson et al., eds., *King Papers*, I, 34 and 53–54; Carson et al., eds., *King Papers*, II, 1–2; Baldwin, *Balm*, 168–174; Watley, *Roots*, 17–45; and J. Michael Parker, "The Theology of Martin Luther King, Jr.," *San Antonio Express-News*, 6 January 1996, 9–10B.

154. Ahlstrom, *Religious History*, 1076.

155. Ling, *King*, 23.

156. King, *Stride*, 91; and Carson, ed., *King Autobiography*, 17–18.

157. The sheer impact of Mordecai Johnson's sermon on King was far more decisive than scholars have acknowledged. King himself noted that Johnson's "message was so profound and electrifying that I left the meeting and bought a half-dozen books on Gandhi's life and works." See King, *Stride*, 96.

158. One of the most brilliant treatments of these matters is found in Watley, *Roots*, 19–45.

159. Carson, ed., *King Autobiography*, 13.

160. King, *Stride*, 99; and Ling, *King*, 23.

161. Carson et al., eds., *King Papers*, I, 274; and Ling, *King*, 23.

162. A similar claim is made in Watley, *Roots*, 19.

163. King, *My Life*, 83.

164. Miller, *Voice*, 134.

165. King scholars have advanced a range of arguments regarding the source of King, Jr's tendency to plagiarize in his sermons and writings. David Garrow claims that King, Jr., "was a southern-church black man who was essentially out of his" place in a northern academic environment, and that his "efforts to play the role of a worldly, sophisticated young philosopher were in good part a way of coping with an intellectual

setting that was radically different from his own heritage." The explanation that seems most compelling and convincing is rejected by most King scholars, and especially David Garrow, David Lewis, and Richard Lischer. That argument is set forth by Keith Miller and Lewis V. Baldwin, both of whom contend that King, Jr.'s attitude toward borrowing resulted from his black church and cultural background. Contrary to what Garrow argues, it is not "unrespectful [sic] of both King's impressive intelligence" and "top-notch undergraduate training" to acknowledge this and more. The point is, as Lawrence H. Mamiya has suggested, that some of "King's weaknesses and moral shortcomings," like his strengths and/or virtues, can be explained in light of his cultural background and heritage. Preaching in the black experience is "an imitative art," and, historically, black preachers have been known to purchase copies of the sermons of other preachers at church meetings and conventions, or to roam from church to church in search of sermonic content and illustrations. King, Jr., never escaped the full impact of this culture. See Lischer, *Preacher King*, 62–64; Lawrence H. Mamiya, "A Review of Baldwin, *There Is a Balm in Gilead*," *Georgia Historical Quarterly*, 75, no. 4 (Winter 1991), 876; Miller, *Voice*, 134–136; and Lewis V. Baldwin, *To Make the Wounded Whole: The Cultural Legacy of Martin Luther King, Jr.* (Minneapolis: Fortress Press, 1992), 298–300.

166. King, *Stride*, 21–22; King, *My Life*, 58; and Baldwin, *Balm*, 41.

167. King, *Daddy King*, 147; and King, *My Life*, 63.

168. King, *My Life*, 83.

CHAPTER 2

1. See Clayborne Carson et al., eds., *The Papers of Martin Luther King, Jr., Volume II: Rediscovering Precious Values, July 1951–November 1955* (Berkeley: University of California Press, 1994), 232–233; James M. Washington, ed., *A Testament of Hope: The Essential Writings and Speeches of Martin Luther King, Jr.* (New York: HarperCollins, 1991), 501–502; and Martin Luther King, Jr. *Why We Can't Wait* (New York: New American Library, 1964), 89–92.

2. Martin Luther King, Jr., "The Philosophy of Life Undergirding Christianity and the Christian Ministry," an unpublished essay, Crozer Theological Seminary, Chester, Pennsylvania (n.d.), Martin Luther King, Jr. Papers Project, Stanford University, Stanford, California, 1–2; and Martin Luther King, Jr., "Transformed Nonconformist," unpublished sermon notes, Montgomery, Alabama (November 1954), The King Papers Project, 1.

3. Martin Luther King, Jr., *Strength to Love* (Philadelphia: Fortress Press, 1981), 61–63.

4. See Lewis V. Baldwin et al., *The Legacy of Martin Luther King, Jr.: The Boundaries of Law, Politics, and Religion* (Notre Dame, Ind.: University of Notre Dame Press, 2002), 77–211; and Michael G. Long, *Against Us, But for Us: Martin Luther King, Jr. and the State* (Macon, Ga.: Mercer University Press, 2002), 3–229.

5. King's training at Morehouse still awaits sufficient attention from scholars, some of whom treat King's intellectual sources and categories as if Crozer and Boston were the only major contexts for his academic development. Only fleeting attention is

given to Morehouse, even in the most important intellectual biographies of King. See John J. Ansbro, *Martin Luther King, Jr.: Nonviolent Strategies and Tactics for Social Change* (New York: Madison Books, 2000), 15, 76, 106, 110, 166, 180, and 283; and Kenneth L. Smith and Ira G. Zepp, Jr., *Search for the Beloved Community: The Thinking of Martin Luther King, Jr.* (Valley Forge, Pa.: Judson Press, 1998), 3–4, 6, 11, 42, and 123. We need studies of Morehouse that build on the treatments provided in Lewis V. Baldwin, *There Is a Balm in Gilead: The Cultural Roots of Martin Luther King, Jr.* (Minneapolis: Fortress Press, 1991), 25–29, 32–33, 114–116, and 278–279; and Lawrence E. Carter, Sr., *Walking Integrity: Benjamin Elijah Mays, Mentor to Martin Luther King, Jr.* (Macon, Ga.: Mercer University Press, 1998), 197–214.

6. The best sources for analyzing King's thoughts on the church at Crozer and Boston are Clayborne Carson et al., eds., *The Papers of Martin Luther King, Jr., Volume I: Called to Serve, January 1929–June 1951* (Berkeley: University of California Press, 1992), 1–57, 129–137, 181, and 211–439; and Carson et al., eds., *King Papers*, II, 1–53 and 119–255.

7. Carson et al., eds., *King Papers*, I, 130–135; and Clayborne Carson, ed., *The Autobiography of Martin Luther King, Jr.* (New York: Warner Books, 1998), 15–16.

8. Carson et al., eds., *King Papers*, I, 43 and 130–135.

9. I am heavily indebted to Rufus Burrow, Jr., for this idea. See Rufus Burrow, Jr., to Lewis V. Baldwin, (24 March 2005), 3.

10. Carson, ed., *King Autobiography*, 16; and Carson et al., eds., *King Papers*, I, 38.

11. Carson, ed., *King Autobiography*, 15–16; and Carson et al., eds., *King Papers*, I, 43 and 130–135.

12. Carson et al., eds., *King Papers*, I, 363; Carson, ed., *King Papers*, II, 3–25; and Baldwin, *Balm*, 29.

13. Carson et al., eds., *King Papers*, I, 363; Carson, ed., *King Autobiography*, 17–29; and Martin Luther King, Jr., "Preaching Ministry," an unpublished handwritten outline, Crozer Theological Seminary, Chester, Pennsylvania (n.d.), The King Papers Project, 1 and 4.

14. See Rufus Burrow, Jr., "King's Dream and Multiculturalism: A Review Essay," *Encounter*, 67, no.2 (2006), 211.

15. Martin Luther King, Jr., *Stride Toward Freedom: The Montgomery Story* (New York: Harper & Row, 1958), 91–92; and Carson, ed., *King Autobiography*, 18.

16. Carson, ed., *King Autobiography*, 18; and Ansbro, *King*, 163–166.

17. See Baldwin, *Balm*, 167–174; William D. Watley, *Roots of Resistance: The Nonviolent Ethic of Martin Luther King, Jr.* (Valley Forge, Pa.: Judson Press, 1985), 31–36; Garth Baker-Fletcher, *Somebodyness: Martin Luther King, Jr. and the Theory of Dignity* (Minneapolis: Fortress Press, 1993), 59–77; and Richard W. Wills, *Martin Luther King, Jr. and the Image of God* (New York: Oxford University Press, 2009), 139–190.

18. Ansbro, *King*, 18–26 and 167–197.

19. Carson et al., eds., *King Papers*, I, 249.

20. King, "Preaching Ministry," 1–2; Martin Luther King, Jr., "Sincerity is Not Enough," unpublished sermon notes, Atlanta (3 June 1951), The King Papers Project, 1; and Carson et al., eds., *King Papers*, II, 52, 179, 184–187, 214–218, and 232.

21. Carson et al., eds., *King Papers*, II, 52, 179, 184–185, 214–218, and 232; King, "Preaching Ministry," 1–2; King, "Sincerity," 1; and Martin Luther King, Jr., "O That I

Knew Where I Might Find Him!", unpublished sermon notes (n.d.), The King Papers Project, 4–5. King referred to his recent graduation from Crozer in the sermon notes mentioned last in this particular endnote, but there is no indication as to where he wrote these.

22. King, "Preaching Ministry," 1.

23. Carson et al., eds., *King Papers*, I, 211–224, 227–230, and 252–253; King, "Preaching Ministry," 1–2; Carson et al., eds., *King Papers*, II, 212–218; King, "Sincerity," 71; and King, "Oh That I Knew!", 3–4.

24. Carson et al., eds., *King Papers*, II, 212–213 and 217; and Justo L. Gonzalez, *A History of Christian Thought: From Augustine to the Eve of the Reformation*, Vol. II (Nashville: Abingdon Press, 1971), 15.

25. Carson et al., eds., *King Papers*, II, 214–217; and King, "Preaching Ministry," 1 and 3.

26. King, *Can't Wait*, 82.

27. Carson, ed., *King Autobiography*, 17.

28. King, "Preaching Ministry," 1–2; Martin Luther King, Jr., "The Limitation of Experience," an unpublished paper, Crozer Theological Seminary, Chester, Pennsylvania (n.d.), The King Papers Project, 1; and Carson et al., eds., *King Papers*, II, 187.

29. Carson et al., eds., *King Papers*, II, 52, 185, and 187.

30. Gonzalez, *Christian Thought*, II, 50.

31. Quoted in Carson et al., eds., *King Papers*, II, 185.

32. Ibid., 52 and 185–186.

33. Ibid., 185–186.

34. King, *Can't Wait*, 88.

35. King noted: "Wherein Catholic thought found the sole authority in the Church, Calvin, along with the other reformers, found it in the Bible." Quoted in Carson et al., eds., *King Papers*, II, 218.

36. Ibid., 186.

37. Ibid., 218 and 232.

38. Ibid., 232.

39. Carson et al., eds., *King Papers*, I, 285.

40. Carson et al., eds., *King Papers*, II, 132 and 142–145; and Carson, ed., *King Autobiography*, 27.

41. Carson et al., eds., *King Papers*, I, 286.

42. Ibid.

43. Ibid.; and Carson et al., eds., *King Papers*, II, 232.

44. Carson et al., eds., *King Papers*, I, 281.

45. Carson et al., eds., *King Papers*, II, 140.

46. Carson, ed., *King Autobiography*, 13.

47. Martin Luther King, Jr., "Is the Church the Hope of the World?" unpublished notes, Crozer Theological Seminary, Chester, Pennsylvania (n.d.), The King Papers Project, 1–2.

48. Martin Luther King, Jr., "Facing Life's Inescapables," unpublished document, Crozer Theological Seminary, Chester, Pennsylvania (c. 3 March 1949), The King Papers Project, 1.

49. Ibid.; and Carson et al., eds., *King Papers*, I, 46–57.

50. Carson et al., eds., *King Papers*, II, 167.

51. Martin Luther King, Jr., "Cooperative Competition, Noble Competition," unpublished sermon notes, Crozer Theological Seminary, Chester, Pennsylvania (n.d.), The King Papers Project, 1–2.

52. Carson et al., eds., *King Papers*, II, 165.

53. King, "Is the Church the Hope?"1.

54. Martin Luther King, Jr., "Karl Barth," unpublished review of Karl Barth's sermon on "Repentance," Crozer Theological Seminary, Chester, Pennsylvania (n.d.), The King Papers Project, 2; Martin Luther King, Jr., "The Philosophy of Life Undergirding Christianity and the Christian Ministry," unpublished essay, Crozer Theological Seminary, Chester, Pennsylvania (n.d.), The King Papers Project, 1; Martin Luther King, Jr., "Communism's Challenge to Christianity," unpublished manuscript, Atlanta (9 August 1953), The King Papers Project, 2; and King, "Cooperative Competition, Noble Competition," 1–2.

55. Martin Luther King, Jr., "Sermon Conclusions," unpublished notes, Crozer Theological Seminary, Chester, Pennsylvania (c.3 March 1949), The King Papers Project, 1–2.

56. Martin Luther King, Jr., "Men's Day Sermon," unpublished notes, Crozer Theological Seminary, Chester, Pennsylvania (3 March 1949), The King Papers Project, 1; Martin Luther King, Jr., "The Purpose of Religion," an unpublished essay, Crozer Theological Seminary Chester, Pennsylvania (n.d.), The King Papers Project, 1; and Carson et al., eds., *King Papers*, I, 249 and 285–287.

57. King, "Preaching Ministry," 3; and Martin Luther King, Jr., "The Danger of Misguided Goodness," an unpublished sermon outline (n.d.), The King Papers Project, 1.

58. King, "Preaching Ministry," 4.

59. Carson et al., eds., *King Papers*, II, 167; King, "Preaching Ministry," 1 and 4.

60. Carson et al., eds., *King Papers*, II, 144.

61. Ibid., 165.

62. In an earlier work, this author claimed that because King "was more deeply influenced by Western thought, especially Christian theology and ethics," his "earliest assessments of culture lacked the critical edge so characteristic of Malcolm's." A careful review of King's papers at Crozer and Boston seems to suggest otherwise, and the point is most certainly open to debate. See Lewis V. Baldwin and Amiri YaSin Al-Hadid, *Between Cross and Crescent: Christian and Muslim Perspectives on Malcolm and Martin* (Gainesville: University Press of Florida, 2002), 26.

63. King, "Men's Day Sermon," 1; and King, "Purpose of Religion," 1.

64. King, "Purpose of Religion," 1–2.

65. King was obviously paraphrasing Barth at this point. See King, "Karl Barth," 2; and Karl Barth, *Come Holy Spirit: Sermons* (New York: Round Table Press, 1933), 71.

66. King, "The Philosophy of Life," 1–2; and King, "Communism's Challenge," 1–4.

67. King, "Life's Inescapables," 2.

68. Ibid.; and King, "Communism's Challenge," 3.

69. King, "Cooperative Competition," 1–2.

70. Carson et al., eds., *King Papers*, I, 181 and 194.

71. King, "Communism's Challenge," 3; and King, "Is the Church the Hope?" 1.

72. Long, *Against Us*, 1–87; Baldwin et al., *Legacy*, 77–81; and King, *Can't Wait*, 84–92.

73. King, "Communism's Challenge," 1 and 3.

74. Ibid. Also see Martin Luther King, Jr., "Splinters and Planks," unpublished sermon, Atlanta (24 July 1949), The King Papers Project, 2; Martin Luther King, Jr., "Will Capitalism Survive?" unpublished essay, Crozer Theological Seminary, Chester, Pennsylvania (n.d.), The King Papers Project, 1–2; and Carson et al., eds., *King Papers*, II, 156–157.

75. Carson et al., eds., *King Papers*, II, 156–157.

76. See King, *Strength*, 96–105.

77. Coretta Scott King, *My Life with Martin Luther King, Jr.* (New York: Henry Holt, 1993), 58; and King, *Stride*, 21–22.

78. King, *Stride*, 16; Martin Luther King, Jr., to Dr. Dwight Loder (5 August 1958), unpublished document, The Library and Archives of the Martin Luther King, Jr. Center for Nonviolent Social Change, Inc. (KCLA), Atlanta, Georgia, 1–2; and Baldwin, *Balm*, 41–44 and 174–175.

79. Carson et al., eds., *King Papers*, I, 109–111.

80. King actually taught a seminar in social philosophy at Morehouse College in 1961–1962, when he was also fulfilling a pastoral role at Atlanta's Ebenezer Baptist Church. This contribution was consistent with his belief that partnerships between the church and the academy are essential in the struggle for freedom. See Carter, ed., *Walking Integrity*, 209.

81. The Pulpit Committee of the Dexter Avenue Baptist Church to Martin Luther King, Jr. (10 March 1954), unpublished document, The Martin Luther King, Jr. Papers, Special Collections, Mugar Memorial Library, Boston University, Boston, Massachusetts, 1; and Martin Luther King, Jr. to the Dexter Avenue Baptist Church (14 April 1954), unpublished document, Special Collections, Boston University, 1.

82. Carson et al., eds., *King Papers*, II, 287–294; and Baldwin, *Balm*, 177–180.

83. Carson et al., eds., *King Papers*, II, 290; and Baldwin, *Balm*, 178. Speaking of church membership in the NAACP, King urged "other churches in our community to do likewise." See Martin Luther King, Jr., to Roy Wilkins (1 May 1956), KCLA, 1.

84. King, *Stride*, 31–35; and Baldwin, *Balm*, 178–180.

85. King, *Stride*, 25.

86. King lashed out al churches that "get caught up in their exclusivism." See Clayborne Carson and Peter Holloran, eds., *A Knock at Midnight: Inspirations from the Great Sermons of Reverend Martin Luther King, Jr.* (New York: Warner Books, 1998), 176–177; and Martin Luther King, Jr., "The Drum Major Instinct," an unpublished sermon delivered at the Ebenezer Baptist Church, Atlanta (4 February 1968), KCLA, 5.

87. Carson et al., eds., *King Papers*, II, 287.

88. Ibid.

89. Martin Luther King, Jr., "The Man Who was a Fool," an unpublished sermon delivered at the Central United Methodist Church, Detroit Michigan (6 March 1961), The King Papers Project, 6.

90. King, *Can't Wait*, 91–92.

91. Ibid., 86.

92. King went on to note "the fact that worship cannot be confined to the Christian religion neither to the Christian God." He also claimed that "Worship is the type of escape that is both healthy and normal." "Through worship," he continued, "one's worst self comes face to face with his better self, and the better self comes face to face with something still better still. No man can be at his best unless he stands over and over again in the presence of that which is superior to his best." See Martin Luther King, Jr., "Worship," an unpublished paper, Montgomery, Alabama (7 August 1955), The King Papers Project, 1 and 3; Martin Luther King, Jr., "Who are We?" an unpublished sermon delivered at the Ebenezer Baptist Church, Atlanta, Georgia (5 February 1966), KCLA, 3; and Martin Luther King, Jr., "The Un-Christian Christian: SCLC Looks Closely at Christianity in a Troubled Land," *Ebony*, 20, no.10 (August 1965), 78.

93. King, "The Un-Christian," 78.

94. King, "Worship," 2–3. King was always critical of churchpersons who reduced the gospel and worship to "showmanship." "The church is not an entertainment center," he asserted. "Monkeys are to entertain, not preachers." See Martin Luther King, Jr., "Transformed Non-Conformist," an unpublished sermon delivered at the Ebenezer Baptist Church, Atlanta, Georgia (16 January 1966), KCLA, 9; and Carson and Holloran, eds., *Knock*, 106.

95. King probably had some dimension of this side of church life in mind when he spoke of "that realm of spiritual ends" that finds expression "in arts, literature, morals, and religion." See Martin Luther King, Jr., "The Quiet Conviction of Nonviolence," *The Mennonite*, 80, no.1 (5 January 1965), 2.

96. Martin Luther King, Jr., "Pharisee and Publican," an unpublished sermon delivered in Atlanta (9 October 1966), KCLA, 1–2.

97. King, "Worship,".2. King lamented that the Christian church is "filled up with people who pay lip service to God and not life service." See Carson and Holloran, eds., *Knock*, 15.

98. See King, "Worship," 3.

99. Martin Luther King, Jr., "Advice for Living," *Ebony*, 14, no.1 (November 1958), 138.

100. Carson et al., eds., *King Papers*, II, 232; and King, "Worship," 1–3.

101. As King saw it, the church shared this educational function with the other most important institution in the community—namely, the family. See Martin Luther King, Jr., "Training Your Child in Love," unpublished Mother's Day sermon, delivered at Ebenezer Baptist Church, Atlanta, Georgia (8 May 1966), KCLA, 1–11; Martin Luther King, Jr., "The Dignity of Family Life," unpublished address, delivered at Abbott House, West Chester County, New York (29 October 1965), KCLA, 1–11; Martin Luther King, Jr., "The Negro Family," unpublished address, delivered at the University of Chicago, Chicago (27 January 1966), KCLA, 1–28; Martin Luther King, Jr., "What a Mother Should Tell Her Child," unpublished sermon, delivered at the Ebenezer Baptist Church, Atlanta (12 May 1963), KCLA, 1–14; and Baldwin, *Balm*, 91–228.

102. King held that "every revolution must be accompanied by a firm intellectual undergirding" of the resources of the mind. Drawing on the values and resources of

the church to advance his cause, he reported that "Education is a primary concern of the civil rights movement, [for] . . . Nothing is more important to the consolidation of social change than adequate education." See Martin Luther King, Jr., "Address at the Southern Association of Political Scientists," unpublished (13 November 1964), KCLA, 1; Martin Luther King, Jr., "An Address," unpublished version, Syracuse University, Syracuse, New York (15 July 1965), KCLA, 1; Martin Luther King, Jr., "Revolution in the Classroom," unpublished speech, Georgia Teachers and Education Association, Atlanta (31 April 1967), KCLA, 2; and Martin Luther King, Jr., "Field of Education a Battle-ground," unpublished address, United Federation of Teachers, New York (14 March 1964), KCLA, 1–4. King made numerous statements regarding the church's role as teaching agency. As early as 1959, he said that "We must utilize the vast resources of the Churches and Synagogues for the many educational functions they can employ, and for which they have highly developed skills, facilities, and experience. . . . However," he added, "to possess resources is worthless without the will to be effective." King believed that the church could make immense contributions "through its channels of religious education and other methods." Throughout the 1960s, he stated that "The church must lead in the all-important program of . . . education," and that "The church can do a great deal to direct the public mind." See Martin Luther King, Jr., "Address at a Conference of Religious Leaders Under the Sponsorship of the President's Committee on Government Contracts," unpublished, The Sheraton D.C., Washington, D.C. (11 May 1959), KCLA, 5; Martin Luther King, Jr., "America's Chief Moral Dilemma," unpublished speech, United Church of Christ, General Synod, Palmer House, Chicago (6 July 1965), KCLA, 10; Martin Luther King, Jr., "A Challenge to the Churches and Synagogues," unpublished, delivered at The Conference on Religion and Race, Edgewater Beach Hotel, Chicago, Illinois (17 January 1963), KCLA, 10; King, *Strength*, 11; Carson and Holloran, eds., *Knock*, 30; Marvin T. Robinson, "Report of the Installation Service of the Western Christian Leadership Conference," unpublished, Pasadena, California (7–8 May 1963), KCLA, 1; King, Jr., "Advice for Living, November 1958, 138; Martin Luther King, Jr., "Advice for Living," *Ebony*, 13, no. 11 (September 1958), 68; Martin Luther King, Jr., "Advice for Living," *Ebony*, 13, no. 5 (March 1958), 92; Martin Luther King, Jr., "The Mission to Social Frontiers," unpublished (n.d.), KCLA, 8–10; "Hugh Downs Interview with Martin Luther King, Jr.," NBC "Today Show" (18 April 1966), unpublished, KCLA, 4; Martin Luther King, Jr., "A Profound Moral . . . Continued," *New York Amsterdam News*, 3 August 1963, 10; and Martin Luther King, Jr., "Crisis and the Church," *Council Quarterly*, October 1961, 1–4.

103. King, "The Mission to the Social Frontiers," 8–10; Jack Gilbert, "King Urges Youth Join in New Order," *Athens Messenger*, 30 December 1959, 1 and 16; Martin Luther King, Jr., "Beyond Discovery, Love," an unpublished address, International Convention of Christian Churches (Disciples of Christ), Dallas, Texas (25 September 1966), KCLA, 5; King, "A Challenge to the Churches," 11; Lee E. Dirks, "The Essence is Love: The Theology of Martin Luther King, Jr.," *National Observer*, 30 December 1963, 1 and 12; Martin Luther King, Jr., "The Church on the Frontier of Racial Tension," unpublished, delivered as one of the Gay Lectures, Southern Baptist Theological Seminary, Louisville, Kentucky (19 April 1961), KCLA, 7; and Martin Luther King, Jr., "A Realistic Look at the Race Relations," unpublished paper, delivered at the Second

Anniversary of the NAACP Legal Defense and Educational Fund, Waldorf Astoria Hotel, New York, (17 May 1956), KCLA, 6.

104. Martin Luther King, Jr., to Thomas Earl Jordan (31 July 1963), KCLA, 1; Martin Luther King, Jr., "The Crisis of Civil Rights," unpublished address, Operation Breadbasket Meeting, Chicago (10–12 October 1967), KCLA, 1; King, "Church on the Frontier," 1; Martin Luther King, Jr., and Wyatt T. Walker to the Student Interracial Ministry Committee of the National Student Christian Federation (29 March 1961), KCLA, 1; and Baldwin, *Balm*, 335–336.

105. "Hugh Downs Interview," 5–6; and King, *Strength*, 10–13.

106. Dirks, "Essence," 1 and 12; "Hugh Downs Interview," 5–6; King, "The Mission," 8–10; Martin Luther King, Jr., to Mrs. Hester Hocking Campbell (16 June 1964), KCLA, 1; Martin Luther King, Jr., "Answer to a Perplexing Question," unpublished sermon, Atlanta (3 March 1963), KCLA, 5–6; and King, "America's Chief Moral," 4 and 10–11.

107. King, "Church on the Frontier," 1; King, "America's Chief Moral," 1–5; King, "The Mission," 8–9; King and Walker to the Student Interracial Ministry Committee, 1; and Baldwin, *Balm*, 335–336.

108. King, "America's Chief Moral," 2–3; King, *Strength*, 61–63; King, "The Mission," 8–10; and King, "Church on the Frontier," 1 and 3–10.

109. Philip Berrigan, the controversial Catholic priest, once contended that King's "Letter from the Birmingham City Jail" (1963) "silenced his critics, most of whom were Christians, and some of whom were Catholics." It is better to say that the document sparked discussion and debate in many circles (i.e., churches, seminaries, divinity schools, public square, etc.) about the proper roles of the church and ministry in public life. King's "Letter from the Birmingham City Jail" probably affords the best evidence of his capacity to inspire debate and discussion about the church and its proper role in society. Clearly, King wrote this treatise in response to clergymen whose concept of the church and its ministry was different from his own. See S. Jonathan Bass, *Blessed are the Peacemakers: Martin Luther King, Jr., Eight White Religious Leaders, and the "Letter from Birmingham Jail"* (Baton Rouge: Louisiana State University Press, 2001), 110–258; Washington, ed., *Testament*, 289 and 294–300; and Philip Berrigan, *Prison Journals of a Priest Revolutionary* (New York: Ballantine Books, 1971), 15.

110. King, "Answer," 21–22; Martin Luther King, Jr., "'Lost Sheep' or 'The God of the Lost,'" unpublished sermon (18 September 1966), KCLA, 8; Martin Luther King, Jr., "Levels of Love," unpublished sermon, delivered at the Ebenezer Baptist Church, Atlanta (21 May 1967), KCLA, 9; Martin Luther King, Jr., "Unfulfilled Dreams," unpublished sermon, delivered at the Ebenezer Baptist Church, Atlanta (3 March 1965), KCLA, 6–7; Martin Luther King, Jr., "Lazarus and Dives," unpublished sermon (10 March 1963), KCLA, 9; and Martin Luther King, Jr., "The Prodigal Son," unpublished sermon, delivered at the Ebenezer Baptist Church, Atlanta (4 September 1966), KCLA, 9–10.

111. King spoke forcefully of the need "at this time to carry this gospel and carry that message to the streets," a point that seemingly carried implications for missionary activity. At the same time, he did not understand the Christian faith primarily in terms of missionary outreach, much as he refused to see it as doctrinal conformity. See

Martin Luther King, Jr., "I Need Some Victories," unpublished statement, Chicago (12 July 1966), KCLA, 3; Dirks, "Essence," 12; King, "Lost Sheep' or 'God of the Lost," 8; King, "Prodigal Son," 9–10; King, "Levels of Love," 9; King, "Unfulfilled Dreams," 6–7; and King, "Lazarus and Dives," 9.

112. For interesting insights into King's perspective on the ethic of foreign missions as it unfolded with Southern Baptists in the 1960s, see Martin Luther King, Jr., "A Knock at Midnight," unpublished sermon, delivered at the All-Saints Community Church, Los Angeles (25 June 1967), KCLA, 1; and Lewis V. Baldwin, *Toward the Beloved Community: Martin Luther King, Jr. and South Africa* (Cleveland: Pilgrim Press, 1995), 28.

113. King, "Crisis and the Church," 1; King, "Beyond Discovery," 1–2; Martin Luther King, Jr., "Acceptance Speech at the Presentation of the 1963 St. Francis Peace Medal," North American Federation of the Third Order of Saint Francis, unpublished (9 November 1963), KCLA, 1–2; and Martin Luther King, Jr., "Why We are Here," unpublished speech, SCOPE Orientation (15 June 1965), KCLA, 1–8.

114. King, "Beyond Discovery," 1; King, "Address at a Conference," 4; King, "America's Chief Moral," 2; King, "A Challenge to the Churches," 2; "Hugh Downs Interview," 1; and King, "A Profound Moral," 10.

115. Obviously, King was influenced by Reinhold Niebuhr's distinction between individual morality and group morality, and felt that the church could not adequately address one without serious attention to the other. King often preached on those moral virtues integral to Christian life, a point some might consider ironic in light of his own personal, moral failings. But a careful study of King's life reveals a compelling portrait of a flawed but faithful man. He found a way to live faithfully in the context of his own brokenness and that of a broken society, even as he acknowledged that no human being "totally" reaches what he termed "the destination of morality." Moreover, I have long argued that King's own moral failures do not diminish the performative character of his work. For some of his many references to issues of personal morality and ethics, around problems such as adultery, alcoholism, sex promiscuity, drug addiction, etc., see King, "'Lost Sheep' or 'God of the Lost'," 5–6; King, "Prodigal Son," 3; Martin Luther King, Jr., "Judging Others," unpublished sermon, delivered at the Ebenezer Baptist Church, Atlanta (4 June 1967), KCLA, 2; Martin Luther King, Jr., "We Would See Jesus," unpublished sermon, delivered at the Ebenezer Baptist Church, Atlanta (7 May 1967), KCLA, 3 and 6–7; King, "Pharisee and Publican," 2–4; Martin Luther King, Jr., "Is the Universe Friendly?" unpublished sermon, delivered at the Ebenezer Baptist Church, Atlanta (12 December 1965), KCLA, 2–3 and 10; Martin Luther King, Jr., "Some Things We Must Do," unpublished speech (5 December 1957), KCLA, 12; Martin Luther King, Jr., "Advice for Living," *Ebony*, 12, no.11 (September 1957), 74; Martin Luther King, Jr., "Advice for Living," *Ebony*, 12, no.12 (October 1957), 53; Martin Luther King, Jr., "Advice for Living," *Ebony*, 13, no.1 (November 1957), 106; Martin Luther King, Jr., "Advice for Living," *Ebony*, 13, no.3 (January 1958), 34; Martin Luther King, Jr., "Advice for Living," *Ebony*, 13, no.6 (April 1958), 104; Martin Luther King, Jr., "Advice for Living," *Ebony*, 13, no.8 (June 1958), 118; Martin Luther King, Jr., "Advice for Living," *Ebony*, 13, no.9 (July 1958), 86; Martin Luther King, Jr., "Advice for Living," *Ebony*, 13, no.12 (October 1958), 138; and

Baldwin et al., *Legacy*, 81–101. For some of King's most provocative statements on the church and social evil and morality, see King, "Address at a Conference," 4–7; "Hugh Downs Interview," 1–2; King, "A Challenge to the Churches," 1–14; and King, "America's Chief Moral," 1–11.

116. King, "Acceptance Speech," 1; King, "Crisis and the Church," 1; King, "Beyond Discovery," 1–2; and King, "Why We are Here," 1–7.

117. Martin Luther King, Jr., *Where Do We Go from Here: Chaos or Community?* (Boston: Beacon Press, 1968), 96; King, "Acceptance Speech," 1; King, "A Challenge to the Churches," 2; King, "America's Chief Moral," 2–3; and King, "Beyond Discovery," 1–2.

118. King said on another occasion that "I remember where Dante said that the hottest places in hell are reserved for those who in a moment of moral crisis seek to maintain their neutrality." See Martin Luther King, Jr., "Speech at an SCLC Staff Retreat," unpublished, Penn Center, Frogmore, South Carolina (3 May 1967), KCLA, 29; King, *Where Do We Go?* 184; and Martin Luther King, Jr., "Stop the Bombing," *Pacific*, 2, no.1 (May/June 1967), 9.

119. King, "America's Chief Moral," 2; King, "Beyond Discovery," 1; King, "A Challenge to the Churches," 2; and Martin Luther King, Jr., "An Address Before a Dinner Sponsored by the Episcopal Society for Cultural and Racial Unity," The 61st General Convention, Sheraton-Jefferson Hotel, St. Louis, Missouri (12 October 1964), KCLA, 2.

120. King, *Strength*, 17 and 62; King, "Transformed Non-Conformist," 2–4; and Carson and Holloran, eds., *Knock*, 72–73.

121. King, *Strength*, 17–19, 62, and 139–140; "Hugh Downs Interview," 2; King, "Church on the Frontier," 3; and Carson and Holloran, eds., *Knock*, 27–28 and 72–73.

122. No scholar has made this point with more clarity and profundity than J. Deotis Roberts, *Bonhoeffer and King: Speaking Truth to Power* (Louisville: Westminster John Knox Press, 2005), 75–81 and 93–99.

123. King, *Can't Wait*, 92; and Washington, ed., *Testament*, 300.

124. Carson and Holloran, eds., *Knock*, 27; and King, *Can't Wait*, 91–92.

125. Carson and Holloran, eds., *Knock*, 28; King, *Can't Wait*, 84; and Washington, ed., *Testament*, 294.

126. King, *Stride*, 207. Also see Carson and Holloran, eds, *Knock*, 27–28; and Baldwin et al., *Legacy*, 78–81.

127. See King, *Can't Wait*, 90; King, "A Challenge to the Churches,'" 4; and King, "Beyond Discovery," 2.

128. King, "Answer," 5–6; King, "A Challenge to the Churches," 3; King, "Beyond Discovery," 2; and King, "Address at a Conference," 4–5.

129. King, *Where Do We Go?* 96; King, *Strength*, 62; King, "A Challenge to the Churches," 3; King, "Beyond Discovery," 2; King, *Can't Wait*, 91–92; and Carson and Holloran, eds., *Knock*, 73.

130. I am greatly indebted to Rufus Burrow, Jr., for much of this idea. See Rufus Burrow, Jr., to Lewis V. Baldwin, 24 March 2005, 3. Also see Baldwin, *Balm*, 298 and 322–330. One young scholar rightly suggests that King used the "rhetoric" or "language of conscience" when explaining the significance of the prophetic role. See Christophe D. Ringer, "Let Your Conscience Be Your Guide: The Idea of Conscience in

the Theology and Ethics of Martin Luther King, Jr.," unpublished paper, Vanderbilt University (Spring 2006), 15–16.

131. King, "Speech at SCLC," 20; Baldwin, *Balm*, 298 and 322–330; Peter J. Paris, "The Bible and the Black Churches," in Ernest R. Sandeen, ed., *The Bible and Social Reform* (Philadelphia: Fortress Press, 1982), 140–144; Burrow, "King's Dream," 209–210; and Burrow to Baldwin, 24 March 2005, 3.

132. King, "Speech at SCLC," 30; Martin Luther King, Jr., "Transcript of an Interview with Local Newscasters," KNXT TV, Los Angeles, unpublished (10 July 1965), KCLA, 2; King, *Can't Wait*, 77; Baldwin, *Balm*, 322; and Lewis V. Baldwin, "The Minister as Preacher, Pastor, and Prophet: The Thinking of Martin Luther King, Jr.," *American Baptist Quarterly*, 7, no.2 (June 1988), 79–97.

133. Here King was speaking specifically of the prophetic witness against racial discrimination, but his comments are clearly revealing in terms of his general definition of a prophet. See King, "A Profound Moral," 10. King said as early as 1958 that:

> Any discussion of the role of the Christian minister today must ultimately emphasize the need for prophecy. Not every minister can be a prophet, but some must be prepared for the ordeals of this high calling and be willing to suffer courageously for righteousness.

See King, *Stride*, 210. Also see Baldwin, *Balm*, 322–330.

134. King, "Address before a Dinner," 2. Also see King, *Can't Wait*, 90.

135. See Gilbert H. Caldwell, "Martin Luther King, Jr.: Ministry Despite the Contradictions," *The African American Pulpit*, 2, no.1 (Winter 1998–99), 10. Inspired by the biblical-prophetic tradition, King engaged in prophetic participation in society while issuing prophetic claims concerning America. Obviously, he lifted a vision of the biblical prophets and Jesus, particularly in terms of doing justice, caring for others, and denouncing the hypocrisy of society. See Baldwin, *Balm*, 322–330; and King, *Stride*, 210.

136. King, "Speech at SCLC," 20. Also see Baldwin, *Balm*, 322–330.

137. Baldwin et al., *Legacy*, 81–101; Baldwin, *Balm*, 322–330; Andrew M. Manis, "'Dying from the Neck Up': Southern Baptist Resistance to the Civil Rights Movement," in *Baptist History and Heritage*, 34, no.1 (Winter 1999), 33–46; and Bill J. Leonard, "A Theology for Racism: Southern Fundamentalists and the Civil Rights Movement," in Ibid, 49–65.

138. "Address before a Dinner," 1–2; and Ansbro, *King*, 163–197.

139. King, *Stride*, 207; King, "Address before a Dinner," 4–5; King, "Beyond Discovery," 4–5; and King, "America's Chief Moral," 10–11.

140. King, "America's Chief Moral," 11; and King, "Beyond Discovery," 5.

141. King, "Address at a Dinner," 2 and 4–6; King, "Beyond Discovery," 2 and 4–7; King, "America's Chief Moral," 2–11; and King, "A Challenge to the Churches," 2–4.

142. King, *Where Do We Go?* 124; King, "A Challenge to the Churches," 2–14; King, "Crisis and the Church," 1–2; and King, "Church on the Frontier," 1–10.

143. For interesting insights into King's Kingdom of God concept, see Smith and Zepp, *Search*, 2, 8–9, 101, 125, 138, and 153–156; and Ansbro, *King*, 172–182.

144. See Ansbro, *King*, 158; King, *Strength*, 110; and Smith and Zepp, *Search*, 155–156.

145. Although the concept of the beloved community extends back to the American absolutistic personalist Josiah Royce (1855–1916) in the late nineteenth century, it was King who gave it living sinew in the 1950s and 1960s. See Rufus Burrow, Jr., *God and Human Dignity: The Personalism, Theology, and Ethics of Martin Luther King, Jr.* (Notre Dame, Ind.: University of Notre Dame Press, 2006), 161–173; Ansbro, *King*, 187–197; and Smith and Zepp, *Search*, 129–156. Rufus Burrow notes that King thought of the church as "this most beloved entity." See Burrow, "King's Dream," 212.

146. Smith and Zepp, *Search*, 141–142; and Burrow, *God and Human*, 167.

147. Walter E. Fluker, *They Looked for a City: A Comparative Analysis of the Ideal of Community in the Thought of Howard Thurman and Martin Luther King, Jr.* (Lanham, Md.: University Press of America, 1989), 150; Ansbro, *King*, 187–189; Washington, ed., *Testament*, 501; Martin Luther King, Jr., "A Statement," unpublished, St. Augustine, Florida (17 June 1964), KCLA, 2; and King, "America's Chief Moral," 19.

148. Baldwin, *Beloved Community*, 165; Ansbro, *King*, 187–188; Smith and Zepp, *Search*, 130–131; and Burrow, *God and Human*, 167–173.

149. King, "America's Chief Moral," 2–5; King, "Advice for Living" (October 1958), 138; King, "Address at a Conference," 4–6; King, "Beyond Discovery," 1–4; King, "A Challenge to the Churches," 2–14; King, "Crisis and the Church," 1–2; and King, "Church on the Frontier," 2–9.

150. Smith and Zepp, *Search*, 132; Burrow, *God and Human*, 169; and Ansbro, *King*, 187–197.

151. Burrow, *God and Human*, 155 and 169; and Smith and Zepp, *Search*, 130–132.

152. King, "Some Things," 3; and King, *Strength*, 110–111.

153. King, "Speech at SCLC," 28; and Martin Luther King, Jr., *The Measure of a Man* (Philadelphia: Fortress Press, 1998), 37.

154. For insights that associate King with "The prophetic or cross-bearing church," see Mary A. Mulligan and Rufus Burrow, Jr., *Daring to Speak in God's Name: Ethical Prophecy in Ministry* (Cleveland: Pilgrim Press, 2002), 197–198. King had a keen sense of the symbolic significance of the cross and the ideal of the sacrificial life in the whole history of the church, and he urged that institution to produce persons who were both vision-bearers and cross-bearers.

155. Carson and Holloran, eds., *Knock*, 108; Martin Luther King, Jr., "Annual Address," unpublished, delivered at the First Annual Institute on Nonviolence and Social Change Under the Auspices of the Montgomery Improvement Association, Holt Street Baptist Church, Montgomery, Alabama (3 December 1956), KCLA, 14; King, "America's Chief Moral," 17–18; and Martin Luther King, Jr., "Interview," unpublished, for USINFO Channels, IPS Telegraph Desk, Oslo (9 December 1964), KCLA, 2. One scholar of the American evangelical traditions persuasively concludes that King saw the cross as "exemplary rather than propitiatory or expiatory." See Donald G. Bloesch, *Essentials of Evangelical Theology: God, Authority, and Salvation*, Vol. I (New York: Harper & Row, 1982), 156.

156. King, "Interview," for USINFO Channels, 2; and King, "Advice for Living" (December 1958), 154.

157. King, "America's Chief Moral," 17–18; King, "Beyond Discovery," 8; and King, *Strength*, 25.

158. King, *Strength*, 21–22 and 25; King, "America's Chief Moral," 2 and 18; and King, "Acceptance Speech," 6.

159. King, "Acceptance Speech," 6; King, "Interview," for USINFO Channels, 2; King, "Speech at SCLC," 31–32; and Washington, ed., *Testament*, 41–42.

160. King, *Strength*, 111; and Washington, ed., *Testament*, 507.

161. Baldwin, *Balm*, 320; and King, "Speech at SCLC," 31–32. Interestingly enough, King's own lived experience in the context of a racist and oppressive society often intersected in his consciousness with the meaning of the cross. As he saw it, his own willingness to pay the ultimate price for justice and peace was not only redemptive for himself and his society, but also instructive for the church. See King, "Interview," for USINFO Channels, 2; and King, "Acceptance Speech," 6.

162. King, "Interview," for USINFO Channels, 2; and Martin Luther King, Jr., "Advice for Living," *Ebony*, 14, no.2 (December 1958), 154. King saw the cross as "an eternal symbol of the love of God, operating in time," a perspective that had profound meaning in light of the mission of the church. See King, "Levels," 7.

163. King, *Can't Wait*, 91; and King, *Strength*, 17–25.

164. King criticized the church for having "failed Christ miserably," for so many worship "Christ emotionally but not morally." See King, "A Challenge to the Churches," 2; and King, "Pharisee and Publican," 2.

165. Martin Luther King, Jr., "Press Conference USA: Transcript from a Video Tape Recording," unpublished, Press Conference USA (5 July 1963), KCLA, 7; and King, *Strength*, 63.

166. Speaking of those "with broken hearts, " King commented: "They need a word of hope. And the church has an answer—if it doesn't, it isn't the church." See king, *Strength*, 63; and Carson and Holloran, eds., *Knock*, 108.

167. King, "America's Chief Moral," 4; and "Sunday with Martin Luther King," WAAF-AM, Transcript of Radio Statement, Chicago (17 April 1966), KCLA, 3.

168. King, "A Statement," St. Augustine, Florida (17 June 1964), 2; King, "Church on the Frontier," 3; King, *Measure*, 35 and 56; King, "Annual Address," First Annual Institute, 14; Martin Luther King, Jr., "The Desirability of Being Maladjusted," unpublished sermon, Chicago (13 January 1958), KCLA, 6; King, "A Realistic Look," 5; and King, "Acceptance Speech," 6.

169. Martin Luther King, Jr., "A Lecture," unpublished, delivered Under the Auspices of the Federation Protestante de France Mutualite, Paris, France (24 October 1965), KCLA, 6; and "Sunday with Martin Luther King, Jr.," WAAF-AM, transcript of a radio statement, Chicago (10 April 1966), KCLA, 1.

170. King, "Annual Address," First Annual Institute, 14; and "Sunday with Martin Luther King" (10 April 1966), 1–2.

171. King, *Can't Wait*, 91; and Washington, ed., *Testament*, 299.

172. The African American theologian J. Deotis Roberts offers brilliant insights into King's effort to weave a thick unity of thought and action in the day-to-day life of the church. Roberts declares that "Martin Luther King, Jr., saw in his ministry the relation between faith and action," between "faith and massive acts of liberation." In a

similar vein, Jim Wallis concludes that "The illuminating oratory of Martin Luther King, Jr. and the other preacher-activists of the movement made the integral connection between faith and politics clear." See J. Deotis Roberts, *A Black Political Theology* (Philadelphia: Westminster Press, 1974), 153; and Jim Wallis, *The Soul of Politics: Beyond "Religious Right" and "Secular Left"* (New York: Harcourt Brace & Company, 1995), 37.

173. For Tolstoy's reflections on the Sermon on the Mount, see Leo Tolstoy, *The Kingdom of God is Within You: Christianity Not as a Mystic Religion but as a New Theory of Life* (Lincoln: University of Nebraska Press, 1984; originally published in 1894), 48–84; and Leo Tolstoy, *Writings on Civil Disobedience and Nonviolence* (Philadelphia: New Society Publishers, 1987), 208–215. One finds hints of the same point of view in Mohandas K. Gandhi's thoughts on Christianity. See Robert Ellsberg, ed., *Gandhi on Christianity* (Maryknoll, N.Y.: Orbis Books, 1991), 12–13 and 19–23; and Ignatius Jesudasan, S.J., *A Gandhian Theology of Liberation* (Maryknoll, N.Y.: Orbis Books, 1984), 130–134.

174. Martin Luther King, Jr. to Chaplain Vernon P. Bodein (3 September 1960), Morehouse KCLA, 1; and Baldwin, *Balm*, 227 n.198.

175. Martin Luther King, Jr., "Speech Made in Savannah," unpublished, Savannah (1 January 1961), KCLA, 13.

176. It was also reported in 1964 that "Both Dr. King and all of the SCLC's 217 affiliate churches, believe there is a pressing need for the weight of the religious and moral forces of the nation to be felt in full strength at the polls." The account went on to quote King, noting that over "the past two years," some of the "major religious bodies of our nation have demonstrated as never before that not only do they have the responsibility to seek redemptive social change in our society, but that they have the responsibility to influence public opinion servants to find creative solutions to pressing social problems." See "SCLC to Launch Religious Vote Mobilization Drive," an unpublished press release (3 October 1964), KCLA, 1–2; and "Statement Regarding SCLC Sponsored Voter Registration Drive," unpublished, Atlanta (12 October 1964), KCLA, 1. Also in 1964, King spoke to the Washington, D.C.-based Second Precinct Clergymen's Association, commending it "for the excellent leadership you have given in the undramatic yet vitally important door-to-door work of getting out registration in the always difficult central city." King essentially agreed with the statement of one of his affiliate organizations, the Western Christian Leadership Conference, which asserted that "The church must lead in the all important program of citizenship," which included voting. Moreover, King worked with organizations aside from the church, such as the Gandhi Society for Human Rights, "to increase the number of Negro registered voters."See Martin Luther King, Jr., "Statement to the Second Precinct Clergymen's Association," unpublished, Washington, D.C. (26 March 1964), KCLA, 1; Robinson, "Report of the Installation Service of the Western Christian Leadership Conference," 1; and Martin Luther King, Jr. to Dr. Harold E. Fey (23 June 1962), KCLA, 2. For a lengthy discussion of the relationship between King's politics and churchmanship, see Baldwin et al., *Legacy*, 125–251.

177. Frederick L. Downing, "A Review" of David J. Garrow, *Bearing the Cross: Martin Luther King, Jr. and the Southern Christian Leadership Conference* (1986), in *Theology Today*, 44, no.3 (October 1987), 391; and Baldwin et al., *Legacy*, xv (Introduction).

178. Baldwin et al., *Legacy*, xvi (Introduction). King also asserted that the church "must grapple with our idea" that neither "legislation" nor "laws" can, in and of themselves, "change internal prejudiced attitudes" and "certain false notions." See King, "Advice for Living" (December, 1958), 154; and King, "Address before a Dinner," 5.

179. Lewis V. Baldwin, "The Public Perversion of Religion," in *Orbis*, 5, no.7 (April 2006), 13 and 18; and Martin Luther King, Jr., "Press Conference after Ministers' Leadership Training Program," unpublished, Chicago (11 July 1967), KCLA, 6. King was quick to respond to those who counseled the church to follow Paul's admonition to "obey duly constituted authorities," as set forth in Romans 13. See King, "Advice for Living" (October 1957), 53; and Baldwin et al., *Legacy*, 85–86.

180. Baldwin et al., *Legacy*, 77–101; and Baldwin, *Balm*, 159–228.

181. King taught the nation a lot about the political dimensions of the religious life, and his own thought and activities afford an illuminating look at the complex interrelationship between religion, morality, law, and politics. Thus, it is not surprising that Andrew Young, an aide to King, called the civil rights leader "a political theologian." See Baldwin et al., *Legacy*, xv–xvi (Introduction); Wallis, *Soul*, 37; Andrew Young, "Martin Luther King as Political Theologian," in Theodore Runyon, ed., *Theology, Poiltics, and Peace* (Maryknoll, N.Y.: Orbis Books, 1989), 79–85.

182. Robert N. Bellah and Phillip E. Hammond, *Varieties of Civil Religion* (San Francisco: Harper & Row, 1980), 194.

183. It is no accident that Robert N. Bellah's initial essay on American civil religion appeared in 1967, as King's leadership in the struggle to transform the nation was triggering much debate, in the academy and in the public square. Bellah, Peter Berger, Sidney Mead, and other scholars of civil religion in America shared their insights against the background of the civil rights crusade, and so did James H. Cone and the first generation of black liberation theologians. See Baldwin, "Perversion," 12; Baldwin et al., *Legacy*, 42–51; Bellah and Hammond, *Varieties*, 15, 171–172, and 194–195; Andrew M. Manis, *Southern Civil Religions in Conflict: Civil Rights and the Culture Wars* (Macon, Ga.: Mercer University Press, 2002), 4–186; John D. Elder, "Martin Luther King and American Civil Religion," in *Harvard Divinity Bulletin*, New Series, I, no.3 (Spring 1968), 17–18; and David Howard-Pitney, *The African American Jeremiad: Appeals for Justice in America*, Revised and Expanded Edition (Philadelphia: Temple University Press, 2005), 1–3, 139–160, and 185–216. For significant references to King's influence on black liberation theology, which challenged both the black and white churches, see James H. Cone, *For My People—Black Theology and the Black Church: Where Have We Been and Where are We Going?* (Maryknoll, N.Y.: Orbis Books, 1984), 6–7; and "James Cone Interview: Liberation, Black Theology, and the Church," in *Radix Magazine*, 14, no.2 (September/October 1982), 9–12.

184. Martin Luther King, Jr., "Address at a Public Meeting of the Southern Christian Ministers Conference of Mississippi," unpublished (23 September 1959), KCLA, 5.

185. The role that King envisioned for intellectuals, and especially social scientists, in coalitions for much-needed change is most interesting, for he suggests a comparison between them and religious leaders. "Every revolution must be accompanied by a firm intellectual undergirding as well as the moral zeal and courage of the masses,"

King declared. He added: "The social analysts and political scientists of a civilization are at best prophets which continue to redeem the civilization and protect it from danger within and without." King, "Address at the Southern Association," 2–3 and 14–15; and R. Drew Smith, ed., *Freedom's Distant Shores: American Protestants and Post-Colonial Alliances with Africa* (Waco, Texas: Baylor University Press, 2006), 53 and 238 n.1.

186. King, "Interview," for USINFO Channels, 5. Also see King, "Address at the Southern Association," 2–3 and 15; King, "A Statement" (17 June 1964), 3; Martin Luther King, Jr., "Draft of a Statement Regarding Deaths of Schwerner, Goodman, and Chaney" (4 August 1964), KCLA, 1; Martin Luther King, Jr., "Statement to the Second Precinct Clergymen's Association," unpublished, Washington, D.C. (26 March 1964), KCLA, 1; and Israel Goldstein, "Martin Luther King, Jr.'s Jewish Associations," *Jerusalem Post*, 22 October 1964, 3.

187. King, *Where Do We Go?* 9; and Smith and Zepp, *Search*, 132.

188. Smith and Zepp, *Search*, 132; Martin Luther King, Jr., *The Trumpet of Conscience* (San Francisco: Harper & Row, 1987), 69–70; Martin Luther King, Jr., "Remarks at a Tribute from City of Atlanta," unpublished, Atlanta (28 January 1965), KCLA, 5; and "Hugh Downs Interview," 2.

189. King, *Can't Wait*, 91.

190. King knew that if the church became just another institution completely subject to its own political whims, it would cease to be the church. In other words, it would become like Pontius Pilate, whose "greatest weakness," according to King, "was that he was a slave to his own self-interest." By its very nature, the church, King thought, has a more noble calling in the political realm. As an advocate of a democratic ethic rooted in Christian (or religious) realism, King insisted that the church should be a pivotal force in the extension of democracy across the country. At the same time, he understood that the church had long been a part of a mythical America that still lacked the courage and the will to live out the true meaning of its democratic creed. See Martin Luther King, Jr., "Outline for a Sermon on Pontius Pilate," unpublished (15 March 1964), KCLA, 1; and Baldwin et al., *Legacy*, 125–148.

191. King, *Stride*, 208; King, *Strength*, 141; King, "Address before a Dinner," 1–2; Martin Luther King, Jr., to Dr. J Oscar Lee (2 July 1962), KCLA, 1; King to Fey (23 June 1962), 1–5; King, "Transformed Non-Conformist," 8; and King, "Press Conference USA," 3.

192. Martin Luther King, Jr., "The Christian Way of Life in Human Relations," unpublished sermon delivered at the General assembly of the National Council of Churches, St. Louis, Missouri (4 December 1957), The King Papers Project, 5; King, "America's Chief Moral," 1–5; King, *Stride*, 205; and James P. Brown, "Another Opinion: Dr. King's Moral Stand," *New York Times*, 23 April 1967, 191.

193. King, "Remarks at a Tribute," 5; King, "The Christian Way," 1 and 5; King, *Stride*, 210; and King, "A Challenge to the Churches," 2.

194. King, *Strength*, 27–29.

195. Martin Luther King, Jr., "Segregation and the Church," *New York Amsterdam News*, 2 February 1963, 8; Martin Luther King, Jr., "The Church and the Race Crisis," *Christian Century*, 75, no.41 (8 October 1958), 1140–1141; King, "A Challenge to the Churches," 2–3; Martin Luther King, Jr., "The Role of the Church," *New York*

Amsterdam News, 15 September 1962, 11 and 14; King, "Beyond Discovery," 1–2; and King, "An Address before a Dinner," 1–4.

196. King often said that "As a minister of the gospel," he was "ashamed to affirm" that this was indeed the case. King, "Church and the Race Crisis," 1141; King, "Church on the Frontier," 6–7; King, "An Address before a Dinner," 5; King, "Press Conference USA," 7; Martin Luther King, Jr., "Advice for Living," *Ebony*, 13, no.4 (February 1958), 84; and Martin Luther King, Jr., "Address to the National Press Club," Washington, D.C., unpublished (19 July 1962), KCLA, 1.

197. King, *Strength*, 141.

198. "Martin Luther King, Jr.," *Church Times*, 25 September 1964; and King, "Address to the National Press Club," 5.

199. King, "A Challenge to the Churches," 5–12; King, "Address before a Dinner," 2–5; King, *Strength*, 142–143; King, *Stride*, 205–209; King, "Role of the Church," 11 and 14; King, "Church and the Race Crisis," 1140–1141; King, "Church on the Frontier," 3–7; King, "Crisis and the Church," 1–4; King, "Beyond Discovery," 1–7; Gilbert, "King Urges Youth," 1 and 16; "Dr. King Urges Church," *St. Louis Post-Dispatch*, 13 October 1964; Martin Luther King, Jr., "The Future of Integration," a speech delivered at the State University of Iowa, Iowa City, Iowa, unpublished (11 November 1959), KCLA, 4–7; Martin Luther King, Jr., "The Role of the Church in Facing the Nation's Chief Moral Dilemma," a speech at the Conference on Christian Faith and Human Relations, Nashville, Tennessee (25 April 1957), typed version issued as part of the Proceedings of the Conference on Christian Faith and Human Relations, KCLA, 29–32; Martin Luther King, Jr., "For All—A Non-Segregated Society," a message for Race Relations Sunday, published by the Department of Racial and Cultural Relations, National Council of Churches, New York (10 February 1957), KCLA, 1–3; Martin Luther King, Jr., "Moral and Religious Imperatives for Brotherhood," excerpts from an address at Congregation B'nai Jeshurun, New York, unpublished (9 February 1963), KCLA, 1–3; Martin Luther King, Jr., "An Analysis of the Ethical Demands of Integration," an address at the Nashville Consultation, Nashville, Tennessee, unpublished (27 December 1962), KCLA, 4–6; Martin Luther King, Jr., "Out of Segregation's Long Night: An Interpretation of a Racial Crisis," *Churchman*, 172 (February 1958), 7; and Martin Luther King, Jr., "How the Civil Rights Struggle Challenges Our Churches," *Redbook*, August 1965, 57 and 131.

200. Kind pointed out that the "evil" of segregation "persists in most of the local churches, church schools, church hospitals, and other church institutions." See King, "For All—A Non-Segregated Society," 1–3.

201. King, "Address before a Dinner," 5; King, "Acceptance Speech," 3; King, "Church and the Race Crisis," 1140; King, "America's Chief Moral," 2; King, "Beyond Discovery," 7; King, "Moral and Religious Imperatives," 1–3; King, "An Analysis of the Ethical Demands," 5 and 11; King, "For All—A Non-Segregated Society," 1–3; "Dr. King Urges Church"; King, "A Challenge to the Churches," 2 and 14; and King, *Stride*, 206.

202. Gilbert, "King Urges Youth," 1 and 16; "Hugh Downs Interview," 5–6; Martin Luther King, Jr., "The Meaning of Hope," unpublished sermon, Dexter Avenue Baptist

Church, Montgomery, Alabama (10 December 1967), KCLA, 17–18; Baldwin, "Perversion," 12; Carson and Holloran, eds., *Knock*, 109; and "James Cone Interview," 9–12.

203. Carson and Holloran, eds., *Knock*, 29–30 and 73; King, "A Statement," St. Augustine, Florida (17 June 1964), 2; King, *Stride*, 105–106, 205–206, 209–210, and 219–220; Carson et al., eds., *King Papers*, II, 232; Washington, ed., *Testament*, 501; King, *Can't Wait*, 45; and Martin Luther King, Jr., "Interview," St. Augustine, Florida, unpublished (17 June 1964), KCLA, 2.

204. King, "Advice for Living," (February 1958), 84. In 1964, King said in London that "We are getting more support from the churches in the United States than ever before, but that is not to say that we are getting enough." At another point he observed that "we have seen the church of Jesus Christ rise up as never before and join the thunderous procession of committed souls in behalf of racial justice." "Here and there," he remarked on yet another occasion, "churches are courageously making attacks on segregation, and actually integrating their congregations." He rejoiced also that "many ministerial associations are integrating," and he concluded that "As the church continues to take a forthright stand on this issue, the transition from a segregated to an integrated society will be infinitely smoother." See William Duck, "The Fine Art of Answering Loaded Questions—Demonstrated Yesterday by Dr. Martin Luther King, Jr.," *Sheffield Telegraph*, London, England, 22 September 1964; Martin Luther King, Jr., "Closing Address before the National Conference on Religion and Race," Chicago, unpublished (17 January 1963), 1; King, "Address to the National Press Club," 6; King, "The Future of Integration," 4 and 7; Gilbert, "King Urges Youth," 1 and 16; King, "Church and the Race Crisis," 1141; Martin Luther King, Jr., "Nonviolence: The Christian Way in Human Relations," *Presbyterian Life*, 8 February 1958, 11–13; and King, "Segregation and the Church," 8. As early as 1957, King came up with a number of suggestions on how "local churches can take action within their own organization" around the issue of race. See King, "For All—A Non-Segregated Society," 1–2.

205. King, "Press Conference USA," 7; King, "Segregation and the Church," 8; and "Hugh Downs Interview," 1. Given the fact that King was steeped in liberal Christian theology, it is not surprising that he saw "endless possibilities for the fulfillment of brotherhood in history." See Carson et al., eds., *King Papers*, II, 140.

206. King, "Segregation and the Church," 8; King, "A Challenge to the Churches," 3–4; and Martin Luther King, Jr., "We are Still Walking," *Liberation*, December 1956, 8.

207. King, "Segregation and the Church," 8; King, "We are Still Walking," 8; King, "Advice for Living" (June 1958), 118; and King, "Remarks at a Tribute," 5.

208. King, "A Challenge to the Churches," 3–4; King, "Segregation and the Church," 8; and King, "Church and the Race Crisis," 1140–1141.

209. King, *Strength*, 102; and King, *Stride*, 208.

210. "Integration Leader Wary of Being Tricked Out of Jail," in *Jet*, 23 August 1962, 14 and 21; Martin Luther King, Jr., "Paul's Letter to American Christians," a printed version of a sermon preached in the Dexter Avenue Baptist Church, Montgomery, Alabama (4 November 1956), KCLA, 3 King, "Church and the Race Crisis," 1141; Martin

Luther King, Jr., "New Wine in Old Bottles," an unpublished sermon, Ebenezer Baptist Church (2 January 1966), KCLA, 4; and King, "Role of the Church in Facing," 31.

211. Martin Luther King, Jr., "A Cry of Hate or a Cry for Help?" unpublished statement (August 1965), KCLA, 4. King often spoke of "the least of these" in his sermons and mass meeting speeches. This became his way of referring to the poor and oppressed generally. See King, "America's Chief Moral," 19; Martin Luther King, Jr., "Revolution and Redemption," unpublished closing address at the European Baptist Assembly, Amsterdam, Holland (16 August 1964), KCLA, 9; King, "Lecture," Federation Protestante, 16; King, "Crisis of Civil Rights," 15–16; and King, "Closing Address," 1.

212. King, "Advice for Living" (April 1958), 104; Carson and Holloran, eds., Knock, 109; and King, "Speech at SCLC," 30.

213. King, "Revolution and Redemption," 9.

214. King, "'Lost Sheep' or 'God of the Lost,'" 1–8.

215. King, "A Challenge to the Churches," 4; King, Stride, 210; Carson and Holloran, eds., Knock, 109; King, "Speech at SCLC," 30; Martin Luther King, Jr., "An Address at the Synagogue Council of America," unpublished (5 December 1965), KCLA, 8–9; and King, "Transformed Non-Conformist," 13.

216. Martin Luther King, Jr., "The Church Must be Firm!," New York Amsterdam News, 23 November 1963, 10; King, "Address at a Conference," 4–5; and King, "A Profound Moral," 10.

217. King, "Address at a Conference," 6–7; King, "The Church Must be Firm!," 10; King, Strength, 102; and King, "A Profound Moral," 10.

218. Watley, Roots, 89; King, "Crisis of Civil Rights," 15; and "Civil Rights in its Second Phase: An Interview with Martin Luther King, Jr.," unpublished, "Arlene Francis Show," New York, (19 June 1967), KCLA, 2.

219. King, Strength, 102.

220. Martin Luther King, Jr., "A Statement," unpublished, Friendship Baptist Church, Chicago (26 July 1967), KCLA, 1; and Martin Luther King, Jr., "My Dream," Chicago Defender, 19–25 February 1966, 1.

221. Martin Luther King, Jr., "Address at Mason Temple Mass Meeting," unpublished, Mason Temple Church of God in Christ, Memphis, Tennessee (18 March 1968), KCLA, 1.

222. Lawrence L. Knudson, "King Threatens Demonstration at Conventions," Atlanta Constitution, 1 April 1968, 2.

223. "Sunday with Martin Luther King, Jr." (17 April 1966), 3; King, "Who are We?" 5; and King, "Answer," 8.

224. Carson and Holloran, eds., Knock, 72.

225. King, "Advice for Living" (April 1958), 104; King, Stride, 25; Carson and Holloran, eds., Knock, 72; and King, "Drum Major Instinct," 5.

226. King frequently noted that "Dives' sin" was "his inordinate self-love . . . his refusal to use his wealth to bridge the gulf between the extremes of superfluous inordinate wealth and abject deadening poverty, . . . [or his decision to become] a conscientious objector in the war against poverty," an assessment applicable, at least to some extent, to the institutional church as well. See Martin Luther King, Jr., "To Serve

the Present Age," unpublished sermon (25 June 1967), KCLA, 1–2; Martin Luther King, Jr., "Pre-Washington Campaign," unpublished speech before the Mississippi Leaders on the Washington Campaign, St. Thomas AME Church, Birmingham, Alabama (15 February 1968), KCLA, 9; King, "Lazarus and Dives," 4–8; and King, *Strength*, 67–68 and 102.

227. King reminded his hearers that Jesus "was born in an obscure village, the child of a poor peasant woman, [and] grew up in still another obscure village where he worked as a carpenter until he was thirty years old." King added: "He was thirty-three when the tide of public opinion turned against him. They called him a rabble-rouser. They called him a troublemaker. They called him an agitator. He practiced civil disobedience; he broke injunctions. And so he was turned over to his enemies, and went through the mockery of a trial." In King's understanding, Jesus identified with the poor and oppressed, the despised and rejected, a view that would course through liberation theologies. See King, "Drum Major Instinct," 8.

228. King, "Address at a Conference," 5; King, "A Challenge to the Churches," 4; and King, *Where Do We Go?* 186.

229. Martin Luther King, Jr., "Draft of an Article on the Status of the Civil Rights Movement in 1965," unpublished (February 1965), KCLA, 15.

230. King, "An Analysis of the Ethical Demands," 12.

231. King, "Who are We?" 5.

232. King, "We Would See Jesus," 5; King, "Segregation and the Church," 8; "Hugh Downs Interview," 2; King, *Strength*, 32 and 35; and King, "Closing Address," 1.

233. King, "Is the Universe Friendly?" 2–3; Martin Luther King, Jr., "A Letter regarding the Mississippi Freedom Democratic Party," unpublished (c. 24 December 1964), KCLA, 1; and King, "Advice for Living" (November 1957), 106.

234. King, "A Cry of Hate?" 12.

235. "Integration Leader Wary of Being Tricked," 20–21; and King, "To Serve the Present Age," 2. King made essentially this same point as early as 1949, while still in seminary. See Clayborne Carson et al., eds., *The Papers of Martin Luther King, Jr., Volume VI: Advocate of the Social Gospel, September 1948–March 1963* (Berkeley: University of California Press, 2007), 88.

236. Carson and Holloran, eds., *Knock*, 72.

237. "Hugh Downs Interview with Martin Luther King, Jr.," 2–3; King, "We are Still Walking," 8; and Martin Luther King, Jr., "What is Your New Year's Resolutions?" unpublished statement, New York (7 January 1968), KCLA, 3. Referring to "preachers who raise their voices in favor of war," King asserted: "I've made my decision. I'm going to follow Christ on this issue." See King, "To Serve the Present Age," 2.

238. King was opposed to war generally as a consequence of pragmatic, moral, and spiritual considerations. See Brown, "Another Opinion: Dr. King's Moral Stand," 191; "As We See It: Dr. King Strengthens an Anti-War Coalition," *Detroit Free Press*, 6 April 1967; King, "To Serve the Present Age," 2; "Hugh Downs Interview," 2–3; Martin Luther King, Jr., to Sam Wyler (20 July 1967), KCLA, 2–3; King, "What are Your New Year's Resolutions?" 3; and "Newsmakers: Featuring Martin Luther King, Jr.," unpublished transcript of an interview on Channel 2, KNXT-TV, Los Angeles (10 July 1965), KCLA, 2.

239. Washington, ed., *Testament*, 39–40.

240. In a paper King wrote as a seminary student, he stated: "Though I cannot accept an absolute pacifist position, I am as anxious as any to see wars end and have no desire to take part in one." See Martin Luther King, Jr., "War and Racifism," unpublished paper, Crozer Theological Seminary, Chester, Pennsylvania (1951), KCLA, 1. Also see "Hugh Downs Interview," 2–3; and King, "To Serve the Present Age," 2.

241. King, "Transformed Non-Conformist," 9–10. For some of King's many comments on the power, richness, and social relevance of the early church, see King, "What are Your New Year's Resolutions?" 3; King, "Advice for Living," (October 1957), 53; King, "Drum Major Instinct," p. 8; King, *Can't Wait*, 84 and 92; King, *Strength*, 78–79 and 95; King, "Press Conference USA," 6; and "Martin Luther King Explains Nonviolent Resistance," in William L. Katz, *Eyewitness: The Negro in American History* (New York: Pitman Publishing, 1967), 512.

242. King obviously drank from the wellsprings of that Christian pacifist tradition stretching back to the early church, but he also acknowledged other intellectual and experiential sources to which he turned. He explained that "Nonviolence blended the ethics of Jesus, the philosophies of Hegel and Thoreau, with the teachings of Gandhi. This amalgam of philosophy and practice proved to be an excellent way to attack the inadequacies existing in the American social system." See Martin Luther King, Jr., "Montgomery Sparked a Revolution," unpublished manuscript prepared for *Southern Courier* (11–12 December 1965), KCLA, 5; and King, "An Analysis of the Ethical Demands," 17.

243. "Martin Luther King Explains Nonviolent Resistance," 512.

244. King often said that "the aftermath of nonviolence is the creation of the beloved community, while the aftermath of violence is tragic bitterness." King, "Out of Segregation's Long Night," 7; King, "Nonviolence: The Christian Way," 12; and King, "An Analysis of the Ethical Demands," 1.

245. Martin Luther King, Jr., "When Peace Becomes Obnoxious," *Louisville Defender*, 29 March 1956; and Carson and Holloran, eds., *Knock*, 32.

246. King," Press Conference USA," 6; and King, *Can't Wait*, 92.

247. "Hugh Downs Interview," 3.

248. In 1967, King actually announced "the largest coalition of religious, civic and public leaders so far organized in protest against U.S. escalation in Vietnam." See James A. Wechsler, "An Un-Patriot?" *New York Post*, 25 April 1967.

249. King felt that the church should reflect the presence of God as a healing community, not as a body that blesses or sanctions the killing of human beings and the destruction of the environment or property. See Martin Luther King, Jr., "An Address at Local 1199, Salute to Freedom," unpublished, Hunter College, New York (10 March 1968), KCLA, 2; and Martin Luther King, Jr., "Transcript of an Interview on the 'Merv Griffin Show' with Harry Belafonte," unpublished, New York (6 July 1967), KCLA, 4.

250. Washington, ed., *Testament*, 40; King, "Revolution and Redemption," 10; and King, "An Address at the Synagogue Council," 11.

251. King, "An Address at the Synagogue Council," 11.

252. King, *Can't Wait*, 92.

CHAPTER 3

1. Martin Luther King, Jr., *Why We Can't Wait*, (New York: New American Library, 1964), 91; and James M. Washington, ed., *A Testament of Hope: The Essential Writings and Speeches of Martin Luther King, Jr.* (New York: HarperCollins, 1986), 299–300.

2. Clayborne Carson et al., eds., *The Papers of Martin Luther King, Jr., Volume III: Birth of a New Age, December 1955–December 1956* (Berkeley: University of California Press, 1997), 74; Martin Luther King, Jr., "Statement Issued from Harlem Hospital," unpublished version, New York (30 September 1958), KCLA, 2; Martin Luther King, Jr., "Great Day for Negroes," *New York Amsterdam News*, 12 October 1963, 10; Martin Luther King, Jr., "Speech Concerning Southern Civil Rights at a Mississippi Freedom Democratic Party Meeting," unpublished, Jackson, Mississippi (23 July 1964), KCLA, 4; Martin Luther King, Jr., "Address at the Southern Association of Political Scientists," unpublished (13 November 1964), KCLA, 4; Martin Luther King, Jr., "Statement to the Press Regarding Trip to Receive Nobel Peace Prize," unpublished, Sheraton-Atlantic Hotel, Atlantic City, New Jersey (4 December 1964), KCLA, 1; Martin Luther King, Jr., *Stride toward Freedom: The Montgomery Story* (New York: Harper & Row, 1958), 224; Martin Luther King, Jr., "Segregation," unpublished statement, Montgomery, Alabama (24 May 1961), KCLA, 1; Martin Luther King, Jr., to Major J. Jones (5 November 1960), KCLA, 1; Martin Luther King, Jr., "Address at a Mass Meeting," unpublished, Laurel, Mississippi (19 March 1968), KCLA, 4; Martin Luther King, Jr., "The Negro and the American Dream," an address at an NAACP Public Meeting, unpublished, Charlotte, North Carolina (25 September 1960), KCLA, 2; and Martin Luther King, Jr., "Speech Made in Savannah," unpublished, Savannah, Georgia (1 January 1961), KCLA, 5 and 7.

3. Martin Luther King, Jr., *Strength to Love* (Philadelphia: Fortress Press, 1981), 62; Martin Luther King, Jr., to Dr. Truman Douglas (28 June 1965), KCLA, 1–2; Martin Luther King, Jr., "A Lecture," unpublished, delivered under the auspices of the Federation Protestante de France Mutualite, Paris (24 October 1965), KCLA, 12; Martin Luther King, Jr., "Remarks at a Tribute from City of Atlanta," unpublished, Atlanta (28 January 1965), KCLA, 5; Martin Luther King, Jr., "Interview," unpublished, for USINFO channels, IPS Telegraph Desk, Oslo (9 December 1964), KCLA, 5; and "SCLC to Launch Religious Vote Mobilization Drive," unpublished press release, Atlanta (3 October 1964), KCLA, 2.

4. King variously referred to the civil rights movement as "a Christian social movement," "a reform movement," "a movement of Christian nonviolent reform," "the Christian social struggle," and as a crusade rooted in "spiritual and moral forces." See Martin Luther King, Jr., to David C. Dautzer (9 May 1961), KCLA, 1; King to Douglas (28 June 1965), 2; Martin Luther King, Jr., "Speech at an SCLC Staff Retreat," unpublished, Penn Center, Frogmore, South Carolina (2 May 1967), KCLA, 8; Martin Luther King, Jr., "An Ambitious Dream Confronts Reality," unpublished version of an essay written for *New York Amsterdam News*, (c. 23 June 1965), KCLA, 1; Martin Luther King, Jr., "Statement in Response to an *Atlanta Constitution* Article Alleging Communist Ties," unpublished (25 July 1963), KCLA, 2; Martin Luther King, Jr., "Meaning of Georgia Elections," *New York Amsterdam News*, 3 July 1965, 16; Martin

Luther King, Jr., to Chaplain Vernon P. Bodein (3 September 1960), KCLA, 1; Martin Luther King, Jr., "Remarks on Fear," unpublished, Montgomery, Alabama (23 March 1956), KCLA, 1; Martin Luther King, Jr., "Statement on the Method of Protest in Montgomery," unpublished, Montgomery, Alabama (21 March 1956), KCLA, 1; and Glenn E. Smiley, "An Interview with Martin Luther King, Jr.," unpublished version (February-March, 1956), KCLA, 2. The term "Christian social movement" has been employed in reference to the Social Gospel movement of the late ninetenth and early twentieth centuries. See Daniel G. Reid et al., eds., *Dictionary of Christianity in America* (Downers Grove, Ill.: InterVarsity Press, 1990), 1104.

5. King, *Strength*, 62; Washington, ed., *Testament*, 501; Clayborne Carson and Peter Holloran, eds., *A Knock at Midnight: Inspirations from the Great Sermons of Reverend Martin Luther King, Jr.* (New York: Warner Books, 1998), 73; and Clayborne Carson et al., eds., *The Papers of Martin Luther King, Jr., Volume I: Called to Serve, January 1929-June 1951* (Berkeley: University of California Press, 1992), 281.

6. King, *Strength*, 43; Carson et al., eds., *King Papers*, I, 131 and 142; Washington, ed., *Testament*, 211; and Martin Luther King, Jr., "Honoring Dr. DuBois," *Freedomways*, 8 (1968), 104–111. Apparently, King knew something quite profound about the historical circumstances that resulted in religious traditions being transmitted from Africa to New World societies—namely, Latin America, the Caribbean, and the United States. He was prepared to think historically and comparatively about the ways in which different slave cultures took shape. In one of his rare references to the different ways in which slavery developed in Latin America and the U.S., he noted:

> Latin America did maintain a little dignity for the slave—they could get married and other things. But slavery in the United States intentionally broke up the family. It sought, and went out of the way to immobilize, and break up the family. It broke up the very structure, which will keep a people together. This is what our forebears went through.

This and other scattered statements in King's writings, speeches, and sermons are useful for getting at the impact of African religious and cultural traditions on the slave church and on slave societies in various parts of the New World. See Martin Luther King, Jr., "The Meaning of Hope," unpublished sermon, Dexter Avenue Baptist Church, Montgomery, Alabama (10 December 1967), KCLA, 14.

7. Drawing on the insights of W. E. B. DuBois, King called the Negro spirituals "that most original and beautiful of all American music." See King, "Hope," 16; Martin Luther King, Jr., "Pre-Washington Campaign: A Speech on the Washington Campaign to Mississippi Leaders," unpublished version, St. Thomas AME Church, Birmingham, Alabama (15 February 1968), KCLA, 12; and Lewis V. Baldwin and Amiri YaSin Al-Hadid, *Between Cross and Crescent: Christian and Muslim Perspectives on Malcolm and Martin* (Gainesville: University Press of Florida, 2002), 384 n.72.

8. King, *Can't Wait*, 61; Washington, ed., *Testament*, xii, 220, 348, and 502–503; Martin Luther King, Jr., "My Dream: Message for the People," unpublished statement

(c. 1 January 1966), KCLA, 1; Clayborne Carson et al., eds., *The Papers of Martin Luther King, Jr., Volume V: Threshold of a New Decade, January 1959–December 1960* (Berkeley: University of California Press, 2005), 249; Martin Luther King, Jr., "Overcoming an Inferiority Complex," unpublished sermon, delivered at the Dexter Avenue Baptist Church, Montgomery, Alabama (14 July 1957), Martin Luther King, Jr. Papers Project, Stanford University, Stanford, California, 10; Martin Luther King, Jr., "Living Under the Tensions of the Modern Life," unpublished sermon, Montgomery, Alabama (1956), The King Papers Project, 1; Martin Luther King, Jr., "Annual Report," unpublished version, delivered at the Eighth Annual Convention of the Southern Christian Leadership Conference, Savannah, Georgia (September 28–October 2, 1964), KCLA, 2; Martin Luther King, Jr., "Early Days," unpublished excerpts from "Thou Fool," a sermon delivered at the Mt. Pisgah Missionary Baptist Church, Chicago, Illinois (27 August 1967), KCLA, 4; Martin Luther King, Jr., "A Knock at Midnight," unpublished version of a sermon delivered at the All Saints Community Church, Los Angeles, California (25 June 1967), KCLA, 16; Martin Luther King, Jr., "Interruptions," unpublished sermon, Ebenezer Baptist Church, Atlanta (21 January 1968), KCLA, 8–9; Martin Luther King, Jr., "The Birth of a New Nation," unpublished version of a sermon, Dexter Avenue Baptist Church, Montgomery, Alabama (April 1957), KCLA, 9–10; King, "Hope," 16; Martin Luther King, Jr., "Speech at a Rally," unpublished, Crawfordville, Georgia (11 October 1965), KCLA, 1–2; Martin Luther King, Jr., "Address at a Mason Temple Mass Meeting," unpublished, Mason Temple Church of God in Christ, Memphis, Tennessee (18 March 1968), KCLA, 11; Martin Luther King, Jr., "Rally Speech on the Georgia Tour and 'Pre-Washington Campaign,'" unpublished, Albany, Georgia (22 March 1968), KCLA, 8–9; and Martin Luther King, Jr., "The Quiet Conviction of Nonviolence," *The Mennonite*, 80, no.1 (5 January 1965), 2.

9. King, *Can't Wait*, 61; King, "Hope," 16; Washington, ed., *Testament*, 348; and King, "My Dream: Message for My People," 1.

10. Martin Luther King, Jr., "Dives and Lazarus," unpublished sermon (10 March 1963), KCLA, 13; Martin Luther King, Jr., "Facing Life's Inescapables," unpublished document, Crozer Theological Seminary, Chester, Pennsylvania (c. 3 March 1949), The King Papers Project, 2; Martin Luther King, Jr., "Accepting Responsibility for Your Actions," unpublished sermon, Ebenezer Baptist Church, Atlanta (26 July 1953), The King Papers Project, 2; Carson et al., eds., *King Papers*, I, 109–110; Washington, ed., *Testament*, 212; Clayborne Carson et al., eds., *The Papers of Martin Luther King, Jr., Volume IV: Symbol of the Movement, January 1957–December 1958* (Berkeley: University of California Press, 2000), 255–256; Carson et al., eds., *King Papers*, III, 270; Carson et al., eds., *King Papers*, V, 285 and 339–340; Martin Luther King, Jr., *Where Do We Go from Here: Chaos or Community?* (Boston: Beacon Press, 1968), 126–127; and Martin Luther King, Jr., "Training Your Child in Love," unpublished sermon, Ebenezer Baptist Church, Atlanta (8 May 1966), KCLA, 5.

11. Martin Luther King, Jr., "Discerning the Signs of History," unpublished sermon, Ebenezer Baptist Church, Atlanta (15 November 1964), KCLA, 4–5.

12. King, *Strength*, 94–95.

13. Carson et al., eds., *King Papers*, IV, 155; Martin Luther King, Jr., "A Christian Movement in a Revolutionary Age," unpublished speech (Fall 1966), KCLA, 1–2; King, "Lecture," The Federation Protestante, 3–5; Martin Luther King, Jr., "But, If Not . . . ," unpublished sermon, Ebenezer Baptist Church, Atlanta, Georgia (5 November 1967), KCLA, 2; and Martin Luther King, Jr., "Why We Must Go to Washington," unpublished statement, SCLC Staff Retreat, Ebenezer Baptist Church, Atlanta (15 January 1968), KCLA, 14.

14. King, "Lecture," The Federation Protestante, 3–5; and King, "Christian Movement," 1–2. Also see King, *Strength*, 80–82; Clayborne Carson and Kris Shepard, eds., *A Call to Conscience: The Landmark Speeches of Dr. Martin Luther King, Jr.* (New York: Warner Books, 2001), 17–18; and Washington, ed., *Testament*, 281 and 495.

15. Interestingly enough, scholars like Albert J. Raboteau and Eddie S. Glaude have offered rich and hard insights into the historical uses of the Exodus by both African Americans and white Americans, and how this fed into their different conceptions of themselves and of nationhood as a whole. Glaude brilliantly explains how the biblical story of the Exodus inspired a pragmatic tradition of racial advocacy among African Americans in the nineteenth century, an approach that is essential for locating King in the black church tradition. See Albert J. Raboteau, *A Fire in the Bones: Reflections on African-American Religious History* (Boston: Beacon Press, 1995), 17–36; Albert J. Raboteau, "African-Americans, Exodus, and the American Israel," in Paul E. Johnson, ed., *African-American Christianity: Essays in History* (Berkeley: University of California Press, 1994), 9–17; Albert J. Raboteau, "Martin Luther King, Jr., and the Tradition of Black Religious Protest," in Rowland A. Sherrill, ed., *Religion and the Life of the Nation: American Recoveries* (Urbana and Chicago: University of Illinois Press, 1990), 50–61; Henry Goldschmidt and Elizabeth McAlister, eds., *Race, Nation, and Religion in the Americas* (New York: Oxford University Press, 2004), 9–11, 143, and 155 n.55; and Eddie S. Glaude, Jr., *Exodus!: Religion, Race, and Nation in Early Nineteenth-Century Black America* (Chicago: University of Chicago Press, 2000), 3–167. Also see King, "Christian Movement," 1–2; and King, "Lecture," The Federation Protestante, 4–6.

16. In employing the image of the Exodus church, King was standing in a long-established and/or time-honored tradition. The AME preacher Daniel Coker evoked this image by implication in a sermon in 1816. Coker argued that the situation of Africans in white churches and under white ecclesiastical domination in the nineteenth century was analogous to that of the Jews in Babylon, and he compared the black church freedom movement under Richard Allen and others to the freedom of the Jews from Babylonian captivity. One detects in Coker's language the seeds of a diasporan ecclesiology that would find some expression in King's thoughts on the antebellum Negro church. See Daniel Coker, "Sermon Delivered Extempore in the African Methodist Episcopal Church in the City of Baltimore, on the 21st of January, 1816, to a Numerous Concourse of People, on Account of the Coloured People Gaining their Church (Bethel) in the Supreme Ct. of the State of Pennsylvania," in Herbert Aptheker, ed., *A Documentary History of the Negro People in the United States* (New York: Citadel Press, 1951), 67–69; and Carol V. R. George, *Segregated Sabbaths: Richard Allen and the Rise of Independent Black Churches, 1760–1840* (New York: Oxford University Press, 1973), 85–86.

17. Martin Luther King, Jr., "The Crisis of Civil Rights," unpublished address, Operation Breadbasket Meeting, Chicago, Illinois (10–12 October 1967), KCLA, 10; Martin Luther King, Jr., "Transforming a Neighborhood," unpublished speech at the NATRA Convention, RCA Dinner, Atlanta, Georgia (11 August 1967), KCLA, 7–8; and King, "Christian Movement," 1–2.

18. King, "Crisis of Civil Rights," 10; King, "Transforming Neighborhood" 7–8; King, "Christian Movement," 1; King, Strength, 64–65; and King, "Hope," 16–17.

19. King, Can't Wait, 61; King, Where Do We Go? 123; and Lewis V. Baldwin, There is a Balm in Gilead: The Cultural Roots of Martin Luther King, Jr. (Minneapolis: Fortress Press, 1991), 58, 88, and 201.

20. E. Franklin Frazier, The Negro Church in America (New York: Schocken Books, 1963), 13–14.

21. Martin Luther King, Jr., to the Reverend Jerry M. Chance (9 May 1961), KCLA, 1; King, Strength, 62; and Carson and Holloran, eds., Knock, 73. King actually made a rare reference to the Underground Railroad in King, "Hope," 16–17.

22. King to Chance (9 May 1961), 1.

23. Washington, ed., Testament, 119; King, Where Do We Go? 78–80; and John J. Ansbro, Martin Luther King, Jr.: Nonviolent Strategies and Tactics for Social Change (Lanham, Md.: Madison Books, 2000), 161–162 and 215. The emphasis placed by the antebellum black church on moral suasion and nonviolence as approaches to social evil has not been seriously treated by most King scholars, an oversight of enormous proportions, especially since that tradition is essential for understanding the civil rights leader. Significant references to the subject can be found in works by Peter Paris and Greg Moses. "Although black churches have a long history of opposition to violence," writes Paris, "they have frequently vacillated between violence and nonviolence, especially during periods of intense racial hostility." Paris goes on to say that

> the concept of nonviolence as promulgated by Martin Luther King, Jr., was not alien to the black churches. None resisted it. In fact, King was merely explicating and implementing the traditional means of protest long practiced by black churches under the black Christian tradition. King's novelty was in his method of mass demonstrations and bringing Gandhi's thought about nonviolent resistance into positive relationship with the black Christian tradition.

Moses challenges the common view that King's nonviolent ethic was imported to black America from foreign, nonblack sources, suggesting instead that King's greatest indebtedness is perhaps to the African American intellectual tradition, beginning with Frederick Douglass and extending to A. Philip Randolph, Howard Thurman, Ralph J. Bunche, and others who preceded King. Moses's claims conflict at points with those of Sudarshan Kapur, who "locates King's nonviolence within the context of a larger tradition of African American encounters with Gandhism. "See Peter J. Paris, The Social Teaching of the Black Churches (Philadelphia: Fortress Press, 1985), 24 n.21 and 50 and also 14–15, 74, and 111; Greg Moses, Revolution of Conscience: Martin Luther King, Jr., and the Philosophy of Nonviolence (New York: Guilford Press, 1997), 3, 5–10, and 34–35; Sudarshan Kapur, *Raising Up a Prophet: The African-American Encounter with Gandhi* (Boston: Beacon Press, 1992), 1–165; and John A. Kirk, "State of the Art: Martin Luther King, Jr.," *Journal of American Studies*, 38, no.2 (2004), 345. The conclusions by both Paris and Moses are supported in large measure by Jacob Neusner's. He observes that "Although the black churches were implicated occasionally in slave revolts, in general they were committed to nonviolent resistance long before the term was popularized by Martin Luther King, Jr." See Jacob Neusner, ed., *World Religions in America: An Introduction* (Louisville: Westminster John Knox Press, 2000), 62. King himself occasionally pointed out that "the Negro himself created the theory of nonviolence and its application to American conditions," or that nonviolence "is consistent with the deeply religious traditions of Negroes." See Martin Luther King, Jr., "Statement on Nonviolence," unpublished (1964), KCLA, 2; and Martin Luther King, Jr., "The Burning Truth in the South," *Progressive*, 24 (May 1960), 9.

24. King, *Where Do We Go?* 56; and Ansbro, *King*, 233. King reminded his people that resistance among African captives began in Africa, aboard slave ships, and extended through the so-called Middle Passage to the plantations of the New World. He urged them to ignore claims that their slave forebears were passive and accommodative: "Let nobody tell you that they didn't resist. They did resist, but they couldn't do anything about it. They didn't have any armies because they had no expansionistic desires." See King, "Hope," 13–18; Martin Luther King, Jr., "The Dignity of Family Life," unpublished address, Abbott House, Westchester County, New York (29 October 1965), KCLA, 9; and Martin Luther King, Jr., "The Negro Family," unpublished address, University of Chicago, Chicago, Illinois (27 January 1966), KCLA, 19–20.

25. Martin Luther King, Jr., "True Dignity," unpublished statement (n.d.), KCLA, 5–7; King, "Hope," 13–18; King, *Where Do We Go?* 78–80; and Baldwin and Al-Hadid, *Cross and Crescent*, 19 and 365 n.39. We have reason to believe that King was somewhat familiar with David Walker's work. In one of his speeches, he referred to "Daniel Walker" in 1829, obviously meaning David Walker. See Martin Luther King, Jr., "Demonstrating Our Unity." unpublished address, Civil Rights Rally, Hurt Park, Atlanta (15 December 1963), KCLA, 2; and King, "My Dream," 1.

26. King was of the opinion that Negroes "have suffered at the hands of writers of American history." "The Negro is belittled and dehumanized in the pages of books," he reasoned, "but in the truth of history he was one of the nation's priceless and exceptional builders and creators." See Martin Luther King, Jr., "Address before the Illinois State Convention of the AFL-CIO," unpublished, Springfield, Illinois (7 October 1965), KCLA, 1; and King, "Dignity," 4.

27. King, *Strength*, 62; King, *Where Do We Go?* 123; and King, "Hope," 13–18.

28. King, "Hope," 16–17; and Carson et al., eds., *King Papers*, I, 281. For similar references to the slave preacher, see Martin Luther King, Jr., "Is the Universe Friendly?" unpublished sermon, delivered at the Ebenezer Baptist Church, Atlanta, Georgia (12 December 1965), KCLA, 6; King, "Overcoming," 9–10; and King, "Southern Civil Rights Speech," 2. King obviously drew on the insights of the African

American scholar Howard Thurman in making this observation. See Howard Thurman, *Deep River and the Negro Spiritual Speaks of Life and Death* (Richmond, Ind.: Friends United Press, 1975), 17–18; and Baldwin, *Balm*, 301–302. William Watley offers brilliant insights into the black church's significant role in developing personality, and I am heavily indebted to him. See William D. Watley, *Roots of Resistance: The Nonviolent Ethic of Martin Luther King, Jr.* (Valley Forge, Pa.: Judson Press, 1985), 32–36.

29. King, "Remarks at a Tribute," 1; Martin Luther King, Jr., "A Speech at a Dinner Honoring Him as a Nobel Prize Recipient," unpublished, the Dinkler Plaza Hotel, Atlanta (27 January 1965), KCLA, 6–7; Baldwin, *Balm*, 88; and Stephen B. Oates, *Let the Trumpet Sound: The Life of Martin Luther King, Jr.* (New York: Harper & Row, 1982), 253.

30. King, *Where Do We Go?* 123; Martin Luther King, Jr., "Annual Address," unpublished, delivered at the First Annual Institute on Nonviolence and Social Change Under the Auspices of the Montgomery Improvement Association," Holt Street Baptist Church, Montgomery, Alabama (3 December 1956), KCLA, 19; and Baldwin, *Balm*, 58.

31. King, "Universe Friendly?" 6; King, "Hope," 16–17; and King, "Overcoming," 9–10.

32. King, "Universe Friendly?" 6; and King, "Overcoming," 9–10. In an earlier work, I mistakenly argued that *"Christian hope* and *Christian optimism* are virtually synonymous in King's rhetoric, and can therefore be used interchangeably to describe his vision concerning the future of humanity and human society." A closer reading of King refutes that contention. King once declared:

> Let me say first that hope is not to be identified with optimism. A lot of people feel that hope is optimism. Now let me change your view, if you have that view, a little at this point. I must distinguish between magic hope, and realistic hope. Now magic hope is sheer optimism. It is the notion that tomorrow, everything will be all right. That's magic hope. Tomorrow, everything will automatically be better. It is the notion that in the very flow of time itself, is a miraculous quality that automatically makes things better. Now, the thing that's wrong with that view is that it is insensitive to the possibility of tragedy. Tomorrow, everything may not be all right. Change is not always for the best. And so optimism is not genuine hope. And this is why I must speak of realistic hope. Now, realistic hope is based on a willingness to face the risk of failure, and embrace an "in spite of" quality. That's realistic hope. Genuine hope involves the recognition that what is hoped for is in some sense already present. Let me kind of illustrate this for you. What is hoped for is not present, and it is present. It's not present in the sense that it is not fulfilled. But what you really hope for is present in the sense that it is in you as a power that drives you to fulfill that hope.

See King, "Hope," 7 and 16–18; and Baldwin, *Balm*, 302 and 339.

33. King, "Hope," 13–18; King, "Universe Friendly?" 5–6; King, *Strength*, 64; Carson and Holloran, eds., *Knock*, 75; King, *Where Do We Go?* 113; Washington, ed., *Testament*, 502–503; Martin Luther King, Jr., "Living Under the Tensions of the Modern Life," unpublished sermon, Montgomery, Alabama (1956), The King Papers Project, 1; and Martin Luther King, Jr. to Dr. J. A. Middleton (17 March 1960), KCLA, 1. Vivian Green is correct in reminding us that "Still segregated largely from the Whites, Black religion, flourishing particularly among Black Southern Baptists and in the Black Methodist Episcopal Church, became more and more significantly a medium for emphasizing Black identity and synthesizing Black hopes." See Vivian Green, *A New History of Christianity* (New York: Continuum, 1996), 371–372.

34. King, "Transforming Neighborhood," 9; King, "Dignity of Family," 6–7; King, "Hope," 15; King, "Negro Family," 11–12; and Washington, ed., *Testament*, 217.

35. King, *Where Do We Go?* 126 and 129; Washington, ed., *Testament*, 20, 212, and 436; King, "Transforming Neighborhood," 10–12; and Martin Luther King, Jr., "The Sword that Heals," *The Critic*, 22 (June-July 1964), 9–10.

36. King had a deep love of history, and especially church history, but his undergraduate training was in sociology, and this explains why he, like W. E. B. DuBois and others, was most apt to speak of the black church as a social institution. Although King wrote papers on various historical trends in the church in seminary and graduate school, he never regarded himself as a church historian. See Carson et al., eds., *King Papers*, I, 144;King to Chance (9 May 1961), 1; King, *Strength*, 62–63; and King, *Can't Wait*, 25, 42, and 47.

37. King to Chance (9 May 1961), 1; and Gayraud S. Wilmore, ed., *African American Religious Studies* (Durham, N.C.: Duke University Press, 1989), xi (General Introduction).

38. King, *Can't Wait*, 33; King, *Where Do We Go?* 126 and 129; King, "Transforming Neighborhood," 10–12; Washington, ed., *Testament*, pp. 20, 212, and 436; Carson et al., eds., *King Papers*, V, 285 and 339; King, "Sword," 9–10; and Ansbro, *King*, 198–203, 209–210, 226, 232, and 322–323.

39. King, *Can't Wait*, 33; King, "Sword," 9; and Ansbro, *King*, 202–204. Interestingly enough, King's maternal grandfather, A. D. Williams, endorsed "a strategy that combined elements of Washington's emphasis on black business development and W. E. B. DuBois's call for civil rights activism." King himself highly respected DuBois's activities in the civil rights field, even as he took issue with his notion of "the talented tenth." See Carson et al., eds., *King Papers*, I, 10; Carson et al., eds., *King Papers*, IV, 357; and Carson et al., eds., *King Papers*, III, 180.

40. King, *Can't Wait*, 33; and King, "Sword," 9.

41. King, *Can't Wait*, 33–34; and King, "Sword," 9–10.

42. King, "Sword," 9–10; and King, *Can't Wait*, 33–34. For significant references to the NAACP's connections to the black church almost from its beginnings, see Gayraud S. Wilmore, *Black Religion and Black Radicalism: An Interpretation of the Religious History of Afro-American People*, Second Edition (Maryknoll, N.Y.: Orbis Books, 1983), 138, 145, and 180–182.

43. King, "Sword," 10; and King, *Can't Wait*, 35.

44. King, "Sword," 10; and King, *Can't Wait*, 35.

45. King to Chance (9 May 1961), 1; and Baldwin, *Balm*, 224.

46. King, "Sword," 10; King to Chance (9 May 1961), 1; King, *Stride*, 20–21; and Baldwin, *Balm*, 224.

47. King to Chance (9 May 1961), 1; Clayborne Carson, ed., *The Autobiography of Martin Luther King, Jr.* (New York: Warner Books, 1998), 1, 3, 13, and 16; King, *Stride*, 18–21; King, "Early Days," 1–4; and Carson et al., eds., *King Papers*, I, 359–363.

48. Robert Penn Warren, *Who Speaks for the Negro?* (New York: Random House, 1965), 209; King, *Stride*, 18–21; Carson, ed., *King Autobiography*, 6–7, 14, and 16; Carson et al., eds., *King Papers*, I, 359–363; "An Interview with Martin Luther King, Jr.," George A. Towns Elementary School, Atlanta (11 March 1964), unpublished document, KCLA, 1; John Freeman, "Face to Face: BBC Interview with Martin Luther King, Jr.," U.K., London, England, transcribed from a TV telediphone recording (29 October 1961), unpublished document, KCLA, 1; and Baldwin, *Balm*, 91–228. A number of scholars have referred to King's role in reviving the activist Christianity that has periodically resurfaced in black church life from the time of Richard Allen. Albert Raboteau suggests that King saw the civil rights movement in the tradition of both the slave church and the Apostolic church, a view sustained in this chapter. Catherine Albanese sees King as "the product of the black church with its history of slavery and freedom." Andrew Manis convincingly contends that "King's work expressed an ongoing ferment in the black church and community." In a similar vein, Mary Sawyer concludes that King was part of "an enduring impulse of activism and cultural revitalization in the black religious tradition." See Wilmore, *Black Religion*, 174–175; Raboteau, "Martin Luther King, Jr.," 58; Catherine L. Albanese, *America: Religion and Religions* (Belmont, Calif.: Wadsworth Publishing Company, 1999), 213; Andrew M. Manis, *Southern Civil Religions in Conflict: Black and White Baptists and Civil Rights* (Athens: University of Georgia Press, 1987), 16; and Mary R. Sawyer, *Black Ecumenism: Implementing the Demands of Justice* (Valley Forge, Pa.: Trinity Press International, 1994), 34.

49. For example, see King to Chance (9 May 1961), 1; Warren, *Who Speaks?* 209; and King, "Christian Movement," 1.

50. A careful study of slave literature and art shows that these were also powerful images in the antebellum black church. See Lawrence W. Levine, *Black Culture and Black Consciousness: Afro-American Folk Thought from Slavery to Freedom* (New York: Oxford University Press, 1978), 19–35; and Thomas L. Webber, *Deep Like the Rivers: Education in the Slave Quarter Community, 1831–1865* (New York: W. W. Norton, 1978), 86.

51. King, *Stride*, 224; Carson et al., eds., *King Papers*, III, 74; Baldwin, *Balm*, 229–272; and Baldwin and Al-Hadid, *Cross and Crescent*, 29–30 and 369 n.71.

52. Peter Paris is right in identifying King with "the prophetic strand" of the black church tradition, which is "that of criticism, subjecting the prevailing institutions, beliefs, and practices to scrutiny in order to uncover their racist bias." See Peter J. Paris, "The Bible and the Black Churches," in Ernest R. Sandeen, ed., *The Bible and Social Reform* (Philadelphia: Fortress Press, 1982), 140–144.

53. Carter G. Woodson, "The Negro Church, All-Comprehending Institution," in *The Negro History Bulletin*, 3, no.1 (October 1939), 7; and Lewis V. Baldwin, "Revisiting

the 'All-Comprehending Institution': Historical Reflections on the Public Roles of Black Churches," in R. Drew Smith, ed., *New Day Begun: African American Churches and Civic Culture in Post-Civil Rights America* (Durham, N.C.: Duke University Press, 2003), 33.

54. Woodson, "The Black Church," 7; Baldwin, "Revisiting," 33; and King to Chance (9 May 1961), 1.

55. But West's assertion could apply to figures in the antebellum black church as well, such as Denmark Vesey and Nat Turner. See Cornel West, "The Prophetic Tradition in Afro-America," in *The Drew Gateway*, 55, nos. 2 and 3 (Winter 1984–Spring 1985), 104.

56. Wilmore, *Black Religion*, 174.

57. See Ronald S. Flowers, *Religion in Strange Times: The 1960s and 1970s* (Macon: Mercer University Press, 1984), 187; and C. Eric Lincoln, *The Black Church Since Frazier* (New York: Schocken Books, 1974), 106–110.

58. Martin Luther King, Jr., to Dr. Dwight Loder (5 August 1958), KCLA, 1–2; and King, *Stride*, 25–34.

59. King, *Stride*, 25; and Carson, ed., *King Autobiography*, 46–47.

60. King, *Stride*, 25–26; Carson, ed., *King Autobiography*, 47–49; and Carson et al., eds., *King Papers*, II, 288–293.

61. "The Baptist Youth Fellowship of Dexter Avenue Baptist Church Presents a Symposium on 'The Meaning of Integration for American Society," a flyer (13 March 1955), KCLA, 1; Baldwin, *Balm*, 179; Martin Luther King, Jr., "Advice for Living," *Ebony*, 13, no.9 (July 1958), 86; and Carson et al., eds., *King Papers*, II, 288–293.

62. King, *Stride*, 27–29; and Carson et al., eds., *King Papers*, II, 288–293.

63. Carson, ed., *King Autobiography*, 47–49. King stated in a 1956 letter to Roy Wilkins, the Executive Secretary of the NAACP, that "My church has just taken out a life membership in the NAACP, and I am urging other churches in our community to do likewise." According to the notes taken by the Montgomery NAACP secretary Rosa L. Parks, King was introduced on one occasion by Dexter Church's clerk Robert B. Nesbitt in these terms: "He is a great asset to Montgomery by activity in everything for the betterment of the community. He has launched an intensive campaign in the church for NAACP membership and voters." King declared in 1961 that "Any Negro who is not a member of the National Association for the Advancement of Colored People should be ashamed of himself." See Martin Luther King, Jr., to Roy Wilkins (1 May 1956), KCLA, 1; King, *Stride*, 29–36; Carson et al., eds., *King Papers*, II, 290–291; Martin Luther King, Jr., "The Peril of Superficial Optimism in the Area of Race Relations," unpublished outline for a speech before "an afternoon mass meeting" of the Montgomery NAACP (19 June 1955?), The King Papers Project, 1–2; King, "Savannah Speech," 15; and Donald M. Schwartz, "The Making of an Integration Leader," *Chicago Sun Times*, 21 January 1963, 29.

64. King, *Stride*, 32–36; and Carson et al., eds., *King Papers*, II, 290.

65. Carson et al., eds., *King Papers*, III, 74; King, "Great Day,"10; and King, "Savannah Speech," 7. Gardner C. Taylor put it best when he said that King "saw something special in black people, an internal courage and resilience," despite "all that was debased and dehumanized." As Taylor put it, King "spoke to that special quality"

or "that grandeur in black people." See Gardner C. Taylor, "The Strange Ways of God," a tape-recorded sermon at an event honoring Martin Luther King, Jr., at Harvard University, Cambridge, Massachusetts in January 1972 in *Essential Taylor* (Valley Forge, Pa.: Judson Press, 2000); and Gardner C. Taylor with Edward L. Taylor, *The Words of Gardner Taylor: Special Occasions and Expository Sermons* (Valley Forge, Pa.: Judson Press, 2001), 4, 103–108. King stood in a long tradition in which African American leaders and thinkers had asserted in biblical and messianic terms that moral leadership in the struggle for a better society and world rested with the black church. See Baldwin, *Balm*, 230–243 and 252–268.

66. King, "Great Day," 10; King, *Stride*, 63 and 224; Carson et al., eds., *King Papers*, III, 74 and 137–138; King, "Statement to Press, Nobel Prize," 1; and King, "Statement from Harlem," 1–2.

67. Despite claims to the contrary, King never saw the Montgomery protest as a drama involving only himself, or "only one actor." "Occasionally you see the name of Martin Luther King in the newspaper and occasionally you see his picture," said King on one occasion, "but Martin Luther King must never forget that there would not be a Martin Luther King with a picture in the paper or a name in the paper, if there had not been a Rosa Parks and 50,000 Negro citizens." See King, *Stride*, 9–10; and Martin Luther King, Jr., "Speech at Guardian Association," unpublished, New York (9 January 1958), KCLA, 1.

68. King, *Stride*, 34–38 and 177–178; and Baldwin, *Balm*, 191–192.

69. King, "Annual Address," First Annual Institute, 3. Also see "Executive Board of the Montgomery Improvement Association, Inc.," an unpublished list (1955–56), KCLA, 1–2; and Carson et al., eds., *King Papers*, III, 453. King once said that "I think I can say without fear of successful contradiction that in proportion to size we had a larger percentage of A.M.E. Zion ministers who served as active participants in our movement than any other denomination." See Martin Luther King, Jr., to Bishop W. J. Walls (31 December 1958), KCLA, 2.

70. Washington, ed., *Testament*, 447–448; King, *Stride*, 85–86; and Martin Luther King, Jr., "Some Things We Must Do," unpublished speech (5 December 1957), KCLA, 2.

71. King, "Annual Address," First Annual Institute, 2; and Carson et al., eds., *King Papers*, III, 452.

72. Washington, ed., *Testament*, 101, 108, and 137; and Baldwin, *Balm*, 87–88.

73. King, *Stride*, 85; and Washington, ed., *Testament*, 447.

74. King, *Stride*, 75 and 77; King, *Strength*, 65–66; Martin Luther King, Jr., "Our Struggle," *Liberation*, 1, no.2 (April 1956), 3; Carson et al., eds., *King Papers*, III, 448–450; and Carson and Holloran, eds., *Knock*, 77.

75. Martin Luther King, Jr., "East or West—God's Children," unpublished speech, Berlin, Germany (13 September 1964), KCLA, 7; and King, *Stride*, 85.

76. King, *Stride*, 85; Washington, ed., *Testament*, 447; and Baldwin, *Balm*, 185–186. King knew that there was something in the background of his people that made them receptive to Christian-Gandhian ideas and methods. Also, he knew that white southerners could never have embraced such ideas and methods in the same way and to the same extent. In my view, King would accept Nathan Huggins'

assessment of why blacks in Montgomery and throughout the South were open to the appeal of nonviolence:

> But the tactic worked in the Southern setting because of the deep tradition of Christian stoicism in the black community. Blacks had long appreciated the moral superiority of those who continued to do right despite violence and oppression. When King repeated again and again that "undeserved suffering is redemptive," he was merely iterating a value that his Southern black audiences had lived their lives by. Christian stoicism was the traditional base on which Southern blacks engrafted King's message of nonviolence.

See Nathan I. Huggins, "Martin Luther King, Jr.: Charisma and Leadership," *The Journal of American History*, 74, no.2 (September 1987), 480–481.

77. King, "Statement on Nonviolence," 2; King, "The Burning Truth," 9; and Baldwin, *Balm*, 186. Albert J. Raboteau observes that "King's doctrine of redemptive suffering awakened old themes within Afro-American religious culture, in particular the theme of the suffering servant with all its associations in the slave past." See Raboteau, "Martin Luther King, Jr.," 58.

78. Perhaps King had this in mind when he stated that "nonviolence in so many ways has given the Negro a new sense of somebodiness." See King, "America's Chief Moral," 12; and Martin Luther King, Jr., "Nobel Lecture," unpublished version, Aula of the University, Oslo (11 December 1964), KCLA, 9–10.

79. Adam Fairclough, "The Southern Christian Leadership Conference and the Second Reconstruction, 1957–1973," *South Atlantic Quarterly*, 80, no.2 (Spring 1981), 177–194; David J. Garrow, *Bearing the Cross: Martin Luther King, Jr., and the Southern Christian Leadership Conference* (New York: William Morrow, 1986), 83–125; and Carson et al., eds., *King Papers*, III, 424–433.

80. Michael Eric Dyson, *I May Not Get There with You: The True Martin Luther King, Jr.* (New York: Simon & Schuster, 2000), 204–205.

81. Adam Fairclough, *To Redeem the Soul of America: The Southern Christian Leadership Conference and Martin Luther King, Jr.* (Athens: University of Georgia Press, 1987), 1–2; Baldwin, *Balm*, 192–193; Martin Luther King, Jr., to Dr. P. J. Ellis (6 February 1960), KCLA, 1; King to Bodein (3 September 1960), 1; Samuel S. Hill, "Religion and Politics in the South," in Charles R. Wilson, ed., *Religion in the South* (Jackson: University Press of Mississippi, 1985), 144; and Martin Luther King, Jr., to Reverend R. A. Battles, Jr. (18 July 1961), KCLA, 1. I agree very much with Richard King's contention that "Fairclough's *To Redeem the Soul of America* is . . . the most successful of . . . the books on King and SCLC." See Richard H. King, "Martin Luther King: Problems of History and Biography," *Southern Review*, 24, no.4 (Autumn 1988), 981.

82. Fairclough, *To Redeem*, 1–35; and Carson et al., eds., *King Papers*, IV, 2–7.

83. This term, "redemptive experiences," is used in Donald C. Swift, *Religion and the American Experience* (Armonk, N.Y.: M. E. Sharpe, 1998), 171.

84. King to Jones (5 November 1960), 1; Martin Luther King, Jr., "A Proposed Statement to the South," unpublished, presented at the Southern Negro Leaders

Conference on Transportation and Nonviolent Integration, Atlanta (10–11 January 1957), KCLA, 3; and Baldwin, *Balm*, 231–243; Raboteau, "Martin Luther King, Jr.," 58; and Martin E. Marty, *Pilgrims in Their Own Land: 500 Years of Religion in America* (New York: Viking Penguin, 1986), 440.

85. Carson et al., eds., *King Papers*, IV, 74 and 94–95; Carson et al., eds., *King Papers*, III, 442, 449, 494–495; King to Ellis (6 February 1960), 1; *Southern Christian Leadership Conference: Plans of Action for Southwide, Year-Round Voter-Registration Program*, typed version, Atlanta (February 1959), KCLA, 5–7; and Martin Luther King, Jr. and Ralph D. Abernathy to Friends of the Montgomery Improvement Association (27 November 1956), KCLA, 1.

86. King and Abernathy to Friends (27 November 1956), 1; King to Ellis (6 February 1960), 1; *Southern Christian Leadership Conference*, 1–7; and Carson et al., eds., *King Papers*, III, 442–443 and 449–450. In 1959, King noted that "a majority of our people are affiliated with some church," a claim that made his point about the continuing relevance of the church in the Negro community all the more significant. See Carson et al., eds., *King Papers*, V, 129.

87. Robert M. Franklin claims that King did not allow "his public visibility to compromise his pastoral duties." This claim is most certainly open to debate, especially in light of King's own observation about his failures as a pastor at Dexter Avenue Baptist Church in Montgomery in 1957:

> They hadn't had much of a pastor in the last two years. Hadn't had much of a pastor. The pastor has neglected his responsibilities and his duties, and yet I haven't heard any complaints. If I had had a church where the members would have argued all the time, 'what are you goin' for, you're supposed to be here,' I never would have been able to make it, but they had the vision to see that this trouble is bigger than Montgomery. And they have been willing to share me with this nation and the world. And I'm grateful to them.

See Robert M. Franklin, "The Safest Place on Earth: The Culture of Black Congregations," in James P. Wind and James W. Lewis, eds., *American Congregations: New Perspectives in the Study of Congregations*, Vol. II (Chicago: University of Chicago Press, 1994), 269; King, "Some Things," 4; and "King Calls Visit 'Gratifying Day'," *Frontier Post*, 1 January 1960, 4.

88. James Lawson, the black preacher and nonviolent advocate from whom King learned a lot, supposedly said that King should never have left Montgomery. See Martin Luther King, Sr. et al., to Dr. Martin Luther King, Jr. (17 November 1959), KCLA, 1; Martin Luther King, Jr., to Mr. P. O. Watson (19 November 1959), KCLA, 1; and Baldwin, *Balm*, 194–195. King said the following concerning his move to Ebenezer: "I am becoming co-pastor with my father, so that I will have more time to devote to the total struggle in the South. In Atlanta, I will have time to organize and train my people to use nonviolence in their struggle for social justice." See "King Calls Visit," 4. Also see Carson et al., eds., *King Papers*, V, 20, 323–324, and 326–327. Interestingly enough, even after moving to Ebenezer Church, King insisted on preaching twice a month, which was an indication of the significance that he still

attached to his pastoral role. For an example, see "Preaching Schedule for Ebenezer from July, 1962 through August, 1963," unpublished document, KCLA, 1–7.

89. King, "Why We Must Go," 1.

90. King to Ellis (6 February 1960), 1–2.

91. King to Chance (9 May 1961), 1.

92. All of these concerns are treated to some extent in Baldwin, *Balm*, 159–228; and Baldwin and Al-Hadid, *Cross and Crescent*, 200–240.

93. Carson, ed., *King Autobiography*, 135 and 140; Washington, ed., *Testament*, 94; John Lewis, *Walking with the Wind: A Memoir of the Movement*, with Michael D'Orso (New York: Simon & Schuster, 1998), 114; and Carson et al., eds., *King Papers*, V, 426–427.

94. Carson, ed., *King Autobiography*, 166; and David Halberstam, *The Children* (New York: Random House, 1998), 272–273.

95. Watley, *Roots*, 65–90; Lewis, *Walking*, 362–363; and King, *Can't Wait*, 61.

96. King, *Can't Wait*, 61; Washington, ed., *Testament*, 535–536; and Carson, ed., *King Autobiography*, 177–178.

97. Lewis V. Baldwin, *To Make the Wounded Whole: The Cultural Legacy of Martin Luther King, Jr.* (Minneapolis: Fortress Press, 1992), 278.

98. In Montgomery, several black churches were bombed during the bus boycott (1955–56), among them the Bell Street and Mt. Olive Baptist Churches. Numerous other black churches in Alabama, Georgia, and Mississippi were either bombed or burned in the 1960s, thus calling to mind the situation in nineteenth-century America. Black churches were occasionally destroyed or closed in antebellum times owing to suspicions about their connections to slave conspiracies or uprisings. In the late nineteenth century, black churches were torched at times because of their role as arenas of political activity in the South. King was quite aware of this history, and it most certainly figured into his sense of the black church as a cross-bearing church. See King, *Stride*, 176; Martin Luther King, Jr., "The Terrible Cost of the Ballot," unpublished statement (1 September 1962), KCLA, 1; Martin Luther King, Jr., "Statement at a Prayer Rally at a Wrecked Church," unpublished, Albany, Georgia (15 August 1962), KCLA, 1; "Dr. King and Jackie Robinson Head Rebuilding for Burned Churches," an unpublished SCLC Press Release, Atlanta, Georgia (12 September 1962), KCLA, 1–2; "Jackie Robinson Heads SCLC Drive to Rebuild Burned Churches," *Southern Christian Leadership Conference Newsletter*, 1, no.7 (September 1962), 3–4; Martin Luther King, Jr., "Statement at a Church Groundbreaking," unpublished, Dawson, Georgia (4 February 1963), KCLA, 1; and Martin Luther King, Jr., to Rev. Leroy Freeman (8 October 1962), KCLA, 1.

99. King, "The Terrible Cost," 1; and Martin Luther King, Jr., "Statement Before the Credentials Committee of the Democratic National Committee," unpublished (22 August 1964) KCLA, 1.

100. Washington, ed., *Testament*, 346–347.

101. King, *Can't Wait*, 87; Washington, ed., *Testament*, 346–347; Mathew Ahmann, ed., *Race: Challenge to Religion* (Chicago: Henry Regnery, 1963), 164–165; and King, "America's Chief Moral," 13–14.

102. King, *Stride*, 142–150; and "Religious Leaders Arrested in Albany, Georgia," unpublished list (28 August 1962), KCLA, 1–2.

103. King reported that when the SCLC began its campaign in Birmingham in 1963, "we encountered numerous Negro church reactions that had to be overcome. Negro ministers were among other Negro leaders who felt they were being pulled into something that they had not helped to organize. This is almost always a problem. Negro community unity was the first requisite if our goals were to be realized." See King, *Can't Wait*, 67; and Washington, ed., *Testament*, 346.

104. Washington, ed., *Testament*, 221–222; and Martin Luther King, Jr., "Sermon Regarding the Bombing of the Sixteenth Street Baptist Church," unpublished version, Birmingham, Alabama (22 September 1963), KCLA, 1.

105. Washington, ed., *Testament*, 347–348.

106. King said on another occasion that "Their positive belief in the dawn was the growing edge of hope that kept the slaves faithful amid the most barren and tragic circumstances," a point made by one who routinely turned to the resources of his heritage in difficult times. See King, *Can't Wait*, 61; Carson, ed., *King Autobiography*, 177–178; and Washington, ed., *Testament*, 502–503 and 535. King's observations concerning the songs support Albert Raboteau's contention that "The demonstrations themselves took on the feel of church services." See Raboteau, "Martin Luther King, Jr.," 58.

107. See Carson, ed., *King Autobiography*, 285 and 287; Martin Luther King, Jr., "Integration Story," unpublished statement, Selma, Alabama (2 February 1965), KCLA, 1–4; Martin Luther King, Jr., "Speaking Out Against Sheriff Clark," unpublished statement, Selma, Alabama (20 January 1965), KCLA, 1; Martin Luther King, Jr., "Plans for Selma," unpublished statement, Selma, Alabama (19 January 1965), KCLA, 1–3; Washington, ed., *Testament*, 127–131; and Baldwin, *Balm*, 204–205.

108. Carson, ed., *King Autobiography*, 287–289 and 299.

109. Kenneth L. Smith, "The Radicalization of Martin Luther King, Jr.: The Last Three Years," *Journal of Ecumenical Studies*, 26, no.2 (Spring 1989), 270.

110. King once said that "You must realize that a very great part of Negro life is church-centered, and thusly, his native religious appetite would not be prone to a godless system such as communism." See King to Dautzer (9 May 1961), 1; and Lewis V. Baldwin et al., *The Legacy of Martin Luther King, Jr.: The Boundaries of Law, Politics, and Religion* (Notre Dame, Ind.: University Press of Notre Dame, 2002), 97, 118–119 n.89–90.

111. Carson, ed., *King Autobiography*, 298–299, 303–304, 306–307, and 312.

112. Martin Luther King, Jr., "Why Chicago is the Target," *New York Amsterdam News*, 11 September 1965, 16; Martin Luther King, Jr., "Going to Chicago," *New York Amsterdam News*, 15 January 1966, 10; Martin Luther King, Jr., "A Prayer for Chicago," *Chicago Defender*, 16 April 1966, 10. Hak Joon Lee has raised questions about my claims regarding the significance of King's southern roots for understanding him and his vision and effectiveness as a civil rights leader. Lee writes:

> Yet Baldwin's approach poses several questions. If the source of King's spirituality was the southern African American culture and religion, where

did the latter originate? If southernness is such an important factor, how did
King's appeal spread to African Americans in other regions? If the distinctive
southern culture and ethos were the dominant sources, why have white
Christians in the South failed to develop a spirit of communal orientation,
inclusiveness, and nonviolence similar to that of African Americans?
Although Baldwin notices a communal disposition within King, he delimits
it to the individual person of King and his family and a particular regional
environment, rather than identifying its influence from the broader African
American spiritual tradition.

Although I appreciate the bold and provocative spirit of Lee's book, I feel that it is not
based on a thorough reading of my work, and that it also raises questions that are not
grounded in a broad knowledge of African American history, culture, and political
thought. Black southern culture moved northward and to other regions of the
country with escaped slaves in the nineteenth century, and this continued with the
massive migration of southern blacks to the North and Midwest in the twentieth
century. With these trends, black culture in the North and other regions also
became largely southern in character. Southern black culture and African cultural
forms were never mutually exclusive, as Lee seems to suggest. Black southern
culture originated out of a blending of African and American influences, but it was
never entirely "African," as Lee also appears to conclude at points. Moreover, we
must remember that regionalism meant little as far as King's appeal to black
America was concerned, for all blacks in the country suffered from racism and
economic injustice. At least one of Lee's questions ignores the difference between
southern whites as oppressors and southern blacks as the oppressed. Why would
oppressors be interested in developing "a spirit of communal orientation, inclusiveness, and nonviolence," especially in their dealings with a race they considered
inferior and undesirable? As oppressors, southern whites had a different ethos, for
they believed that violence was absolutely necessary to sustain their position and
privileges over blacks—socially, politically, and economically. Let me also say that any
serious reading and understanding of my work will show that there is absolutely no
suggestion that King's "communal disposition" was limited to his person, family, and
"a particular regional environment," for I have repeatedly stated that even as King
reflected a sense of regional identity and regional responsibility in a southern context,
his beloved community vision had national and international meaning and
implications, and so did his efforts to actualize that vision. Lee's suggestion that
blacks in other regions were entirely different from black southerners is not supported
by the sources, and it goes far beyond James H. Cone's tendency to distinguish
between the South and the North when discussing King's background, vision, and
impact. I respectfully disagree with both Lee and Cone. See Hak Joon Lee, *We Will Get
to the Promised Land: Martin Luther King, Jr.'s Communal-Political Spirituality*
(Cleveland: Pilgrim Press, 2006), 6; Baldwin, *Balm*, 1–228; Baldwin, *Wounded*,
163–317; Baldwin and Al-Hadid, *Cross and Crescent*, 9–42; and James H. Cone, *Martin
& Malcolm & America: A Dream or a Nightmare* (Maryknoll, N.Y.: Orbis Books, 1991),
41 and 58.

113. King, "Going to Chicago," 10; Carson, ed., *King Autobiography*, 298; and Martin Luther King, Jr., "I Need Some Victories," unpublished statement, Chicago (12 July 1966), KCLA, 1–3.

114. From the time of King's stay in Montgomery, he had urged his people to "pool their economic resources through various cooperative enterprises," including the church. See Martin Luther King, Jr., "Advice for Living," 13, no.5 (March 1958), 92. King spoke of "All-black organizations" as "only a contemporary way station on the road to freedom," which suggests something quite profound about what he regarded as the potential for the realization of his communitarian ideal. He also insisted that "There is no separate black path to power and fulfillment that does not intersect with white roots, and there is no separate white path to power and fulfillment short of social disaster that does not recognize the need of sharing that power with black aspirations for freedom and justice." See Washington, ed., *Testament*, 317; and Martin Luther King, Jr., "Speech at an Operation Breadbasket Meeting," unpublished, Chicago Theological Seminary, Chicago (25 March 1967), KCLA, 1.

115. Carson, ed., *King Autobiography*, 347 and 351; "King Threatens Demonstrations at Conventions," *Atlanta Constitution*, 1 April 1968, 2; Martin Luther King, Jr., "Statement regarding Goals of Poor People's Campaign," unpublished, Selma, Alabama (1968), KCLA, 2; Fairclough, *To Redeem*, 367–372; Ralph D. Abernathy, *And the Walls Came Tumbling Down: An Autobiography* (New York: Harper & Row, 1989), 414–415; and Gerald D. Knight, *The Last Crusade: Martin Luther King, Jr., the FBI, and the Poor People's Campaign* (Boulder, Co.: Westview Press, 1998), 25.

116. Abernathy, *And the Walls*, 417, 430–431; Joan T. Beifuss, *At the River I Stand: Memphis, the 1968 Strike, and Martin Luther King* (Memphis: B & W Books, 1985), 60–64; and Garrow, *Bearing*, 603–613.

117. King, "Address," Laurel, Mississippi, 4; and King, *Where Do We Go?* 57.

118. Baldwin, *Balm*, 174–206.

119. Kenneth L. Smith and Ira G. Zepp, Jr., *Search for the Beloved Community: The Thinking of Martin Luther King, Jr.* (Valley Forge, Pa.: Judson Press, 1998), 1.

120. King's rhetorical use of the Exodus narrative, with a specific focus on the idea of freedom, is examined in Gary S. Selby, *Martin Luther King, Jr. and the Rhetoric of Freedom: The Exodus Narrative in America's Struggle for Civil Rights* (Waco: Baylor University Press, 2008), 13–172.

121. Baldwin, *Balm*, 243–252.

122. King, *Can't Wait*, 87; and Washington, ed., *Testament*, 296.

123. King, "A Challenge," 4–5; Martin Luther King, Jr., "Answer to a Perplexing Question," unpublished sermon, Atlanta (3 March 1963), KCLA, 8–9; and "Sunday with Martin Luther King, Jr.," WAAF-AM, transcript of radio statement, Chicago (17 April 1966), KCLA, 3.

124. King, *Strength*, 62–63; Washington, ed., *Testament*, 501–502; and Carson and Holloran, eds., *Knock*, 73–74.

125. King, *Stride*, 35–36; and Carson et al., eds., *King Papers*, II, 330.

126. King, *Stride*, 35–36.

127. Ibid.

128. In King's "Advice for Living," a column that appeared in *Ebony* in 1957–58, the civil rights leader frequently stated that the church and religion could not be logically separated from the work of the NAACP and other civic and political involvements. See Martin Luther King, Jr., "Advice for Living," *Ebony*, 13, no.2 (December 1957), 120; Martin Luther King, Jr., "Advice for Living," *Ebony*, 13, no.7 (May 1958), 112; and Martin Luther King, Jr., "Advice for Living," *Ebony*, 13, no.11 (September 1958), 68.

129. Martin Luther King, Jr., "Remember Who You Are," unpublished sermon notes, Ebenezer Baptist Church, Atlanta (7 July 1963), KCLA, 1–2; King, "Answer," 8; and Baldwin, *Wounded*, 47.

130. King rejected "the virgin birth of Christ as a literal fact," noting that this was a "devised mythological story" employed by the ancient church to emphasize "Jesus' biological uniqueness." King once said that "I do not believe in hell as a place of a literal burning fire. Hell, to me, is a condition of being out of fellowship with God. It is Man's refusal to accept the Grace of God. It is a state in which the individual continues to experience the frustrations, contradictions, and agonies of earthly life. Hell is as real as absolute loneliness and isolation." At another point, King expressed satisfaction that religious liberalism had "thrown out [very] traditional concepts like the damnation of infants and a hell with a fiery furnace." See Lee E. Dirks, "The Essence is Love: The Theology of Martin Luther King," *National Observer*, 30 December 1963, 1 and 12; Martin Luther King, Jr., "Man's Sin and God's Grace," an unpublished sermon outline (1954–1960?), The King Papers Project, 2; and Era B. Thompson, "Current Opinions Regarding Hell: A Telephone Interview with Martin Luther King, Jr.," unpublished version for *Ebony*, Chicago (January 1961), The King Papers Project, 1.

131. King, *Where Do We Go?* 124; Martin Luther King, Jr., "Cooperative Competition, Noble Competition," unpublished sermon notes, Crozer Theological Seminary, Chester, Pennsylvania (n.d.), The King Papers Project, 1; King, "Some Things," 2; King, *Strength*, 141; and Carson and Holloran, eds., *Knock*, 29–30. King was as knowledgeable as anyone in his time about the unique function of denominationalism in American ecclesiastical life. He knew that denominationalism had long been an important method of organizing local, regional, and national church life.

132. King, *Where Do We Go?* 124.

133. King, *Strength*, 62–63; and King, *Stride*, 35–37.

134. Martin Luther King, Jr., "Transformed Nonconformist," unpublished version of sermon, Ebenezer Baptist Church, Atlanta (16 January 1966), KCLA, 9.

135. King lashed out at ministers who "too often judge the success of our ministry by the size of the wheelbase on our automobile, the bigness of our houses, and the bigness of our salaries." See King, "Answer," 7–8; and King, "Transformed Noncomformist," 8–9.

136. King, "Advice for Living" (December 1957), 120.

137. Washington, ed., *Testament*, 346.

138. The claim that King was "'anathema' to the urban Negroes in the North" is open to debate, and it must be made with some qualifications. See William G. McLoughlin and Robert N. Bellah, eds., *Religion in America* (Boston: Beacon Press, 1968), 64.

139. Reverend C. Fain Kyle to Martin Luther King, Jr. (29 January 1964), KCLA; and "Clergyman's Challenge to King Unanswered," *San Francisco Examiner*, 13 February 1964.

140. When SCLC joined the Chicago Freedom Movement against slums in the late 1960s, the Reverend Henry Mitchell, pastor of the North Star Missionary Baptist Church on Chicago's West Side, told King to "get the hell out of" Chicago. Mitchell charged that the King-led marches in the city's "white neighborhoods created hate." The references here are not to the Reverend Dr. Henry H. Mitchell, who has written extensively on black preaching and who was supportive of King's efforts. See "Negro Pastor Urges King to Leave Town," *The Plain Dealer*, 20 April 1967, 14; and Peter J. Ling, *Martin Luther King, Jr.* (New York: Routledge, 2002), 224.

141. Carson et al., eds., *King Papers*, V, 31–32; "Powell Warns on King," *New York Amsterdam News*, 14 August 1965, 1–2; and Martin Luther King, Jr., to Mr. James J. Phelan (6 December 1965), KCLA, 1–5.

142. William D. Booth, "Dr. L. Venchael Booth and the Origin of the Progressive National Baptist Convention, Inc.," *American Baptist Quarterly*, 20, no.1 (March 2001), 72–90; and Baldwin, *Balm*, 206–224.

143. Charles H. King, "Quest and Conflict: The Untold Story of the Power Struggle Between King and Jackson," *Negro Digest*, May 1967, 6–9 and 71–79.

144. Baldwin, *Balm*, 206–224; Booth, "Dr. L. Venchael Booth and the Origin of the Progressive National Baptist Convention, Inc.," 72–90; Baldwin, *Wounded*, 15–19; King, "Quest and Conflict," 6–9 and 71–79; and Malcolm Nash, "Calls Self Victim of Press: Dr. Jackson Explains to Martin Luther King," *New York Amsterdam News*, 14 October 1961, 1 and 13.

145. Martin Luther King, Jr., to Reverend T. Y. Rogers, Jr. (8 March 1962), KCLA, 1–2.

146. C. Eric Lincoln, *The Black Muslims in America*, Third Edition (Grand Rapids, Mich.: William B. Eerdmans and Trenton, N.J.: African World Press, 1994), 147–150; and Baldwin and Al-Hadid, *Cross and Crescent*, 25–30 and 107–114.

147. "Black Power for Whom?" *The Christian Century*, 83, no.29 (20 July 1966), 903.

148. King once declared that "There is no set of propositions that I could disagree with more strongly than I do the assumptions of black nationalism." Here, he had in mind the nationalist stress on racial separatism and retaliatory violence. See Martin Luther King, Jr., to Mr. Joseph B. Cummings, Jr. (22 December 1961), KCLA, 2; Washington, ed., *Testament*, 296–297, 323, and 362–363; and Martin Luther King, Jr., "A Cry of Hate or Cry of Help," unpublished statement (August 1965), KCLA, 7.

149. King, *Where Do We Go?* 125.

150. Baldwin, *Balm*, 224–225.

CHAPTER 4

1. Martin Luther King, Jr., *Strength to Love* (Philadelphia: Fortress Press, 1981), 62.

2. Martin Luther King, Jr., "Address at a Mass Meeting," unpublished, the Maggie Street Baptist Church, Montgomery, Alabama (16 February 1968), The

Library and Archives of the Martin Luther King, Jr. Center for Nonviolent Social Change, Inc. (KCLA), Atlanta, 3; Martin Luther King, Jr., "The Negro Speaks—The Negro is the Most Glaring Evidence of White America's Hypocrisy," *St. Louis Post Dispatch*, 25 August 1963, 1 and 3; "Civil Rights in its Second Phase: An Interview with Martin Luther King, Jr.," unpublished, "The Arlene Francis Show," New York City (19 June 1967), KCLA, 4 and 7; and Martin Luther King, Jr., "Speech at an SCLC Staff Retreat," unpublished, Penn Center, Frogmore, South Carolina (3 May 1967), KCLA, 21. King undoubtedly had the white church in view when he submitted that "The church has a schism in its own soul that it must close." See King, *Strength*, 102.

3. King, *Strength*, 29; King, "Negro Speaks," 1 and 3; "Civil Rights in Second Phase," 4 and 7; and King, "Speech at SCLC," 21.

4. Martin Luther King, Jr., *Stride toward Freedom: The Montgomery Story* (New York: Harper & Row, 1958), 18–21; Clayborne Carson et al., eds., *The Papers of Martin Luther King, Jr., Volume I: Called to Serve, January 1929–June 1951* (Berkeley: University of California Press, 1992), 362.

5. Carson et al., eds., *King Papers*, I, 110–112; and Clayborne Carson, ed., *The Autobiography of Martin Luther King, Jr.* (New York: Warner Books, 1998), 9–10.

6. Carson et al., eds., *King Papers*, I, 327–329.

7. Martin Luther King, Jr., "Mastering Our Evil Selves and Mastering Ourselves," unpublished version of sermon, Ebenezer Baptist Church, Atlanta (5 June 1949), The Martin Luther King, Jr. Papers Project, Stanford University, Stanford, California, 1–2; and Martin Luther King, Jr., "Is the Church the Hope of the World?" unpublished notes, Crozer Theological Seminary, Chester, Pennsylvania (n.d.), The King Papers Project, 1.

8. Martin Luther King, Jr., "Splinters and Planks," unpublished sermon, Atlanta, Georgia (24 July 1949), The King Papers Project, 1.

9. Martin Luther King, Jr., "Communism's Challenge to Christianity," unpublished manuscript, Atlanta (9 August 1953), The King Papers Project, 3; and Martin Luther King, Jr., "Can a Christian Be a Communist?" unpublished sermon, Ebenezer Baptist Church, Atlanta (30 September 1962), The King Papers Project, 4–5.

10. Martin Luther King, Jr., "Statement Regarding Kyle Haselden's *Mandate for White Christians*," unpublished version of a foreword (2 December 1965 and 15 December 1965), KCLA, 1–2; and Martin Luther King, Jr., "Foreword," in Kyle Haselden, *Mandate for White Christians* (Richmond, Va.: John Knox Press, 1966), 5.

11. Martin Luther King, Jr., "The Un-Christian Christian: SCLC Looks Closely at Christianity in a Troubled Land," in *Ebony*, 20, no.10 (August 1965), 78.

12. Significantly, King suggested this kind of contrast in his challenge to the white church and its ministry in his "Letter from the Birmingham City Jail" (1963). See King, *Can't Wait*, 89–92; and James M. Washington, ed., *A Testament of Hope: The Essential Writings and Speeches of Martin Luther King, Jr.* (New York: HarperCollins Publishers, 1986), 295–300.

13. Martin Luther King, Jr., "The Church on the Frontier of Racial Tension," unpublished, delivered as one of the Gay Lectures, Southern Baptist Theological Seminary, Louisville, Kentucky (19 April 1961), KCLA, 1–2.

14. On one occasion, King brought a bit of humor to his reflections on how the Hamitic myth or hypotheses was employed in white church culture to justify slavery:

> And, I've often wondered about that passage, why they use that one. Even if they are Biblical literate, literalists, they would interpret that a little better, because it tells us that before Noah pronounced the curse, he was drunk, and when he did pronounce it he had a hangover. (laughter) And I don't think, and although God can work in diverse ways and diverse manners, I don't think He will entrust anything that important to a man with a hangover. (laughter) I don't think He will. And it states very clearly that Noah pronounced the Curse, not God (Yeah), you see.

See Washington, ed., *Testament*, 211; King, "Church on the Frontier," 1–2; Martin Luther King, Jr., "An Address Before a Dinner Sponsored by the Episcopal Society for Cultural and Racial Unity," unpublished, 61st General Convention, the Sheraton-Jefferson Hotel, St. Louis, Missouri (12 October 1964), KCLA, 4; Martin Luther King, Jr., "Address at Valedictory Service," unpublished, University of the West Indies, Mona, Jamaica (20 June 1965), KCLA, 9–10; Clayborne Carson et al., eds., *The Papers of Martin Luther King, Jr., Volume IV: Symbol of the Movement, January 1957–December 1958* (Berkeley: University of California Press, 2000), 335; Clayborne Carson et al., eds., *The Papers of Martin Luther King, Jr., Volume III: Birth of a New Age, December 1955–December 1956* (Berkeley: University of California Press, 1997), 300 and 323; Jack Gilbert, "King Urges Youth Join New Order," *Athens Messenger*, 30 December 1959, 1 and 16; and Martin Luther King, Jr., to Mr. William E. Newgent (20 October 1959), unpublished, KCLA, 1. King found the concept of sin in most white churches in pre-Civil War times to be totally escapist, declaring that "During the days of slavery it was a sin to gamble but it was all right to own slaves." See Martin Luther King, Jr., "Pharisee and Publican," unpublished sermon, incomplete transcript edited for broadcast, Atlanta (9 October 1966), KCLA, 2–4. Speaking of the use of scripture to sanction racism and the old segregated order in the South from the time of *Brown v. Board of Education* (1954), one scholar has noted that

> Those who supported the racial status quo with scripture quickly became popular in a region that prided itself on religious piety and biblical literalism. Some resurrected the old defense of slavery by arguing that Noah's curse on Ham condemned the black race to perpetual servitude. Others quoted portions of Acts 17, which told of God's determining the "bounds of their habitations," a passage that quickly became one of the key pieces of evidence to show that "god was the original segregationist." One Episcopal priest argued that the social structure under attack from liberals was "more in accord with the will of God" than a "society of forced integration," for in the

South, "where the kingdom of God is taken seriously," a "very workable social order" had developed under segregation.

See Michael B. Friedland, *Lift Up Your Voice Like a Trumpet: White Clergy and the Civil Rights and Antiwar Movements, 1954–1973* (Chapel Hill: University of North Carolina Press, 1998), 20.

15. Martin Luther King, Jr., "A Realistic Look at Race Relations," unpublished paper, delivered at the Second Anniversary of the NAACP Legal Defense and Educational Fund, Waldorf Astoria Hotel, New York City (17 May 1956), KCLA, 3; and Carson et al., eds., *King Papers*, III, 300. King felt that slavery in the United States was perpetuated not only due to "human badness" and "blindness," but, perhaps more importantly, by "spiritual and intellectual blindness." See King, *Strength*, 41–43.

16. Martin Luther King, Jr., "A Lecture," unpublished, delivered under the auspices of the Federation Protestante de France Mutualite, Paris, France (24 October 1965), KCLA, 4–5; "Sunday with Martin Luther King, Jr.," WAAF-AM, transcript of a radio statement, Chicago (10 April 1966), KCLA, 2–4; Martin Luther King, Jr., "A Christian Movement in a Revolutionary Age," unpublished speech (Fall 1966), KCLA, 1; and Carson et al., eds., *King Papers*, IV, 155.

17. King was familiar with the work of the southern churchman Kyle Haselden, and actually wrote the foreword for one of Haselden's books. See King, "Statement Regarding Kyle Haselden's *Mandate*," 1–4; King, "Foreword," 5–7; Miss D. McDonald to Dr. Tadashi Akaishi (2 December 1965), KCLA, 1; Martin Luther King, Jr., "The Vision of a World Made Knew," unpublished speech, at the Meeting of the Women's Auxiliary of the National Baptist Convention, St. Louis, Missouri (9 September 1954), The King Papers Project, 1 and 3; Martin Luther King, Jr., "Transformed Nonconformist," unpublished sermon, delivered at the Dexter Avenue Baptist Church, Montgomery, Alabama (November 1954), The King Papers Project, 2–3; and Kyle Haselden, *The Racial Problem in Christian Perspective* (New York: Harper & Row, 1959), 29.

18. King, *Strength*, 62; Washington, ed., *Testament*, 501; Carson et al., eds., *King Papers*, I, 281; and Clayborne Carson and Peter Holloran, eds., *A Knock at Midnight: Inspiration from the Great Sermons of Reverend Martin Luther King, Jr.* (New York: Warner Books, 1998), 73.

19. King, "Statement Regarding Kyle Haselden's *Mandate*," 2; and King, "Foreword," 6.

20. Ibid.

21. Ibid., 1.

22. "Sunday with Martin Luther King, Jr." (10 April 1966), 3.

23. Martin Luther King, Jr., *Where Do We Go from Here: Chaos or Community* (Boston: Beacon Press, 1968), 11; King, *Can't Wait*, 131 and 138; "Sunday with Martin Luther King, Jr." (10 April 1966), 2–3; and Lewis V. Baldwin et al., *The Legacy of Martin Luther King, Jr.: The Boundaries of Law, Politics, and Religion* (Notre Dame, Ind.: University of Notre Dame Press, 2002), 47.

24. DuBois called "the color line" "an ethical question that confronts every religion and every conscience," and King said essentially the same as he thought of the church in relation to what he labeled "the color bar." See "Dr. DuBois Hits Church

Attitude on Color Line: Behind in Bettering Race Relations Says Scholar," *The Atlanta World*, 27 December 1931, 1; William E. B. DuBois, "Will the Church Remove the Color Line?" *Christian Century*, 48 (9 December 1931), 1556; David M. Reimers, *White Protestantism and the Negro* (New York: Oxford University Press, 1965), 180; King, *Where Do We Go?* 173–176; and Lewis V. Baldwin, *To Make the Wounded Whole: The Cultural Legacy of Martin Luther King, Jr.* (Minneapolis: Fortress Press, 1992), 304.

25. Carson, ed., *King Autobiography*, 13. In later years, King was known to quote Dubois's ideas on "the color line" when discussing race as a challenge to the church and the nation. See King, *Where Do We Go?* 173.

26. King, "Pharisee and Publican," 2–3.

27. See Lee E. Dirks, "The Essence is Love: The Theology of Martin Luther King," *National Observer*, 30 December 1963, 1 and 12; Martin Luther King, Jr., "Man's Sin and God's Grace," an unpublished sermon outline (1954–1960?), The King Papers Project, 2; and Era B. Thompson, "Current Opinions Regarding Hell: A Telephone Interview with Martin Luther King, Jr.," unpublished version for *Ebony*, Chicago (January 1961), The King Papers Project, 1.

28. King was not always consistent in his comments on the image of the white Jesus. In 1957, he suggested that Jesus was a white man, but quickly noted that "The color of Jesus' skin is of little or no consequence." In 1968, he explained that "Jesus Christ was not a white man," implying that the widely promoted symbol amounted to nothing more than cultural imperialism. See Martin Luther King, Jr., "Advice for Living," *Ebony*, 12, no.12 (October 1957), 53; Martin Luther King, Jr., "An Address," unpublished, delivered at the Ministers' Leadership Training Program, Miami (19–23 February 1968), KCLA, 5; Baldwin, *Wounded*, 57; and Lewis V. Baldwin and Amiri YaSin Al-Hadid, *Between Cross and Crescent: Christian and Muslim Perspectives on Malcolm and Martin* (Gainesville: University Press of Florida, 2002), 97–98.

29. King, *Stride*, 91 and 98–99; King, *Strength*, 147–148 and 150; and Carson, ed., *King Autobiography*, 18.

30. For the best intellectual biography of King, which offers a decisively critical focus on his intellectual sources and categories, See Rufus Burrow, Jr., *God and Human Dignity: The Personalism, Theology, and Ethics of Martin Luther King, Jr.* (Notre Dame, Ind.: University of Notre Dame Press, 2006), 1–265.

31. For King's interesting but brief reflections on the impact of what he called "the 'God is Dead' theologians," see Martin Luther King, Jr., "The Meaning of Hope," unpublished sermon, Dexter Avenue Baptist Church, Montgomery, Alabama (10 December 1967), KCLA, 17–18; "Hugh Downs Interview with Martin Luther King, Jr.," "NBC Today Show" (18 April 1966), unpublished, KCLA, 5–6; and Carson and Holloran, eds., *Knock*, 15.

32. Martin Luther King, Jr., "Who is Their God?" *The Nation*, 195, no.11 (13 October 1962), 209–211; and Martin Luther King, Jr., "An Address at the Twenty-Fifth Anniversary Dinner of the National Maritime Union," unpublished (23 October 1962), KCLA, 9.

33. King, "Statement regarding Kyle Haselden's *Mandate*", 3–4; and King, "Foreword," 6–7.

34. King, *Can't Wait*, 90; Washington, ed., *Testament*, 298–299; and John J. Ansbro, *Martin Luther King, Jr.: Nonviolent Strategies and Tactics for Social Change* (Lanham, Md.: Madison Books, 2000), 181.

35. Martin Luther King, Jr., "The Christian Way of Life in Human Relations," unpublished sermon, delivered at the General Assembly of the National Council of Churches, St. Louis, Missouri (4 December 1957), The King Papers Project, 1–5; Martin Luther King, Jr., "We Are Still Walking," *Liberation*, 1 (December 1956), 6; Carson et al., eds., *King Papers*, III, 449; and Martin Luther King, Jr., "Sermons for Future Weeks," unpublished sketches of planned sermon topics and texts (May 1959), The King Papers Project, 1.

36. Interestingly enough, King scholars have generally accepted King's comments concerning his early optimism regarding white church support for the movement without raising serious questions. Such an approach must be subjected to critical scrutiny, especially in light of what King knew about the whole history of the white church and its role in preserving the values and structures of white supremacy. For example, see Ansbro, *King*, 181.

37. King's reaction to E. Stanley Frazier's comments and demeanor was far more insightful and persuasive. See King, *Stride*, 116–117. In another primary King source, the name is recorded as G. Stanley Frazier. See Carson et al., *King Papers*, III, 124. Also see Franklin H. Littell, *From State Church to Pluralism: A Protestant Interpretation of Religion in American History* (New York: MacMillan, 1971), 161–162. As late as 1968, King received letters from conservative churchmen who echoed the Reverend Frazier's perspective, an experience that reminded him of the sheer difficulty of getting church people to understand the need for the church to address social ills:

> I receive many letters as I usually do when we engage in a campaign. Many of them, I would say most of them, are friendly. But I remember one in particular. This brother was saying to me, "You claim to be a so-called preacher, and now you're getting ready to cause some more trouble. If you were really a preacher, you would be busy doing the work of the ministry and the work of the church. And you wouldn't be getting out here messing up things in the social and the economic realm." And I wish I had time to answer him this morning. And I would tell him that Jesus said that he was anointed. Anointed to do some specific things to release those in captivity. He was anointed . . . to open the eyes of the blind. He was anointed . . . to heal the sick. When a religion fails to do this, it loses its soul.

See Martin Luther King, Jr., "Who are We?" an unpublished sermon delivered at the Ebenezer Baptist Church, Atlanta, Georgia (5 February 1966), KCLA, 4.

38. This subject is examined at some length in Baldwin et al., *Legacy*, 77–109. Strangely, it is not treated seriously in the few studies that claim to explore dimensions of King's attitude toward the church. See Philip A. Rahming, "The Church and the Civil Rights Movement in the Thought of Martin Luther King, Jr.," unpublished M.Th. thesis, Southern Baptist Theological Seminary, Louisville, Kentucky (July 1971), 1–92; and Randall G. Anderson, "The Beloved Community: A Contemporary Model for

the Mission of the Church in America," unpublished D.Min. dissertation, Claremont School of Theology, Claremont, California (May 1978), iv–64.

39. Baldwin et al., *Legacy*, 77–100.

40. The most extensive treatment of King's letter and the white pastors to whom it was addressed is afforded by S. Jonathan Bass, *Blessed are the Peacemakers: Martin Luther King, Jr., Eight White Religious Leaders, and the "Letter from Birmingham Jail"* (Baton Rouge: Louisiana State University Press, 2001), 1–258. Also see Ansbro, *King*, 181.

41. When it came to questions about the nature and purpose of the church in society, the Birmingham letter was quintessentially Kingian in language and outlook. Lewis V. Baldwin, *There Is a Balm in Gilead: The Cultural Roots of Martin Luther King, Jr.* (Minneapolis: Fortress Press, 1991), 315–316. This view seems to be supported in Malinda Snow, "Martin Luther King's 'Letter from Birmingham Jail' as Pauline Epistle," *Quarterly Journal of Speech*, 71 (1985), 318–334. Giving special attention to how King fused elements of the religious and political in his "Letter from the Birmingham City Jail," Stephen Carter calls the letter an "unapologetically religious document." See Stephen L. Carter, *The Culture of Disbelief: How American Law and Politics Trivialize Religious Devotion* (New York: Anchor Books, 1994), 228.

42. King, *Can't Wait*, 89–90; Washington, ed., *Testament*, 298–299; and Ansbro, *King*, 181.

43. King, *Can't Wait*, 90.

44. The Birmingham letter actually highlights King's challenging portrait of the early church, or the true *ekklesia*. He was very clear on the difference between the New Testament *ekklesia* and the institutionalized church of his time. See Washington, ed., *Testament*, 293–300; and King, *Can't Wait*, 82–92.

45. Philip Berrigan, *Prison Journals of a Priest Revolutionary* (New York: Ballantine Books, 1971), 15.

46. These general categories are patterned largely after those identified by Harvey Cox back in 1967, and I am heavily indebted to him and Michael Friedland for these ideas. See Harvey Cox, "The 'New Breed' in American Churches: Sources of Social Activism in American Religion," *Daedalus*, 96 (Winter 1967), 137; and Friedland, *Lift Voice*, 6. The term "establishment evangelicals" was borrowed from Richard Quebedeaux, *The Young Evangelicals: The Story of the Emergence of a New Generation of Evangelicals* (New York: Harper & Row, 1974), 28–37.

47. On one occasion, Bob Jones, Jr., stated: "There is no such thing as a social Gospel. That's a joke! There is only the Gospel of the Grace of God, and it's an individual Gospel. Whosoever comes, whosoever believes. The Lord's message is always a message to the individual." Jones went on to call the Social Gospel "pure socialism." When King was killed, Jones referred to King as "an apostate," and refused to honor President Lyndon Johnson's request to lower his university's flag to half-mast in memory of the civil rights leader. See Martin E. Marty and R. Scott Appleby, *The Glory and the Power: The Fundamentalist Challenge to the Modern World* (Boston: Beacon Press, 1992), 49–50; and Baldwin et al., *Legacy*, 91, 101, and 120 n.104. For insights into the Joneses view of King, one might also view the PBS television series "The Glory and the Power," which is a companion to the volume by Marty and Appleby.

48. Like the Joneses, Falwell was profoundly antipathetic to even the idea that Christianity has social implications. In March 1965, Falwell actually preached a sermon at his church called "Ministers and Marches," in which he reported that King was "known to have left-wing associations," and he concluded that black ministers like King were guilty of misinterpreting the Exodus story in support of protest activities. "The 400 years of Egyptian bondage is a type of the sinners experience before he is converted," Falwell asserted. "We all live in bondage to sin until we know the truth of the new birth." Strangely, Falwell stated, in a CNN "Crossfire" debate on "Battle Over Ten Commandments Monument Intensifies," aired on 21 August 2003, that, "You know, I supported Martin Luther King, Jr., who did practice his civil disobedience." All of the evidence suggests that this statement was simply false. This author immediately faxed a letter to Falwell after the debate, pleading for him to set the record straight, but there was no response. As he became more politically involved in the decades after King's death, Falwell reversed his position on the role of the church and the minister in society, claiming that, "I feel that what King was doing is exactly what we are doing." Even so, most white politically active preachers today still have not acknowledged the extent of the influence of King and the civil rights movement on them, an oversight that is undoubtedly attributable to lingering racism. See Perry D. Young, *God's Bullies: Native Reflections on Preachers and Politics* (New York: Holt, Rinehart and Winston, 1982), 310–312; CNN.com transcripts (21 August 2003), 4; Lewis V. Baldwin to the Reverend Dr. Jerry Falwell (22 August 2003), The author's files, 1–3; Ansbro, *Martin Luther King, Jr.,* 315 n.115; Carol Flake, *Redemptorama: Culture, Politics, and the New Evangelicalism* (New York: Penguin Books, Viking Penguin, 1984), 226–227; Richard J. Neuhaus and Michael Cromartie, eds., *Piety & Politics: Evangelicals and Fundamentalists Confront the World* (Washington, D.C.: Ethics and Public Policy Center, 1987), 12; Donald C. Swift, *Religion and the American Experience: A Social and Cultural History, 1765–1997* (Armonk, N.Y.: M. E. Sharpe, 1998), 273; Walter H. Capps, *The New Religious Right: Piety, Patriotism, and Politics* (Columbia: University of South Carolina Press, 1994), 202; Gabriel Fackre, *The Religious Right and Christian Faith* (Grand Rapids, Mich.: William B. Eerdmans, 1982), 14; Flo Conway and Jim Siegelman, *Holy Terror: The Fundamentalist War on America's Freedoms in Religion, Politics, and Our Private Lives* (New York: Dell, 1984), 85–86; Baldwin et al., *Legacy,* 91–92 and 115–116 n.57; Baldwin, *Wounded,* 237–238; and Lewis V. Baldwin, *Toward the Beloved Community: Martin Luther King, Jr. and South Africa* (Cleveland: Pilgrim Press, 1995), 131–132.

49. Lyons is reported to have been among the first white preachers to take aim at King. See Andrew M. Manis, "'Dying from the Neck Up': Southern Baptist Resistance to the Civil Rights Movement," *Baptist History and Heritage,* 34, no.1 (Winter 1999), 33–41; and Bill J. Leonard, "A Theology for Racism: Southern Fundamentalists and the Civil Rights Movement," *Baptist History and Heritage,* 34, no.1 (Winter 1999), 49–65.

50. Manis, "'Dying'," 33–46; Leonard, "A Theology," 49–65; and Baldwin et al., *Legacy,* 77–109.

51. King actually spoke at the Southern Baptist Theological Seminary in Louisville, Kentucky, in 1961, and some Southern Baptists, outraged by the invitation, vowed that they would no longer support the institution financially. Significantly, King

spoke of "The great expressions of moral support that I received from Southern Baptist Theological Seminary." However, an Alabama layman's group did circulate a critical statement concerning King's visit to the seminary, and he "wondered if this group represented the attitude of the Southern Baptist leadership." See Martin Luther King, Jr., to Dr. Henlee Barnette (3 May 1961), The Martin Luther King, Jr. Papers, Special Collections, Mugar Memorial Library, Boston University, Boston, Massachusetts, 1.

52. Martin Luther King, Jr., "Rally Speech," unpublished, Gadsden, Alabama (21 June 1963), KCLA, 2; and Martin Luther King, Jr., "Transcript of an Interview on the 'Merv Griffin Show' with Harry Belafonte," unpublished, New York, New York (6 July 1967), KCLA, 3.

53. Leonard, "A Theology," 57; and Clay Cooper, "Church Found 'Meddlin' in Rights Crisis," The Fundamentalist, November 1963, 5.

54. It is not enough to dismiss these attacks on King as the natural tendency of persons caught up in the multi-sensory world of images. King was publicly condemned, unjustly maligned, and challenged at virtually every turn by Southern Baptist leaders, and opposition to his tactics remained strident and relentless. The power of celebrity could not protect him. Apparently, there were many in the white churches who were passionate, almost obsessive, in their hatred for King and the values for which he stood, and they targeted him with ruthless zeal. Their unrelenting hostility toward King matched that of the FBI Director J. Edgar Hoover and his racist determination to destroy the civil rights leader. See Baldwin et al., Legacy, 81–109; Leonard, "A Theology," 49–65; and Manis, "'Dying,'" 33–46.

55. King, "Lecture," Federation Protestante, 2.

56. Martin Luther King, Jr., "The Role of the Church in Facing the Nation's Chief Moral Dilemma," a speech at the Conference on Christian Faith and Human Relations, Nashville, Tennessee (25 April 1957), typed version issued as part of the Proceedings of the Conference on Christian Faith and Human Relations, KCLA, 31.

57. W. W. Bottoms, "'I Still Stand by Nonviolence', Says Luther King," The Baptist Times, 24 September 1964, 9.

58. King, Can't Wait, 89–91; Carson, ed., King Autobiography, 284; and King, "Foreword," 5–7.

59. King accused the defenders of white supremacy of segregating the "Southern churches from Christianity." See Carson, ed., King Autobiography, 284.

60. King, Strength, 42. King at times exchanged letters with white bigots who justified segregation by claiming, as did one such person, that "The Negroes could never be equal to the whites—even the least of them—that's God's decision and not the white man's." See Sally Canada to Martin Luther King, Jr. (September 1956), The King Papers, Boston University, 1; and Martin Luther King, Jr., to Sally Canada (19 September 1956), The King Papers, Boston University, 1.

61. Manis, "'Dying,'" 39; and King, Strength, 42.

62. King dismissed this tendency to use the story of Ham to justify segregation as "blasphemy," and he insisted that "This is against everything that the Christian religion stands for." See Martin Luther King, Jr., "Paul's Letter to American Christians," a printed version of a sermon preached in the Dexter Avenue Baptist

Church, Montgomery, Alabama (4 November 1956), KCLA, 4; Carson et al., eds., *King Papers*, IV, 335; and King to Newgent (20 October 1959), 1. David Chappell has argued, in a recent book on prophetic religion and the civil rights movement, that white supremacists and pro-segregationist thinkers in the South were unsuccessful in getting their churches to actively support their cause. Pro-slavery advocates in antebellum times, the argument continues, were much more successful in fashioning a profoundly coherent and persuasive mode of thought in favor of their cause. Contrary to Chappell's claims, I would suggest that white supremacists in both antebellum times and during the modern civil movement received strong support from white churches, and in both cases biblical literalism was employed toward this end. Chappell's claim that white southern churches provided little support for segregation is most disturbing, for it shows a stunning lack of insight into the history of those institutions. The findings of this study suggest that King would be the first to disagree with Chappell's claim. Many white southern churches and their leaders appealed to scripture and the Christian faith in developing what Bill Leonard calls "a theology for racism." Moreover, white churches and their leadership supported the status quo by their silence and lack of sympathy in the face of black oppression, by their noncommitment to the struggle for equal rights and social justice, and by their rejection of an open-door policy. The debate about which was more successful—pro-slavery thinkers in antebellum times or pro-segregationist thinkers in the modern civil rights era—will probably be ongoing. However, we must bear in mind that despite the nature, extent, and effectiveness of the claims on both sides of this debate, both slavery and Jim Crow ended as legal systems. Although Jim Crow faded as a legal system, the continued segregation and re-segregation of the American society leaves one wondering if the pro-segregationist cause actually failed. The jury may still be out on this. In any case, the positions set forth by scholars like Bill Leonard and Andrew Manis are far more persuasive than those advanced by Chappell. See David L. Chappell, *A Stone of Hope: Prophetic Religion and the Death of Jim Crow* (Chapel Hill: University of North Carolina Press, 2004), 6 and 320; Leonard, "A Theology," 49–65; Manis, "'Dying,'" 33–46; Lewis V. Baldwin, "A Review of Chapell, *A Stone of Hope*," in *The Alabama Review*, 58, no.1 (January, 2005), 72–73; and Andrew M. Manis, *Southern Civil Religions in Conflict: Civil Rights and the Culture Wars* (Macon, Ga.: Mercer University Press, 2002), 1–148.

63. Martin Luther King, Jr., "Levels of Love," unpublished sermon, delivered at the Ebenezer Baptist Church, Atlanta (21 May 1967), KCLA, 6.

64. Martin Luther King, Jr., "A Knock at Midnight," unpublished sermon, delivered at the All Saints Community Church, Los Angeles, California (25 June 1967), KCLA, 8. Andrew Manis writes about the separate civic creeds of black southerners and white southerners—"one based on freedom by law and equality under God; the other finding in the Constitution a guarantee of states' rights and in the Bible a divine sanction of segregation." He uses the Southern Baptist Convention and the traditionally black National Baptist Convention as case studies, thus making his claims in a very convincing fashion. I found Manis's work immensely useful in framing my discussion of King and the Southern Baptist Convention. See Manis, *Southern Civil Religions*, xii (preface).

65. King, *Strength*, 102; and Carson, ed., *King Autobiography*, 284.

66. Bottoms, "I Still Stand," 9.

67. See Carson et al., eds., *King Papers*, IV, 45, 238, 264–266, and 457–458; and *Billy Graham and the Black Community* (Minneapolis: World Wide Publications, 1973), 24. Graham's relationship to King and the civil rights movement is increasingly finding a place in the scholarship in the field. See Edward L. Moore, "Billy Graham and Martin Luther King, Jr.: An Inquiry into White and Black Revivalistic Traditions," unpublished Ph.D. dissertation, Vanderbilt University, Nashville, Tennessee (May 1979), 453–480; Baldwin et al., *Legacy*, 85, 87, 89, 91–93, 95–96, and 101–102; Michael G. Long, *Billy Graham and the Beloved Community: America's Evangelist and the Dream of Martin Luther King, Jr.* (New York: Palgrave McMillan, 2006), 1–232. Long's treatment of Graham and King is by far the best provided so far. For a study that offers a saccharine and thus largely unreliable depiction of King's response to Billy Graham, see Chappell, *Stone*, 96–97, 140–144, and 317.

68. Carson et al., eds., *King Papers*, IV, 238 n.3.

69. Long, *Billy Graham*, 113; Carson et al., eds., *King Papers*, IV, 238; and Taylor Branch, *Parting the Waters: America in the King Years, 1954–1963* (New York: Simon and Schuster, 1988), 227–228. Branch affords rich information on Graham's associations with King and other black pastors.

70. Carson et al., eds., *King Papers*, IV, 265; and Long, *Billy Graham*, 8.

71. Clayborne Carson et al., eds., *The Papers of Martin Luther King, Jr., Volume V: Threshold of a New Decade, January 1959–December 1960* (Berkeley: University of California Press, 2005), 193.

72. *Billy Graham and the Black Community*, 24.

73. Long, *Billy Graham*, 8.

74. Carson et al., eds., *King Papers*, IV, 457–458; and Long, *Billy Graham*, 112.

75. Long seems to make this point, and I agree wholeheartedly with him. Long says that "the possibility of cooperation for a Graham-and-King crusade" eventually broke down over "the emphasis between politics and pure religion." See Long, *Billy Graham*, 112–113.

76. Strangely enough, Professor Edward T. Ladd of Emory University referred to King in these terms in a script for a taped interview. See "Profile Series: The Script for a Taped Interview with Martin Luther King, Jr.," Emory University and Station WAII-TV (Channel 11), Atlanta (9 April 1964), unpublished document, KCLA, 1; and Dora Byron to Martin Luther King, Jr. (4 April 1964), KCLA, 1.

77. "Billy Graham Urges Restraint in Sit-ins," *New York Times*, 18 April 1963, 21.

78. Graham at times appeared more concerned about what he saw as "extremism" in the movement than he was about the extremism of terrorist groups like the Ku Klux Klan. See Baldwin et al., *Legacy*, 92; and "State Trooper Protection in Ala.," *Jet*, 28, no.5 (13 May 1965), 49.

79. Edward B. Fiske, "Billy Graham Links Concern with Social Issues to Religious Conversion," *New York Times*, 6 December 1966, 38.

80. On this point, I agree essentially with Michael Long and Rufus Burrow, Jr., not David Chappell, whose approach to Graham lacks a decisively critical focus. At points, Chappell's treatment borders on hagiography. See Long, *Billy Graham*, 1–232; Rufus Burrow, Jr., "Graham, King, and the Beloved Community," in Michael G. Long,

ed., *The Legacy of Billy Graham: Critical Reflections on America's Greatest Evangelist* (Louisville: Westminster John Knox Press, 2008), 161–177; and Chappell, *Stone*, 96–96 and 140–144.

81. King, "Address at Mass Meeting" (16 February 1968), 5.

82. I take issue with the way in which some scholars have handled King's directive to Graham. David Chappell fails to adequately analyze what King was possibly thinking at this point, and he retreats instead to the questionable view that King and other civil rights leaders admired Graham's techniques. Michael Long's claims are generally more analytical and persuasive. In explaining why King did not invite Graham "to join the marches," or to "leave behind the relatively safe confines of the stadium pulpit" to support the movement "in the dangerous streets and jails of the South," Long writes: "The absence of this invitation most likely reflected not only King's social manners, as well as his practical sensibilities about the movement, but also his awareness and acceptance of Graham's particular vocation as a Christian evangelist." Long goes on to assert that King, as one with deep roots in the black church, "must have found Graham's calling to be alien, counter-intuitive, and perhaps suspect." See Chappell, *Stone*, 97; and Long, *Billy Graham*, 9–10.

83. As was commonly said in black church circles during King's time, it is impossible to sit at Pharaoh's table and to be a prophet at the same time. Moses had to leave Pharaoh's household before realizing and actualizing his calling to lead the oppressed. When faced with the choice between the needs of the oppressed and the lure of the seductive halls of power, Graham chose the later. His contributions to the civil rights movement amounted mostly to paying lip service and preaching to an integrated audience here and there. For the most critical treatments of Graham, see Baldwin et al., *Legacy*, 89–96, and 101–102; and Long, *Billy Graham*, 1–232.

84. In light of King's definition of a prophet, I find it strange that anyone could seriously treat Graham in a major work on prophetic religion and the demise of Jim Crow, especially in a highly uncritical fashion. See Chappell, *Stone*, 96–97 and 140–144.

85. Martin Luther King, Jr., "Creative Non-Conformist," *Chicago Defender*, 2 April 1966, 14. This same account also appears in *New York Amsterdam News*, 26 March 1966, 12; and in Martin Luther King, Jr., "Transformed Nonconformist," unpublished sermon, delivered at the Ebenezer Baptist Church, Atlanta (16 January 1966), KCLA, 5. The silence of the white church in the face of evil, declared King, represented a betrayal of both Christ and the mission to which it was called:

> Segregation could not exist today in the United States if the church took a stand against it. (Yeah) Mr. Meredith would be in the University of Mississippi right now if the churches of Mississippi had taken a stand against segregation. (Preach brother) The tragic fact is that in spite of Mr. Barnett's defiance of the Supreme Court of the land and the moral law of the universe, we haven't heard a single word from the churches of Mississippi.

See King, "Can a Christian Be a Communist?" 4–5.

86. Martin Luther King, Jr., "Answer to a Perplexing Question," unpublished sermon, Ebenezer Baptist Church, Atlanta (3 March 1963), KCLA, 6–7; and Martin

Luther King, Jr., "Remember Who You Are," unpublished sermon, Ebenezer Baptist Church, Atlanta, Georgia (7 July 1963), KCLA, 1.

87. King, "Knock," 3; and King, *Strength*, 21.

88. King made this suggestion in the strongest terms in his sermon, "How Should a Christian View Communism?" which was known in some circles in white churches. See King, *Strength*, 99–100.

89. Swift, *Religion*, 241; William Bradford Huie, *He Slew the Dreamer: My Search, with James Earl Ray, for the Truth About the Murder of Martin Luther King* (New York: Delacorte, 1970), 207–211; Baldwin et al., *Legacy*, 28; Baldwin, *Balm*, 76; and Washington, ed., *Testament*, xvi (Introduction). Senator Hillary Clinton recalls that as a youngster, her youth minister took her and other youngsters to hear King deliver a speech at Orchestra Hall in Chicago, "despite some church members' suspicion that King was a Communist." See Hillary Rodham Clinton, *It Takes a Village and Other Lessons Children Teach Us* (New York: Simon & Schuster, 1996), 176.

90. Martin Luther King, Jr., "Beyond Condemnation," unpublished sermon, Montgomery, Alabama (November 1954), The King Papers, Project, 1.

91. Martin Luther King, Jr., "The Impassable Gulf (The Parable of Dives and Lazarus)," unpublished sermon, Montgomery, Alabama (2 October 1955), The King Papers Project, 3–4.

92. Washington, ed., *Testament*, 298–299; King, *Can't Wait*, 89–90; King, *Where Do We Go?* 96; Martin Luther King, Jr., *The Trumpet of Conscience* (New York: Harper & Row, 1987), 13; and King, "Role of the Church in Facing," 31.

93. Washington, ed., *Testament*, 500–502; King, *Strength*, 21–22, 35, and 61–63; King, "Address Before a Dinner," 3–4; King, "Role of the Church in Facing," 31; and Martin Luther King, Jr., "Address at a Conference of Religious Leaders Under the Sponsorship of the President's Committee on Government Contracts," unpublished, the Sheraton D.C., Washington, D.C. (11 May 1959), KCLA, 3–7.

94. Leonard, "A Theology," 63 and 68 n.85.

95. Martin Luther King, Jr., to Dr. Harold E. Fey (23 June 1962), KCLA, 1–5.

96. King, "Pharisee and Publican," 2–3; and King, "Address Before a Dinner," 4.

97. Clayborne Carson et al., eds., *The Papers of Martin Luther King, Jr., Volume VI: Advocate of the Social Gospel, September 1948–March 1963* (Berkeley: University of California Press, 2007), 250.

98. King, "Pharisee and Publican," 2–3; King, "An Address Before a Dinner," 4; Martin Luther King, Jr., "Nonviolence: The Christian Way in Human Relations," *Presbyterian Life*, 8 February 1958, 12–13; and King, "We Are Still Walking," 6–8.

99. Stephen E. Berk, *A Time to Heal: John Perkins, Community Development, and Racial Reconciliation* (Grand Rapids, Mich.: Baker Books, 1997), 150 and 195; and Baldwin et al., *Legacy*, 101–102.

100. "Hugh Downs Interview," 3; Martin Luther King, Jr., "Revolution and Redemption," unpublished closing address at the European Baptist Assembly, Amsterdam, Holland (16 August 1964), KCLA, 10; Washington, ed., *Testament*, 39–40; Martin Luther King, Jr., "Address at the Closing Session of the Mobilization of Clergy and Laymen Concerned About the War in Vietnam," printed version delivered at the New York Avenue Presbyterian Church, Washington, D.C. (5–6

February 1968), KCLA, 1–17; and *Dr. Martin Luther King, Jr.: Speak on the War in Vietnam*, a pamphlet issued by Clergy and Laymen Concerned About Vietnam (April 1967), 2–30.

101. King, "Transformed Nonconformist" (16 January 1966), 9–10; and Martin Luther King, Jr., "What Are Your New Year's Resolutions?" unpublished sermon, New York (7 January 1968), KCLA, 3.

102. This is essentially what King was saying in his challenge to the white church in his famous "Letter from the Birmingham City Jail" (1963). See King, *Can't Wait*, 89–92.

103. Manis, *Southern Civil Religions*, 186. Also see "Join the Protest Demonstration Against Martin Luther King," a flyer (1967), KCLA, 1; *Hear Julia Brown, Former FBI Undercover Operative, Expose Martin Luther King's Communist Affiliations*, a pamphlet (c. 1967), KCLA, 1–4; and Washington, ed., *Testament*, 231–243.

104. Martin Luther King, Jr., "Address at the Southern Association of Political Scientists," unpublished (13 November 1964), KCLA, 1–2.

105. David T. Morgan, *The New Crusades, The New Holy Land: Conflict in the Southern Baptist Convention, 1969–1991* (Tuscaloosa: University of Alabama Press, 1996), 46; and Manis, *Southern Civil Religions*, 166 and 186.

106. Ralph W. McGill to Rev. Martin Luther King, Jr. (1 May 1967), KCLA, 1; and King, "What Are Your New Year's Resolutions?" 2.

107. King, "Speech at SCLC," 32.

108. Martin Luther King, Jr., "Advice for Living," *Ebony*, 12, no.12 (October 1957), 53; Carson et al., eds., *King Papers*, IV, 280–281; and Baldwin et al., *Legacy*, 85–86. For the best and most extensive treatment of King's thoughts on the relationship of the Christian to the state, or to temporal authority, see Michael G. Long, *Against Us, But for Us: Martin Luther King, Jr. and the State* (Macon, Ga.: Mercer University Press, 2002), 1–229. A serious study of the different ways in which King and conservative white Christians approached the question of the relationship of the church to the state would constitute a major contribution to the scholarship on both King and the American churches. For an interesting essay that offers insights along these lines, see David John Marley, "Martin Luther King, Jr., Pat Robertson, and the Duality of Modern Christian Politics," *Fides et Historia: Journal of the Conference on Faith and History*, 32, no.2 (Summer/Fall 2000), 67–81.

109. Martin Luther King, Jr., "America's Chief Moral Dilemma," unpublished speech, United Church of Christ, General Synod, Palmer House, Chicago (6 July 1965), KCLA, 3.

110. Stephen Carter persuasively makes this observation, using King's "Letter from the Birmingham City Jail" (1963) as his support. See Stephen L. Carter, *The Culture of Disbelief: How American Law and Politics Trivialize Religious Devotion* (New York: Anchor Books, 1994), 38.

111. Carter, *Culture of Disbelief*, 38. David Howard-Pitney is correct in saying that King articulated the nation under God version of civic faith. See David Howard-Pitney, *The Afro-American Jeremiad: Appeals for Justice in America* (Philadelphia: Temple University Press, 1990), 144–145.

112. Andrew Shanks, *Civil Society, Civil Religion* (Cambridge, Mass.: Blackwell Publishers, 1995), 6. There is some debate about the extent to which King invoked

American civil religion in his struggle. For some sense of this debate, see David Howard-Pitney, *The African American Jeremiad: Appeals for Justice in America*, Revised and Expanded Edition (Philadelphia: Temple University Press, 2005), 213–214.

113. Charles Wilson seems to suggest that King fits squarely into this tradition. He notes that "King used the language of the nineteenth-century Lost Cause, speaking of suffering, tragedy, honor, the need for virtuous behavior, the need of a defeated people to achieve dignity, and the search for group identity and destiny," but Wilson fails to explain that these concepts and values did not mean the same thing for King and southern whites. See Charles R. Wilson, *Judgment & Grace in Dixie: Southern Faiths from Faulkner to Elvis* (Athens: University of Georgia Press, 1995), 31–32. For a critique of Wilson's approach, see Baldwin et al., *Legacy*, 45–49.

114. Baldwin et al., *Legacy*, 45–59; and King, *Where Do We Go?* 11. The best and most reliable treatment of the differences between the civic-religious faiths of white and black southerners is provided by Andrew Manis. Manis uses the Southern Baptist Convention and the predominantly black National Baptist Convention as case studies in setting forth his claims and conclusions. See Manis, *Southern Civil Religions*, ix–148.

115. Martin Luther King, Jr., "An Address," unpublished, delivered at the 47th NAACP Annual Convention, San Francisco, California (24 June 1956), The King Papers, Boston University, 8–9; Martin Luther King, Jr., "An Announcement of His Decision to Move from Montgomery to Atlanta," unpublished, Dexter Avenue Baptist Church, Montgomery, Alabama (29 November 1959), The King Papers, Boston University, 2; Baldwin, *Balm*, 64; and Baldwin et al., *Legacy*, 46–47.

116. Carson et al., eds., *King Papers*, III, 429.

117. King, *Stride*, 32–33; and Carson, ed., *King Autobiography*, 48–49.

118. King, *Stride*, 32–33; and Carson, ed., *King Autobiography*, 48.

119. King, *Stride*, 32–33; and Friedland, *Lift Voice*, 29.

120. King, *Stride*, 33 and 108–109; Clayborne Carson et al., eds., *The Papers of Martin Luther King, Jr, Volume II: Recovering Precious Values, July 1951–November 1955* (Berkeley: University of California Press, 1994), 44 and 621; Carson et al., eds., *King Papers*, III, 194, 353, 468–469, 504, 536, and 543; Carson et al., eds., *King Papers*, IV, 179–180 and 570; Friedland, *Lift Voice*, 27–32; Robert S. Graetz, *A White Preacher's Memoir: The Montgomery Bus Boycott* (Montgomery, Ala.: Black Belt Press, 1998; originally published in 1991), 49, 51, 99, 112, 115, and 142; and Robert S. Graetz, *A White Preacher's Message on Race and Reconciliation: Based on His Experiences Beginning With the Montgomery Bus Boycott* (Montgomery, Ala.: New South Books, 2006), 54, 89, 113, 116–117, and 145.

121. King, *Stride*, 33, 74, 161, 169, 175, and 209; Washington, ed., *Testament*, 440, 456, 459, and 464; Carson et al., eds., *King Papers*, III, 28–29, 50, 184, 193, 357, 369, 381–382, 389, 391, 424 502–503, 505, 508, 533, and 535; Carson et al., eds., *King Papers*, IV, 46, 69, 110, 144, 155, 398, 558, 566, 570, 572, 586, and 614; Ansbro, *King*, 315–316; Friedland, *Lift Voice*, 28–30 and 47; Coretta Scott King, *My Life with Martin Luther King, Jr.*, Revised Edition (New York: Henry Holt, 1993), 128, 131, and 136; Graetz, *White Preacher's Message*, 9 and 29–271; Graetz, *A White Preacher's Memoir*, 9–156; King, "We Are Still Walking," 6; and Private Interview with the Reverend Robert S. Graetz (26 July 1988).

122. Carson, ed., *King Autobiography*, 97; King, *Stride*, 163 and 173; King, *My Life*, 127 and 135–136; Washington, ed., *Testament*, 5, 82, 458, and 462; Carson et al., eds., *King Papers*, III, 14, 17–18–20, 30, 151, 211, 213–214, 245, 311–312, 353, 388–390, 435–436, and 485–486; Carson et al., eds., *King Papers*, V, 27, 213, 218, 397, 587, 590, 601, 603, and 618; and Carson et al., eds., *King Papers*, IV, 3, 99, 110–111, 141–143, 181, 207, 279, 290–291, 523, 550–551, 581, 601–602, 604, 610, and 612.

123. King, *Stride*, 176–177.

124. For a careful exploration of King's vision of the "New South," which places the civil rights leader squarely in southern intellectual history, see Baldwin et al., *Legacy*, 1–41.

125. Carson et al., eds., *King Papers*, III, 449.

126. Merrill M. Hawkins, Jr., *Will Campbell: Radical Prophet of the South* (Macon, Ga.: Mercer University Press, 1997), 42.

127. King, "Role of the Church in Facing," 31.

128. King, *Stride*, 210; and Washington, ed., *Testament*, 89 and 93.

129. Washington, ed., *Testament*, 346; Ansbro, *King*, 316 n.116; William D. Watley, *Roots of Resistance: The Nonviolent Ethic of Martin Luther King, Jr.* (Valley Forge, Pa.: Judson Press, 1985), 65; King, *Can't Wait*, 92; and "Religious Leaders Arrested in Albany, Georgia" unpublished list (28 August 1962), KCLA, 1–2.

130. King, *Can't Wait*, 89; and Ansbro, *King*, 316 n.116.

131. Carson, ed., *King Autobiography*, 222.

132. Martin Luther King, Jr., "transcript of an interview on the WINS-News Conference," Radio 1010, New York, unpublished (31 May 1964), The King Papers, Boston University, 4; and Stan Brooks to the Reverend Martin Luther King, Jr. (1 June 1964), unpublished, The King Papers, Boston University, 1.

133. Bottoms, "I Still Stand," 9.

134. Martin Luther King, Jr., "An Address at the Synagogue Council of America," unpublished (5 December 1965), KCLA, 2; and Baldwin and Al-Hadid, *Cross and Crescent*, 122. One Catholic scholar notes that the Catholics who marched with King constituted "the Catholic left." See James Hennesey, S.J., *American Catholics: A History of the Roman Catholic Community in the United States* (New York: Oxford University, Press, 1983), 315; and King,"Lecture," The Federation Protestante, 12.

135. King, *Where Do We Go?* 9; King, "America's Chief Moral,"19; and Martin Luther King, Jr., "Closing Address before the National Conference on Religion and Race," Chicago, unpublished (17 January 1963), KCLA, 2. King felt that the church had much to learn from the communitarian ethics of southern-based groups like the Highlander Folk School, a unique embodiment of unionism, democracy, and Christian socialism, established by Myles Horton in Monteagle, Tennessee, in 1932; and the Koinonia Farm, a racially integrated expression of Christian community, started by Clarence Jordan in Americus, Georgia, in 1942. See Baldwin et al., *Legacy*, 32–33.

136. Carson, ed., *King Autobiography*, 289.

137. Mary Stanton, *From Selma to Sorrow: The Life and Death of Viola Liuzzo* (Athens: University of Georgia Press, 1998), 46–51; Carson, ed., *King Autobiography*,

270, 282, 289, 294, and 324; King, *Where Do We Go?* 34; Martin Luther King, Jr., "Draft of a Statement Regarding the Death of Rev. James Reeb," unpublished (11 March 1965) KCLA, 1–6; Martin Luther King, Jr., "Tribute to James Reeb," unpublished, Montgomery, Alabama (16 March 1965), KCLA, 1; and Martin Luther King, Jr., "Draft of a Statement Regarding the Deaths of Schwerner, Goodman, and Cheney," unpublished (4 August 1964), The King Papers, Boston University, 1–2.

138. King, "Statement Regarding James Reeb," 1–2 and 6. King often said that:

> One of the most inspirational moments of my life was the memorial
> service for the Rev. James Reeb when an Episcopal Bishop, a Methodist
> Bishop, a Greek Orthodox Archbishop, the President of the Unitarian-
> Universalist National Conference, a Roman Catholic Monsignor, and two
> Baptist preachers conducted services in an A.M.E. Church, with twenty or
> thirty top ranking officials of labor and civil rights organizations seated in the
> choir stand saying "Amen."

See King, "America's Chief Moral," 18–19; and King, "Closing Address," 2. King also addressed the significance of Reeb's death for the South in particular:

> They will be ministers of the gospel—priests, rabbis and nuns—who are
> willing to march for freedom and go to jail for conscience sake. One day the
> South will know that when these dedicated children of God courageously
> protested segregation, they were in reality standing up for the best in the
> American dream, standing up for the most sacred values in our Judeo-Chris-
> tian heritage, thereby carrying our whole nation back to those great well
> springs of democracy, which were dug deep by the founding fathers in the
> formulation of the Constitution and the Declaration of Independence. When
> this glorious story is written, the name of James Reeb will stand as the
> shining example of manhood at its best.

See King, "Tribute to Reeb," 1.

139. "Hugh Downs Interview," 1–3; and Washington, ed., *Testament*, 658–659.

140. A study of the various religious organizations and agencies with which King had ties would significantly enhance our knowledge of how he related to the church nationwide and worldwide. Such a study might find a model in James F. Findlay, Jr., *Church People in the Struggle: The National Council of Churches and the Black Freedom Movement, 1950–1970* (New York: Oxford University Press, 1993), 11–190.

141. Martin Luther King, Jr., to Dr. William H. Rhodes (26 January 1962), KCLA, 1. For other sources that shed light on this issue, see Dr. William H. Rhodes to Martin Luther King, Jr. (31 January 1962), KCLA, 1; Clifford G. Hansen to Dr. Martin Luther King, Jr. (1 February 1962), KCLA, 1; Martin Luther King, Jr., to Dr. Clifford G. Hansen (10 July 1962), KCLA, 1; Clifford G. Hansen to Martin Luther King, Jr. (20 June 1962), KCLA, 1; Charles N. Forsberg to Martin Luther King, Jr. (27 July 1962), KCLA, 1–2; Martin Luther King, Jr. to the Board of Education & Publication of the American Baptist Convention (17 October 1963), KCLA, 1; Elizabeth J. Miller to Dr. Martin Luther King, Jr. (11 November 1963), KCLA, 1; Martin Luther King, Jr. to the Department of

Management and Organization of the American Baptist Convention (16 January 1964), KCLA, 1; Edwin H. Tuller to Dr. Martin Luther King, Jr. (3 March 1964), KCLA, 1–3; Martin Luther King, Jr., to Mr. Edwin H. Tuller (2 April 1964), KCLA, 1; Miss D. McDonald to the Rev. Robert W. Towner (11 May 1964), KCLA, 1; Robert W. Towner to Dr. Martin Luther King, Jr. (4 May 1964), KCLA, 1; and Rev. Newton E. Woodbury to Reverend Martin Luther King, Jr. (15 March 1967), KCLA, 1.

142. Martin Luther King, Jr., "Advice for Living," *Ebony*, 13, no.9 (July 1958), 86; and "Martin Luther King, Jr. on 'Meet the Press,'" produced by Lawrence E. Spivak, 4, no.16, 17 April 1960 (Washington, D.C.: Merkle Press, 1960), 11.

143. King to Rhodes (26 January 1962), 1.

144. Friedland, *Lift Voice*, 29; King, "Nonviolence: The Christian Way," 13; King, *Stride*, 208; and Ansbro, *King*, 180.

145. Ansbro, *King*, 180; Martin Luther King, Jr., to Dr. Oscar Lee (2 July 1962), The King Papers, Boston University, 1; Martin Luther King, Jr., "Press Conference USA: Transcript from a Video Tape Recording," unpublished, Press Conference USA (5 July 1963), KCLA, 5; and "Hugh Downs Interview," 1–2.

146. King to Lee (2 July 1962), 1; Mathew Ahmann, ed., *Race: Challenge to Religion* (Chicago: Henry Regnery, 1963), iv–ix and 155–169; and Martin Luther King, Jr., "On Interfaith Conference on Civil Rights," unpublished statement (15 January 1963), KCLA, 1.

147. Martin Luther King, Jr., "Segregation and the Church," *New York Amsterdam News*, 2 February 1963, 8.

148. Harold E. Fey to Rev. P. Malcolm Hammond (10 December 1963), KCLA, 1; Martin Luther King, Jr. to Dr. Truman Douglas (28 June 1965), KCLA, 1–2; and Martin Luther King, Jr. to Dr. Wesley A. Hotchkiss (1 March 1966), KCLA, 1–2.

149. Martin Luther King, Jr., and Wyatt Tee Walker to the Student Interracial Ministry Committee (29 March 1961), KCLA, 1; Martin Luther King, Jr., to Thomas E. Jordan (31 July 1963), KCLA, 1; and Baldwin, *Balm*, 335–336.

150. King, "Transformed Nonconformist" (16 January 1966), 8; and Friedland, *Lift Voice*, 6–236.

151. King, "Address at the Closing Session," 1–17; and *Dr. Martin Luther King, Jr.: oSpeak*, 2–31; and Friedland, *Lift Voice*, 148, 155, 170, 180–182, and 202–203.

CHAPTER 5

1. Martin Luther King, Jr., *The Trumpet of Conscience* (San Francisco: Harper & Row, 1987; originally published in 1968), 31. McLoughlin and Bellah include King among what they call "world-oriented clerics." See William G. McLoughlin and Robert N. Bellah, eds., *Religion in America* (Boston: Beacon Press, 1970), 178.

2. Martin Luther King, Jr., "Statement Regarding the Legitimacy of the Struggle in Montgomery, Alabama," unpublished (4 May 1956), The Martin Luther King, Jr. Papers, Special Collections, Mugar Memorial Library, Boston University, Boston, 1. Before the 1990s, it was commonly held among scholars that King developed an international vision after he received the Nobel Peace Prize in December 1964, or

during the last three years of his life. This view has been challenged in much of the recent scholarship on King. See Lewis V. Baldwin, *To Make the Wounded Whole: The Cultural Legacy of Martin Luther King, Jr.* (Minneapolis: Fortress Press, 1992), 247–257; and Lewis V. Baldwin, *Toward the Beloved Community: Martin Luther King, Jr. and South Africa* (Cleveland: Pilgrim Press, 1995), 7–24.

3. Although King spoke at churches throughout the world, made occasional references to the work of the World Council of Churches (WCC) and the World Convention of the Churches of Christ (WCCC), and challenged the Christian Church to seriously engage the range of religions and/or faith traditions worldwide, there is no serious scholarly treatment of his views on how the ministry and mission of the church should unfold on a global scale. Scattered references to the subject can be found in Baldwin, *Beloved Community*, 7–63.

4. Martin Luther King, Jr., "What a Mother Should Tell Her Child," unpublished sermon, Ebenezer Baptist Church, Atlanta (12 May 1963), The Library and Archives of the Martin Luther King, Jr. Center for Nonviolent Social Change, Inc. (KCLA), Atlanta, Georgia, 4; Martin Luther King, Jr., "A Challenge to the Churches and Synagogues," unpublished, delivered at The Conference on Religion and Race, Edgewater Beach Hotel, Chicago (17 January 1963), KCLA, 10; and Martin Luther King, Jr., "The Church on the Frontier of Racial Tension," unpublished, delivered as one of The Gay Lectures, Southern Baptist Theological Seminary, Louisville, Kentucky (19 April 1961), KCLA, 3–7.

5. King, "What a Mother," 4; and Jack Gilbert, "King Urges Youth Join in New Order," *Athens Messenger*, 30 December 1959, 1 and 16.

6. Even as a seminary student, King praised those in the American churches who did not worship what he labeled "the god of nationalism." See Martin Luther King, Jr., "False God of Nationalism," unpublished sermon, Atlanta (12 July 1953), The Martin Luther King, Jr. Papers Project, Stanford University, Stanford, California, 1–2.

7. Martin Luther King, Jr., "Paul's Galatians: You Are Called to Freedom, Brethren," unpublished sermon (n.d.), KCLA, 3; Martin Luther King, Jr., "Revolution and Redemption," unpublished closing address at the European Baptist Assembly, Amsterdam (16 August 1964), KCLA, 5; and Martin Luther King, Jr., "A Christian Movement in a Revolutionary Age," unpublished speech (Fall 1966), KCLA, 8.

8. "Dexter Avenue Baptist Church Covenant," unpublished, presented to the Congregation by The June Club in Memory of Mrs. Katie Owens and Miss Nellie Williams (14 June 1959), KCLA, 1–2.

9. Martin Luther King, Jr., "Propagandizing Christianity," unpublished sermon, Dexter Avenue Baptist Church, Montgomery (12 September 1954), The King Papers Project, 1–2.

10. Martin Luther King, Jr., "Redirecting Our Missionary Zeal," unpublished sermon notes, Montgomery (22 January 1956), The King Papers Project, 1; and Clayborne Carson et al., eds., *The Papers of Martin Luther King, Jr., Volume VI: Advocate of the Social Gospel, September 1948–March 1963* (Berkeley: University of California Press, 2007), 249–250.

11. King, "Revolution and Redemption," 1–2.

12. Carson et al., eds., *King Papers*, VI, 106; and Martin Luther King, Jr., "A Knock at Midnight," unpublished version, delivered at the All Saints Community Church, Los Angeles (25 June 1967), KCLA, 8.

13. Carson et al., eds., *King Papers*, VI, 105–106, 181–184, and 249–250.

14. Martin Luther King, Jr., "Communism's Challenge to Christianity," unpublished sermon (9 August 1953), The King Papers Project, 1–4; and Martin Luther King, Jr., *Strength to Love* (Philadelphia: Fortress Press, 1981), 96. King credited communism with challenging "the social conscience of the churches" in a global context, and he noted that it was "a corrective for a Christianity that has been all too passive." See Martin Luther King, Jr., *Stride toward Freedom: The Montgomery Story* (New York: Harper & Row, 1958), 95.

15. Martin Luther King, Jr., "Is Direct Action Necessary?," *Current*, August 1963, 19.

16. King, *Strength*, 58–59; James M. Washington, ed., *A Testament of Hope: The Essential Writings and Speeches of Martin Luther King, Jr.* (San Francisco: HarperCollins, 1991), 498–499; and Clayborne Carson and Peter Holloran, eds., *A Knock at Midnight: Inspiration from the Sermons of Reverend Martin Luther King, Jr.* (New York: Warner Books, 1998), 68. As early as 1958, King declared that "As a Baptist I am especially interested to be in contact with the large number of practicing Baptists within the Soviet Union." King went on to praise "the continued existence of religious conviction among millions of Soviet citizens, all of whom have been subjected to varying degrees of oppression and discouragement by powerful agencies of propaganda and anti-religious education." King had initially planned to visit the Soviet Union while also visiting India in 1959 because he was "anxious to examine the reactions of the people in a society which for so many years has sought to deny the basic spiritual and moral doctrines of Christianity." However, King's plans were altered "due to the state of his health after he was stabbed" in New York, and also "the urgency of racial conflict in the South." See Martin Luther King, Jr., to Dr. Darrell Randall (13 November 1958), The King Papers, Boston University, 1–2; and "Dr. King Calls Off Russian Part of Trip," *Los Angeles Times*, 6 February 1959.

17. Martin Luther King, Jr., "People to People," unpublished version of an essay prepared for *New York Amsterdam News*. 17 September 1964, KCLA, 2–3.

18. Carson et al., eds., *King Papers*, VI, 442.

19. King, "Knock," 8; Martin Luther King, Jr., "Levels of Love," unpublished, delivered at Ebenezer Baptist Church, Atlanta (21 May 1967), KCLA, 6–7; and Carson et al., eds., *King Papers*, VI, 94 and 250.

20. Carson et al., eds., *King Papers*, VI, 105–106, 181–184, and 249–250.

21. Martin Luther King, Jr., "I Sat Where They Sat," unpublished sermon notes (1948–54), The King Papers Project, 1.

22. King's reference here is to J. W. Milan and Roy Bryant, the two white men involved in the brutal lynching of Emmett Till, the fourteen-year-old black boy from Chicago, in Mississippi in August 1955. See Carson et al., eds., *King Papers*, VI, 250.

23. Martin Luther King, Jr., to Mr. M. Bernard Resnikoff (17 September 1961), unpublished, KCLA, 1.

24. "An Interview with Martin Luther King, Jr.," unpublished version prepared for *Redbook*, 5 November 1964, KCLA, 3.

25. King to Resnikoff (17 September 1961), 1; Martin Luther King, Jr. to Dr. Harold E. Fey (23 June 1962), unpublished, KCLA, 3; and "King Interview," 3.

26. Apparently, this tendency existed in black churches almost from the point of their origins in the late eighteenth century. Walter Williams is one scholar who brilliantly treats this topic, especially the struggles of African Americans to reconcile their interest in and identification with African cultures with their participation in white Western missionary expansionist practices on the African continent. See Walter L. Williams, *Black Americans and the Evangelization of Africa, 1877–1900* (Madison: University of Wisconsin Press, 1982), 104–194.

27. King, *Stride*, 224; Martin Luther King, Jr., "Speech Made in Savannah," unpublished (1 January 1961), KCLA, 7; Martin Luther King, Jr., "Great Day for Negroes," *New York Amsterdam News*, 12 October 1963, 10; Martin Luther King, Jr., "Statement Issued from Harlem Hospital," New York, unpublished (30 September 1958), KCLA, 1; and Lewis V. Baldwin, *There is a Balm in Gilead: The Cultural Roots of Martin Luther King, Jr.* (Minneapolis: Fortress Press, 1991), 230–272. This image of the black church as a possible messianic presence and instrument was discussed more among black church activists than one would perhaps imagine in the 1950s and 1960s. Charles R. Lawrence, who, like King, graduated from Morehouse College, and was national chair of the Fellowship of Reconciliation (FOR), said the following to King in a letter in February, 1956: "Providence may have given the Negroes of Montgomery the historic mission of demonstrating to the world the practical power of Christianity, the unmatched vitality of a nonviolent, loving approach to social protest." See Clayborne Carson et al., eds., *The Papers of Martin Luther King, Jr., Volume III: Birth of a New Age, December 1955–December 1956* (Berkeley: University of California Press, 1997), 74 and 137–138. Coretta King has reported that King felt that "there was a great opportunity for black people to redeem Christianity in America." See Coretta Scott King, *My Life with Martin Luther King, Jr.* (New York: Henry Holt, 1993; originally published in 1969), 239.

28. King, "Statement from Harlem," 1; and Washington, ed., *Testament*, 490.

29. Martin Luther King, Jr., "Statement on Invitation Received from Prime Minister Kwame Nkrumah," unpublished (1957), KCLA, 1.

30. King, "People to People," 2.

31. John Hope Franklin, ed., *The Souls of Black Folk in Three Negro Classics* (New York: Avon Books, 1965), 215; and Baldwin, *Balm*, 262.

32. Lewis V. Baldwin et al., *The Legacy of Martin Luther King, Jr.: The Boundaries of Law, Politics, and Religion* (Notre Dame, Ind.: University of Notre Dame Press, 2002), 21.

33. In making this observation, King was not guilty of a kind of arrogant triumphantism, for he also acknowledged that such an achievement on the part of his people "would not have been possible were it not for the goodwill of a great segment of the white community." See Martin Luther King, Jr., "Statement for the Press," unpublished, Sheraton-Atlantic Hotel, New York (4 December 1964), KCLA, 1–2.

34. Martin Luther King, Jr., "Dreams of Brighter Tomorrows," unpublished (March 1965), KCLA, 1.

35. Martin Luther King, Jr., "Nobel Lecture," unpublished, delivered at Aula of the University, Oslo (11 December 1964), KCLA, 10; and Martin Luther King, Jr., "True Dignity," unpublished (n.d.), KCLA, 3.

36. King, "Dreams of Brighter Tomorrows," 4–5.

37. Martin Luther King, Jr., to Mr. Sam Wyler (20 July 1967), KCLA, 2.

38. Martin Luther King, Jr., *Where Do We Go from Here: Chaos or Community?* (Boston: Beacon Press, 1968), 57; and Baldwin, *Beloved Community*, 54.

39. King used both of these metaphors from time to time to explain his vision of world community, or what he meant by *beloved community* in universal terms. See Martin Luther King, Jr., "Desireability of Being Maladjusted," unpublished sermon (13 January 1958), KCLA, 1; Carson et al., eds., *King Papers*, III, 429; and King, *Strength*, 82–83.

40. King felt that blacks had already made significant strides in this direction, often with the support of allies from the ranks of the white church. See Martin Luther King, Jr., *Where Do We Go from Here?*, unpublished manuscript (1967), KCLA, 9–10; and Baldwin, *Balm*, 242. King actually said on some occasions that "If democracy is to win its place throughout the world, millions of people, Negro and white, must stand before the world as examples of democracy in action, not as vote-less victims of the denial and corruption of our heritage." See Martin Luther King, Jr., "Remarks at the Launching of SCLC's Crusade for Citizenship," unpublished, Miami, Florida (12 February 1958), KCLA, 3.

41. Washington, ed., *Testament*, 40, 239, and 498–499; and King, *Strength*, 61, 141, and 143.

42. Carson et al., eds., *The Papers of Martin Luther King, Jr., Volume IV: Symbol of the Movement, January 1957–December 1958* (Berkeley: University of California Press, 2000), 164–165; and Martin Luther King, Jr., "The Birth of a New Nation," unpublished (April 1957), KCLA, 18–20.

43. King, "Challenge to the Churches," 3; King, *Strength*, 62; and Carson and Holloran, eds., *Knock*, 72.

44. This was precisely the point that King was making in his "Letter from the Birmingham City Jail" (1963), when he criticized the American churches for their "silent and often vocal sanction of things as they are." See Martin Luther King, Jr. *Why We Can't Wait* (New York: New American Library, 1964), 92; and Washington, ed., *Testament*, 300.

45. King, "Knock," 7–8; and Martin Luther King, Jr., "Pharisee and Publican," unpublished sermon, Atlanta (9 October 1966), KCLA, 2.

46. King, "Pharisee and Publican," 2.

47. Carson et al., eds., *King Papers*, VI, 183–184 and 350; and Martin Luther King, Jr., "A Knock at Midnight," unpublished sermon outline (25 June 1967), KCLA, 1.

48. "Conversation in Ghana," *Christian Century*, 74, no. 15 (10 April 1957), 446–448; and Baldwin, *Beloved Community*, 10.

49. Michael Scott to Martin Luther King, Jr., unpublished (23 January 1958), KCLA, 1–2; and Baldwin, *Beloved Community*, 17–18 and 38.

50. King, *Strength*, 61; Carson and Holloran, eds., *Knock*, 71; Carson et al., eds., *King Papers*, VI, 499; Baldwin, *Beloved Community*, 10, 17–18, and 38; and Martin Luther King, Jr., "Introduction," in *Southwest Africa: The U.N.'s Stepchild* (New York: American Committee on Africa, 1958–59), The King Papers, Boston University, 1.

51. "Dr. King Meets Bishop: Southern Leader and Africa's Reeves Discuss Race Issues," *New York Times*, 28 July 1957, 39; and Baldwin, *Beloved Community*, 10.

52. Baldwin, *Beloved Community*, 17; George M. Houser to Julius Mueller, unpublished (18 September 1957), ACOA Collection, Amistad Research Center, Tulane University, 1; George M. Houser, *No One Can Stop the Rain: Glimpses of Africa's Liberation Struggle* (New York: Pilgrim Press, 1989), 124; "Biased Appeal Scored by South Africans," *New York Times*, 13 December 1957, 17; and John Hughes, "South Africa Retorts to Racial Crisis," *Christian Science Monitor*, 13 December 1957, 16.

53. "Report on Declaration of Conscience Campaign," unpublished, American Committee on Africa, New York (1957–58), ACOA Collection, Amistad Research Center, Tulane University, 1–2.

54. J. B. Abrahamsen to Martin Luther King, Jr., unpublished (2 March 1958), KCLA, 1.

55. "King to Develop Non-Violent Integration Movement in the South," *Ohio University Post*, 1 January 1960, 1.

56. W. W. Bottoms, "'I Still Stand by Nonviolence', Says Luther King," *Baptist Times*, 24 September 1964, 9.

57. King and Luthuli exchanged letters from time to time, and each considered the other a major influence on his life, thought, and methods. Luthuli once said that "the greatest inspiration to him was" King's book, *Stride toward Freedom* (1958), and King praised Luthuli, who was frequently under house arrest for standing "amid persecution, abuse, and oppression with a dignity and calmness of spirit seldom paralleled in human history." King mentioned Luthuli in his Nobel Peace Prize speech in 1964, and also in both of the major speeches he gave on South Africa in 1964 and 1965. King's 1965 speech, delivered at Hunter College in New York, carried the title of Luthuli's autobiography, *Let My People Go*, which came right out of the biblical tradition of the Exodus. King said at times that "If I lived in South Africa today in the midst of the white supremacy law in South Africa, I would join Chief Luthuli and others in saying break these unjust laws." King's relationship and friendship with Luthuli were forged in a common cause, since, as far as we know, they never really met each other. See G. McLeod Bryan to Martin Luther King, Jr., unpublished (10 October 1959), KCLA, 1–2; Martin Luther King, Jr. to Albert J. Luthuli, unpublished (8 December 1959), KCLA, 1; James W. King to Martin Luther King, Jr., unpublished (25 March 1964), KCLA, 1; Martin Luther King, Jr. to James W. King, unpublished (6 April 1964), KCLA, 1; Baldwin, *Beloved Community*, 1, 8, 17–21, 35–37, 46–47, 52–55, 62, 67, 78, 86, 91, 103, 155, and 169; and Washington, ed., *Testament*, 50.

58. Albert J. Luthuli to the Friends of the American Committee on Africa, unpublished (6 August 1962), KCLA, 1; "An Appeal for Action Against Apartheid," an ACOA Campaign Flyer (1962), ACOA Collection, Amistad Research Center, Tulane University, 1–4, and KCLA, 1–2.

59. *An Appeal*, 1–4; Houser, *No One Can Stop*, 266; and Baldwin, *Beloved Community*, 36–38.

60. Martin Luther King, Jr., "Statement Announcing Visit with Pope Paul VI," unpublished, KCLA, 1.

61. Martin Luther King, Jr., to His Holiness Pope Paul VI, unpublished (15 October 1964), KCLA, 1; "Martin Luther King to Meet with Pope," unpublished press release given by Barbara Suarez to the Associated Press, *New York Times*, United Press International, and *Atlanta Constitution*, 16 September 1964, KCLA, 1; and John J. Ansbro, *Martin Luther King, Jr.: Nonviolent Strategies and Tactics for Social Change* (Maryknoll, N.Y.: Orbis Books, 2000), 180.

62. "Conversation," 447.

63. Eugene Carson Blake to Dr. Martin Luther King, Jr., unpublished (18 July 1966), KCLA, 1; and Eugene Carson Blake and Others for the Conference on Church and Society of the World Council of Churches to Martin Luther King, Jr., unpublished (19 July 1966), KCLA, 1–2.

64. King, *Where Do We Go?*, 173.

65. King, *Trumpet*, 37–78; and Jim Douglass, "The Crucifixion of Martin Luther King," *The Other Side.* September-October 1996, 45.

66. King, *Where Do We Go?*, 177–179.

67. Drawing an analogy to the parable of Lazarus and Dives, King held that Africa had been "so long exploited and crushed by Western Civilization" that it had become "a beggar at Europe's doorstep." Martin Luther King, Jr., "Dives and Lazarus," unpublished sermon (10 March 1963), KCLA, 1–2.

68. Carson et al., eds., *King Papers*, VI, 174–176; and Martin Luther King, Jr., "Cooperative Competition, Noble Competition," unpublished typed version of a sermon (1948–1954), KCLA, 1–2.

69. Martin Luther King, Jr., "The Crisis of Civil Rights," unpublished speech, Chicago (10–12 July 1967), KCLA, 15–16; and King, *Where Do We Go?*, 177.

70. Martin Luther King, Jr., "The Quiet Conviction of Nonviolence," *The Mennonite*, 80, no. 1 (5 January 1965), 4.

71. Martin Luther King, Jr., "A Statement on America and World Problems," unpublished (1959–60), KCLA, 1–2.

72. Martin Luther King, Jr., "Press Conference and Statement on the Nobel Peace Prize," unpublished transcript, Forneby, Norway (9 December 1964), KCLA, 3; and Martin Luther King, Jr., "Statement Delivered at Stockholm Airport Arrival," Stockholm (12 December 1964), KCLA, 1.

73. King pointed out that "The pope's message and what [he] learned from [Scandinavian] countries have intensified my determination to press even more vigorously for a broad alliance of all forces—Negro and white—dedicated to the achievement of economic justice." See Martin Luther King, Jr., "Statement on Accepting the New York City Medallion," unpublished, New York (17 December 1964), KCLA, 3–4. Even as King praised the pope for his stance on world problems, he was known to be strongly critical of the Catholic Church and how it operated within the global Christian community. King once declared:

I am disturbed about Roman Catholicism. This church stands before the world with its pomp and power, insisting that it possesses the only truth. It incorporates an arrogance that becomes a dangerous spiritual arrogance. It stands with its noble Pope, who somehow rises to the miraculous heights of infallibility when he speaks *ex cathedra*. But I am disturbed about a person or an institution that claims infallibility in this world. I am disturbed about any church that refuses to cooperate with other churches under the pretense that it is the only true church. I must emphasize the fact that God is not a Roman Catholic, and that the boundless sweep of his revelation cannot be limited to the Vatican. Roman Catholicism must do a great deal to mend its ways.

See Carson and Holloran, eds., *Knock*, 30.

74. Blake and Others to King (19 July 1966), 1–2; and Blake to King (18 July 1966), 1; and Martin Luther King, Jr., "My Dream," *Chicago Defender*, 19–25 February 1966, 1.

75. Martin Luther King, Jr., "To Serve the Present Age," unpublished sermon (25 June 1967), KCLA, 2; Martin Luther King, Jr., "What are Your New Year's Resolutions?," unpublished sermon, New York (7 January 1968), KCLA, 2–3; and Washington, ed., *Testament*, 39–40.

76. Washington, ed., *Testament*, 39–40; King, "To Serve the Present Age," 2; Martin Luther King, Jr., "An Address," unpublished, delivered at the Fiftieth Anniversary of the Women's International League for Peace and Freedom, Philadelphia (15 October 1965), KCLA, 11; and Martin Luther King, Jr., "An Address," unpublished, delivered at the Synagogue Council of America (5 December 1965), KCLA, 11.

77. D. McDonald, Secretary to Dr. Martin Luther King, Jr., to Mr. G. Ramachandran, unpublished (20 December 1961), KCLA, 1.

78. Some churches and church leaders abroad actually recommended King for the Nobel Peace Prize. The Norwegian religious magazine *Varr Kirke* (Our Church) strongly supported the recommendation. See "Dr. King Given His Prize: Ceremony in Oslo," *London Times*, 11 December 1964, 10; and "Norwegian Magazine Urges Nobel Prize for Dr. King," *Newsletter: Southern Christian Leadership Conference*, 2, no. 8 (July-August 1964), 9.

79. Washington, ed., *Testament*, 275; "Dr. King Strengthens An Anti-War Coalition," *Detroit Free Press*, 6 April 1967, 6A; Martin Luther King, Jr., "Statement on Vietnam," unpublished, prepared for immediate release (5 October 1965), KCLA, 1–2; and Martin Luther King, Jr., "The Drum Major Instinct," unpublished version, delivered at the Ebenezer Baptist Church, Atlanta (4 February 1968), KCLA, 7.

80. Washington, ed., *Testament*, 239.

81. King, "What are Your New Year's Resolutions?," 3; and Washington, ed., *Testament*, 236 and 240.

82. But ultimately, King called upon persons in both the churches and the government, who would, as he put it, "champion the cause of peace from the perspectives of moral, religious and spiritual orientations." King, "Statement on Vietnam," 2.

83. "An Interview with Martin Luther King, Jr." (5 November 1964), 2.

84. "Hugh Downs Interview with Martin Luther King, Jr.," NBC "Today Show," 18 April 1966, unpublished, KCLA, 3; Martin Luther King, Jr., "Transformed

Nonconformist," unpublished sermon, Ebenezer Baptist Church, Atlanta (16 January 1966), KCLA, 8; King, "An Address," Synagogue Council of America, 5; and King, "Statement on Accepting the New York City Medallion," 4.

85. James A. Wechsler, "An Un-Patriot?," *New York Post*, 25 April 1967. In a statement that was touchingly prudent, King spoke in the most glowing terms about church involvement in the peace movement. See Martin Luther King, Jr., "The Other America," unpublished address, delivered at Local 1199, Salute to Freedom, Hunter College, New York City (10 March 1968), KCLA, 2.

86. "Martin Luther King, Jr. in Holland: An Interview," unpublished transcript (October 1964), KCLA, 1.

87. King, *Where Do We Go?*, 167.

88. King, "People to People," 3.

89. Martin Luther King, Jr., "East or West—God's Children," unpublished address, delivered in Berlin (13 September 1964), KCLA, 1.

90. King, "Religion and Redemption," 1–11; and Martin Luther King, Jr., "A Speech During the European Tour," unpublished (March 1966), KCLA, 1–10; and "Martin Luther King, Jr. in Holland," 1.

91. Kenneth L. Smith and Ira G. Zepp, Jr., *Search for the Beloved Community: The Thinking of Martin Luther King, Jr.* (Valley Forge, Pa.: Judson Press, 1998; originally published in 1974), 156; Baldwin, *Wounded*, 121–122 and 313; John H. Cartwright, "Foundations of the Beloved Community," *Debate and Understanding: A Semestral Review of Black Americans' Political, Economic, and Social Development*, 1, no. 3 (Semester 2, 1977), 171–176; and Rufus Burrow, Jr., *God and Human Dignity: The Personalism, Theology, and Ethics of Martin Luther King, Jr.* (Notre Dame, Ind.: University of Notre Dame Press, 2006), 169.

92. King, *Where Do We Go?*, 167–168.

93. There is no thorough examination of King in relation to inter-religious dialogue and cooperation, even by the most accomplished King scholars. Some attention is given to the subject in Lewis V. Baldwin and Amiri YaSin Al-Hadid, *Between Cross and Crescent: Christian and Muslim Perspectives on Malcolm and Martin* (Gainesville: University Press of Florida, 2002), 115–127.

94. I am indebted to John J. Thatamanil, who specializes in issues of inter-religious dialogue, for much of this idea. See John J. Thatamanil, "The Gandhi-King Encounter and Interreligious Dialogue," unpublished paper outline (2007), the author's files, 1; and A Personal Conversation with John J. Thatamanil, Vanderbilt University, Nashville, Tennessee, 20 March 2007.

95. King made this observation in a paper on Mithraism. See Clayborne Carson et al., eds., *The Papers of Martin Luther King, Jr., Volume I: Called to Serve, January 1929–June 1951* (Berkeley: University of California Press, 1992), 211.

96. Ibid., 281.

97. This point benefited from a reading of Thatamanil, "The Gandhi-King Encounter and Interreligious Dialogue," 7. Gandhi refused to abandon his own Hindu traditions and to convert to Christianity, for he concluded that the two religions shared many great truths, and that "to be a good Hindu also meant that" he "would be a good

Christian." See Robert Ellsberg, ed., *Gandhi on Christianity* (Maryknoll, N.Y.: Orbis Books, 1991), 12 and 14.

98. Carson et al., eds., *King Papers*, IV, 471–472; and Baldwin and Al-Hadid, *Cross and Crescent*, 116.

99. King to Fey (23 June 1962), 3.

100. King, *Where Do We Go?*, 96.

101. Carson et al., eds., *King Papers*, VI, 212.

102. Ibid., 185. At least in principle, King's model of the church was one of female inclusion, but the extent to which he sought to implement this in practical terms is open to question and/or debate.

103. Martin Luther King, Jr., "Sermon Notes and Outlines II," unpublished, The King Papers Project, 1.

104. King to Resnikoff (17 September 1961), 1.

105. Ibid., 1–2. For other statements by King in opposition to religious bigotry, see Martin Luther King, Jr., "An Address Before a Dinner Sponsored by the Episcopal Society for Cultural and Racial Unity," the 61st general Convention, Sheraton-Jefferson Hotel, St. Louis, Missouri (12 October 1964), KCLA, 7; Martin Luther King, Jr., "Why We are Here," unpublished speech, SCOPE Orientation (15 June 1965), KCLA, 2; and King to Fey (23 June 1962), 2–3.

106. Carson et al., eds., *King Papers*, VI, 87.

107. Clayborne Carson, ed., *The Autobiography of Martin Luther King, Jr.* (New York: Warner Books, 1998), 310; Carson et al., eds., *King Papers*, IV, 460; Leo Trepp, *Judaism: Development and Life*, Third Edition (Belmont, Calif.: Wadsworth, 1982), 127; and Rabbi Marc Schneier, *Shared Dreams: Martin Luther King, Jr. and the Jewish Community* (Woodstock, Vt.: Jewish Lights Publishing, 1999), 29–36.

108. Carson et al., eds., *King Papers*, IV, 460. King was careful to note that

> there is absolutely no anti-Semitism in the black community in the historic sense of anti-Semitism. Anti-Semitism historically has been based on two false, sick, evil assumptions. One was unfortunately perpetuated even by many Christians, all too many as a matter of fact, and that is the notion that the religion of Judaism is anathema. That was the first basis for anti-Semitism in the historic sense. . . .
>
> Second, a notion was perpetuated by a sick man like Hitler and others that the Jew is innately inferior. Now in these two senses, there is virtually no anti- Semitism in the black community. There is no philosophical anti-Semitism or anti-Semitism in the sense of the historic evils of anti-Semitism that have been with us all too long.

See Washington, ed., *Testament*, 668–670.

109. King, *Strength*, 27 and 29.

110. Carson et al., eds., *King Papers*, VI, 137.

111. King to Fey (23 June 1962), 3. On another occasion, King asserted that "It may now be that Mahatma Gandhi is God's appeal to this age, an age drifting to its doom. And that appeal is always in the form of a warning: 'He who lives by the sword, will

perish by the sword.'" See "Martin Luther King, Jr. on Gandhi," transcript of a recording, unpublished, WILD Sound, Atlanta (22 March 1959), KCLA, 10; and Clayborne Carson et al., eds., *The Papers of Martin Luther King, Jr., Volume V: Threshold of a New Decade, January 1959–December 1960* (Berkeley: University of California Press, 2005), 156.

112. King to Fey (23 June 1962), 3; "Martin Luther King, Jr. on Gandhi," 1–11; and Carson et al., eds., *King Papers*, V, 145–157.

113. Carson et al., eds., *King Papers*, VI, 113.

114. Because of his admiration for Gandhi and his methods, which owed much to both Hinduism and Jainism, King was seen by some white fundamentalists as gaining the support of "religious infidels" and as promoting heathenism. See Bill J. Leonard, "A Theology for Racism: Southern Fundamentalists and the Civil Rights Movement," in *Baptist History and Heritage*, 34, no. 1 (Winter 1999), 61 and 63.

115. King, *Strength*, 96; and Carson et al., eds., *King Papers*, VI, 146–147.

116. King actually spoke in terms of "the world house" as early as December 1964, when he received the Nobel Peace Prize. See King, "Nobel Lecture," 24; and King, "An Address" (15 October 1965), 6.

117. Again, in developing this sense of King's understanding of inter-religious dialogue, I benefited immensely from my conversation with John J. Thatamanil. See notes from A Personal Conversation with Thatamanil, 20 March 2007; and Thatamanil, "The Gandhi-King Encounter and Interreligious Dialogue," 1.

118. King, *Strength*, 141; and King, *Where Do We Go?*, 124.

119. Amanda Porterfield, *The Transformation of American Religion: The Story of a Late-Twentieth-Century Awakening* (New York: Oxford University Press, 2001), 102; and Avery Dulles, *Models of the Church* (Garden City, New York: Image Books, 1987), 155.

120. Convinced that "God is not a denominational God," King, with superb clarity, addressed the ways in which Protestants and Catholics could collaborate in carrying forward the mission and ministry of the whole church. See Carson et al., eds., *King Papers*, VI, 149; and Martin Luther King, Jr., "Remarks 'En Granslos Kval Pa Operan,'" Stockholm (31 March 1966), KCLA, 3. Robert McAfee Brown says that "If Martin Luther started a revolution in the sixteenth century that drove Catholics and Protestants apart, Martin Luther King, Jr., started a revolution in the twentieth century that is drawing them back together again." See Robert McAfee Brown, *The Ecumenical Revolution*, Revised Edition (Garden City, N.Y.: Doubleday, 1969), 407–408. Also quoted in Dulles, *Models*, 156.

121. Martin Luther King, Jr., "A Lecture," unpublished, delivered under the auspices of the Federation Protestante de France Mutualite, Paris (24 October 1965), KCLA, 12.

122. Unfortunately, church historians have had little to say about King's contribution to ecumenism as concrete action in the twentieth century. See Williston Walker et al., *A History of the Christian Church* (New York: Scribner's, 1985), 704; William G. McLoughlin and Robert N. Bellah, eds., *Religion in America* (Boston: Beacon Press, 1970), 357–358; Edwin Scott Gaustad, *A Religious History of America*, New Revised Edition (New York: HarperCollins, 1990), 331; and Ronald C. White, Jr., et al., *American Christianity: A Case Approach* (Grand Rapids, Mich.: William B. Eerdmans, 1986), 173–178.

123. Here King was speaking of unified struggle, or working toward common goals in a unified fashion. Having a great sense of the history of the church and its

struggles, he alluded to how the Jewish Christians had contributed to the division of the church by spending "all their time opposing Paul," or by majoring in that which "was wholly negative." See Martin Luther King, Jr., "Getting Caught in the Negative, the Peril of Emphasizing a Negative, Accentuating the Positive," unpublished sermon notes (1948–54), The King Papers Project, 1–2.

124. King, "Revolution and Redemption," 11.

125. This subject is examined in Schneier, *Shared Dreams*, 37–47.

126. Ibid., xii (preface).

127. For interesting and rather rich references to how "African American religions have encountered Jewish traditions, beliefs, and spaces," a discussion that highlights "how African American congregations have transformed synagogue paces into churches," see Yvonne Chireau and Nathaniel Deutsch, eds., *Black Zion: African American Religious Encounters with Judaism* (New York: Oxford University Press, 2000), 3–10.

128. Dr. Israel Goldstein, "Martin Luther King's Jewish Associations," *Jerusalem Post*, 22 October 1964, 3.

129. "Where are We Going: Human Rights in 1958?," a flyer circulated concerning the American Jewish Congress—Manhattan Divisions Joint Legislative Conference, New York (8 February 1958), The King Papers, Boston University, 1.

130. King, *Where Do We Go?*, 186; Baldwin, *Wounded*, 258; and Lewis V. Baldwin, "King's 'Triple Evils' Start with Racism," *Sunday Tennessean*, 8 February 1987, 1H and 3H.

131. King, "A Challenge to the Churches and Synagogues," 1–14; and Mathew Ahmann, ed., *Race: Challenge to Religion* (Chicago: Regnery, 1963), 55–71 and 155–169.

132. Martin Luther King, Jr., "An Address," Synagogue Council of America, 1–11.

133. King, "A Lecture," Federation Protestante, 12; King, "An Address," Synagogue Council of America," 2; and Baldwin and Al-Hadid, *Cross and Crescent*, 122.

134. Martin Luther King, Jr., "My Jewish Brother," *New York Amsterdam News*, 26 February 1966, 1.

135. George Houser to Julius Mueller, 18 September 1957, ACOA Collection, Tulane University, 1; and Baldwin, *Beloved Community*, 17.

136. "Liberals Bid U.S. Censure South Africa: ADA Petition Urges Envoy's Recall, Halt in Gold-Buying" *Baltimore Sun*, 17 April 1960, 1; "ADA Asks U.S. Protest on African Apartheid," *Sunday Star*, 17 April 1960; and "Liberals Urge Ambassador to South Africa Be Recalled for Consultation—Suspension of Gold Purchases," press release, Americans for Democratic Action, Washington, D.C., 15 April 1960, KCLA, 1–3.

137. *An Appeal for Action*, 1–4; and Baldwin, *Beloved Community*, 37–38.

138. See "Draft of a Statement on SCLC's Participation at a National Conference on New Politics Regarding Resolution on the Middle East," unpublished document (September 1967), KCLA, 1–2; Tom Jerriel and John Casserly, "Interview with Martin Luther King, Jr.," on "Issues and Answers," an ABC Radio and Television Program, unpublished transcript. 18 June 1967, KCLA, 13–14. This latter source also appeared as "International Evening: Martin Luther King, Jr. on 'Issues and Answers,'" *Publishers' Weekly*, 19 June 1967, 13–14. For important information on King's growing stance on

the Middle East crisis, see Schneier, *Shared Dreams*, 160–165 and 168–169; and Baldwin and Al-Hadid, *Cross and Crescent*, 344–345.

139. Martin Luther King, Jr., to Rabbi Seymour J. Cohen, unpublished (8 September 1965), KCLA, 1; and Rabbi Israel Miller to Martin Luther King, Jr., unpublished (11 November 1966), KCLA, 1–2.

140. Interestingly enough, when the Israeli delegation to the United Nations felt left out of a reception sponsored by the African and Asian delegations for President Tom Mboya of Kenya, who was visiting the United States, King was contacted about his thoughts. Naturally, he opposed all forms of discrimination based on race, ethnicity, and religion, but he, in an irenic spirit, often refused to comment on matters like the one involving the various U.N. delegations. See Isidore W. Ruskin to Martin Luther King, Jr., unpublished (30 November 1959), KCLA, 1–2.

141. Martin Luther King, Jr., to Rabbi Seymour J. Cohen, unpublished (28 December 1965), KCLA, 1–2; and "Synagogue Council to Award Judaism and World Peace Award to Martin Luther King, Jr.," *News: Synagogue Council of America* (1965), 1–2.

142. *Martin Luther King, Jr.: Speak on the War in Vietnam*, a pamphlet issued by Clergy and Laity Concerned (April 1967), 2–30; and Wechsler, "An Unpatriot." Largely because of the extent and power of King's witness for peace in the face of the threat of global conflict, Rabbi Abraham Heschel concluded that "Martin Luther King is a sign that God has not forsaken the United States of America. God has sent him to us. His presence is the hope of America. His mission is sacred, his leadership is of supreme importance to every one of us." See "Conversation with Martin Luther King," in *Conservative Judaism*, 22, no. 3 (Spring 1968), 1; and Washington, ed., *Testament*, 657–658.

143. "Cassius Clay (Muhammad Ali) and MLK Interviewed on SYNC Sound #146 (Roll #175), CBS 35557–7, Louisville, Kentucky, unpublished transcript (29 March 1967), KCLA, 1.

144. Martin Luther King, Jr. and Thich Nhat Hanh, "A Joint Statement," made under the auspices of the International Committee of Conscience on Vietnam, unpublished, Nyack, New York (1966), KCLA, 1–2; Porterfield, *Transformation*, 126; Diana L. Eck, *A New Religious America: How a "Christian Country" Has Now Become the World's Most Religiously Diverse Nation* (San Francisco: HarperCollins, 2001), 204; and Baldwin and Al-Hadid, *Cross and Crescent*, 121.

145. "Statement of the Venerable Nhat Hanh," unpublished, issued by the International Committee of Conscience on Vietnam and the Inter-Universities Committee for Debate on Foreign Policy, Nyack, New York (16 May 1966), KCLA, 1.

146. "Thich Nhat Hanh," *New Yorker*, 25 June 1966, 23.

147. Porterfield, *Transformation*, 126; and Eck, *Religious America*, 204.

148. An e-mail message from John Thatamanil to Lewis V. Baldwin, 12 March 2007, 1; and Thatamanil, "The Gandhi-King Encounter," 1–3.

149. Thatamanil convincingly concludes that "those of us who are committed to interreligious dialogue still have much to learn from Martin Luther King and especially Mahatma Gandhi," a thesis supported by much of this work. See Thatamanil, "The Gandhi-King Encounter," 1, 3, and 12; a personal conversation with Thatamanil, 20 March 2007; and an e-mail message from Thatamanil to Baldwin, 12 March 2007.

150. James R. Wood to Mr. L. F. Palmer, Jr., a letter dictated by Martin Luther King, Jr., unpublished (23 February 1961), KCLA, 2.

151. King, *Where Do We Go?*, 190–191; and Washington, ed., *Testament*, 242.

152. "King Interview" (5 November 1964), 1–2. King once asserted that because of the stress on love and peace in the world's great religions, they could all find meaning in Christmas and especially the celebration of the birth of Jesus Christ: "This is the kind of experience around which the whole world can experience a great unity. Even in the parts of the world that are not traditionally Christian, people know that in the majority of the world people are celebrating the birth of a man called the Son of God, who has come to bring Peace on Earth and Good Will toward all men." See "Interview with Martin Luther King, Jr.," unpublished, Radio Norway (December 1964), KCLA, 1.

153. "King Interview" (5 November 1964), 2.

154. Ibid., 3.

155. Much of this insight came through my conversation with John Thatamanil. See notes from a personal conversation with Thatamanil, 20 March 2007.

156. Roy Money to Lewis V. Baldwin (17 June 2001), unpublished, author's files (17 June 2001), 1–3. King clearly knew a lot about Asian religions and philosophy, including Buddhism, Hinduism, Confucianism, and Taoism, and one finds comments on these and other Asian traditions in King's writings. See Martin Luther King, Jr., "Speech at an SCLC Staff Retreat," unpublished, Penn Center, Frogmore, South Carolina (2 May 1967), KCLA, 12; and Carson et al., eds., *King Papers*, VI, 223–224, 293–294, and 350–351.

157. King, *Can't Wait*, 77.

158. Michael Cromartie and Irving Kristol, eds., *Disciples and Democracy: Religious Conservatives and the Future of American Politics* (Grand Rapids, Mich.: William B. Eerdmans, 1994), 107.

159. There are echoes of Leo Tolstoy in this comment. See Martin Luther King, Jr., "The Meaning of Hope," unpublished sermon, Dexter Avenue Baptist Church, Montgomery (10 December 1967), KCLA, 8.

160. King, "The Quiet Conviction," 4.

CHAPTER 6

1. "Roundup: Foreign Tributes to Dr. King," *The Christian Century*, 85, no.19 (8 May 1968), 629–630; William Bradford Huie, *He Slew the Dreamer: My Search, with James Earl Ray, for the Truth About the Murder of Martin Luther King* (New York: Delacorte Press, 1970), 207–212; Stephen E. Berk, *A Time to Heal: John Perkins, Community Development, and Racial Reconciliation* (Grand Rapids, Mich.: Baker Book House Company, 1997), 150 and 195; and Lewis V. Baldwin et al., *The Legacy of Martin Luther King, Jr.: The Boundaries of Law, Politics, and Religion* (Notre Dame, Ind.: University of Notre Dame Press, 2002), 101–102.

2. Barndt has spoken with startling clarity about the meaning of King's life and death for the church and society as a whole. He linked the images of Jesus' crucifixion and King's assassination in an interview on a film presentation called, "Martin's

Lament: Religion and Race in America." Also see Joseph Barndt, *Dismantling Racism: The Continuing Challenge to White America* (Minneapolis: Augsburg Fortress Press, 1991), 8, 13–14, 59–60, and 65; and James Lawson, "God Still Speaks Through MLK Works," *The Tennessean*, 4 April 2008, 12A.

3. Gerald Miller, "Pope's Pal Mass Deplores Slaying," *Atlanta Constitution*, 8 April 1968, 11; and "Roundup," 629–630. Jim Douglass observes: "And like Jesus, King's choice of nonviolence as the way of life led to crucifixion." See Jim Douglass, "The Crucifixion of Martin Luther King," *The Other Side*, September/October 1996, 42.

4. Much of this idea came from Walter E. Fluker, "A Review of Lewis V. Baldwin's *Who Is Their God? Images of the Church in the Mind of Martin Luther King, Jr.*," unpublished manuscript (3 December 2007), 1.

5. See Gayraud S. Wilmore, *Black Religion and Black Radicalism: An Interpretation of the Religious History of African Americans*, Third Edition (Maryknoll, N.Y.: Orbis Books, 1998), 204.

6. Carlyle F. Stewart, *African American Church Growth: Twelve Principles of Prophetic Ministry* (Nashville: Abingdon Press, 1994), 36 and 39–150.

7. Robert C. Smith, *We Have No Leaders: African Americans in the Post-Civil Rights Era* (Albany: State University of New York Press, 1996), xvi (preface). Before Smith's work emerged, Clarence James had made essentially some of the same conclusions, but with a special focus on our failure to sustain a pattern of strong, energetic, and active young leadership, thus breaking with that era that began with King and the movement in the 1950s and 1960s. See Clarence James, "Leadership Development Patterns in the African-American Community, 1955–1979," unpublished essay, 10.

8. Roger D. Hatch, *Beyond Opportunity: Jesse Jackson's Vision for America* (Philadelphia: Fortress Press, 1988), 3.

9. Clarence Taylor, "The Political Dilemma of the Reverend Al Sharpton," in Felton O. Best, ed., *Black Religious Leadership from the Slave Community to the Million Man March* (Lewiston, N.Y.: Edwin Mellen Press, 1998), 237–238; and Nick Charles, "The New Al Sharpton: New York City's Preacher-Activist is Making a Respectable Run at Politics," *Emerge: Black America's Newsmagazine*, 6, no.2 (November 1994), 34–38.

10. Berk, *A Time to Heal*, 73; Baldwin et al., *Legacy*, 102–103; Lewis V. Baldwin, "The Perversion of Public Religion," *Orbis*, 5, no.7 (April 2006), 12–13; Richard N. Ostling et al., "Jerry Falwell's Crusade: Fundamentalist Legions Seek to Remake Church and Society," *Time*, 126, no.9 (2 September 1985), 48–52, 55, and 57; and Gabriel Fackre, *The Religious Right and Christian Faith* (Grand Rapids, Mich.: William B. Eerdmans, 1983), 1–3.

11. Fackre, *Religious Right*, 1–3; Ostling, "Falwell's Crusade," 48–52, 55, and 57; and Robert Ajemian, "Jerry Falwell Spreads the Word: The Fundamentalist Leader Wages Political War on Immorality," *Time*, 126, no.9 (2 September 1985), 58–59 and 61. Interestingly enough, King, in opposition to Alabama's Governor George Wallace and other right-wingers, supported the Supreme Court's ban on school prayer in 1965, noting that "I endorse" the court's decision because "I think it was correct." King went on to say:

Contrary to what many have said, it sought to outlaw neither prayer nor belief in God. In a pluralistic society such as ours, who is to determine what prayer should be spoken, and by whom? Legally, constitutionally or otherwise, the state certainly has no such right. I am strongly opposed to the efforts that have been made to nullify the decision. They have been motivated, I think, by little more than the wish to harass the Supreme Court. When I saw brother Wallace going up to Washington to testify against the decision at the congressional hearings, it only strengthened my conviction that the decision was right.

See James M. Washington, ed., *A Testament of Hope: The Essential Writings and Speeches of Martin Luther King, Jr.* (New York: HarperCollins, 1986), 373.

12. Baldwin et al., *Legacy*, 156; and John Blake, "Modern Black Church Shuns King's Message," ttp://www.cnn.com/2008/US/04/06mlk.role.church?iref=mpstoryview.

13. David T. Morgan, *The New Crusades, the New Holy Land: Conflict in the Southern Baptist Convention, 1969–1991* (Tuscaloosa: University of Alabama Press, 1996), 116; Oran P. Smith, *The Rise of Baptist Republicanism* (New York: New York University Press, 1997), 222; Jerry Sutton, *The Baptist Reformation: The Conservative Resurgence in the Southern Baptist Convention* (Nashville: Boardman & Holman Publishers, 2000), 320–321; Rufus Burrow, Jr., *God and Human Dignity: The Personalism, Theology, and Ethics of Martin Luther King, Jr.* (Notre Dame, Ind.: University of Notre Dame Press, 2006), 11; and Michael Eric Dyson, *I May Not Get There with You: The True Martin Luther King, Jr.* (New York: Simon & Schuster, 2000), xv–xvi (preface).

14. Baldwin et al., *Legacy*, 102–103; Flo Conway and Jim Siegelman, *Holy Terror: The Fundamentalist War on America's Freedoms in Religion, Politics and Our Private Lives* (New York: Dell Publishing Company, 1984), 85–87; John J. Ansbro, *Martin Luther King, Jr.: Nonviolent Strategies and Tactics for Social Change* (Lanham, Md.: Madison Books, 2000), 315 n.115; Daniel C. Maguire, *The New Subversives: Anti-Americanism of the Religious Right* (New York: Continuum, 1982), 40; George Marsden, ed., *Evangelicalism and Modern America* (Grand Rapids, Mich.: William B. Eerdmans, 1984), 60; Fackre, *Religious Right*, 28; and Richard J. Neuhaus and Michael Cromartie, eds., *Piety and Politics: Evangelicals and Fundamentalists Confront the World* (Washington, D.C.: Ethics and Public Policy Center, 1976), 310.

15. James D. Hunter, *Culture Wars: The Struggle to Define America* (New York: Basic Books, 1991), 17; Baldwin et al., *Legacy*, 103; and Fackre, *Religious Right*, 28.

16. Dyson, *May Not Get There*, xv (preface); Baldwin et al., *Legacy*, 104; and Obery M. Hendricks, Jr., "The Domestication of Martin Luther King, Jr.," *A.M.E. Church Review*, April-June 1998, 53–54.

17. Claims such as this about King came from representatives of the National Black Republican Association (NBRA), and they were quickly refuted by King associates such as Reverend Joseph Lowery and Congressman John Lewis (D-Ga.), who viewed them as an "insult" to King's memory and legacy. See Darryl Fears, "Controversial Ad Links MLK, GOP: Assertion About Civil Rights Leader Angers Liberals—and Conservatives," *Washington Post*, 19 October 2006, A4; and Carolyn

Garris, "Martin Luther King's Conservative Legacy," WebMemo #961, The Heritage Foundation (12 January 2006), 1–3.

18. Vincent Harding, *Martin Luther King: The Inconvenient Hero* (Maryknoll, N.Y.: Orbis Books, 2008), ix.

19. Andy Spillers, "At Least, Pope Benedict Blesses America," *The Tennessean*, 24 April 2008, 21A; Randall C. Bailey, "What's Right with Wright?" unpublished paper, the Interdenominational Theological Center, Atlanta, Georgia (March 2008), 1–2; Martin E. Marty, "Prophet and Pastor," *Chronicle Review*, 54, no.30 (11 April 2008), B1; Percy Johnson, "In Support of Our Brother Jeremiah: Reclaiming the Prophetic Voice Within the African American Pulpit and Church," unpublished paper, the author's files, Atlanta, Georgia (March 2008), 1–20; and Eugene Robinson, "Wright is Wrong: Black Church not Monolith," *Birmingham News*, 30 April 2008, 9A.

20. "Voters Sift through a Pastor's Words," *The Tennessean*, 6 May 2008, 8A; Robinson, "Wright is Wrong," 9A; Johnson, "Our Brother," 1–20; Bailey, "What's Right with Wright?" 1–2; and Marty, "Prophet and Pastor," B1.

21. Peter W. Williams, *America's Religions: From Their Origins to the Twenty-First Century* (Urbana and Chicago: University of Illinois Press, 2002), 384–385; Roderick Townley, "Video Evangelists: The Survivors," *TV Guide*, 35, no.33 (15 August 1987), 4–7; Andrew M. Greeley, "In Defense of TV Evangelism," *TV Guide*, 26, no.26 (9 July 1988), 5–7; Michael Horton, ed., *The Agony of Deceit: What Some TV Preachers are Really Teaching* (Chicago: Moody Press, 1990), 21–251; and Baldwin, "Perversion," 12–13 and 18.

22. The definition of mega church, especially from the standpoint of sheer numbers, varies in the scholarship on the subject, with some scholars meaning at least 2,000 and others at least 5,000 members. See Anthony B. Pinn, *The Black Church in the Post-Civil Rights Era* (Maryknoll, N.Y.: Orbis Books, 2002), 135–139; Charles E. Swann, "Religious Broadcasting," in Samuel S. Hill et al., eds., *The New Encyclopedia of Southern Culture* (Chapel Hill: University of North Carolina Press, 2006), 43; Luisa Kroll, "Megachurches, Megabusinesses," *Christian Capitalism*, 9 September 2003; and Maynard Eaton, "Bishop T. D. Jakes Discusses Mega-Churches," *Sacramento Observer*, 42, no. 40 (22–28 September 2005), C1.

23. Swann, "Religious Broadcasting," 43.

24. Kroll, "Megachurches"; Eaton, "Jakes Discusses," C1; Adelle M. Banks, "Black Megachurches: Serving the Soul of a Rising Middle Class," *San Antonio Express-News*, 17 August 1996, 1; Adelle M. Banks, "Worship Service—Black Megachurches Built on Need for Larger Spiritual Homes," *Chicago Tribune*, 18 August 1996, 5Q; John Blake, "Pastors Choose Sides Over Direction of Black Church," *Atlanta Journal-Constitution*, 15 February 2005, 1A; Jasmyn Connick, "Pimpin Ain't Easy: The New Face of Today's Black Church," *Jacksonville Free Press*, 19, no.40 (20–26 October 2005), 4; Christopher Davis, "With Corporate Approach, Evangelistic Churches Prosper, Study Finds," *University of Florida News* (2 October 2000); Ray Waddle, "Megachurches Arise from Death-of-God Theology's Ashes," *The Tennessean*, 2 April 2005, 3B; Pinn, *The Black Church in the Post-Civil Rights Era*, 133–139; Paula L. McGee, "The New Black Church: 'I Bling Because I'm Happy'," unpublished paper (n.d.), the author's files, 1–24; and

Paula L. McGee, "Pastor or CEO? The New Black Church Leaders," *NBV: The National Baptist Voice*, 5, no.3 (Summer 2006), 64–65.

25. Connick, "Pimpin," 4; Blake, "Pastors Choose," 1A; and Baldwin, "Perversion," 12–13 and 18.

26. Connick, "Pimpin," 4; Blake, ""Pastors Choose," 1A; Banks, "Worship," 5Q; Banks, "Black Megachurches," 1; Baldwin, "Perversion," 12–13 and 18; Eaton, "Jakes Discusses," C1; Kroll, "Megachurches"; John Blake, "Long Not Welcome by All at Seminary: Graduation Invite Provokes Protests," *Atlanta Journal-Constitution*, 5 May 2006; "Our Opinion: The Sin of False Profits—Bishop Eddie Long Shouldn't Count Himself Among the Needy that His Charity was Created to Help," *Atlanta Journal-Constitution*, 30 August 2005; "Poll Shows Americans Split Over Role of Religion in Politics," *Church & State*, 59, no.9 (October 2006), 14; and Robert M. Franklin, *Crisis in the Village: Restoring Hope in African American Communities* (Minneapolis: Fortress Press, 2007), 110–111.

27. Ansbro, *King*, 315 n.115; and Baldwin et al., eds., *Legacy*, 102–103.

28. Rick Warren, "Myths of the Modern Mega-Church," Event Transcript, The Forum on Religion & Public Life, Key West, Florida (23 May 2005), 31.

29. Sridhar Pappu, "The Preacher," *Atlantic Monthly*, March 2006, 92 and 96.

30. "Our Opinion"; Blake, "Long Not Welcome"; Darryl Fears, "King Funeral Site Reflects Changes in Black America," *Washington Post*, 7 February 2006, A1; Earl Ofari Hutchison, "King Would Not Have Marched Against Gay Marriage," *San Francisco Chronicle*, 14 December 2004; and Horace I. Griffin, *Their Own Receive Them Not: African American Lesbians & Gays in Black Churches* (Cleveland: Pilgrim Press, 2006), 88 and 204.

31. Blake, "Pastors Choose," 1A; and Pinn, *Black Church*, 136–139.

32. Blake, "Modern Black Church," 1.

33. Franklin, *Crisis*, 110–111.

34. C. Eric Lincoln and Lawrence H. Mamiya, *The Black Church in the African American Experience* (Durham, N.C.: Duke University Press, 1990), 240–251.

35. In this regard, mega churches today are perhaps as instrumental as Reverdy C. Ransom's Institutional AME Church in Chicago, H. H. Proctor's First Congregational Church in Atlanta, L. K. Williams's Olivet Baptist Church in Chicago, and Adam Clayton Powell, Sr.'s Abyssinian Baptist Church in New York, which, in the early decades of the twentieth century, "became, in effect, social welfare agencies serving a broad spectrum of the needs of the burgeoning urban populations." In 1919, Williams's church had a membership of 8,743, and Powell's later reported 14,000, which means that these were among black America's first mega churches. See Wilmore, *Black Religion*, 190.

36. Faussett and Jarvie, "Funeral Site."

37. Eaton, "Jakes Discusses," C1; and McGee, "Pastor or CEO?" 64–65.

38. Blake, "Modern Black Church," 2.

39. The issues raised here are painfully exposed in Lincoln and Mamiya, *Black Church*, 309–345.

40. Lewis V. Baldwin, "Revisioning the Church: Martin Luther King, Jr. as a Model for Reflection," *Theology Today*, 65, no.1 (April 2008), 26–40; and Dale P.

Andrews, "Global Conflict and the Preaching Tradition of Martin Luther King, Jr.," *The Review of Faith and International Affairs*, 6, no.1 (Spring 2008), 61–63.

41. Baldwin, "Revisioning," 26–40.

42. Martin Luther King, Jr., "Address at the Southern Association of Political Scientists," unpublished (13 November 1964), The Library and Archives of the Martin Luther King, Jr. Center for Nonviolent Social Change, Inc. (KCLA), Atlanta, Georgia, 1–2.

43. Maguire, *Subversives*, 40.

44. Ibid., 39.

45. Ibid., 42.

46. Martin Luther King, Jr., "Transformed Nonconformist," an unpublished sermon delivered at the Ebenezer Baptist Church, Atlanta, Georgia (16 January 1966), KCLA, 4–5.

47. Martin Luther King, Jr., *Strength to Love* (Philadelphia: Fortress Press, 1981; originally published in 1963), 59.

48. Martin Luther King, Jr., "A Speech," unpublished version, delivered to the Mississippi Leaders on the Washington Campaign, St. Thomas AME Church, Birmingham, Alabama (15 February 1968), KCLA, 9.

49. Some mega-church preachers, like Eddie Long and Creflo Dollar, have actually claimed that Jesus was rich, thus challenging the view, advanced in liberation theologies and in the black-church tradition, that Jesus became poor and identified with the oppressed and outcast. Obviously, the stress on "the rich Jesus" is designed to sanction the lavish and/or extravagant lifestyle, which King saw as unbecoming for a religious and/or moral leader, to say the least. See Clayborne Carson and Peter Holloran, eds., *A Knock at Midnight: Inspiration from the Great Sermons of Reverend Martin Luther King, Jr.* (New York: Warner Books, 1998), 183; and McGee, "Pastor or CEO?" 64–65. For interesting insights on how the American churches have raised and spent money on clergy and for other purposes from colonial to contemporary times, see James Hudnut-Beumler, *In Pursuit of the Almighty's Dollar: A History of Money and American Protestantism* (Chapel Hill: University of North Carolina Press, 2007), 1–288.

50. Eddie Long reflects much of this spirit when he, referring to his New Birth Missionary Baptist Church, declares: "We're not just a church, we're an international corporation. We're not just a bumbling bunch of preachers who can't talk and all we're doing is baptizing babies. I deal with the White House. I deal with Tony Blair. I deal with presidents around this world. I pastor a multimillion-dollar congregation." See Connick, "Pimpin," 4.

51. See Martin Luther King, Jr., "Dives and Lazarus," unpublished sermon, Atlanta, Georgia (10 March 1963), KCLA, 8.

52. See Clayborne Carson et al., eds., *The Papers of Martin Luther King, Jr., Volume III: Birth of a New Age, December 1955–December 1956* (Berkeley: University of California Press, 1997), 461; and Washington, ed., *Testament*, 371.

53. King, "Dives and Lazarus," 8; Carson and Holloran, eds., *Knock*, 183–186; and Washington, ed., *Testament*, 371–372.

54. Blake, "Modern Black Church," 2–3.

55. Blake, "Pastors Choose," 1A.

56. King said as much and more as early as the Montgomery bus boycott. See Martin Luther King, Jr., *Stride toward Freedom: The Montgomery Story* (New York: Harper & Row, 1958), 35.

57. "The Souls of Black Folk," *Savoy*, April-May 2005, 72–73.

58. Neela Banerjee, "More Black Clergy Embracing GOP Ideals, Creating Division," *The Tennessean*, 6 March 2005, 17A.

59. Strangely enough, the march led by Long and Bernice King in December 2004 began at the King Center in Atlanta, and they claimed that their protest honored Dr. King's legacy. See Hutchison, "King Would Not Have Marched Against Gay Marriage"; Banerjee, "More Black Clergy Embracing GOP Ideals," 17A; and "The Souls," 74.

60. Karin Miller, "Southern Baptists Battle Gay Rights: Goal is Amendment to Define Marriage for Man, Woman Only," *The Tennessean*, 5 November 2003, 1A.

61. Hutchison, "King Would Not Have Marched"; Fears, "King Funeral Site," A1; Blake, "Pastors Choose," 1A; and Griffin, *Their Own*, 88–89.

62. "The Souls," 74; and Darryl Fears, "Coretta Scott King's Legacy Celebrated in Final Farewell," *Washington Post*, 8 February 2006, A1.

63. Kimberly Blaker has treated this kind of "extremism" in brilliant terms in her edited volume. See Kimberly Blaker, ed., *The Fundamentals of Extremism: The Christian Right in America* (New Boston, Mich.: New Boston Books, 2003); Brian Lewis, "Criticism of Christian Right Short on Objectivity, Documentation," *The Tennessean*, 5 July 2003, 3B; and Stephanie Simon, "Evangelicals Claim Right to Intolerance," *The Tennessean*, 23 April 2006, 17A and 19A.

64. Joe Garofoli, "Move is On to Allow Preaching of Politics from the Pulpit," *The Tennessean*, 22 May 2005, 26A.

65. Hunter, *Culture Wars*, 17 and 49–50; and Frances Meeker, "Police on Alert for Abortion Foe," *Nashville Banner*, Nashville, Tennessee (1 June 1995), A1–2.

66. DeWayne Wickham, "Be Scared of What Robertson Could Unleash," *The Tennessean*, 26 August 2005, 11A; Jeannine F. Hunter, "In the News: Robertson's Remarks Stun Religious Leaders," *The Tennessean*, 27 August 2005, 3B; Christopher Toothhaker, "Venezuela Assails Robertson's Call to 'Take Out' Its President," *The Tennessean*, 24 August 2005, 5A; Leonard Pitts, "'Rev. Ridiculous' Preys on Dover, Pa.," *The Tennessean*, 16 November 2005, 15A; and "Robertson Apologizes for Assassination Remarks," *The Tennessean*, 25 August 2005, 5A.

67. Natalia Mielczarek, "Anti-Gay Activists to Picket Service at Post: Kansans Won't Be Welcome at Fort Campbell," *The Tennessean*, 3 February 2006, 3B; Leon Alligood, "Kansas Church Says Troop Deaths are God's Punishment for U.S. Tolerance of Gays," *The Tennessean*, 9 February 2006, 1B; Leon Pitts, "Pastor Phelps May Be What He Hates: Gay," *The Tennessean*, 3 March 2006, 11A; Jenny Jarvie, "Pastors, Theologians Address Homophobia in Black Churches," *The Tennessean*, 21 January 2006, 16A; and Brian Lewis, "Both Sides Should be Gracious in Debate Over Gay Rights," *The Tennessean*, 24 January 2004, 3B.

68. Martin Luther King, Jr., *Why We Can't Wait* (New York: New American Library, 1964), 88–89.

69. King, "Address at the Southern," 1–2.

70. "The Souls," 72.

71. Ibid.; and Eaton, "Jakes Discusses," C1.

72. "The Souls," 72.

73. "Views on Implementing Faith-Based Initiative Clash," *The Tennessean*, 4 September 2002, 13A; and Linda Bryant, "Churches Reaching Out to Needy through Faith-Based Corporations," *The Tennessean*, 2 August 2002, 2M.

74. Eaton, "Jakes Discusses," C1. One journalist has reported that "Jakes is without political affiliation, and thus has the ability to straddle both Left and Right ('I've never seen an eagle that can soar on one wing', he likes to point out)." While this may hold some truth, Jakes' appearance at the White House could suggest a closer relationship with Bush and the Republican Party than the popular preacher is willing to acknowledge in a public forum. See Pappu, "Preacher," 92.

75. "The Souls," 74; and Connick, "Pimpin'," 4.

76. "The Souls," 74.

77. Jeff O. Carr, "Should We Kill the Preachers: How Negro Ministers Destroy the Legacy of Dr. King and Make a Mockery of Jesus the Christ," *The Third Eye*, January 2001, 9–14. There has long been the conviction in the African American community that the servant of God cannot sit at Pharaoh's table and be a prophet at the same time. The wedding of biblical principles and practical wisdom is quite evident here.

78. Andrews, "Global Conflict," 61.

79. "Our Opinion"; Blake, "Long Not Welcome"; Fears, "King Funeral Site," A1; Ofari, "King Would Not Have Marched"; Griffin, *Their Own*, 88 and 204; and Brentin Mock, "Face Right," *Intelligence Report: The Southern Poverty Law Center*, 125 (Spring 2007), 27.

80. King, *Can't Wait*, 92; and Washington, ed., *Testament*, 501.

81. Blake, "Pastors Choose," 1A; and King, *Strength*, 30.

82. In a statement that seems to minimize the importance of clergy outspokenness on controversial matters, T. D. Jakes recently observed: "In years past the idea of a strong pastor in the community was a pastor who talked the most, who challenged the powers that be. But today we are not measured by how loud we talk; we are measured by how much we do." This comment actually amounts to a subtle denial of what King called prophetic ministry, for it suggests that the "powers that be" and/or structural evil should not be challenged by persons who claim a call from God to minister to the world. See Eaton, "Jakes Discusses," C1.

83. This is obvious from even a casual reading of King's "A Christmas Sermon on Peace." See Martin Luther King, Jr., *The Trumpet of Conscience* (San Francisco: Harper & Row, 1968), 67–78.

84. Baldwin, "Perversion," 12–13 and 18.

85. Excerpts from Religion Programming with Eddie Long, Harry Jackson, Bernice A. King, Joseph E. Lowery, Steven Green, Elizabeth Omilami, Dr. Gloria Ward, and Robert Graetz, Trinity Broadcasting Network (TBN), www.tbn.org (23 April 2008).

86. This is the point that Vincent Harding and Michael Dyson seem to have in mind when they speak of freezing King's legacy, distorting his memory, or trapping him in romantic images. See Harding, *Martin Luther King, Jr.*, vii (introduction); and Dyson, *I May Not Get There*, xv–xvi (preface).

87. Martin Luther King, Jr., "Speech at an SCLC Staff Retreat," unpublished, Penn Center, Frogmore, South Carolina (2 May 1967), KCLA, 32.

88. This view was set forth to some extent by William Ramsay a few years after King's assassination, and his claim that Christians can learn from King's example is still valid. William M. Ramsay, *Four Modern Prophets: Walter Rauschenbusch, Martin Luther King, Jr., Gustavo Gutierrez, Rosemary Radford Ruether* (Atlanta: John Knox Press, 1973), 1–7 and 29–49.

89. I am indebted to Peter Paris for much of this idea. However, he seems to locate the prophetic tradition that produced King primarily "in antebellum opposition to slavery," though he does not ignore scripture and the traditions of the early church. See Peter J. Paris, "The Bible and the Black Churches," in Ernest R. Sandeen, ed., *The Bible and Social Reform* (Philadelphia: Fortress Press, 1982), 140–144.

90. Martin Luther King, Jr., *Where Do We Go from Here: Chaos or Community?* (Boston: Beacon Press, 1968), 177–178; and Washington, ed., *Testament*, 231–244.

91. This is substantiated by even a cursory reading of King's many sermons on the message of Jesus and its challenge to the church. See Carson and Holloran, eds., *Knock*, 105–115; and King, *Strength*, 9–55.

92. "Southern Baptist Resolution Supports Death Penalty," *The Tennessean*, 16 June 2000, 14A.

93. King, *Can't Wait*, 110; King, *Where Do We Go?* 183; and Martin Luther King, Jr., *The Measure of a Man* (Philadelphia: Fortress Press, 1988; originally published in 1959), 18.

94. Some religious institutions known for their racist and segregated practices in the King era are now recruiting blacks, chief among which are Bob Jones University and the Southern Baptist Convention, which constitutes much of the electronic church and media ministries. But these institutions' opposition to affirmative action, reparations, and other policies for black uplift suggests that their attitudes toward race and the need to address racism have not shifted very much. See "Bob Jones Recruits Minorities," *The Tennessean*, 15 February 2002, 7A; Ray Waddle, "SBC Seeks to Increase Minority Membership," *The Tennessean*, 12 January 1987, 1A and 8A; Brian Lewis, "Southern Baptists Reaching Out to Blacks," *The Tennessean*, 7 July 2003, 4B; Colleen McCain Nelson, "Christians Flocking to Religious Media," *Dallas Morning News*, 5 June 2005, 1A and 16A; and Randy Gardner, "GOP Has Right View on Affirmative Action: Letter to the Editor," *The Tennessean*, 24 January 2003, 18A.

95. Susy Buchanan, "Deadly Force," *Intelligence Report of the Southern Poverty Law Center*, 123 (Fall 2006), 13–14; and Brentin Mock, "Smokescreen: Activists Say a Black Anti-Immigration Movement is Gathering Steam," *Intelligence Report of the Southern Poverty Law Center*, 123 (Fall 2006), 18–24.

96. Bill Nichols, "Powell Will Not Attend U.N.'s Conference on Racism," *USA Today*, 27 August 2001, 13A; and "U. S. Will Boycott Racism Meeting," *The Tennessean*, 19 April 2009, 4A. Racism as a global phenomenon has gotten much attention in recent decades, beginning with King's own assault on the problem more than four decades ago. See King, *Where Do We Go?* 173–174; Anthony Arnove, "Racism Fuels the Iraqi Sanctions: An Interview with James Lawson," *Fellowship*, 66, nos. 9–10 (September/October 2000), 6–8; and Ferdinand Protzman, "A Neo-Nazi Powder Keg Blows," *The Tennessean*, 6 September 1992, 2D.

97. King, *Where Do We Go?* 173–174.

98. Clayborne Carson et al., eds., *The Papers of Martin Luther King, Jr., Volume VI: Advocate of the Social Gospel, September 1948–March 1963* (Berkeley: University of California Press, 2007), 212.

99. "Baptists Debate Proposal on Service of Female Pastors: Denomination's Convention Gets Under Way Today," *The Tennessean*, 13 June 2000, 10A; "Southern Baptists Debate Men-Only Clergy Statement," *The Tennessean*, 13 June 2000, 2A and 10A; "Baptists Risk Division Over Women's Role: Pastor Defined as Job for Men," *The Tennessean*, 15 June 2000, 1A–2A; Monica Bryant, "Issue of Female Preachers Divides Baptist Churches," *The Tennessean*, 28 August 2002, 3M; Jim Abrams, "Equal Rights Amendment Stirs Emotion," *The Tennessean*, 4 April 2007, 4A; George Will, "Left Again Wants to Force-Feed Us the Equal Rights Amendment," *The Tennessean*, 4 April 2007, 15A; "Female Bishops to Be Debated," *The Tennessean*, 6 February 2006, 7A; "Push Renewed to Accelerate Women's Rights Worldwide," *The Tennessean*, 4 June 2000, 2A; "U.N. Delegates Struggle with Women's Rights," *The Tennessean*, 10 June 2000, 4A; "Jewish Women Pray Aloud at Wall, Defying Israeli Band," *The Tennessean*, 5 June 2000, 3A; "U.N. Conference Fends Off Efforts to Curb Women's Rights," *The Tennessean*, 11 June 2000, 4A; "Debates Within Islam," *USA Today*, 20 November 2006, 20A; Lisa Anderson, "Service Runs Counter to Muslim Tradition: Scholar's Point is that Men, Women Equal," *The Tennessean*, 2 April 2005, 3B; and Diaa Hadid, "Women of Hamas Make a Play for More Power," *The Tennessean*, 25 November 2006, 15A.

100. Carson et al., eds., *King Papers*, III, 378–379.

101. Lewis V. Baldwin and Amiri YaSin Al-Hadid, *Between Cross and Crescent: Christian and Muslim Perspectives on Malcolm and Martin* (Gainesville: University Press of Florida, 2002), 187–190.

102. Much of the scholarship holds that King was indeed sexist, but Rufus Burrow suggests that the civil rights leader would have "broadened his liberation project to include women's rights" had he "lived into the 1970s and beyond," mainly because he had a nuanced and flexible mind, coupled with "a profound capacity and willingness to broaden his moral field" to include the oppressed generally. See Burrow, *God and Human Dignity*, 152–153.

103. Rachel Zoll, "Lutherans Spurn Gay Clergy Compromise," *The Tennessean*, 13 August 2005, 13A; Laurie Goodstein, "Episcopal Congregations to Cut Ties with Church," *The Tennessean*, 17 December 2006, 11A; Maggie Gallagher, "Black Christians Step Up to Say No," *The Tennessean*, 14 August 2003, 15A; Brian Lewis, "Diocese Leader Won't Recognize Gay Bishop, Priests Say," *The Tennessean*, 20 November 2003, 1B; Chris Jones, "Local Pastors Torn by Ruling to Defrock Gay Minister: United Methodist Church Council Decides 2004 Philadelphia Case," *The Tennessean*, 1 November 2005, 1B-2B; Anita Wadhwani, "Priest: Black Churches Ignore Gay Issues—His Book Likens Homophobia to Racism," *The Tennessean*, 23 January 2007, pp. 1B and 4B; Rachel Zoll, "Split with Parent Church Looms for Episcopalians: Tennessee Conservatives Laud Ultimatum on Gays," *The Tennessean*, 23 February 2007, 11–12A; Rachel Zoll, "Bishops Ask States Not to Recognize Same-Sex Marriage," *The Tennessean*, 13 November 2003, 11A; "Episcopals Divided on Same-Sex Union," *The*

Commercial Appeal, 19 July 2003; "Evangelicals Call for Split," *The Tennessean*, 7 May 2004, 8A; and Errin Haines, "United Church of Christ Set to Consider Gay Marriage," *Clarion Ledger*, 2 July 2005, 3E.

104. Rachel Zoll, "Anglicans Address Gay Issue: Leaders Meet to Work on Preventing Breakup," *The Tennessean*, 15 October 2003, 6A; "Church Cut Ties Over Bishop," *The Tennessean*, 18 November 2003, 3A; Emling, "Anglican Leaders Rebuke U.S. Church on Gay Bishop Issue," 8A; Cheryl Wittenauer, "African Lesbian Fears for Safety, Seeks U.S. Asylum," *The Tennessean*, 1 April 2007, 12A; Alexandra Zavis, "South Africa's Highest Court Rules in Favor of Gay Marriages," *The Tennessean*, 2 December 2005, 6A; Rachel Zoll, "Episcopalians Who Oppose Gay Bishop to Form Network," *The Tennessean*, 18 October 2003, 8A; Ian Fisher and Laurie Goodstein, "Catholic Church May Ban Homosexual Priests," *The Tennessean*, 22 September 2005, 3A; and Victor L. Simpson, "Vatican to Reaffirm Priesthood Barred to Active Homosexuals," *The Tennessean*, 23 November 2005, 13A. The gay artist Elton John holds that "religion has always tried to turn hatred toward gay people," an indictment virtually impossible to refute when one considers the attitudes of various world religions toward gays and lesbians. See "People in the News—Elton John: Religion Turns People Hateful," *The Tennessean*, 13 November 2006, 2A.

105. Susan Wiltshire, "From a Jail Cell, Group Prayed to Change the Anti-Gay Policies of Churches," *The Tennessean*, 9 June 2006, 15A.

106. Pierre Berton, *The Comfortable Pew* (Philadelphia: J. B. Lippincott, 1965), 78–79.

107. Devon W. Carbado and Donald Weise, eds., *Time on Two Crosses: The Collected Writings of Bayard Rustin* (San Francisco: Cleis Press, 2003), 285 and 292–293; and Hutchison, "King Would Not Have Marched."

108. Victor Anderson, "Farewell to Innocence: Can the Black Church Be a Moral Light in its Contestations with Difference," unpublished paper, Vanderbilt Divinity School, Nashville, Tennessee (2 November 2006), author's files, 1–2.

109. King, *Where Do We Go?* 167–168.

110. "Doubts and Certainties Link: An Interview with Martin Luther King, Jr.," unpublished transcript, London, England (Winter 1968), KCLA, 5; and Lewis V. Baldwin, *To Make the Wounded Whole: The Cultural Legacy of Martin Luther King, Jr.* (Minneapolis: Fortress Press, 1992), 286.

111. See King, *Where Do We Go?* 167–202. Also see King, *Trumpet*, 3–78.

112. Amy Green, "Who Will be Allowed Into Heaven's Doors?" *The Tennessean*, 15 January 2005, 3B.

113. Baldwin and Al-Hadid, *Cross and Crescent*, 357–358.

114. Anita Wadhwani, "Religious Right's Agenda Endangers Liberty, Author Says," *The Tennessean*, 14 November 2006, B1. For an interesting perspective on how born-again Christians use religion to sway the functions of democracy, see Dwight Lewis, "Religion Can Sway the Workings of Democracy," *The Tennessean*, 12 November 2006, 23A.

115. This point is made at a number of points in a recent work by the Princeton Theologian Mark L. Taylor. See Mark L. Taylor, *Where the Christian Right Goes Wrong* (Minneapolis: Augsburg-Fortress Press, 2005), 1–200.

116. Martin Luther King, Jr., "A Cry of Hate or a Cry for Help?" unpublished statement (August, 1965), KCLA, 4.

117. Baldwin et al., *Legacy*, 77–109.

118. King, "Address at the Southern," 15.

119. This category in my typology grew in part out of my reading of Richard Deats, "The Audacious Challenge: A Decade for a Culture of Peace and Nonviolence," *Fellowship*, 65, no.5–6 (May/June 1999), 3; and "International Decade for a Culture of Peace and Nonviolence for the Children of the World (2001–2010)," *Fellowship*, 65, no.5–6 (May/June 1999), 6.

120. A report commissioned by the United States Conference of Catholic Bishops (USCCB) shows that 4, 392 priests nationwide were accused of sexually abusing 10,667 minors between 1950 and 2002. See Rachel Zoll, "Abuse Has Cost Catholic Church $1B," *The Tennessean*, 10 June 2005, 1A-2A; Holly Edwards, "Bishop Says Church's Sex Abuse Problem Mirrors Society's: Reports 'Shocking' Numbers Show Church's Effort to Uncover It, He Says," *The Tennessean*, 28 February 2002, 1A-2A; Alessandra Eizzo, "Pope Breaks Silence on Sex Abuse by Clergy," *The Tennessean*, 29 October 2006, 5A; "Victims of Abuse Call on Bishops to Remove All Priest Offenders," *The Tennessean*, 13 June 2002, 4A; Fred Bayles, "Abuse Response Varies by Diocese: Catholic Church Structure Tends to Complicate Reform Efforts," *USA Today*, 25 February 2002, 3A; Anita Wadhwani, "Sex Abuse Victims Turn Focus to Baptists: Advocate Group Calls on Church to Face Problem," *The Tennessean*, 29 February 2007, 1A and 14A; Rose French, "Group Asks Southern Baptists to Review Sexual Abuse Charges," *The Tennessean*, 22 February 2007, 4B; Brian Lewis, "SBC Holds Pastors to High 'Sexual Integrity' Standard," *The Tennessean*, 13 June 2002, 14A; and Rev. Neely Williams, "Children in Foster Care Need Support of Christians," *The Tennessean*, 5 May 2007, B5.

121. Arnove, "Racism Fuels the Iraqi Sanctions: An Interview with James Lawson," *Fellowship*, 66, nos.9–10 (September/October 2000), 6–8; Robert Parham, "President is Ignoring People of Faith in This Audacious Walk to War," *The Tennessean*, 17 February 2003, 13A; Molly Ivins, "'Culture of Life' Doesn't Extend to Baghdad," *The Tennessean*, 2 June 2005, 11A; Don Beisswenger and Judy Pilgrim, "'Ribbons and Bows' Cover Up an Ugly War: Letters to the Editor," *The Tennessean*, 25 April 2005, 10A; "U.N. War Crimes Tribunal Gets Milosevic," *The Tennessean*, 29 June 2001, 3A; Alexander G. Higgins, "U.N. Team Says World Response to Darfur Inadequate," *The Tennessean*, 13 March 2007, 5A; and Jimmy Carter, *Our Endangered Values: America's Moral Crisis* (New York: Simon & Schuster, 2005), 112–114.

122. A newspaper commentator recently raised the same question regarding Mohandas K. Gandhi. See Saritha Prabhu, "What Would Gandhi Think of All This Violence?" *The Tennessean*, 14 November 2005, 9A.

123. Martin Luther King, Jr., "Revolution and Redemption," unpublished, closing address at the European Baptist Assembly, Amsterdam (16 August 1964), KCLA, 10; King, "Transformed" (16 January 1966), 3; Martin Luther King, Jr., "What are Your New Year's Resolutions?" unpublished sermon, New York, New York (7 January 1968), KCLA, 3; and Martin Luther King, Jr., "An Address at the Fiftieth Anniversary of the Women's International League for Peace and Freedom," unpublished, Philadelphia (15 October 1965), KCLA, 11.

124. A recent book by a former lawyer of King gives the strange impression that if King were alive today, he would be advising the U.S. to take out the terrorists and fight the war in Iraq. The book offers a highly questionable analysis of how King might frame the relationship between war and the poor. See Clarence B. Jones, *What Would Martin Say?* with Joel Engel (New York: HarperCollins, 2008), 69–99 and 143–178.

125. Clayborne Carson et al., eds., *The Papers of Martin Luther King, Jr., Volume IV: Symbol of the Movement, January 1957–December 1958* (Berkeley: University of California Press, 2000), 88 and 166; Carson et al., eds., *King Papers*, III, 462 and 278–479.

126. For statements that highlight King's sense of sacrificial servant-hood, see King, *Stride*, 94–95; Washington, ed., *Testament*, 41–42; and Alex Ayres, ed., *The Wisdom of Martin Luther King, Jr.: An A-to-Z Guide to the Ideas and Ideals of the Great Civil Rights Leader* (New York: Penguin Books, 1993), 205. Rufus Burrow uses the term "servant-hood" in a discussion of "King's dream and the church." See Rufus Burrow, Jr., "King's Dream and Multiculturalism: A Review Essay," *Encounter*, 67, no.2 (2006), 212.

127. Washington, ed., *Testament*, 41–42.

128. King, *Strength*, 26–46.

129. Washington, ed., *Testament*, 41–42.

130. Baldwin, "Revisioning," 39.

131. Anthony B. Pinn, *Why Lord? Suffering and Evil in Black Theology* (New York: Continuum, 1995), 17 and 75–78; and Delores S. Williams, *Sisters in the Wilderness: The Challenge of Womanist God-Talk* (Maryknoll, N.Y.: Orbis Books, 1993), 200; and Baldwin and Al-Hadid, *Cross and Crescent*, 195–196. Williams and Pinn are critical of King's concept of the cross and redemptive suffering. In contrast, Kelly B. Douglass and JoAnne M. Terrell provide more positive views, and are therefore more useful for discussing King in relation to the need for a culture of sacrificial servant-hood. See Kelly Brown Douglass, *What's Faith Got to Do with It? Black Bodies/Christian Souls* (Maryknoll, N.Y.: Orbis Books, 2005), 93–96; and JoAnne Marie Terrell, *Power in the Blood? The Cross in the African American Experience* (Maryknoll, N.Y.: Orbis Books, 1998), 77–83.

132. King, *Strength*, 26–46.

133. King, *Can't Wait*, 89–92.

134. Lewis V. Baldwin, *There is a Balm in Gilead: The Cultural Roots of Martin Luther King, Jr.* (Minneapolis: Fortress Press, 1991), 327–328.

135. Walter Harrelson, "Martin Luther King, Jr. and the Hebrew Prophets," a lecture given in a Martin Luther King, Jr. class at Vanderbilt University, Nashville, Tennessee (6 February 1986), 1–10; and Baldwin, *Balm*, 327–328.

136. Harrelson, "Martin Luther King, Jr.," 1–10; and Baldwin, *Balm*, 327–328.

137. This is strongly suggested in King's "Letter from the Birmingham City Jail" (1963). See King, *Can't Wait*, 90–91.

138. In statements in which King referred to the Negro church, the black press, and other establishments, the civil rights leader described "self-criticism" as evidence of a certain depth of maturity. See King, *Where Do We Go?* 124–125.

139. King must have been thinking along these lines when he noted how worship should prepare the believer for service to humanity. See Carson et al., eds., *King Papers*, VI, 224–225.

140. Carson and Holloran, eds., *Knock*, 108–112; and Washington, ed., *Testament*, 101, 107–108, and 447–448.

141. Jay Sekulow, "Should Congress Scrap a Law that Prevents Churches from Engaging in Political Activities," *The Tennessean*, 30 August 2004, 7A.

142. King consistently spoke to this issue in powerful ways. See King, *Can't Wait*, 92.

143. Carson and Holloran, eds., *Knock*, 72–73; and King, *Can't Wait*, 91–92.

144. King, *Strength*, 21.

145. Ibid., 29–35.

146. King, "Address at SCLC," 20; and King, *Where Do We Go?* 96.

147. Many of King's sermons are unpublished, and the published ones can be found in King, *Measure*, 9–59; King, *Strength*, 9–146; and Carson et al., eds., *King Papers*, VI, 69–600. Other volumes of the King Papers also contain sermons and sermon outlines.

148. Washington, ed., *Testament*, 286.

149. Baldwin, "Revisioning," 40; and Lewis V. Baldwin, "Beyond Hoopla, We Must Act on Legacy," *The Tennessean*, 4 April 2008, 12A.

Index